BRUNEI

CRIMINAL LAWS, REGULATIONS AND PROCEDURES HANDBOOK
STRATEGIC INFORMATION, REGULATIONS, PROCEDURES

International Business Publications, USA
Washington DC, USA - Bandar Seri Begawan

BRUNEI
CRIMINAL LAWS, REGULATIONS AND PROCEDURES HANDBOOK
STRATEGIC INFORMATION, REGULATIONS, PROCEDURES

UPDATED ANNUALLY

We express our sincere appreciation to all government agencies and international organizations which provided information and other materials for this handbook

Cover Design: International Business Publications, USA

International Business Publications, USA. *has used its best efforts in collecting, analyzing and preparing data, information and materials for this unique handbook. Due to the dynamic nature and fast development of the economy and business environment, we cannot warrant that all information herein is complete and accurate. IBP does not assume and hereby disclaim any liability to any person for any loss or damage caused by possible errors or omissions in the handbook.*
This handbook is for individual use only. Use this handbook for any other purpose, included but not limited to reproducing and storing in a retrieval system by any means, electronic, photocopying or using the addresses or other information contained in this handbook for any commercial purposes requires a special written permission from the publisher.

2017 Updated Reprint International Business Publications, USA
ISBN

For additional analytical, business and investment opportunities information,
please contact Global Investment & Business Center, USA
at (703) 370-8082. Fax: (703) 370-8083. E-mail: ibpusa3@gmail.com
Global Business and Investment Info Databank - www.ibpus.com

Printed in the USA

BRUNEI
CRIMINAL LAWS, REGULATIONS AND PROCEDURES HANDBOOK
STRATEGIC INFORMATION, REGULATIONS, PROCEDURES

TABLE OF CONTENTS

STRATEGIC AND BUSINESS PROFILE 7
   BRUNEI DARUSSALAM 7
      Stable, conducive environment 9
      Pioneer industry incentives 10
      Geography 10
      People 10
      Government 12
      Economy 14
      Energy 17
      Communcation 19
      Transportation 20
      Military 20
      Transnational Issues 20

IMPORTANT INFORMATION FOR UNDERSTANDING BRUNEI 21
   PROFILE 21
      PEOPLE 21
      HISTORY 22
      GOVERNMENT AND POLITICAL CONDITIONS 22
      ECONOMY 23
      DEFENSE 26
      FOREIGN RELATIONS 26
      U.S.-BRUNEI RELATIONS 26
      TRAVEL AND BUSINESS INFORMATION 27

BRUNEI LEGAL SYSTEM BASICS 28
   THE CONSTITUTION 31
      Statutes/Legislative Enactments 31
      Islamic Laws 32
      Subsidiary Legislation 33
      Case Law/Judicial Precedent 33
      Common Law of England 33
   GOVERNMENT AND THE STATE 34
      The Executive 34
      The Legislative Council 34

For additional analytical, business and investment opportunities information,
please contact Global Investment & Business Center, USA
at (703) 370-8082. Fax: (703) 370-8083. E-mail: ibpusa3@gmail.com
Global Business and Investment Info Databank - www.ibpus.com

The Judiciary	*35*
Syariah Court	*40*
LEGAL PROCEDURE	43
Criminal Prosecution	*43*
Criminal Procedure	*44*
Civil Procedure	*48*
Procedure in the High Court	*51*
Reciprocal enforcement of foreign judgments and foreign maintenance orders	*54*
LEGAL PROCEDURE IN THE SYARIAH COURTS	*55*
THE LEGAL PROFESSION	57
Legal Qualifications	*57*
Practitioners	*57*
The Law Society	*60*
Legal Qualifications for Syariah Lawyers	*61*
Legal Education	*62*
CRIMINAL PROCEDURE CODE	**64**
PART I PRELIMINARY	64
Chapter I Citation and application	*64*
PART II CONSTITUTION AND POWERS OF CRIMINAL COURTS	66
Chapter II Criminal Courts generally	*66*
PART III GENERAL PROVISIONS	70
Chapter III Aid and information to Magistrates and police and persons making arrests	*70*
Chapter IV Arrest, escape and re-taking	*71*
Chapter V Processes to compel appearance	*76*
Chapter VI Processes to compel production of documents and other movable property and for discovery of persons wrongfully confined	*80*
PART IV PREVENTION OF OFFENCES	84
Chapter VII Security for keeping peace and for good behaviour	*84*
Chapter VIII Unlawful assemblies	*88*
Chapter IX Public nuisances	*89*
Chapter X Temporary orders in urgent cases of nuisance	*91*
Chapter XI Disputes as to immovable property	*92*
Chapter XII Preventive action of police	*93*
PART V INFORMATION TO POLICE AND THEIR POWERS TO INVESTIGATE	94
Chapter XIII Duties of police officer on receiving information about offences	*94*
PART VI PROCEEDINGS IN PROSECUTIONS	106
Chapter XIV Jurisdiction of criminal Courts in inquiries and trials	*106*
Chapter XV Complaints	*107*
Chapter XVI Commencement of proceedings	*108*
Chapter XVII Preliminary inquiries into cases triable by High Court	*108*
Chapter XVIII Charge	*114*
Chapter XIX Trials without aid of assessors	*120*
Chapter XX Trials of capital offences	*126*
Chapter XXI Assessors	*127*
Chapter XXII General provisions as to inquiries and trials	*127*
Table of offences	*129*
Chapter XXIII Mode of taking and recording evidence in inquiries and trials	*131*
Chapter XXIIIA Recording of proceedings by mechanical means	*135*
Chapter XXIV Judgment	*137*
Chapter XXV Submission of sentences of death to	*139*
Chapter XXVI Execution of sentences	*140*
Chapter XXVII Previous acquittals or convictions	*147*
PART VII APPEALS, REFERENCE AND REVISION	148

Chapter XXVIII Appeals *148*
Chapter XXIX Reference and revision *153*
PART VIII SPECIAL PROCEEDINGS 154
Chapter XXX Inquests *154*
Chapter XXXI Persons of unsound mind *158*
Chapter XXXII Proceedings in case of certain offences affecting administration of justice *162*
Chapter XXXIII Maintenance of wives and children *164*
Chapter XXXIV Directions of nature of habeas corpus *164*
PART IX SUPPLEMENTARY PROVISIONS 165
Chapter XXXV Bail *165*
Chapter XXXVI Bonds *167*
Chapter XXXVII Disposal of property subject of offences *168*
Chapter XXXVIII Transfer of criminal cases *170*
Chapter XXXIX Irregularities in proceedings *170*
Chapter XL Public Prosecutor *172*
Chapter XLI General *174*
PART X JURISDICTION OF COURT OF APPEAL 178
Chapter XLII (Repealed by S 63/2002) *178*
Chapter XLIII Reference *178*
Chapter XLIV Appeals by persons convicted *181*
Chapter XLIVA Appeals by Public Prosecutor *217*
Chapter LXV General *222*
FIRST SCHEDULE TABULAR STATEMENT OF OFFENCES UNDER THE PENAL CODE 224
CHAPTER V — ABETMENT *224*
CHAPTER VA — CRIMINAL CONSPIRACY *229*
CHAPTER VI — OFFENCES AGAINST THE STATE *229*
CHAPTER VII — OFFENCES RELATING TO ARMY, NAVY, AIR FORCE AND POLICE *230*
CHAPTER VIII — OFFENCES AGAINST THE PUBLIC TRANQUILLITY *231*
CHAPTER IX — OFFENCES BY OR RELATING TO PUBLIC SERVANTS *233*
CHAPTER X — CONTEMPTS OF LAWFUL AUTHORITY OF PUBLIC SERVANTS *234*
CHAPTER XI — FALSE EVIDENCE AND OFFENCES AGAINST PUBLIC JUSTICE *238*
CHAPTER XII — OFFENCES RELATING TO COIN AND GOVERNMENT STAMPS *246*
CHAPTER XIII — OFFENCES RELATING TO WEIGHTS AND MEASURES *249*
CHAPTER XIV — OFFENCES AFFECTING PUBLIC HEALTH, SAFETY, CONVENIENCE, ... *249*
CHAPTER XV — OFFENCES RELATING TO RELIGION *254*
CHAPTER XVI — OFFENCES AFFECTING THE HUMAN BODY *255*
CHAPTER XVII — OFFENCES AGAINST PROPERTY *266*
CHAPTER XVIII — OFFENCES RELATING TO DOCUMENTS, FALSE DOCUMENTS AND CURRENCY NOTES AND BANK NOTES *278*
CHAPTER XX — OFFENCES RELATING TO MARRIAGE *281*
CHAPTER XXI — DEFAMATION *282*
CHAPTER XXII — CRIMINAL INTIMIDATION, INSULT AND ANNOYANCE *282*
CHAPTER XXIII — ATTEMPTS TO COMMIT OFFENCES *283*
OFFENCES AGAINST OTHER LAWS *283*

TRAVEL TO BRUNEI **285**

TRAVEL TO BRUNEI **285**

US STATE DEPARTMENT SUGGESTIONS 285
Holidays *289*
BUSINESS CUSTOMS 291

SUPPLEMENTS **293**

IMPORTANT LAWS OF BRUNEI 293

STRATEGIC GOVERNMENT CONTACT IN BRUNEY 304
FOREIGN MISSIONS 305
   Brunei's Missions in ASEAN, China, Japan and Korea 308
   FOOD AND RESTAURANTS 310
   Travel Agents 312
   Bandar Seri Begawan 312
   Kuala Belait 312
SELECTED COMPANIES 312
BASIC TITLES ON BRUNEI 314

STRATEGIC AND BUSINESS PROFILE
BRUNEI DARUSSALAM

Capital and largest city	Bandar Seri Begawan 4°53.417′N 114°56.533′E4.890283°N 114.942217°E
Official languages	Malay
Recognised	English
Other languages	<ul><li>Brunei Malay</li><li>Tutong</li><li>Kedayan</li><li>Belait</li><li>Murut</li><li>Dusun</li><li>Bisaya</li><li>Melanau</li><li>Iban</li><li>Penan</li></ul>
Ethnic groups (2004)	<ul><li>66.3% Malays</li><li>11.2% Chinese</li><li>3.4% Indigenous</li><li>19.1% other</li></ul>
Demonym	Bruneian
Government	Unitary Islamic absolute monarchy
- Sultan	Hassanal Bolkiah
- Crown Prince	Al-Muhtadee Billah
Legislature	Legislative Council
Formation	
- Sultanate	14th century
- British protectorate	1888
- Independence from the United Kingdom	1 January 1984
Area	
- Total	5,765 km^2 (172nd) 2,226 sq mi
- Water (%)	8.6
Population	
- Jul 2013 estimate	415,717 (175th)
- Density	67.3/km^2 (134th) 174.4/sq mi
GDP (PPP)	2012 estimate
- Total	$21.907 billion
- Per capita	$50,440
GDP (nominal)	2012 estimate
- Total	$17.092 billion
- Per capita	$39,355
HDI (2013)	▲0.855 very high · 30th
Currency	Brunei dollar (BND)
Time zone	BDT (UTC+8)

For additional analytical, business and investment opportunities information, please contact Global Investment & Business Center, USA at (703) 370-8082. Fax: (703) 370-8083. E-mail: ibpusa3@gmail.com Global Business and Investment Info Databank - www.ibpus.com

Drives on the	left
Calling code	+673
ISO 3166 code	BN
Internet TLD	.bn

Brunei officially the **Nation of Brunei, the Abode of Peace** is a sovereign state located on the north coast of the island of Borneo in Southeast Asia. Apart from its coastline with the South China Sea, it is completely surrounded by the state of Sarawak, Malaysia; and it is separated into two parts by the Sarawak district of Limbang. It is the only sovereign state completely on the island of Borneo; the remainder of the island's territory is divided between the nations of Malaysia and Indonesia. Brunei's population was 408,786 in July 2012.

At the peak of Bruneian Empire, Sultan Bolkiah (reigned 1485–1528) is alleged to have had control over the northern regions of Borneo, including modern-day Sarawak and Sabah, as well as the Sulu archipelago off the northeast tip of Borneo, Seludong (modern-day Manila), and the islands off the northwest tip of Borneo. The maritime state was visited by Spain's Magellan Expedition in 1521 and fought against Spain in 1578's Castille War.

During the 19th century the Bruneian Empire began to decline. The Sultanate ceded Sarawak to James Brooke as a reward for his aid in putting down a rebellion and named him as rajah, and it ceded Sabah to the British North Borneo Chartered Company. In 1888 Brunei became a British protectorate and was assigned a British Resident as colonial manager in 1906. After the Japanese occupation during World War II, in 1959 a new constitution was written. In 1962 a small armed rebellion against the monarchy was ended with the help of the British.

Brunei regained its independence from the United Kingdom on 1 January 1984. Economic growth during the 1990s and 2000s, averaging 56% from 1999 to 2008, has transformed Brunei into a newly industrialised country. It has developed wealth from extensive petroleum and natural gas fields. Brunei has the second-highest Human Development Index among the South East Asia nations after Singapore, and is classified as a developed country. According to the International Monetary Fund (IMF), Brunei is ranked fifth in the world by gross domestic product per capita at purchasing power parity. The IMF estimated in 2011 that Brunei was one of two countries (the other being Libya) with a public debt at 0% of the national GDP. *Forbes* also ranks Brunei as the fifth-richest nation out of 182, based on its petroleum and natural gas fields

Brunei can trace its beginnings to the 7th century, when it was a subject state of the Srivijayan empire under the name Po-ni. It later became a vassal state of Majapahit before embracing Islam in the 15th century. At the peak of its empire, the sultanate had control that extended over the coastal regions of modern-day Sarawak and Sabah, the Sulu archipelago, and the islands off the northwest tip of Borneo. The thalassocracy was visited by Ferdinand Magellan in 1521 and fought the Castille War in 1578 against Spain. Its empire began to decline with the forced ceding of Sarawak to James Brooke and the ceding of Sabah to the British North Borneo Chartered Company. After the loss of Limbang, Brunei finally became a British protectorate in 1888, receiving a resident in 1906. In the post-occupation years, it formalised a constitution and fought an armed rebellion. Brunei regained its independence from the United Kingdom on 1 January 1984. Economic growth during the 1970s and 1990s, averaging 56% from 1999 to 2008, has transformed Brunei Darussalam into a newly industrialised country.

Brunei has the second highest Human Development Index among the South East Asia nations, after Singapore and is classified as a Developed Country. According to the International Monetary Fund (IMF), Brunei is ranked 4th in the world by gross domestic product per capita at purchasing power parity.

According to legend, Brunei was founded by Awang Alak Betatar. His move from Garang [location required] to the Brunei river estuary led to the discovery of Brunei. His first exclamation upon landing on the shore, as the legend goes, was "Baru nah!" (Which in English loosely-translates as "that's it!" or "there") and thus, the name "Brunei" was derived from his words.

It was renamed "Barunai" in the 14th Century, possibly influenced by the Sanskrit word varunai (वरुण), meaning "seafarers", later to become "Brunei". The word "Borneo" is of the same origin. In the country's full name "Negara Brunei Darussalam" "Darussalam" means "Abode of Peace" in Arabic, while "Negara" means "Country" in Malay. "Negara" derives from the Sanskrit Nagara , meaning "city".

Brunei Darussalam, the host of the 1995 BIMP-EAGA EXPO is a stable and prosperous country which offers not only a well-developed infrastructure but also a strategic location within the Asean region. The country is chugging full steam ahead to diversify its economy away from an over-dependence on oil and gas, and has put in place flexible and realistic policies to facilitate foreign and local investment. The cost of utilities are the lowest in the region, while political stability, extensive economic and natural resources and a business environment attuned to the requirements of foreign investors go towards making Brunei an excellent investment choice

At present the country's economy is dominated by the oil and liquefied natural gas industries and government expenditure patterns. Brunei exports crude oil, petroleum products and LNG mainly to Japan, the United States and the Asean countries. The second most important industry is construction, a direct result of the government's investment in development and infrastructure projects. Gearing up towards putting on the mantle of a developed country in January 1996, Brunei allocated in its 1991-95 Five Year Plan a hefty B$5 billion for national development, over a billion dollars more than in the previous budget. About B$510 million was allotted for 619 projects while B$550 million or 10 percent of the development budget went to industry and commerce. Some B$100 million alone was reserved for industrial promotion and development.

STABLE, CONDUCIVE ENVIRONMENT

The oil-rich country, lying on the north-western edge of the Borneo island, has never experienced typhoons, earthquakes or severe floods. Profitable investment can be had as the country levies no personal income tax, no sales tax, payroll, manufacturing or export tax.

Competitive investment incentives are available for investors throughout the business cycle marked by the start up, growth, maturity and expansion stages. The tax advantages at start up and the on-going incentives during growth and expansion are among the most competitive around. There is no difficulty in securing approval for foreign workers, from labourers to managers. With a small labour pool of 284,500 Brunei people and Bruneians showing a marked preference for the public sector as employer, the country has had to rely on foreign workers. These make up a third of its work force.

In line with moves to promote the private sector, it is encouraging to note the contribution from the non-oil and gas sector of the economy has risen, contributing about 25 percent to GDP compared to the oil and gas sector's 46 percent. In terms of infrastructure, Brunei is ready for vigorous economy activity. At its two main ports at Muara and Kuala Belait, goods can be shipped direct to Hong Kong, Singapore and other Asian destinations. Muara, a deep-water port 29 km away from the capital of Bandar Seri Begawan, has seen continual increase in container traffic over the past two decades.

The Brunei International Airport at Bandar offers expanded passenger and cargo facilities. Its new terminal can accommodate 1.5 million passengers and 50,000 tonnes of cargo a year, which is expected to suffice till the end of the decade. A 2,000-km road network serving the whole country undergoes continual expansion. A main highway runs the entire length of its coastline, linking Muara, the port entry point at one end, and Belait, the oil-production centre, at another end.

Telecommunications-wise, Brunei has one of the best systems in the region with plans for major upgrading. Telephone availability is about one to every three people.

Two earth satellite stations provide direct telephone, telex and facsimile links to most parts of the world. Operating systems include an analogue telephone exchange, fibreoptic cable links with Singapore and Manila, a packet switching exchange for access to high-speed computer bases overseas, cellular mobile telephone and paging systems. Direct phone links are also available in the more remote parts of the country via microwave and solar-powered telephones.

PIONEER INDUSTRY INCENTIVES

Companies granted pioneer status enjoy tax holidays of up to eight years. Brunei's regulations governing foreign participation in equity are the most flexible in the region, with 100 percent foreign ownership permitted. A pioneer company is also exempt from customs duty on items to be installed in the pioneer factory and from paying import duties on raw materials not available locally or produced in Brunei for the manufacture of pioneer products.

GEOGRAPHY

Location: Southeastern Asia, bordering the South China Sea and Malaysia
Geographic coordinates: 4 30 N, 114 40 E
Map references: Southeast Asia

Area:
total: 5,770 sq km
land: 5,270 sq km
water: 500 sq km

Area—comparative: slightly smaller than Delaware

Land boundaries:
total: 381 km
border countries: Malaysia 381 km

Coastline: 161 km
Land use:
arable land: 1%
other: 12%

permanent crops: 1%
permanent pastures: 1%
forests and woodland: 85%

Irrigated land: 10 sq km
Natural hazards: typhoons, earthquakes, and severe flooding are very rare
Environment—current issues: seasonal smoke/haze resulting from forest fires in Indonesia

Environment—international agreements:
party to: Endangered Species, Law of the Sea, Ozone Layer Protection, Ship Pollution
signed, but not ratified: none of the selected agreements

Geography—note: close to vital sea lanes through South China Sea linking Indian and Pacific Oceans; two parts physically separated by Malaysia; almost an enclave of Malaysia

PEOPLE

Population: 322,982

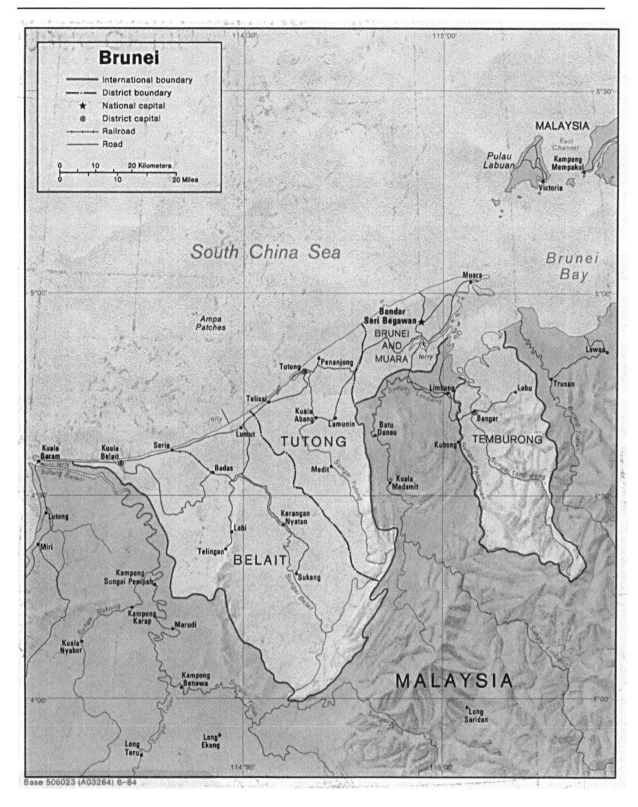

Age structure:
0-14 years: 33% (male 54,154; female 51,766)

15-64 years: 63% (male 106,492; female 95,921)
65 years and over: 4% (male 7,945; female 6,704)

Population growth rate: 2.38%
Birth rate: 24.69 births/1,000 population
Death rate: 5.21 deaths/1,000 population
Net migration rate: 4.35 migrant(s)/1,000 population

Sex ratio:
at birth: 1.06 male(s)/female
under 15 years: 1.05 male(s)/female
15-64 years: 1.11 male(s)/female
65 years and over: 1.19 male(s)/female
total population: 1.09 male(s)/female

Infant mortality rate: 22.83 deaths/1,000 live births

Life expectancy at birth:
total population: 71.84 years
male: 70.35 years
female: 73.42 years

Total fertility rate: 3.33 children born/woman

Nationality:
noun: Bruneian(s)
adjective: Bruneian

Ethnic groups: Malay 64%, Chinese 20%, other 16%
Religions: Muslim (official) 63%, Buddhism 14%, Christian 8%, indigenous beliefs and other 15% (1981)
Languages: Malay (official), English, Chinese

Literacy:
definition: age 15 and over can read and write
total population: 88.2%
male: 92.6% *female:* 83.4%

GOVERNMENT

Country name:
conventional long form: Negara Brunei Darussalam
conventional short form: Brunei

Data code: BX
Government type: constitutional sultanate
Capital: Bandar Seri Begawan

Administrative divisions: 4 districts (daerah-daerah, singular—daerah); Belait, Brunei and Muara, Temburong, Tutong

Independence: 1 January 1984 (from UK)
National holiday: National Day, 23 February (1984)

Constitution: 29 September 1959 (some provisions suspended under a State of Emergency since December 1962, others since independence on 1 January 1984)

Legal system: based on English common law; for Muslims, Islamic Shari'a law supersedes civil law in a number of areas

Suffrage: none

Executive branch:
Brunei

Sultan	HASSANAL Bolkiah, Sir
Prime Minister	HASSANAL Bolkiah, Sir
Min. of Communications	Awang ABU BAKAR bin Apong
Min. of Culture, Youth, & Sports	MOHAMMAD bin Daud, Gen. (Ret.)
Min. of Defense	HASSANAL Bolkiah, Sir
Min. of Development	ABDULLAH bin Begawan
Min. of Education	Abdul RAHMAN bin Mohamed Taib
Min. of Energy	YAHYA bin Begawan
Min. of Finance	HASSANAL Bolkiah, Sir
Min. of Finance II	ABDUL RAHMAN bin Ibrahim
Min. of Foreign Affairs	MOHAMED Bolkiah, Prince
Min. of Foreign Affairs II	LIM Jock Seng
Min. of Health	SUYOI bin Osman
Min. of Home Affairs	ADANAN bin Begawan
Min. of Industry & Primary Resources	AHMAD bin Jumat, Dr.
Min. of Religious Affairs	MOHD ZAIN bin Serudin, Dr.
Senior Min. in the Prime Minister's Office	Al Muhtadee BILLAH, Crown Prince
Ambassador to the US	PUTEH ibni Mohammad Alam
Permanent Representative to the UN, New York	SHOFRY bin Abdul Ghafor

Legislative branch: unicameral Legislative Council or Majlis Masyuarat Megeri (a privy council that serves only in a consultative capacity; NA seats; members appointed by the monarch)
elections: last held in March 1962
note: in 1970 the Council was changed to an appointive body by decree of the monarch; an elected Legislative Council is being considered as part of constitutional reform, but elections are unlikely for several years

Judicial branch: Supreme Court, chief justice and judges are sworn in by the monarch for three-year terms

Political parties and leaders: Brunei Solidarity National Party or PPKB in Malay [Haji Mohd HATTA bin Haji Zainal Abidin, president]; the PPKB is the only legal political party in Brunei; it was registered in 1985, but became largely inactive after 1988; it has less than 200 registered party members; other parties include Brunei People's Party or PRB (banned in 1962) and Brunei National Democratic Party (registered in May 1985, deregistered by the Brunei Government in 1988)

International organization participation: APEC, ASEAN, C, CCC, ESCAP, G-77, IBRD, ICAO, ICRM, IDB, IFRCS, IMF, IMO, Inmarsat, Intelsat, Interpol, IOC, ISO (correspondent), ITU, NAM, OIC, OPCW, UN, UNCTAD, UPU, WHO, WIPO, WMO, WTrO

Diplomatic representation in the US:
chief of mission: Ambassador Pengiran Anak Dato Haji PUTEH Ibni Mohammad Alam
chancery: Watergate, Suite 300, 3rd floor, 2600 Virginia Avenue NW, Washington, DC 20037
telephone: (202) 342-0159
FAX: (202) 342-0158

Diplomatic representation from the US:
chief of mission: Ambassador Craig B. Allen
embassy: Third Floor, Teck Guan Plaza, Jalan Sultan, Bandar Seri Begawan
mailing address: PSC 470 (BSB), FPO AP 96534-0001
telephone: [673] (2) 229670 *FAX:* [673] (2) 225293

Flag description: yellow with two diagonal bands of white (top, almost double width) and black starting from the upper hoist side; the national emblem in red is superimposed at the center; the emblem includes a swallow-tailed flag on top of a winged column within an upturned crescent above a scroll and flanked by two upraised hands

ECONOMY

Brunei is an energy-rich sultanate on the northern coast of Borneo in Southeast Asia. Brunei boasts a well-educated, largely English-speaking population; excellent infrastructure; and a stable government intent on attracting foreign investment. Crude oil and natural gas production account for approximately 65% of GDP and 95% of exports, with Japan as the primary export market.

Per capita GDP is among the highest in the world, and substantial income from overseas investment supplements income from domestic hydrocarbon production. Bruneian citizens pay no personal income taxes, and the government provides free medical services and free education through the university level.

The Bruneian Government wants to diversify its economy away from hydrocarbon exports to other industries such as information and communications technology and halal manufacturing, permissible under Islamic law. Brunei's trade in 2016 was set to increase following its regional economic integration in the ASEAN Economic Community, and the expected ratification of the Trans-Pacific Partnership trade agreement.

GDP (purchasing power parity):

$32.76 billion (2016 est.)
$33.17 billion (2015 est.)
$32.95 billion (2014 est.)
note: data are in 2016 dollars
country comparison to the world: 127

GDP (official exchange rate):
$11.4 billion (2016 est.)

GDP - real growth rate:
-2.5% (2016 est.)
-0.4% (2015 est.)
-2.5% (2014 est.)
country comparison to the world: 209

GDP - per capita (PPP):
$77,500 (2016 est.)
$80,600 (2015 est.)
$81,900 (2014 est.)
note: data are in 2016 dollars
country comparison to the world: 10

Gross national saving:
43.5% of GDP (2016 est.)
51.3% of GDP (2015 est.)
58.1% of GDP (2014 est.)
country comparison to the world: 6

GDP - composition, by end use:
household consumption: 22.5%
government consumption: 26.6%
investment in fixed capital: 35.3%
investment in inventories: 0%
exports of goods and services: 52.1%
imports of goods and services: -36.5% (2016 est.)

GDP - composition, by sector of origin:
agriculture: 1.2%
industry: 56.5%
services: 42.4% (2016 est.)

Agriculture - products:
rice, vegetables, fruits; chickens, water buffalo, cattle, goats, eggs

Industries:
petroleum, petroleum refining, liquefied natural gas, construction, agriculture, transportation

Industrial production growth rate:
-2.9% (2016 est.)
country comparison to the world: 179

Labor force:
203,600 (2014 est.)
country comparison to the world: 169

Labor force - by occupation:
agriculture: 4.2%
industry: 62.8%
services: 33% (2008 est.)

Unemployment rate:
6.9% (2016 est.)
9.3% (2011 est.)
country comparison to the world: 90

Budget:
revenues: $2.679 billion
expenditures: $4.561 billion (2016 est.)

Taxes and other revenues:
24% of GDP (2016 est.)
country comparison to the world: 123

Budget surplus (+) or deficit (-):

-16.8% of GDP (2016 est.)
country comparison to the world: 213

Public debt:
3.1% of GDP (2016 est.)
3% of GDP (2015 est.)
country comparison to the world: 203

Fiscal year:
1 April - 31 March

Inflation rate (consumer prices):
-0.7% (2016 est.)
-0.4% (2015 est.)
country comparison to the world: 24

Commercial bank prime lending rate:
5.5% (31 December 2016 est.)
5.5% (31 December 2015 est.)
country comparison to the world: 130

Stock of narrow money:
$3.232 billion (31 December 2016 est.)
$3.31 billion (31 December 2015 est.)
country comparison to the world: 115

Stock of broad money:
$10.08 billion (31 December 2016 est.)
$10.16 billion (31 December 2015 est.)
country comparison to the world: 105

Stock of domestic credit:
$4.066 billion (31 December 2016 est.)
$5.323 billion (31 December 2015 est.)
country comparison to the world: 131

Current account balance:
$1.091 billion (2016 est.)
$2.071 billion (2015 est.)
country comparison to the world: 41

Exports:
$5.023 billion (2016 est.)
$6.126 billion (2015 est.)
country comparison to the world: 105

Exports - commodities:
mineral fuels, organic chemicals

Exports - partners:
Japan 36.5%, South Korea 16.8%, Thailand 10.6%, India 9.8%, Malaysia 6.6%, China 4.6% (2016)

Imports:

$3.119 billion (2016 est.)
$3.216 billion (2015 est.)
country comparison to the world: 140

Imports - commodities:
machinery and mechanical appliance parts, mineral fuels, motor vehicles, electric machinery

Imports - partners:
US 28.4%, Malaysia 24%, Singapore 7.1%, Indonesia 5.7%, Japan 5.3%, China 4.9%, Australia 4.3% (2016)

Debt - external:
$0 (2014)
$0 (2013)
note: public external debt only; private external debt unavailable
country comparison to the world: 207

Exchange rates:
Bruneian dollars (BND) per US dollar -
1.3814 (2016 est.)
1.3814 (2015 est.)
1.3749 (2014 est.)
1.267 (2013 est.)
1.25 (2012 est.)

ENERGY

Electricity - production:
3.723 billion kWh (est.)
country comparison to the world: 126

Electricity - consumption:
3.391 billion kWh (est.)
country comparison to the world: 127

Electricity - exports:
0 kWh (est.)
country comparison to the world: 111

Electricity - imports:
0 kWh (est.)
country comparison to the world: 123

Electricity - installed generating capacity:
759,000 kW (est.)
country comparison to the world: 129

Electricity - from fossil fuels:
100% of total installed capacity (est.)
country comparison to the world: 9

Electricity - from nuclear fuels:
0% of total installed capacity (est.)
country comparison to the world: 57

Electricity - from hydroelectric plants:
0% of total installed capacity (2010 est.)
country comparison to the world: 161

Electricity - from other renewable sources:
0% of total installed capacity (est.)
country comparison to the world: 162

Crude oil - production:
141,000 bbl/day (est.)
country comparison to the world: 45

Crude oil - exports:
147,900 bbl/day (est.)
country comparison to the world: 35

Crude oil - imports:
0 bbl/day (est.)
country comparison to the world: 166

Crude oil - proved reserves:
1.1 billion bbl (1 January 2013 est.)
country comparison to the world: 41

Refined petroleum products - production:
13,500 bbl/day (est.)
country comparison to the world: 101

Refined petroleum products - consumption:
14,640 bbl/day (est.)
country comparison to the world: 144

Refined petroleum products - exports:
0 bbl/day (est.)
country comparison to the world: 159

Refined petroleum products - imports:
3,198 bbl/day (est.)
country comparison to the world: 169

Natural gas - production:
12.44 billion cu m (est.)
country comparison to the world: 38

Natural gas - consumption:

2.97 billion cu m (est.)
country comparison to the world: 73

Natural gas - exports:
9.42 billion cu m (est.)
country comparison to the world: 25

Natural gas - imports:
0 cu m (est.)
country comparison to the world: 167

Natural gas - proved reserves:
390.8 billion cu m (1 January 2013 est.)
country comparison to the world: 35

Carbon dioxide emissions from consumption of energy:
8.656 million Mt (2011 est.)

COMMUNCATION

Telephones - main lines in use:
70,933
country comparison to the world: 154

Telephones - mobile cellular:
469,700
country comparison to the world: 170

Telephone system:
general assessment: service throughout the country is good; international service is good to Southeast Asia, Middle East, Western Europe, and the US
domestic: every service available
international: country code - 673; landing point for the SEA-ME-WE-3 optical telecommunications submarine cable that provides links to Asia, the Middle East, and Europe; the Asia-America Gateway submarine cable network provides new links to Asia and the US; satellite earth stations - 2 Intelsat (1 Indian Ocean and 1 Pacific Ocean)

Broadcast media:
state-controlled Radio Television Brunei (RTB) operates 5 channels; 3 Malaysian TV stations are available; foreign TV broadcasts are available via satellite and cable systems; RTB operates 5 radio networks and broadcasts on multiple frequencies; British Forces Broadcast Service (BFBS) provides radio broadcasts on 2 FM stations; some radio broadcast stations from Malaysia are available via repeaters (2009)

Internet country code:
.bn

Internet hosts:
49,457
country comparison to the world: 96

Internet users:
314,900
country comparison to the world: 128

TRANSPORTATION

Railways:
total: 13 km (private line)
narrow gauge: 13 km 0.610-m gauge

Highways:
total: 1,150 km *paved:* 399 km *unpaved:* 751 km

Waterways: 209 km; navigable by craft drawing less than 1.2 m
Pipelines: crude oil 135 km; petroleum products 418 km; natural gas 920 km
Ports and harbors: Bandar Seri Begawan, Kuala Belait, Muara, Seria, Tutong
Merchant marine:
total: 7 liquefied gas tankers (1,000 GRT or over) totaling 348,476 GRT/340,635 DWT

Airports: 2

Airports—with paved runways:
total: 1
over 3,047 m: 1
Airports—with unpaved runways:
total: 1 *914 to 1,523 m:* 1 **Heliports:** 3

MILITARY

Military branches: Land Forces, Navy, Air Force, Royal Brunei Police
Military manpower—military age: 18 years of age
Military manpower—availability:
males age 15-49: 88,628
Military manpower—fit for military service:
males age 15-49: 51,270
Military manpower—reaching military age annually:
males: 3,078
Military expenditures—dollar figure: $343 million
Military expenditures—percent of GDP: 6%

TRANSNATIONAL ISSUES

Disputes—international: possibly involved in a complex dispute over the Spratly Islands with China, Malaysia, Philippines, Taiwan, and Vietnam; in 1984, Brunei established an exclusive fishing zone that encompasses Louisa Reef in the southern Spratly Islands, but has not publicly claimed the island.

IMPORTANT INFORMATION FOR UNDERSTANDING BRUNEI

PROFILE

OFFICIAL NAME: Negara Brunei Darussalam

Geography
Area: 5,765 sq. km. (2,226 sq. mi.), slightly larger than Delaware.
Cities: *Capital*--Bandar Seri Begawan.
Terrain: East--flat coastal plain rises to mountains; west--hilly lowland with a few mountain ridges.
Climate: Equatorial; high temperatures, humidity, and rainfall.

People
Nationality: *Noun and adjective*--Bruneian(s).
Population : 383,000.
Annual growth rate: 3.5%.
Ethnic groups: Malay, Chinese, other indigenous groups.
Religion: Islam.
Languages: Malay, English, Chinese; Iban and other indigenous dialects.
Education: *Years compulsory*--9. *Literacy* (2006)--94.7%.
Health: *Life expectancy (years)*--74.4 (men), 77.4 (women) yrs. *Infant mortality rate* --12.25/1,000.

Government
Type: Malay Islamic Monarchy.
Independence: January 1, 1984.
Constitution: 1959.
Branches: *Executive*--Sultan is both head of state and Prime Minister, presiding over a fourteen-member cabinet. *Legislative*--a Legislative Council has been reactivated after a 20-year suspension to play an advisory role for the Sultan. *Judicial* (based on Indian penal code and English common law)--magistrate's courts, High Court, Court of Appeals, Judicial Committee of the Privy Council (sits in London).
Subdivisions: *Four districts*--Brunei-Muara, Belait, Tutong, and Temburong.

Economy
Natural resources: Oil and natural gas.
Trade: *Exports*--oil, liquefied natural gas, petroleum products, garments. Major markets--Japan, Korea, ASEAN, U.S. *Imports*--machinery and transport equipment, manufactured goods. *Major suppliers*--ASEAN, Japan, U.S., EU.

PEOPLE

Many cultural and linguistic differences make Brunei Malays distinct from the larger Malay populations in nearby Malaysia and Indonesia, even though they are ethnically related and share the Muslim religion. Brunei has hereditary nobility, carrying the title Pengiran. The Sultan can award to commoners the title Pehin, the equivalent of a life peerage awarded in the United Kingdom. The Sultan also can award his subjects the Dato, the equivalent of a knighthood in the United Kingdom, and Datin, the equivalent of damehood.

Bruneians adhere to the practice of using complete full names with all titles, including the title Haji (for men) or Hajah (for women) for those who have made the Haj pilgrimage to Mecca. Many Brunei Malay women wear the tudong, a traditional head covering. Men wear the songkok, a traditional Malay cap. Men who have completed the Haj can wear a white songkok.
The requirements to attain Brunei citizenship include passing tests in Malay culture, customs, and language. Stateless permanent residents of Brunei are given International Certificates of Identity, which allow them to travel overseas. The majority of Brunei's Chinese are permanent residents, and many are stateless. An amendment to the National Registration and Immigration Act of 2002 allowed female Bruneian citizens for the first time to transfer their nationality to their children.

Oil wealth allows the Brunei Government to provide the population with one of Asia's finest health care systems. Malaria has been eradicated, and cholera is virtually nonexistent. There are five general hospitals--in Bandar Seri Begawan, Tutong, Kuala Belait, Bangar, and Seria--and there are numerous health clinics throughout the country.

Education starts with preschool, followed by 6 years of primary education and up to 7 years of secondary education. Nine years of education are mandatory. Most of Brunei's college students attend universities and other institutions abroad, but approximately 3,674 study at the University of Brunei Darussalam. Opened in 1985, the university has a faculty of more than 300 instructors and is located on a sprawling campus overlooking the South China Sea.

The official language is Malay, but English is widely understood and used in business. Other languages spoken are several Chinese dialects, Iban, and a number of native dialects. Islam is the official religion, but religious freedom is guaranteed under the constitution.

HISTORY

Historians believe there was a forerunner to the present Brunei Sultanate, which the Chinese called Po-ni. Chinese and Arabic records indicate that this ancient trading kingdom existed at the mouth of the Brunei River as early as the seventh or eighth century A.D. This early kingdom was apparently conquered by the Sumatran Hindu Empire of Srivijaya in the early ninth century, which later controlled northern Borneo and the Philippines. It was subjugated briefly by the Java-based Majapahit Empire but soon regained its independence and once again rose to prominence.

The Brunei Empire had its golden age from the 15th to the 17th centuries, when its control extended over the entire island of Borneo and north into the Philippines. Brunei was particularly powerful under the fifth sultan, Bolkiah (1473-1521), who was famed for his sea exploits and even briefly captured Manila; and under the ninth sultan, Hassan (1605-19), who fully developed an elaborate Royal Court structure, elements of which remain today.

After Sultan Hassan, Brunei entered a period of decline due to internal battles over royal succession as well as the rising influences of European colonial powers in the region that, among other things, disrupted traditional trading patterns, destroying the economic base of Brunei and many other Southeast Asian sultanates. In 1839, the English adventurer James Brooke arrived in Borneo and helped the Sultan put down a rebellion. As a reward, he became governor and later "Rajah" of Sarawak in northwest Borneo and gradually expanded the territory under his control.

Meanwhile, the British North Borneo Company was expanding its control over territory in northeast Borneo. In 1888, Brunei became a protectorate of the British Government, retaining internal independence but with British control over external affairs. In 1906, Brunei accepted a further measure of British control when executive power was transferred to a British resident, who advised the ruler on all matters except those concerning local custom and religion.

In 1959, a new constitution was written declaring Brunei a self-governing state, while its foreign affairs, security, and defense remained the responsibility of the United Kingdom. An attempt in 1962 to introduce a partially elected legislative body with limited powers was abandoned after the opposition political party, Parti Rakyat Brunei, launched an armed uprising, which the government put down with the help of British forces. In the late 1950s and early 1960s, the government also resisted pressures to join neighboring Sabah and Sarawak in the newly formed Malaysia. The Sultan eventually decided that Brunei would remain an independent state.

In 1967, Sultan Omar abdicated in favor of his eldest son, Hassanal Bolkiah, who became the 29th ruler. The former Sultan remained as Defense Minister and assumed the royal title Seri Begawan. In 1970, the national capital, Brunei Town, was renamed Bandar Seri Begawan in his honor. The Seri Begawan died in 1986.

On January 4, 1979, Brunei and the United Kingdom signed a new treaty of friendship and cooperation. On January 1, 1984, Brunei Darussalam became a fully independent state.

GOVERNMENT AND POLITICAL CONDITIONS

Under Brunei's 1959 constitution, the Sultan is the head of state with full executive authority, including emergency powers since 1962. The Sultan is assisted and advised by five councils, which he appoints. A Council of Ministers, or cabinet, which currently consists of 14 members (including the Sultan himself), assists in the administration of the government. The Sultan presides over the cabinet as Prime Minister and also holds the positions of Minister of Defense and Minister of Finance. His son, the Crown Prince, serves as Senior Minister. One of the Sultan's brothers, Prince Mohamed, serves as Minister of Foreign Affairs.

Brunei's legal system is based on English common law, with an independent judiciary, a body of written common law judgments and statutes, and legislation enacted by the sultan. The local magistrates' courts try most cases. More serious cases go before the High Court, which sits for about 2 weeks every few months. Brunei has an arrangement with the United Kingdom whereby United Kingdom judges are appointed as the judges for Brunei's High Court and Court of Appeal. Final appeal can be made to the Judicial Committee of the Privy Council in London in civil but not criminal cases. Brunei also has a separate system of Islamic courts that apply Sharia law in family and other matters involving Muslims.
The Government of Brunei assures continuing public support for the current form of government by providing economic benefits such as subsidized food, fuel, and housing; free education and medical care; and low-interest loans for government employees.

The Sultan said in a 1989 interview that he intended to proceed, with prudence, to establish more liberal institutions in the country and that he would reintroduce elections and a legislature when he "[could] see evidence of a genuine interest in politics on the part of a responsible majority of Bruneians." In 1994, a constitutional review committee submitted its findings to the Sultan, but these have not been made public. In 2004 the Sultan re-introduced an appointed Legislative Council with minimal powers. Five of the 31 seats on the Council are indirectly elected by village leaders.

Brunei's economy is almost totally supported by exports of crude oil and natural gas. The government uses its earnings in part to build up its foreign reserves, which at one time reportedly reached more than $30 billion. The country's wealth, coupled with its membership in the United Nations, Association of Southeast Asian Nations (ASEAN), the Asia Pacific Economic Cooperation (APEC) forum, and the Organization of the Islamic Conference give it an influence in the world disproportionate to its size.

Principal Government Officials
Sultan and Yang di-Pertuan, Prime Minister, Minister of Defense, and Minister of Finance--His Majesty Sultan Hassanal Bolkiah
Senior Minister--His Royal Highness Crown Prince Billah
Minister of Foreign Affairs--His Royal Highness Prince Mohamed Bolkiah
Ambassador to the United States--Pengiran Anak Dato Haji Puteh
Ambassador to the United Nations--Dr. Haji Emran bin Bahar
Brunei Darussalam maintains an embassy in the United States at 3520 International Court, NW, Washington, DC 20008; tel. 202-237-1838.

ECONOMY

Currency	Brunei dollar BND
Fixed exchange rates	1 Brunei dollar = 1 Singapore dollar
Fiscal year	1 April – 31 March (from April 2009)
Trade organisations	APEC, ASEAN, WTO. BIMP-EAGA
	Statistics
GDP	$20.38 billion PPP Rank: 123rd
GDP growth	2.8% Q1
GDP per capita	$51,600
GDP by sector	agriculture (0.7%), industry (73.3%), services (26%)
Inflation (CPI)	1.2%
Population below poverty line	1000 person
Labour force	188,800

Labour force by occupation	agriculture 4.5%, industry 63.1%, services 32.4%
Unemployment	3.7%
Main industries	petroleum, petroleum refining, liquefied natural gas, construction
Ease-of-doing-business rank	83rd
External	
Exports	$10.67 billion
Main export partners	Japan 46.5% South Korea 15.5% Australia 9.3% India 7.0% New Zealand 6.7% (est.)
Imports	$12.055 billion c.i.f.
Main import partners	Singapore 26.3% China 21.3% United Kingdom 21.3% Malaysia 11.8%
Public finances	
Public debt	$0
Revenues	$10.49 billion
Expenses	$5.427 billion
Credit rating	Not rated

Main data source: CIA World Fact Book *All values, unless otherwise stated, are in US dollars.*

Brunei is a country with a small, wealthy economy that is a mixture of foreign and domestic entrepreneurship, government regulation and welfare measures, and village tradition. It is almost totally supported by exports of crude oil and natural gas, with revenues from the petroleum sector accounting for over half of GDP. Per capita GDP is high, and substantial income from overseas investment supplements income from domestic production. The government provides for all medical services and subsidizes food and housing. The government has shown progress in its basic policy of diversifying the economy away from oil and gas. Brunei's leaders are concerned that steadily increased integration in the world economy will undermine internal social cohesion although it has taken steps to become a more prominent player by serving as chairman for the 2000 APEC (Asian Pacific Economic Cooperation) forum. Growth in 1999 was estimated at 2.5% due to higher oil prices in the second half.

Brunei is the third-largest oil producer in Southeast Asia, averaging about 180,000 barrels per day (29,000 m^3/d). It also is the fourth-largest producer of liquefied natural gas in the world.

Brunei is the fourth-largest oil producer in Southeast Asia, averaging about 219,000 barrels a day in 2006. It also is the ninth-largest exporter of liquefied natural gas in the world. Like many oil producing countries, Brunei's economy has followed the swings of the world oil market. Economic growth has averaged around 2.8% in the 2000s, heavily dependent on oil and gas production. Oil production has averaged around 200,000 barrels a day during the 2000s, while liquefied natural gas output has been slightly under or over 1,000 trillion btu/day over the same period. Brunei is estimated to have oil reserves expected to last 25 years, and enough natural gas reserves to last 40 years.

Brunei Shell Petroleum (BSP), a joint venture owned in equal shares by the Brunei Government and the Royal Dutch/Shell group of companies, is the chief oil and gas production company in Brunei. It also operates the country's only refinery. BSP and four sister companies--including the liquefied natural gas producing firm BLNG--constitute the largest employer in Brunei after the government. BSP's small refinery has a distillation capacity of 10,000 barrels per day. This satisfies domestic demand for most petroleum products.

The French oil company Total (then known as ELF Aquitaine) became active in petroleum exploration in Brunei in the 1980s. The joint venture Total E&P Borneo BV currently produces approximately 35,000 barrels per day and 13% of Brunei's natural gas.

In 2003, Malaysia disputed Brunei-awarded oil exploration concessions for offshore blocks J and K (Total and Shell respectively), which led to the Brunei licensees ceasing exploration activities. Negotiations between the two countries are continuing in order to resolve the conflict. In 2006, Brunei awarded two on-shore blocks--one to a Canadian-led and the other to a Chinese-led consortium. Australia, Indonesia, and Korea were the largest customers for Brunei's oil exports, taking over 67% of Brunei's total crude exports. Traditional customers Japan, the U.S., and China each took around 5% of total crude exports.
Almost all of Brunei's natural gas is liquefied at Brunei Shell's Liquefied Natural Gas (LNG) plant, which opened in 1972 and is one of the largest LNG plants in the world. Some 90% of Brunei's LNG produced is sold to Japan under a long-term agreement renewed in 1993.

The agreement calls for Brunei to provide over 5 million tons of LNG per year to three Japanese utilities, namely to TEPCo, Tokyo Electric Power Co. (J.TER or 5001), Tokyo Gas Co. (J.TYG or 9531) and Osaka Gas Co. (J.OSG or 9532). The Japanese company, Mitsubishi, is a joint venture partner with Shell and the Brunei Government in Brunei LNG, Brunei Coldgas, and Brunei Shell Tankers, which together produce the LNG and supply it to Japan. Since 1995, Brunei has supplied more than 700,000 tons of LNG to the Korea Gas Corporation (KOGAS) as well. In 1999, Brunei's natural gas production reached 90 cargoes per day. A small amount of natural gas is used for domestic power generation. Since 2001, Japan remains the dominant export market for natural gas. Brunei is the fourth-largest exporter of LNG in the Asia-Pacific region behind Indonesia, Malaysia, and Australia.

The government sought in the past decade to diversify the economy with limited success. Oil and gas and government spending still account for most of Brunei's economic activity. Brunei's non-petroleum industries include agriculture, forestry, fishing, aquaculture, and banking. The garment-for-export industry has been shrinking since the U.S. eliminated its garment quota system at the end of 2004. The Brunei Economic Development Board announced plans in 2003 to use proven gas reserves to establish downstream industrial projects. The government plans to build a power plant in the Sungai Liang region to power a proposed aluminum smelting plant that will depend on foreign investors. A second major project depending on foreign investment is in the planning stage: a giant container hub at the Muara Port facilities.

The government regulates the immigration of foreign labor out of concern it might disrupt Brunei's society. Work permits for foreigners are issued only for short periods and must be continually renewed. Despite these restrictions, the estimated 100,000 foreign temporary residents of Brunei make up a significant portion of the work force. The government reported a total work force of 180,400 in 2006, with a derived unemployment rate of 4.0%.

Oil and natural gas account for almost all exports. Since only a few products other than petroleum are produced locally, a wide variety of items must be imported. Nonetheless, Brunei has had a significant trade surplus in the 2000s. Official statistics show Singapore, Malaysia, Japan, the U.S., and the U.K. as the leading importers in 2005. The United States was the third-largest supplier of imports to Brunei in 2005.

Brunei's substantial foreign reserves are managed by the Brunei Investment Agency (BIA), an arm of the Ministry of Finance. BIA's guiding principle is to increase the real value of Brunei's foreign reserves while pursuing a diverse investment strategy, with holdings in the United States, Japan, Western Europe, and the Association of Southeast Asian Nations (ASEAN) countries.

The Brunei Government encourages more foreign investment. New enterprises that meet certain criteria can receive pioneer status, exempting profits from income tax for up to 5 years, depending on the amount of capital invested. The normal corporate income tax rate is 30%. There is no personal income tax or capital gains tax.

One of the government's priorities is to encourage the development of Brunei Malays as leaders of industry and commerce. There are no specific restrictions of foreign equity ownership, but local participation, both shared capital and management, is encouraged. Such participation helps when tendering for contracts with the government or Brunei Shell Petroleum.

Companies in Brunei must either be incorporated locally or registered as a branch of a foreign company and must be registered with the Registrar of Companies. Public companies must have a minimum of seven shareholders. Private companies must have a minimum of two but not more than 50 shareholders. At least half of the directors in a company must be residents of Brunei.

The government owns a cattle farm in Australia through which the country's beef supplies are processed. At 2,262 square miles, this ranch is larger than Brunei itself. Eggs and chickens are largely produced locally, but most of Brunei's other food needs must be imported. Agriculture, aquaculture, and fisheries are among the industrial sectors that the government has selected for highest priority in its efforts to diversify the economy.

Recently the government has announced plans for Brunei to become an international offshore financial center as well as a center for Islamic banking. Brunei is keen on the development of small and medium enterprises and also is investigating the possibility of establishing a "cyber park" to develop an information technology industry. Brunei has also promoted ecotourism to take advantage of the over 70% of Brunei's territory that remains primal tropical rainforest.

DEFENSE

The Sultan is both Minister of Defense and Supreme Commander of the Armed Forces (RBAF). All infantry, navy, and air combat units are made up of volunteers. There are two infantry battalions equipped with armored reconnaissance vehicles and armored personnel carriers and supported by Rapier air defense missiles and a flotilla of coastal patrol vessels armed with surface-to-surface missiles. Brunei has ordered, but not yet taken possession of, three offshore patrol vessels from the U.K.
Brunei has a defense agreement with the United Kingdom, under which a British Armed Forces Ghurka battalion (1,500 men) is permanently stationed in Seria, near the center of Brunei's oil industry. The RBAF has joint exercises, training programs, and other military cooperation with the United Kingdom and many other countries, including the United States. The U.S. and Brunei signed a memorandum of understanding (MOU) on defense cooperation in November 1994. The two countries conduct an annual military exercise called CARAT.

FOREIGN RELATIONS

Brunei joined ASEAN on January 7, 1984--one week after resuming full independence--and gives its ASEAN membership the highest priority in its foreign relations. Brunei joined the UN in September 1984. It also is a member of the Organization of the Islamic Conference (OIC) and of the Asia-Pacific Economic Cooperation (APEC) forum. Brunei hosted the APEC Economic Leaders' Meeting in November 2000 and the ASEAN Regional Forum (ARF) in July 2002.

U.S.-BRUNEI RELATIONS

Relations between the United States and Brunei date from the 1800s. On April 6, 1845, the U.S.S. Constitution visited Brunei. The two countries concluded a Treaty of Peace, Friendship, Commerce and Navigation in 1850, which remains in force today. The United States maintained a consulate in Brunei from 1865 to 1867.

The U.S. welcomed Brunei Darussalam's full independence from the United Kingdom on January 1, 1984, and opened an Embassy in Bandar Seri Begawan on that date. Brunei opened its embassy in Washington in March 1984. Brunei's armed forces engage in joint exercises, training programs, and other military cooperation with the U.S. A memorandum of understanding on defense cooperation was signed on November 29, 1994. The Sultan visited Washington in December 2002.

Principal U.S. Embassy Officials
Ambassador-- Craig Allen

Ambassador Craig Allen was sworn in as the United States ambassador to Brunei Darussalam on December 19, 2014.

Deputy Chief of Mission--John McIntyre
Management Officer--Michael Lampel

The U.S. Embassy in Bandar Seri Begawan is located on the third & fifth floors of the Teck Guan Plaza, at the corner of Jalan Sultan and Jalan MacArthur; tel: 673-2229670; fax: 673-2225293; e-mail: usembassy_bsb@state.gov

TRAVEL AND BUSINESS INFORMATION

The U.S. Department of State's Consular Information Program advises Americans traveling and residing abroad through Consular Information Sheets, Public Announcements, and Travel Warnings. **Consular Information Sheets** exist for all countries and include information on entry and exit requirements, currency regulations, health conditions, safety and security, crime, political disturbances, and the addresses of the U.S. embassies and consulates abroad. **Public Announcements** are issued to disseminate information quickly about terrorist threats and other relatively short-term conditions overseas that pose significant risks to the security of American travelers. **Travel Warnings** are issued when the State Department recommends that Americans avoid travel to a certain country because the situation is dangerous or unstable.

For the latest security information, Americans living and traveling abroad should regularly monitor the Department's Bureau of Consular Affairs Internet web site at http://www.travel.state.gov, where the current Worldwide Caution, Public Announcements, and Travel Warnings can be found. Consular Affairs Publications, which contain information on obtaining passports and planning a safe trip abroad, are also available at http://www.travel.state.gov. For additional information on international travel, see http://www.usa.gov/Citizen/Topics/Travel/International.shtml.

The Department of State encourages all U.S citizens traveling or residing abroad to register via the State Department's travel registration website or at the nearest U.S. embassy or consulate abroad. Registration will make your presence and whereabouts known in case it is necessary to contact you in an emergency and will enable you to receive up-to-date information on security conditions.

Emergency information concerning Americans traveling abroad may be obtained by calling 1-888-407-4747 toll free in the U.S. and Canada or the regular toll line 1-202-501-4444 for callers outside the U.S. and Canada.

The National Passport Information Center (NPIC) is the U.S. Department of State's single, centralized public contact center for U.S. passport information. Telephone: 1-877-4USA-PPT (1-877-487-2778). Customer service representatives and operators for TDD/TTY are available Monday-Friday, 7:00 a.m. to 12:00 midnight, Eastern Time, excluding federal holidays.

Travelers can check the latest health information with the U.S. Centers for Disease Control and Prevention in Atlanta, Georgia. A hotline at 877-FYI-TRIP (877-394-8747) and a web site at http://www.cdc.gov/travel/index.htm give the most recent health advisories, immunization recommendations or requirements, and advice on food and drinking water safety for regions and countries. A booklet entitled "Health Information for International Travel" (HHS publication number CDC-95-8280) is available from the U.S. Government Printing Office, Washington, DC 20402, tel. (202) 512-1800.

**For additional analytical, business and investment opportunities information,
please contact Global Investment & Business Center, USA
at (703) 370-8082. Fax: (703) 370-8083. E-mail: ibpusa3@gmail.com
Global Business and Investment Info Databank - www.ibpus.com**

BRUNEI LEGAL SYSTEM BASICS

The British Residential system was introduced in Brunei Darussalam by virtue of the Courts Enactment of 1906. Another enactment was later introduced, known as the 1908 Enactment and had repealed the 1906 Enactment. The purpose of this second Enactment was to amend the law relating to the constitution and powers of the Civil and Criminal Courts and the law and procedures to be administered in Brunei Darussalam (hereafter called the "State").

By virtue of section 3 of the 1908 Enactment, five courts were constituted in the State for the administration of Civil and Criminal justice. There were:

(1) The Court of the Resident

(2) Courts of Magistrate of the First Class

(3) Courts of Magistrate of the Second Class

(4) Courts of Native Magistrates

(5) Courts of Kathis.

The first court would be the Court of the Resident, which had and exercised original and appellate jurisdiction in civil and criminal matters. The Officer, which presided the Court of the Resident, should either be the Resident; or the District Judge of the District Court of Labuan or any District Judge of the Colony of the Straits Settlements[1].

The Court of the Resident had jurisdiction in all suits, matters and questions of a civil nature except the power to authorize any Court in the State to dissolve or annul a marriage lawfully solemnised in the United Kingdom of Great Britain and Ireland or in any British Colony, Protectorate or Possession[2].

Its appellate jurisdiction in both civil and criminal matters would be to hear and determine all appeals from the decisions of the lower Courts; and in doing so might exercise full powers or supervision and revision in respect of all proceedings in such Courts[3].

Section 8A of the 1908 Enactment stated that the Courts of Magistrates was of two kinds

i.e. Courts Magistrates of the First Class, and Courts Magistrates of the Second Class.

For the Court of Magistrate of the First Class, its criminal jurisdiction would be to try all offences for which the maximum term of imprisonment provided by law did not exceed a term of 7 years imprisonment of either description or which were punishable with fine only and for any other offence in respect of which jurisdiction was given by law; whereas

[1] Section 4 of the 1908 Enactment. [2] Section 5(i) of the 1908 Enactment. [3] Section 7 of the 1908 Enactment.

for civil jurisdiction it would hear and determine all suits when the amount in dispute or the value of the subject matter did not exceed $1,000 [4].

In addition to that, such Court had power to grant, alter, revoke and annul probates of wills and letters of administration in the estate of all persons leaving movable or immovable property in the State or the time of death having a fixed place of abode within the State where such estate does not exceed in value $2,500[5]. Such Court also had power to appoint and control guardians of infants and lunatics[6].

For its appellate jurisdiction, the Court of Magistrate of the First Class had power to hear and determine all appeals from the decisions of inferior Courts both in civil and criminal matters, and had power for revision and supervision in respect of all proceedings in such Courts[7].

For the Court of Magistrate of the Second Class, its criminal jurisdiction would be to try all offences for which the maximum term of imprisonment provided by law does not exceed 3 years imprisonment of either description or which were punishable with fine only of a sum not exceeding $100 and any offence in respect of which jurisdiction is given to the Court of a Magistrate of the Second Class.[8]

In its civil jurisdiction, the Court of Magistrate of the Second Class would hear and determine all suits when the amount in dispute or the value of the subject matter does not exceed $ 100.[9]

Unlike the Court of Magistrate of the First Class, the Court of Magistrate of the Second Class had no power to grant probate of wills or letters of administration, to appoint and control guardians of infants and lunatics, or even to hear appeals in civil or criminal matters[10].

As for the Court of a Native Magistrate, it could hear and determine all suits brought by or against Malays or other Asiatics in which the amount in dispute or the subject matter does not exceed $25 while its criminal jurisdiction would be to try and determine cases in which the maximum amount of imprisonment prescribed by law did not exceed three months[11].

And lastly, the Court of a Kathi that had such powers in all matters concerning Islamic religion, marriage and divorce as may be defined in his "Kuasa."[12].

[4] Section 8B (i) of the 1908 Enactment. [5] Section 8B (ii)(a) of the 1908 Enactment. [6] Section 8B (ii)(b) of the 1908 Enactment. [7] Section 8B (iii) of the 1908 Enactment. [8] Section 8C (i) of the 1908 Enactment. [9] Section 8C (i) of the 1908 Enactment. [10] Section 8C (ii) of the 1908 Enactment. [11] Section 9 of the 1908 Enactment. [12] Section 9 of the 1908 Enactment.

Sentences that might be imposed by the various Courts:

(1) Court of the Resident – any sentence authorized by law.

(2) Courts of Magistrate of the First Class – Imprisonment for a term not exceeding two years. Fine not exceeding $1,000. Whipping not exceeding 12 strokes.

(3) Courts of Magistrate of the Second Class – Imprisonment for a term not exceeding fourteen days. Fine not exceeding $50.

(4) Courts of Native Magistrates and Kathis – Fine not exceeding $10.[13]

Apart from the five courts mentioned earlier, there was the Supreme Court. The is court or any Judge thereof would have the original jurisdiction in the case of any offence charged to had been committed within the State for which the punishment of death is authorised by law[14].

The Supreme Court had civil appellate jurisdiction for an appeal from the final decision of the Court of the Resident in any civil action or proceeding where the amount in dispute or the subject matter exceeded$1,000 except in any of the following cases where no such appeal might be made:

(1) where the judgment or order was made by the consent of parties;

(2) where the judgment or order relates to costs only;

(3) where by any Enactment for the time being in force the judgment or order of the Court of the Resident was expressly declared to be final[15].

The criminal appellate jurisdiction of the Supreme Court would be to hear appeal from any decision of the Court of the Resident in the exercise of its original jurisdiction whereby any person had been convicted and sentenced to not less than two years imprisonment or to a fine of not less than $ 500[16]. To make an appeal, the appellant would lodge a petition of appeal at the Court of the Resident addressed to the Supreme Court within seven days from the date when the judgment or order was pronounced or within such further time as may be allowed by the Court of the Resident[17]. Any judgment of order of the Court of Appeal or of the Supreme Court made under this Enactment should be executed, enforced and be given effect by the Court of the Resident[18].

However, under this Enactment there was still scope for an appeal against any judgment or order of the Court of Appeal in any civil matter. This appeal might be made to His Britannic Majesty in Council (i.e. Privy Council) subject to such rules and regulations as may be prescribed by order of His Majesty in Council[19].

[13] Section 13 of the 1908 Enactment. [14] Section 14 (i) of the 1908 Enactment. [15] Section 15 (i) of the 1908 Enactment. [16] Section 16 (1) of the 1908 Enactment. [17] Section 16(2) of the 1908 Enactment. [18] Section 17 of the 1908 Enactment. [19] Section 18 of the 1908 Enactment.

THE COMING OF ISLAM TO BRUNEI DARUSSALAM

Being a state where majority of the populations are Muslims, Islam has been made the official religion of Brunei Darussalam. To say that Islam has only been practiced in this country in recent years are quite incorrect as there are sources, which date the establishment of a Muslim sultanate rule. In fact, Islamic laws have always been the governing laws in Brunei Darussalam even before the coming of the British.

There are evidences which show that Islam had come to Brunei since the 10th century. However, its reception was slow probably because most of the populations during that time were still holding on to their beliefs in Hinduism. Muslims were comprised of just a small section of the population including those traders who came to Brunei[20]. And it was believed that the acceptance of the Sultans and nobles had started the spread of Islam among the community. Awang Alak Betatar, the first ruler of Brunei, embraced Islam when he married the princess of Johore[21]. He changed his name to Sultan Mohammad Shah and since then Islam slowly spread within Brunei.

Islam was quickly spread among most of the people in Brunei when Sultan Sharif Ali, the third Sultan of Brunei, ascended to the throne. Believed to be a descendant of the Prophet Muhammad (Peace Be Upon Him)[22], he was a pious person and was the one who had started to build mosque and had been the one who determined the direction of the Qiblat[23]. From then on Islam has become an important aspect in the life of people in Brunei where eventually it has become the official religion of Brunei Darussalam.

Other evidence that shows Brunei was indeed been governed by Islamic law can be seen in written and codified form. There exist two manuscripts, the first manuscript was called the "Hukum Kanun Brunei" which, contained 96 pages and is kept at the Language and Literature Bureau, whilst copy for reference can be found at the Brunei Museum reference no. A/BM/98/90[24]. While the second manuscript was known as "Undang-Undang dan Adat Brunei Lama" (Old Brunei Law and Custom). It consists of 68 pages and is now reserved in the Sarawak Museum[25].

The content of the first manuscript covered a wide range of laws including the Islamic laws of hudud and qisas. The overall content of the manuscript is in harmony with the Islamic law. For example: Clause One of the manuscript talks about relationship between people and its ruler, conditions of becoming a ruler, responsibilities of the people towards

[20] Prof. Dato Dr. Haji Mahmud Saedon A. Othman, *Ke Arah Pelaksanaan Undang-Undang Di Negara Brunei Darussalam*, Jurnal Undang-Undang Syariah Brunei Darussalam, Januari-Jun 2002 Jilid 2 Bil. 2 p.

[21] Pehin Jawatan Dalam Seri Maharaja Dato Seri Utama Dr. Haji Awang Mohd. Jamil Al-Sufri, *Tarsilah Brunei: Sejarah Awal dan Perkembangan Islam*, Jilid 1, Pusat Sejarah Brunei 2001, p. 33. [22] Ibid p. 80. [23] Ibid p. 90. [24] Prof. Dato' Dr. Hj Mahmud Saedon bin Awang Othman, *Undang-Undang Islam Dalam Kesultanan Melayu Brunei hingga Tahun 1959*, International Seminar on Brunei Malay Sultanate in Nusantara 1999, p.

its rulers; Clause Four talks about various kind of offences such as murder, stabbing, slaying, hitting, robbery, stealing and many other though no punishment for those offences were stated in this Clause; Clause Five talks about the punishment of qisas for murder and also for the murderer to be killed in return for his crime; Clause Seven talks about offence of stealing, the punishment of which would be to cut off certain part of his hand; Clause Twenty-Five talks about marriage, requirements of marriage and the words to be uttered during the marriage contract; Clause twenty-Six talks about number of witnesses in a marriage contract; Clause Thirty-One talks about the rule and conditions in sale and purchase contract; and other clauses which talks about wide ranges of laws that is in accordance with Islamic laws.[26]

The *Hukum Kanun Brunei* was written during the reign of Sultan Hassan though it was believed that it had been started even earlier than that. It was completed and enforced during the reign of Sultan Jalilul Akbar and then continued during the reign of his son, Sultan Jalilul Jabbar. With the enforcement of this law, Islamic law has been enforced and that it had became the basic law and policy of Brunei Darussalam at that time[27].

THE CONSTITUTION

The governing structure of Brunei Darussalam rests on the country's written Constitution along with the three pillars of its national philosophy, namely Malay, Islam and Monarchy.

Brunei Darussalam's written Constitution sets out its governing authorities along with their respective functions and responsibilities. Specifically, the Constitution sets out the executive authority over the affairs of Brunei Darussalam and further creates the Council of Ministers, the Religious Council, the Privy Council, the Legislative Council, the *Adat Istiadat* (Customs and Traditions) Council and the Council of Succession. The basic order, structure, functions, responsibilities and underlying principles of the governing authorities are premised on what is prescribed in the Constitution. In relation to the law making process, it sets out the procedure within Brunei Darussalam with the recent rejuvenation of the Legislative Council, which will be discussed in detail later.

The Constitution of Brunei Darussalam was originally enacted in September 1959 much to the efforts of our then Sultan, Al-Marhum Sultan Haji Omar Ali Saifuddien Sa'adul Khairi Waddien, who is also the present Sultan's late father. The enactment of the 1959 Constitution represented the country's primary stepping stone in its move towards full independence, which eventually came in 1984.

Since 1959, the Constitution has been subject to a number of important amendments, in particular in 1971, 1984 and most recently in 2004. In fact, a newly revised Constitution was published in 2004 incorporating all the amendments that have been made since its birth year of 1959.

STATUTES/LEGISLATIVE ENACTMENTS

Brunei Darussalam has in place a set of acts compiled in volumes called "Laws of Brunei." At present, there are 193 Acts in place which are in loose leaf form kept in ring binder volumes that consist of legislations that were passed prior to Independence Day and those that were enacted after it. Some of the legislations are also Acts that were extended from the United Kingdom, some dating back as early as 1958. However, some have been notably repealed, either in whole or in part to reflect updates in the development of the law. There are however some old enactments that have been merely omitted from the Laws of Brunei as authorized by

His Majesty for the Attorney General to omit. Nevertheless, its omission does not mean that they do not have the force of law and hence would still be considered valid unless it is otherwise provided.[1]

There are also a number of *Government Gazettes* which consists of: i) new laws that has not been revised to become an Act;

Since Brunei Darussalam at present pass their laws in accordance with article 83(3) of the Constitution, any new laws that has been approved by His Majesty will be published in *Government Gazette* form and will come into force on the date His Majesty approves of. Hence that new law will for the time being be referred to as an Order and not an Act.

The Law Revision Act is in place to govern the revision of such *Gazettes* to turn into Acts. After the 1st of January of every year, the Attorney General revises the law and publishes a revised edition of the new law to be included in the Laws of Brunei volumes. He also does this with existing law that has been amended so he will publish a new revised edition of that law incorporating all the recent amendments.[2]

The following constitutional and legislative documents are also considered part of the Laws of Brunei.[3] They are:

i) Treaty of Friendship and Co-operation between Brunei Darussalam and the

United Kingdom dated 7th January 1979;

ii) The Continental Shelf Proclamation 1954

iii) The North Borneo (Definition of Boundaries) Order in Council 1958; and

iv) The Sarawak (Definition of Boundaries) Order in Council 1958.

ISLAMIC LAWS

In Islam, the main source of law is the Holy Qur'an then followed by the tradition of the Prophets or Hadith as the second source of the Islamic Laws[4]. Other sources of law in Islam includes *Ijma'* or consensus of opinion[5], *Qiyas* (Analogical Deduction)[6], *Istihsan* or Equity in Islamic Law[7], *Maslahah Mursalah* (Consideration of Public Interest)[8], *'Urf* (Custom)[9], *Istishab* (presumption of Continuity)[10], *Saad al-Dhara'i* (Blocking the Means)[11].

Similarly, Islamic laws in Brunei Darussalam are guided mainly by the principles in the Holy Qur'an and the Prophet's tradition or Hadith as well as other sources mentioned earlier. Islam as the official religion in Brunei Darussalam is clearly stated in the Constitution of Brunei Darussalam:

[2] Section 7 of the Law Revision Act [3] Schedule to the Law Revision Act [4] Mohammad Hashim Kamali, *Principles of Islamic Jurisprudence*, Second Revised Edition, Ilmiah Publishers Sdn. Bhd., Kuala Lumpur 1998, p. 58. [5] ibid p.168. [6] ibid p.197. [7] ibid p.245. [8] ibid p.267. [9] ibid p.283. [10] ibid p.297. [11] ibid p.310.

"The official religion of Brunei Darussalam shall be the Islamic Religion: Provided that all other religions may be practiced in peace and harmony by the persons professing them.[12]"

Islamic law in Brunei is still governed under the Religious Council and Kadis Courts Act (Chapter 77), an Act which consolidates the law relating to the Religious Council and the Kadis Courts, the constitution and organization of religious authorities and the regulation of religious affairs.

Apart from this Act, there are also other legislations enforced in Brunei Darussalam to govern the conduct of Muslims in this country, these legislations are for example:

i) the Syariah Courts Act (Chapter 184), an Act which make specific provisions in respect of the establishment of Syariah Courts, appointments, powers of Syar'ie Judge and jurisdiction of Syariah Courts and other matters connected with the proceedings of Syariah Courts, and for the determination and confirmation of the new moon;

ii) the Syariah Courts Evidence Order, 2001, an Order relating to the law of evidence for the Syariah Courts;

iii) the Emergency (Islamic Family Law) Order, 1999, an Order that make certain provisions relating to Islamic family law in respect of marriage, divorce, maintenance, guardianship and other matters connected with family life;

iv) the Islamic Adoption of Children Order, 2001, an Order to make certain provisions on the law of adoption of children according to Islam; and

v) the Halal Meat Act (Chapter 183) an Act which regulate the supply and importation of halal meat and related matters.

SUBSIDIARY LEGISLATION

We also have in place as part of the Laws of Brunei, a number of subsidiary legislations which include rules, regulations, orders, proclamations or other documents that has the force of law and annexed to their relevant parent Acts. Other government departments whose work is relevant to that particular legislation would usually prepare the drafts for subsidiary legislations.

The power to make subsidiary legislation is conferred under section 13 of the Interpretation and General Clauses Act (CAP. 4). Section 16 further states that the subsidiary legislation should be published in the *Government Gazette*.

CASE LAW/JUDICIAL PRECEDENT

The Supreme Court of Brunei Darussalam is largely guided by the written Constitution and the Laws of Brunei in executing their responsibility of upholding the law in Brunei Darussalam. However where there are no written laws on a particular matter, the courts would then turn to principles of law that are found in case law or judicial precedent.

[12] Article 3(1) of the Constitution of Brunei Darussalam.

Cases heard in Brunei Darussalam are compiled in annual volumes of what are called "Judgments of Brunei Darussalam." Similar to other members in the family practicing the English Legal System, Brunei Darussalam also practice the doctrine of *stare decisis*, where decisions of a higher court are binding on the lower courts. The advantages of following binding precedent include certainty, flexibility, comprehensiveness and practicality in its practice. However, it is recognized that sometimes it can be difficult for lower courts that are bound by the decision and therefore cannot alter it. For that reason also, it may create more appeals.

The courts of Brunei Darussalam would also occasionally refer to cases from Malaysia, Singapore, India and the United Kingdom, all practicing the English legal system though the decisions in those cases would not be binding but instead would only be regarded as "persuasive authority" in the courts of Brunei Darussalam.

COMMON LAW OF ENGLAND

Under the Application of Laws Act, the Common Law of England and the doctrine of equity, together with the statutes of general application that are administered or in force in England, also have the force of law in Brunei Darussalam. This provision is however on the condition that the said common law, doctrine of equity and statutes of general application does not contradict the circumstances of Brunei Darussalam, its inhabitants and subject to such qualifications or local circumstances and custom may render necessary.

GOVERNMENT AND THE STATE

THE EXECUTIVE

As stated under section 4 of the Constitution, the supreme executive authority of Brunei Darussalam is vested in and shall be exercised by His Majesty the Sultan and Yang Di-Pertuan of Brunei Darussalam who is also the Prime Minister of Brunei Darussalam. Nevertheless, His Majesty the Sultan may still appoint Ministers or Deputy Ministers to exercise that executive authority whilst solely being responsible to him in the course of their duties. These appointed ministers shall also assist and advise His Majesty the Sultan in the event His Majesty discharges his executive authority.

THE LEGISLATIVE COUNCIL

Under the Constitution, any member of the Legislative Council may introduce any bill and a bill will only become law when His Majesty the Sultan has assented, signed and sealed the bill with the Seal of the State.

The Legislative Council was temporarily suspended in 1983 but was recently reestablished at its first official meeting in September 2004. During the period where the Council was inactive, laws were passed in the form of emergency orders by His Majesty in accordance with article 83(3) of the Constitution. The normal procedure of the law making process during this period would be initiated by a particular Ministry or Government Department who would either propose or prepare the draft legislation and would then pass it to the Attorney General's Chambers to give legal advice on. Where a Ministry or Governmental Department merely propose the drafting of such legislation, the Attorney General's Chambers will then prepare the draft based on substantive points the former provides. Once the draft is ready to be adopted, it will be presented to His Majesty for his approval. The draft legislation that His Majesty approves of will be passed in an **Emergency Order** form and will be published in the *Government Gazette.*

Every order made under article 83(3) however are deemed to have been validly made, to be fully effectual and to have had full force from the date on which such Proclamation or Order was declared or made and they are deemed to have been passed by the Legislative Council.[1]

The law making process by the Legislative Council is prescribed under Part VII of the Constitution. Basically, any member of the Legislative Council may

(i) introduce a new bill;
(ii) propose a motion for the Council to debate on; or

(iii) present any petition to the Council. The bill, motion or petition will then be debated on and disposed of in accordance with the Standing Orders of the Legislative Council.

[1] Article 83A

Every bill that is going to be introduced needs to be published in the gazette and within 7 days of the publication of the bill in a gazette, the bill shall then be laid before the Legislative Council.[2]

There are certain matters however that are generally excluded from being discussed by the Legislative Council, unless His Majesty the Sultan approves otherwise, and these include matters relating to the issue of bank notes, the establishment of any bank association, amendment of the constitution in relation to both those matters. Matters that would also be disqualified are where the issues are inconsistent with any obligations imposed upon His Majesty under any international treaty or agreement with another power of state. Other disqualified matters include those having the effect of lowering or adversely affecting the rights, positions, discretions, powers, privileges, sovereignty or prerogatives of His Majesty, the standing or prominence of Brunei Darussalam's national philosophy that is Malay Islamic Monarchy and the finances or currency of Brunei Darussalam.[3]

All questions proposed to the Legislative Council to decide upon shall be concluded by way of majority vote taken from the members that are present and voting. Once a bill has been debated on, the Legislative Council will then make a decision whether or not to pass it. If the Council rejects it, which is called a "negative resolution", the Speaker of the Council will then have to submit a report to His Majesty the Sultan incorporating a summary of the debate and the reasons why the Council reached such a resolution. Nevertheless, His Majesty may still declare the Bill to have effect, notwithstanding the negative resolution and he may order it to have effect either as an Act in the form in which it was introduced or to include any amendments that he may think fit to include.[4]

When the Legislative Council decides to pass the Bill, such Bill will only become law if His Majesty the Sultan assents to it, signs it and thereafter seals the Bill with the official State Seal. Again, the bill might take effect as an Act either in its original form as to how it was introduced or His Majesty the Sultan may still make amendments to it as he thinks fit. Such law once assented, signed and sealed by His Majesty shall come into operation on the date on which such assent shall be given.[5]

All the laws made through the Legislative Council shall be styled as "Acts" which will always have the enacting words as follows: "Be it enacted by His Majesty the Sultan and Yang DI-Pertuan with the advice and consent of the Legislative Council as follows."[6]

His Majesty the Sultan also has reserved powers over any bills that was not or has not yet been passed by the Legislative Council if in his opinion, the passing or expedited passing of the Bill is in the interests of public order, good faith and good government. In such

[2] Article 41, the Constitution [3] Article 42 [4] Article 43 [5] Article 45 [6] Article 46

cases, he can declare that bill/motion/petition /business to have effect as if it had been passed or carried by that Council even though it has not been done so.[7]

THE JUDICIARY

THE SUPREME COURT

The Supreme Court of Brunei Darussalam is the body wholly responsible for the administration of justice in civil law (as opposed to "syariah law") and strictly speaking has within its hierarchical structure, the Court of Appeal and the High Court. Within the same building of the Supreme Court, we can also find the Intermediate Courts and the Courts of Magistrates (also known as the Subordinates Courts).

The head of administration for the Judiciary Department is the Chief Registrar whereas the entire judicial system is presided over and supervised by the Chief Justice.

Introduction

The Supreme Court is governed by the Supreme Court Act[8] along with its Rules annexed to the Act. The Rules of the Supreme Court regulates the practice and procedure of the High Court and the Court of Appeal. The Supreme Court consists of the President of the Court of Appeal, the Chief Justice, the Judges and the Judicial Commissioners of the Supreme Court. The jurisdiction of the Supreme Court is over any original and appellate criminal and civil cases by the High Court and also appellate criminal and civil jurisdiction by the Court of Appeal.[9]

The judges of the High Court at present consist of the Chief Justice along with two judges who are often referred to as Justices. The Court of Appeal judges are the President and two other appellate judges.

Jurisdiction

The civil jurisdiction of the High Court consists of the original jurisdiction and authority similar to that held and exercised by the Chancery, Family and Queen's Bench Divisions of the High Court of England and shall also include any other jurisdiction, original or appellate as may be conferred upon it by any other written law.[10]

The criminal jurisdiction of the High Court consists of such jurisdiction, original or appellate, as may be conferred upon it by any written law, which includes the Penal Code, the Criminal Procedure Code or the Criminal Conduct (Recovery of Proceeds) Order. In the Criminal Procedure Code specifically,[11] the High Court will have jurisdiction over any offence that was committed wholly or partly within Brunei Darussalam, or committed on board any ship or aircraft registered in Brunei Darussalam,

[7] Article 47, The Constitution [8] CAP 5 of the Laws of Brunei [9] Section 6, Supreme Court Act [10] Section 16, Supreme Court Act [11] Section 7 of the Criminal Procedure Code

or committed on the high seas if the offence is one of piracy by the law of nations. The Court will also have jurisdiction over an offence whether or not it was committed in Brunei Darussalam if it was committed by a subject of His Majesty the Sultan or by a person who abets, or enters a conspiracy to commit, an offence of Brunei Darussalam whether or not any overt act in furtherance of such conspiracy takes place within Brunei Darussalam. The High Court may also pass any sentence authorized by law.[12]

Any civil or criminal appeals from the High Court can be brought to the Court of Appeal.

The civil jurisdiction of the Court of Appeal consists of appeals from a judgment or order of the High Court in a civil cause or matter and again, such other jurisdiction conferred upon it by any other written law. The criminal jurisdiction of the Court of Appeal consists of appeals from the High Court.[13]

Appeals

Any civil appeals made from the Court of Appeal can only be referred by His Majesty the Sultan to the Judicial Committee of Her Britannic Majesty's Privy Council. For criminal cases however, no such appeals from the Court can be further made. There can be no civil appeals made if the appeal is[14]:

(i) against an order made allowing for an extension of time for appealing against a judgment or order;
(ii) a judgment that has been expressed to be final by any law;

(iii) any order made with the consent of all parties to the case;

(iv) any order relating only to costs;
(v) made without leave of the High Court of the Court of Appeal where the amount or value of the subject matter does not exceed $10,000 or where it is from any interlocutory order of judgment.

Extended jurisdiction of the High Court

Along with the exercise of its own jurisdiction as mentioned above, the High Court also has a general supervisory and revisionary jurisdiction over the Intermediate Courts and the Magistrates' Courts. Any time during a proceeding in an Intermediate Court or a Magistrates' Court, a High Court judge can always call for and check the record of proceedings and thereafter can either transfer the matter or proceedings to the High Court of he could also give directions as to the further conduct of the proceeding by the Intermediate or Magistrates' Court. Upon the High Court calling for any record in this instance, all such proceedings in the Intermediate or Subordinate Courts shall be stayed pending further what the High Court will order later on. The High Court may also feel the need to call on any decision recorded or passed by the Intermediate or

Magistrates' Courts to assess the correctness, legality or propriety of the decision recorded. If they are not satisfied with their findings, they can direct for a new trial or whatever action that is necessary to secure that substantial justice is done.[15]

[12] Section 10 of the Criminal Procedure Code [13] Section 18, 19, Supreme Court Act [14] Section 20, Supreme Court Act [15] Section 20A to 20E, Supreme Court Act

INTERMEDIATE COURTS

Introduction

The Intermediate Court is governed by the Intermediate Courts Act.[16] It is an open court to which the public generally has access to.[17] However, the same provisions with regards to power to hear proceedings in camera that was are mentioned below for Magistrates Court likewise applies to the Intermediate Courts. The Intermediate Court is presided over by a Judge who sits alone.[18] There are also registrars and deputy registrar who shall also be ex-officio commissioners for oaths and notaries public.[19]

Jurisdiction

The Intermediate Court's criminal jurisdiction[20] runs concurrently with the High Court. Hence, it has all the jurisdiction, powers, duties and authority as are vested, conferred and imposed on the High Court in the exercise of its **original** criminal jurisdiction.

The Court however does not have jurisdiction in respect of any offence that is punishable with death or with imprisonment for life. Nor does it have jurisdiction in respect of any offence that imposes a period of imprisonment that is longer than 20 years. If it so happens that after the trial ends and a conviction is secured, and it appears to the Court that the imprisonment imposed should be longer than 20 years or should carry a more serious penalty, then the Intermediate Court may commit the case to the High Court for sentencing.

Where the High Court and the Intermediate Court has concurrent jurisdiction in respect of any prosecution or proceeding, the Public Prosecutor or any person expressly authorized by him in writing, can direct in which those courts the proceeding should be instituted in.

The Intermediate Court exercises its original civil jurisdiction[21] in every action where the amount claimed or the value of the subject matter in dispute exceeds $15, 000 but does not exceed $100,000 or any higher sum that the Chief Justice may further prescribe. Similarly to the provisions for the Magistrate Court, to obtain this jurisdiction, one has to further prove that the cause of action arose in Brunei Darussalam or the defendant at the time the proceedings were instituted has some form of connection with Brunei Darussalam, be it being a resident or carrying on a business etc, or the facts of the case the proceedings are based on must be alleged to have occurred in Brunei Darussalam.

[16] CAP 162 of the Laws of Brunei [17] Section 7, Intermediate Courts Act [18] Section 10, Intermediate Courts Act [19] Section 11, Intermediate Courts Act [20] See Part IV of the Intermediate Courts Act [21] See Part V of the Intermediate Courts Act

The Court does not have civil jurisdiction over the recovery of immovable property or where there is a dispute as to a title registered under the Land Code, over the interpretation of a trust instrument, the grant or revocation of probate, over the interpretation of a will, over a declaratory decree, over the legitimacy of any person, over the guardianship or custody of a minor and over the validity or dissolution of any marriage.

In an action concerning immovable property that commenced in the Intermediate Court, a defendant may within one month apply to the High Court for the action to be transferred to the High Court if he feels that there is a dispute as to a title registered under the Land code. If a High Court judge is satisfied, he may order the action to be transferred to the High Court.

Also, not taking into account that the amount claimed should not be more than $100,000, an Intermediate Court has jurisdiction over any action for the recovery of immovable property with or without a claim for rent or profits if there is no dispute as to title registered under the Land Code.

Any judgement of an Intermediate Court should be regarded by the Parties as final and conclusive between themselves.

The Intermediate Court also has jurisdiction to grant probate and letters of administration in respect of the estate within Brunei Darussalam of a deceased person and the estate in respect of which the grant is applied for but it must be exclusive of what the deceased possessed of and over what the applicant is entitled to as a trustee and not a beneficiary, and without deducting anything on the account of debts due or owing, the amount claimed must not exceeds $250,000.

When a plaintiff has a cause of action for more than $100,000, which the Intermediate Court does not have jurisdiction over, it is possible for him to abandon the excess amount in order to bring it within the jurisdiction of the Intermediate Court. However he will not be able to recover any of the excess amounts that he abandoned. Nevertheless, if the amount is more than $100,000, the Intermediate Court can still have jurisdiction when and if the parties concerned agree by a signed memorandum filed in the Intermediate Court that it shall have jurisdiction, even though the amount claimed exceeds $100,000.

In an Intermediate Court proceeding, if the counterclaim or defence of any defendant involves a matter beyond the Intermediate Court's jurisdiction, any party may apply to the High Court within one month of being served the counterclaim, for an order that the whole proceedings, or just proceedings on the counterclaim defence to be transferred to the High Court.

Appeals

Civil appeals goes straight to the Court of Appeal as if it was an appeal from the High Court. However there will be no right of appeal entertained if the parties to the action have agreed in writing that the judgment of the court shall be final and conclusive between them.[22]

Criminal appeals also go to the Court of Appeal. The Court of Appeal can also review any sentencing that has been passed by the Intermediate Court on any person or provide an opinion on a point of law that has been referred to it.[23] The practice and procedure as contained in the Supreme Court Rules for the High Court and the Court of Appeal shall also apply to the Intermediate Court.

MAGISTRATES' COURT

Introduction

The Magistrate Courts are governed by the Subordinate Courts Act[24], in terms of its civil jurisdiction and by the Criminal Procedure Code[25] in the exercise of its criminal jurisdiction. There is also in place a set of Subordinate Courts Rules regulating and prescribing the procedure (including methods for pleading) and the practice in the Magistrate Courts in the exercise of its civil jurisdiction. These Rules of Court extends to all matters of procedures, practice relating to or concerning the effect or operation in law of any procedure or practice, enforcement of judgments or orders, in any case within the cognizance of the Magistrate Court.

All magistrate courts are deemed to be open and allow public access, however there are some instances when a Court may still direct to have the whole proceedings or only in part to be in camera sitting only[26]. In particular, where references are made, whether orally or in writing, directly to any act, decision, grant, revocation, suspension, refusal, omission, authority or discretion by His Majesty the Sultan or if there are cases that intends to refer to any issue that may directly or indirectly concerns the inviolability, sanctity or interests of the position, dignity, standing, honour, eminence or sovereignty of His Majesty the Sultan, then the Magistrate Court shall hold such proceedings in camera, so long as His Majesty the Sultan has not himself issued a direction that such proceedings need not be heard in camera.

Jurisdiction

The Magistrate Court exercises its civil jurisdiction[27] over every civil proceeding where the amount claimed or the value of the subject matter in dispute does not exceed B$30,000. However, if the matter is heard before the Chief Magistrate, Chief Registrar, Deputy Chief Registrar, Senior Magistrate or the Senior Registrar this prescribed limit would be B$50,000.

[22] Section 26, Intermediate Courts Act [23] Section 27, Intermediate Courts Act [24] CAP 6 of the Laws of Brunei [25] CAP 7 of the Laws of Brunei [26] Section 7, Subordinate Courts Act [27] See Section 17 of the Subordinate Courts Act

For the court to have jurisdiction of the case, the cause of action need to have arose in Brunei Darussalam, the defendant at the time the proceedings were instituted has some form of connection with Brunei Darussalam, be it being a resident or carrying on a business etc, and the facts of the case the proceedings are based on must be alleged to have occurred in Brunei Darussalam.

Furthermore, a Magistrate Court also has jurisdiction in any proceedings for the recovery of immovable property where the rent payable in respect of such property does not exceed $500 per month. This excludes cases where there is a genuine dispute as to title registered under the Land Code.

A Magistrate Court does not have any civil jurisdiction over acts done by the order of His Majesty the Sultan, over the recovery of immovable property where there is a genuine dispute as to the title registered under the Land Code, over cases involving specific performance and rescission of contracts, over the cancellation or rectification of instruments, over the interpretation of trust instruments and the enforcement of administration of trusts, the grant of probate or letters of administration in respect of a deceased person, over the interpretation of wills, administration of estate of any deceased person and lastly it does not have civil jurisdiction over declaratory decrees.

The Magistrate's court criminal jurisdiction[28] is similar to the High Court's criminal jurisdiction as mentioned above. Namely, the court will have jurisdiction over any offence that was committed wholly or partly within Brunei Darussalam, or committed on board any ship or aircraft registered in Brunei Darussalam, or committed on the high seas if the offence is one of piracy by the law of nations. The Court will also have jurisdiction over an offence whether or not it was committed in Brunei Darussalam if it was committed by a subject of His Majesty the Sultan or by a person who abets, or enters a conspiracy to commit, an offence of Brunei Darussalam whether or not any overt act in furtherance of such conspiracy takes place within Brunei Darussalam. Furthermore, the types of offences the magistrate court may try are any offence that is shown in the eighth column of the First Schedule of the Criminal Procedure Code to be so triable. However, if the offence it is given the power to try carries a maximum punishment the court has no power to award, it shall then commit the defendant for trial by the High Court if it holds the opinion that the punishment it has power to award is inadequate.

The criminal jurisdiction of magistrates conferred by the Criminal Procedure Code include hearing, trying, determining and disposing of summarily prosecutions for offences cognized by such magistrate and inquiring into offences committed with a view to committal for trial by the High Court. Magistrates also have the power and authority to inquire into complaints of offences, summon and examine relevant witnesses, summon and issue warrants for the apprehension of criminals and offenders, and deal with them according to law, issue search warrants, hold inquests and do all other matters and things which a magistrate is empowered to do by this Code or any other Act.

[28] See section 7 of the Criminal Procedure Code

Appeals

Any appeal in a civil matter in the Magistrate Court goes to the High Court.[29] Such appeals that has right to do so are cases where a Magistrate Court has given a final judgment in any proceedings for the recovery of immovable property or in any proceedings where the amount in dispute exceeds $500. Leave for appeal is needed from a judge with respect of an interlocutory order, from a final judgment of a Magistrate Court where the amount claimed or the value of the subject matter in dispute does not exceed $500. Leave from the judge is also required from an order relating to costs and also for any orders that were made by consent of the parties.

It is important for the appellant to keep in mind that he must also fulfill all other conditions of appeal imposed in accordance with the Rules of Court of the Supreme Court Act.

In a criminal matter, if a defendant, the complainant or the Public Prosecutor is not satisfied with any judgment, sentence or order given by the magistrate, he may appeal to the High Court against such judgment, sentence or order for any error in law or in fact, or on the ground that the sentence is either to extensive or too inadequate.

A Magistrate Court can also, at any time before or during any civil proceeding, request a legal opinion from the High Court if it desires to do so. Either the Magistrate initiates the request or it can also be made on the application of any of the parties. They shall forward a statement of the facts of the case and specify the exact points on which legal opinion is being sought. The High Court will then make a declaration or order in response to the query as it thinks fit.[30]

APPOINTMENT OF JUDGES, REGISTRARS AND OTHER RELEVANT PERSONS WITHIN THE SUPREME COURTS, INTERMEDIATE COURTS AND SUBORDINATE COURTS

The High Court and Court of Appeal judges are appointed by His Majesty the Sultan by instrument under his sign manual and the State Seal.[31] To become a judge of the Supreme Court, one has to be or has been a judge of a Court having unlimited jurisdiction over civil and criminal matters in some part of the Commonwealth or a Court having jurisdiction in appeals from any such Court. He must also have been entitled to practice as an advocate in such a court for a period of not less than 7 years. The judges of the Supreme Court hold their positions until the age of 65 or at a later time where His Majesty may approve of.

His Majesty may also from time to time appoint someone who satisfies the same conditions as mentioned above for the Supreme Court judges to be a Judicial Commissioner of the Supreme Court.[32] The Judicial Commissioner has the power to act as a Judge of the Supreme Court and all things done by him in accordance with the terms

[29] Section 17, Subordinate Courts Act [30] Section 22, Subordinate Courts Act [31] Section 7, Supreme Court Act [32] Section 11, Supreme Court Act

of this appointment will be deemed to have the same validity and effect as if it has been done by a judge.

An Intermediate Court judge is also appointed by His Majesty. To qualify for appointment, he must have been entitled to practice in a court having unlimited jurisdiction in civil and criminal matters in Brunei Darussalam or some part of the Commonwealth for not less then 5 years.[33]

Finally, magistrates are also appointed by His Majesty, in particular a Chief Magistrate who shall have seniority over all other Magistrates and Coroners. His Majesty can also appoint any fit and proper person to be a Coroner who shall have the same power to act as a Magistrate for the purpose of discharging the functions of a Magistrate. Hence, their actions shall have the same validity and effect as if they had been done by a Magistrate.[34]

SYARIAH COURT

The Syariah Courts in Brunei Darussalam consist of the Syariah Subordinate Courts, the Syariah High Court and the Syariah Appeal Court. These courts will have such jurisdiction, powers, duties and authority as are conferred and imposed by the Syariah Courts Act (Chapter 184) as well as by any other written law.[35]

For appointment of Judges in the Syariah Courts, Part II of this Act, among others, talks about the appointment of Chief Syar'ie Judge, the Syariah Appeal Court Judges, Syariah High court Judges and Syariah Subordinate Courts Judges.

Section 8(1) of this Act, stated that His Majesty the Sultan and Yang Di-Pertuan may, on the advice of the President of the Majlis Ugama Islam and after consultation with the Majlis, appoint a Chief Syar'ie Judge.[36] To be qualified as a Chief Syar'ie Judge, a person must be a citizen of Brunei Darussalam; and he has served as either a Judge of a Syariah Court, or Kadi, or in both capacities, for a cumulative period of not less than 7 years prior to his appointment or that he is a person learned in *Hukum Syara*[37].

For Syariah Appeal Court Judges, section 9(1) of this Act, stated that His Majesty the Sultan and Yang Di-Pertuan may, on the advice of the President of the Majlis and after consultation with the Majlis, appoint and re-appoint not more than 5 Muslims to form a standing panel of Judges, for a period of not exceeding 3 years. For each proceeding in the Syariah Appeal Court, the Chief Syar'ie Judge shall elect 2 of them to constitute a quorum of Judges. Again, a person qualified to be appointed as one of the Judges in the Syariah Appeal Court must be a citizen of Brunei Darussalam and he has served as either a Judge of a Syariah Court, or Kadi, or in both capacities, for a cumulative period of not

[33] Section 10, Intermediate Courts Act [34] Section 9-11, Subordinate Courts Act [35] Section 6(1) of the Syariah Courts Act (Chapter 184). [36] Section 8(1) of the Syariah Courts Act (Chapter 184). [37] Section 8(2) of the Syariah Courts Act (Chapter 184).

less than 7 years prior to his appointment, or that he is a person learned in *Hukum Syara*[38].

Section 10(1) of this Act provides for appointment of Syariah High court Judges whereby His Majesty the Sultan and Yang Di-Pertuan may, on the advice of the President of the Majlis and after consultation with the Majlis, appoint Judges of the Syariah High Court. To be qualified as one, a person must be a citizen of Brunei Darussalam; and has, for a cumulative of not less than 7 years prior to his appointment, served as either a Judge of a Syariah Subordinate Court, or Kadi, or registrar, or Syar'ie Prosecutor, or in more than one of such capacities; or that he is a person learned in Hukum Syara'[39].

And for appointment of Syariah Subordinate Courts Judges, section 11 of this Act provides that His Majesty the Sultan and Yang Di-Pertuan may, on the advice of the President of the Majlis and after consultation with the Majlis, appoint Judges of the Syariah Subordinate Courts.

Under this Act, the Chief Syar'ie Judge and Syariah High Court Judges shall hold office until the age of 65 years or until such later time as may be approved by His Majesty the Sultan and Yang Di-Pertuan[40]. However, any Syar'ie Judges including the Chief Syar'ie Judge, may at any time resign from his office by sending to His Majesty the Sultan and Yang Di-Pertuan a letter of resignation under his hand, through the Majlis or the Chief Syar'ie Judge, but he may not be removed from his office or his service terminated except in accordance with the provisions of subsections (3), (4) and (5) of section 12(1) of this Act.

As mentioned earlier, Syariah Courts in Brunei Darussalam consists of Syariah Subordinate Courts, the Syariah High Court and the Syariah Appeal Court each with its own jurisdictions.

The Syariah High Court has both criminal and civil jurisdiction. In its criminal jurisdiction it shall try any offence punishable under any written law which provides for syariah criminal offences, under any written law relating to Islamic family law or under any other written law which confers on it jurisdiction to try any offence, and may impose any punishment provided therein[41].

In its civil jurisdiction, the Syariah High Court shall hear and determine all actions and proceedings relating to –

(i) betrothal, marriage (including *ta'at balik*), divorce, *khulu'*, *fasakh*, *cerai ta'liq*, determination of turns, *li'an*, *illa* or any matrimonial matter;

(ii) any disposition of or claim to any property arising out of any matter set out in the above paragraph.

[38] Section 9(2) of the Syariah Courts Act (Chapter 184). [39] Section 10(2) of the Syariah Courts Act (Chapter 184). [40] Section 12(1) of the Syariah Courts Act (Chapter 184). [41] Section 15*(a)* of the Syariah Courts Act (Chapter 184).

(iii) maintenance of dependants, legitimacy (*ithbatun nasab*) or guardianship or custody (*hadanah*) of infants;

(iv) division of or claims to *harta sepencarian*;
(v) wills or gifts during *maradal-maut* of a deceased Muslim;
(vi) gift *inter vivos* (*hibah*), or settlement (*sulh*) made without adequate monetary consideration or value by Muslim;

(vii) *waqaf* or *nazar*;

(viii) division of and inheritance of property, testate or intestate;

(ix) determination or persons entitled to part of the estate of a deceased Muslim or part of the property which such persons are respectively entitled to; or
(x) other matters in respect of which jurisdiction is conferred by any written law.[42]

For Syariah Subordinate Courts, their criminal jurisdiction are to try offence punishable under any written law which provides for syariah criminal offences, prescribing offences where the maximum punishment provided for does not exceed $10,000 or imprisonment for a period not exceeding 7 years or both and may impose any punishment provided therefor[43].

In their civil jurisdiction, the Syariah Subordinate Courts shall hear and determine all actions and proceedings which the Syariah High Court is empowered to hear and determine, where the amount or value of the subject-matter in dispute does not exceed $500,000 or is not capable of estimation in terms of money[44]. This jurisdiction may, form time to time, be increased by His Majesty the Sultan and Yang Di-Pertuan on the recommendation of the Chief Syar'ie Judge, by notifying it in the *Gazette*[45].

Jurisdiction of the Syariah Appeal Court shall be to hear and determine any appeal against any decision made by the Syariah High Court in the exercise of its original jurisdiction[46]. Whenever an appeal against a decision of the Syariah Subordinate Court has been determined by the Syariah High Court, the Syariah Appeal Court may, on application by any party, grant leave for any question of law in the public interest which has arisen in the course of the appeal, and where the decision of the Syariah High Court has affected the determination of the appeal, to be referred to the Syariah Appeal Court for its decision. Whenever leave is granted by the Syariah Appeal Court, it shall hear and determine the questions allowed to be referred for its decision and make any order which the Syariah High Court might have made, and as it thinks just for the disposal of the appeal.

[42] Section 15*(b)* –do-. [43] Section 16(1)*(a)* of the Syariah Courts Act (Chapter 184). [44] Section 16(1)*(b)* Ibid. [45] Section 16(2) Ibid. [46] Section 20(1) Ibid.

Apart from having its original jurisdiction, the Syariah High Court shall have supervisory and revisionary jurisdiction over all Syariah Subordinate Courts[47]. Similarly, the Syariah Appeal Court shall have that same power over the Syariah High Court[48].

OTHER RELEVANT LEGAL DEPARTMENTS

The Attorney General's Chambers

The Attorney General is the principal legal adviser to the Government of His Majesty the Sultan and shall advise on all legal matters connected with the affairs of Brunei Darussalam or by the Government of Brunei Darussalam.[49] He is assisted by the Solicitor General and counsels, in advising the Government and representing the Government in civil and criminal cases. The Attorney General is also responsible for the drafting of legislation. In carrying out the task of legislative drafting, the Attorney General's Chambers work closely with other Government Ministries and Departments.

The Attorney General is vested with the power under the Constitution to institute, proceed and discontinue once instituted, any criminal proceedings. All criminal prosecutions are instituted in the name of the Public Prosecutor. In carrying out this duty, the Attorney General is not subject to the direction or control of any other person or authority. He is assisted by Deputy Public Prosecutors in the conduct of criminal trials held in the Supreme Court and the Subordinate Courts.

The Attorney General basically has the exercisable power to institute, conduct or discontinue, at his discretion, any proceedings of an offence other than proceedings before a Syariah Court or a Court Martial, subject to the provisions of any other written law.

In addition, the Public Prosecutor and his Deputies also advise, and direct prosecution undertaken by the police and other law enforcement departments including rendering advice in their investigations.

Apart from carrying out the above duties, the Attorney General's Chambers also provides services to the public by maintaining the following registries; Companies, Business names, Trade Marks, Industrial designs, Inventions, Power of Attorney, Marriages, Bills of Sales.

There are five legal divisions in the Attorney-General's Chambers: Civil Division, Criminal Justice Division, International Law Division, Legislative Drafting Division and the Registry Division.

Syariah department

In 1980, a Committee of Harmonizing Laws In Accordance With Islam[50], was formed. To increase this effort, a Legal Unit[51] chaired by the Chief Kadi was established in 1988 by the Ministry of Religious Affairs its task mainly to replace the earlier committee. In 1993, a Committee for the establishment of Syariah Supreme Court known as the Action Committee Towards the Establishment of Syariah Supreme Court[52] was formed. Another committee known as the Islamic Family Law Legislative Committee[53] was later established in 1995, its tasks are to study, legislate and prepare Islamic family laws as well as other laws governed by the Kadis Court. This Legal Unit, in 1997, was eventually alleviated to its present position as a separate department in the Ministry of Religious Affairs now known as the Islamic Legal Unit.[54]

Among the duties of this Unit are to study, examine and do research on provisions in the Laws of Brunei now enforced to see whether or not there is any conflict with *Hukum Syara'*; prepare proposed draft amendment for any legal provision that conflict with *Hukum Syara'* and prepare draft legislation in accordance with *Hukum Syara'* if there is no such legislation available yet. This Unit is also appointed secretariat for several committees that had been mentioned above. Apart from that, this Unit also gives advice concerning Islamic laws to the Syariah Courts, the Faith Control Unit (Unit Kawalan Akidah), the Prosecution Section, the Investigation Section, the Family Counseling Section, the Attorney General's Chambers as well as other government departments and private firms.[55]

LEGAL PROCEDURE

CRIMINAL PROSECUTION

As stated in the Criminal Procedure Code, the general direction and control over criminal prosecutions and proceedings in Brunei Darussalam is under the responsibility of the Attorney General who is also the Public Prosecutor. His Majesty may also from time to time appoint Deputy Public Prosecutors who will be under the general control and direction of the Public Prosecutor. Deputy Public Prosecutors are conferred the powers under the Criminal Procedure Code as are delegated to them by the Public Prosecutor.

The Public Prosecutor may also by notification in the *Government Gazette* delegate all or any of his powers vested to him under the Criminal Procedure Code to any Deputy Public Prosecutor. Thus the exercise of these powers by the Deputy Public Prosecutor would be treated as if they had been exercised by the Public Prosecutor so long as Public Prosecutor does not revoke the delegation.

The Criminal Procedure Code also specifically states that every criminal prosecution and every inquiry can also be conducted by some other person expressly authorized in writing by the Public Prosecutor or His Majesty the Sultan. In those cases, a police officer or an officer of a Government Department in relation to minor cases and cases that is relevant to that particular Government Department, such as the Customs Department, the Immigration Department, the Narcotics Control Bureau and the Anti-Corruptions Bureau who do have their own prosecuting officers also conduct criminal prosecution for their relevant cases.

CRIMINAL PROCEDURE

INVESTIGATIONS

The Police are given powers to search a property and in doing so they are required to prepare a list of the things that have been seized and this document is to be signed by the officer in charge of the search and seizure. The owner of the property being searched must be present at the time the search is conducted. [1]

The police officer during the investigation stage can also take a written statement from a witness or a suspect and the person being interviewed is required to answer all questions posed to him in relation to the case being investigated on. The police officer is required to repeat the statement back to the person being questioned and he must thereafter sign the statement. [2] All statements made can be used as evidence if the person questioned becomes a witness during proceedings thereafter. [3]

[1] Section 69 of the Criminal Procedure Code [2] Section 116 of the Criminal Procedure Code [3] Section 117 of the Criminal Procedure Code

When interviewing a potential defendant, the police officer is always required to read out the defendant's rights to him after the charge is explained to him. The Courts only accept voluntarily made statements whether or not the contents of the statement are true. There is no right of silence in Brunei Darussalam as the Courts may as a consequence treat silence as a detrimental factor for the defendant.

Once a suspect is arrested, he shall be placed in remand or released on bail. If the remand is ordered by the Magistrate, the defendant cannot be remanded for more than 15 days. On the other hand, if it was ordered by the High Court, there is no time limit. [4]

PRE-TRIAL PROCEDURE

With the exception of some offences that would need the prior sanction of the Public Prosecutor or the official complaint of a concerned public servant, a Judge or magistrate may take cognizance of an offence upon receiving a complaint launched by a complainant[5], upon his own knowledge or suspicion that an such offence has been committed or when any person who is in custody without process, has been brought before him for committing an offence that the Judge or magistrate has jurisdiction to inquire into or try.[6]

Once the Judge or magistrate takes cognizance of the offence and is satisfied that there is sufficient ground for proceeding, he will either issue a summons for the accused to attend court or if it is in relation to an offence that requires a warrant to be issued first, he would then issue the warrant in the first instance and also issue a summons that specifies the accused to appear at a certain time before him or some other Judge or magistrate having jurisdiction over the case. [7]

Preliminary Inquiries

Preliminary inquiries are always held for offences against the State, murder or any offence which carries a death penalty. [8]

Preliminary Inquiries are generally held for a magistrate to determine whether there is sufficient evidence to commit the case for trial in the High Court (filteration). Other cases like trafficking of drugs and rape cases go straight to the High Court without any preliminary inquiries. All other cases are generally tried summarily in the Magistrate Court.

At a preliminary inquiry, the Prosecutor will present its case and set out all the evidence, including examining witnesses, in support of its case to the Magistrate. The defendant is allowed to cross examine the witnesses who can then also be re-examined by the Prosecutor. If the magistrate, after hearing all the evidence, feels that there are insufficient grounds for committing the accused, he could either discharge him or he can

[4] Section 223 of the Criminal Procedure Code [5] Section 133 of the Criminal Procedure Code [6] Section 131 of the Criminal Procedure Code [7] Section 136 of the Criminal Procedure Code [8] Section 138 of the Criminal Procedure Code

still order that the defendant be tried before himself or before some other magistrate. In the latter case, he will consequently frame a charge and call upon the defendant to plead to those charges. [9] However if the magistrate finds that there are sufficient grounds for committing him for trial, he shall then commit the accused for trial before the High Court. [10]

If the accused is committed to trial to High Court, the magistrate will give the accused the opportunity to give a list of witnesses he wishes to be summoned to give evidence for his trial. The final list of witnesses shall be included in the record of the magistrate. [11]

Once the accused has been committed for trial, the committing magistrate shall then send the original record and all the relevant documents, weapons (if any) or any other thing which is to be produced in evidence to the Court the accused is committed to. A list of all the exhibits is also forwarded with the record. The record will specifically contain the following information[12]:

i) the serial number of the case;

ii) the date of the commission of the offence;

iii) the date of the complaint, if any;

iv) the name, age, sex, residence, if known, and nationality (or race) of the accused;

v) the offence complained of and the offence proved, and the value of the

property, if any, in respect of which the offence has been committed;

vi) the date of the summons or warrant and of the return day of the summons, if any, or on which the accused was first arrested;

vii) the date on which the accused first appeared or was brought before a magistrate;

viii) the name and title of the officer or other person conducting the prosecution;

ix) the date of making each adjournment or postponement, if any, and the date to which such adjournment or postponement was made and the grounds for making the same;

x) the date on which the proceedings terminated;

xi) the order made;

xii) the depositions;

xiii) the statement, if any, of the accused;

xiv) the charge; and

xv) the list of witnesses as provided by the accused.

The law also allows for committal without the consideration of evidence. This method is referred to as paper committal and is done through the submission of written statements only. [13] Hence a written statement can be substituted for oral evidence and it would have

[9] Section 141 of the Criminal Procedure Code [10] Section 144 of the Criminal Procedure Code [11] Section 145 of the Criminal Procedure Code [12] Section 147 of the Criminal Procedure Code [13] Section 151A and 151B of the Criminal Procedure Code

a similar effect to be admissible under the Evidence Act. It must however satisfy the following conditions:

a) the statement must be signed by the person who made it;

b) the statement must contain a declaration by that person that the information he has written is true to the best of this knowledge and belief;

c) a copy of the statement must be given to each of the other parties to the proceedings not less then 7 days before the statement is tendered in evidence;

d) none of the other parties objects to the statement being tendered in evidence.

Bail applications[14]

The defendant or his counsel may also apply for bail (whilst investigations are still being carried out) before a magistrate, High Court Judge or Intermediate Court Judge, depending on the seriousness of the case. In deciding to grant that application, the magistrate will consider two opposing factors. [15] On one hand, the Court must remember that the accused is innocent only until proved otherwise. However, the Court shall also take into consideration that the interests of justice will be perverted if the accused absconds or tampers with the witnesses.

At present, all magistrates have the power to grant bail for all type of cases by virtue of their appointments as Registrars of the Supreme Court. However, in practice, bail applications in serious cases that are triable in the High Court or Intermediate Court will be remitted to either court for such applications to be heard. These particular points will be taken into account on deciding whether or not the defendant should be released on bail:

i) Is the offence bailable or non bailable under Schedule 1 of the Criminal

Procedure Code? However, the Court still has discretion to grant bail for non-bailable offences;

ii) The nature and gravity of the offence;

iii) The number of charges;

iv) The likelihood of the accused absconding;

v) The previous record of the accused;

vi) Strength of evidence; and

vii) Other relevant factors like the age and health of the accused.

The usual conditions attached to bail are cash bail, the duty to report to the nearest police station at a prescribed number of times a week, the assurance that the accused will not tamper with witnesses and to not approach certain places, to surrender his passport and other travel documents and to remain indoors between certain hours.

Pre-Trial Review

Sometimes, a pre-trial review is also held by the High Court Judge prior to the trial. There is no legislative requirement for this and hence is not mandatory but in practice is usually held for High Court and Intermediate Court cases where the Judge will go

[14] Sections 346-353 of the Criminal Procedure Code [15] Public Prosecutor V Haji Sadikin (2000) JCBD Vol. 1 349

through the relevant documents such as the list of witnesses, list of exhibits and agreed facts (if any) with both the prosecution and the defence.

Withdrawal of Charges

At any time before a judgment is entered, charges against the defendant and all evidence against him may be discharged. If the discharge is one not amounting to an acquittal, this would mean that prosecution can be made at another time based on the same factors. [16] The power to withdraw a charge only lies with the prosecution. The person who reported the offence and initiated the prosecution cannot withdraw his claim once a police report or a statement has been prepared.

TRIAL PROCEDURE

Chapter XIX of the Criminal Procedure Code governs the procedure for trials in Brunei Darussalam.

When the defendant first appears before the Court, the charge containing the particulars to the offence or offences he is accused of shall be read out and explained to him and he shall then be asked to enter his plea, guilty or not guilty. If the accused pleads guilty, the plea will be recorded and he may be convicted thereon. However, the Judge would first need to hear the complainant and other evidence first as it considers necessary and he would also make sure the defendant truly understands the nature and consequences of his plea and intends to admit, without qualification, the offence or offences alleged against him.

Where the defendant pleads not guilty, a trial will be held ad witnesses would be called to give evidence. At the start of the trial, the prosecution will first open the case by stating briefly the nature of the offence charged and disclosing the evidence, including the appearance of witnesses, by which he proposed to prove guilt of the defendant. The burden of proof lies with the prosecution beyond reasonable doubt. If the defendant is not represented by counsel, (there is no legal aid in Brunei Darussalam with the exception of cases carrying a death penalty where the defendant will be provided a defence counsel) the Court will assist the defendant in the cross examination of witnesses.

At the close of the prosecution's case, the Court will lay down the choices for the defendant, either to given his own evidence or maintain his silence. Usually, if they choose to keep silent, and where the evidence against him is strong, a conviction will be given. However, if he decides to give his own evidence, he will then in turn open his case by stating the facts or law on which he intends to rely and make whatever comments in response to the evidence put forward by the prosecution. Before summing up his case, he would then be called upon to enter his defence and then produce his own evidence which may include witnesses that are examined on his behalf. The prosecution will then have the right of reply on the whole case.[17]

[16] Section 186 of the Criminal Procedure Code [17] Section 184 of the Criminal Procedure Code

At the end of the trial, if the Court finds the defendant not guilty, the Court shall record an order of acquittal. If the Court finds otherwise or if the defendant entered a plea of guilty, the Court shall pass sentence in accordance with the law. [18]

Sentencing

The types of sentences in Brunei Darussalam are: i) Death Penalty: The most serious punishment in Brunei Darussalam is the death penalty. In sentencing hearings dealing with the death penalty, there must be 2 judges present and both these judges must agree with the sentencing decision. Death penalties are not imposed on pregnant women who would get life imprisonment instead.

ii) Life imprisonment: The defendant will be imprisonment for as long as he shall live.

iii) Whipping: There is also whipping in Brunei Darussalam, usually a maximum of 24 whips for an adult and a maximum of 18 whips for a defendant below the age of 18.[19] Women, men above 50 years old and those that are imposed the death penalty are exempted from whipping.[20]

iv) Fines: Fines are imposed according to the relevant written law. If that does not exist, the court will decide on the appropriate amount.

v) Pay compensation: On top of the above punishments, the Court can order the defendant to pay compensation if it is satisfied that the defendant can afford to pay such amount imposed. He will be imposed imprisonment or further imprisonment on default of payment. [21]

POST-TRIAL PROCEDURE (APPEALS)

If an appeal is made from the Magistrates Court, the appeal will be heard by the High Court. Any party can make an appeal against a judgment or sentence, be it the prosecution or the defendant. Appeals made from the High Court are heard by the Court of Appeal and these are governed by the Criminal Procedure Code (Criminal Appeal Rules) 2002. A person shall commence his appeal by sending a notice of appeal to the Registrar within 14 days of the judgment or sentence made. He can at any time abandon his appeal after serving his notice of appeal by giving notice of abandonment to the Registrar. His appeal should then be dismissed.

CIVIL PROCEDURE

Civil proceedings are usually private matters between parties that relates to breach of contracts or for compensation. The civil procedure in Brunei Darussalam is governed by the Supreme Court Rules for the High Court and the Magistrates' Court Rules (Civil

[18] Section 181 of the Criminal Procedure Code [19] Section 257 of the Criminal Procedure Code [20] Section 258 of the Criminal Procedure Code [21] Section 382 of the Criminal Procedure Code

Procedure and Civil Appeals Procedure) for the Magistrate Courts. These rules mainly prescribe regulations for types of action, procedure, process, addresses and forms.

Procedure in the Magistrate Court

INTRODUCTION

Civil proceedings in the Magistrate Court would include a civil action, an order for payment of any sum or money or an order for doing or abstaining from doing any act or thing not enforceable through a mere fine or by imprisonment. All civil proceedings heard by the Magistrate Court are dealt with summarily.[22]

PRE-HEARING PROCEDURE

A person who wishes to institute civil proceedings in the Magistrate Court would need to register a written statement to the Clerk of the Court to be included in the Civil Cause Book. This written statement is often referred to as the "plaint" and it shall state the names and last known place of residence of the parties and also include a statement on the substance of the action intended to be brought. Upon doing so, he is also required to pay a prescribed fee to the Court. The magistrate has discretion to refuse the plaint if it appears that there is no cause of action. They would naturally refuse the plaint if the matter is outside their jurisdiction. Any person dissatisfied with the magistrate's decision in refusing his plaint is allowed to appeal against that decision as if it was an order of the magistrate.[23]

Once the magistrate registers the plaint, it shall next issue a summons for the defendant requiring him to attend before him at a certain time but normally not more than 7 days after the summons have been served on him. The defendant will also be required to file his written statement of defence in answer to the plaint against him.[24] However, if he decides to admit the claim wholly or partially, he can then sign a statement admitting the amount of the claim or part of the amount of the claim entered against him. If this is the case, the Clerk of the Court shall send a notice regarding this admission to the plaintiff who is then required to prove the aforesaid claim. The magistrate shall then upon proof of the signature of the party enter judgment for the admitted claim.[25]

The defendant will then pay into Court the sum of money in full satisfaction of the claim against him together with the costs incurred by the plaintiff up to the time of such payment and this payment should then be notified to the plaintiff. This payment shall then be paid out to the plaintiff without further delay.[26]

A plaintiff may also apply for the magistrate to make a judgment when no defence or counterclaim has been filed. Once satisfied that the plaint was served on the defendant and yet he did not appear in Court, the Court can then enter judgment for the plaintiff

[22] Rule 3 of the Magistrates' Court (Civil Procedure) Rules 2001 [23] Rule 13 of the Magistrates' Court (Civil Procedure) Rules 2001 [24] Rule 14 of the Magistrates' Court (Civil Procedure) Rules 2001 [25] Rule 38 of the Magistrates' Court (Civil Procedure) Rules 2001 [26] Rule 40 of the Magistrates' Court (Civil Procedure) Rules 2001

with costs. If the defendant manages to file a defence or counterclaim before judgment bas been entered, then a judgment in default cannot be made by the Court.[27]

PROCEDURE AT HEARING[28]

All hearings in the Magistrate Court are heard in public but the magistrate may still decide to hear the matter in the presence of the parties only. The persons permitted to address the Court in a civil proceeding are any party to the proceedings, any advocate and solicitor qualified and admitted under the Legal Profession Act and also any person permitted by the magistrate if he is satisfied that that person is not appearing for fee or reward.

If both the plaintiff and defendant are present at the hearing, the plaint would first be read out to the defendant who will then be required to make his defence. On hearing his defence, the magistrate shall then proceed with the case. During the hearing, the magistrate shall take into consideration any question of law raised, legal submissions made and the substance of the oral evidence given. The party on whom the burden of proof lies shall commence the case before the magistrate. Once he has closed his case, his opponent may adduce his own evidence. If he does not choose to do so, the initiating party shall address the magistrate for the second time and will sum up his evidence. The opponent is then given his right to reply. When the initiating party has concluded his case, the opponent can decide to call his own witnesses and he is free to open his own case, calls his own witnesses and in the end sums up not only on his own evidence but also on his own case. The initiating party will in turn have the right to reply to his opponent. [29]

On the conclusion of the hearing, the magistrate can deliver judgment either at the same or at a subsequent sitting. A certified copy of the judgment can also be delivered to the parties upon payment of a prescribed fee to the court.

However, in the case where only the defendant appears in court either on the day of the hearing or at any continuation the case, the claim or case shall be struck out by the magistrate but excluding any counter-claims that may have been made by the defendant against the plaintiff. But if the defendant admits to the cause of action, the magistrate may then proceed to give judgment, with or without costs, as if the plaintiff were present. Where there has been a counter claim, the magistrate, if satisfied that the counter claim has been served on the plaintiff, may proceed to hear the defendant's case and may give judgment on the evidence adduced by the defendant or may postpone the hearing on the counter claim. Such postponement will be notified to the plaintiff. The magistrate may also award costs to the defendant when the plaintiff fails to appear.

Where the defendant is the party that has failed to appear in court, the magistrate once satisfied with the proof of service on the defendant and that the defendant lacks sufficient excuse for his non attendance, can determine the case and enter judgment. That judgment

[27] Rule 41 of the Magistrates' Court (Civil Procedure) Rules 2001 [28] Part VIII of the Magistrates' Court (Civil Procedure) Rules 2001 [29] Rule 61 of the Magistrates' Court (Civil Procedure) Rules 2001

shall be as valid as if both parties had appeared before him. Otherwise, the magistrate can still adjourn the hearing to a convenient date to allow more time for the defendant.

APPEALS

Any civil appeals are governed by the Magistrates' Courts (Civil Appeal) Rules 2001. Every notice of appeal will be lodged in the magistrates court within a month of the decision appealed from was made and shall be served on all other parties affected by the appeal.[30]

The contents of the notice of appeal should include the reference number of the proceedings, names of parties, date of decision appealed, grounds of appeal and be accompanied by a certified copy of the decision appealed against.[31]

Appeals shall be heard by one Judge of the High Court who may reserve for the consideration of the Court of Appeal ay question of law which may arise on the hearing of such an appeal.[32]

The Registrar will notify the parties the date and time of the appeal hearing. If the appellant fails to appear at the appeal hearing, the case shall then be struck out and the decision shall be affirmed. If the respondent appeared at that appeal where the appellant failed to do so, the appellant shall be ordered to pay the costs of the appeal. But if the respondent did not appear, the High Court will need to consequently decide on the costs of the appeal. [33]

However if the appellant appears and whether or not the respondent appears, the High Court shall proceed with the hearing and determination of the case and shall thereafter give judgment according to the merits of the case. During the hearing, the appellant is not allowed to argue on any other points that are separate from the reasons for appeal and those set forth in his notice of appeal. But the Judge may allow amendments to the notice of appeal if he feels that there are actually other grounds than was not mentioned that should be included and also if he feels that the statement of grounds of appeal is defective.[34]

Once the Judge decides on the appeal, the High Court shall certify the judgment made and notify it to the magistrates' court. The magistrates' court will then act upon the judgment either by making such orders that are necessary and amending its own records in accordance with the judgment. The magistrate shall then have the same jurisdiction and power to enforce the High Court's judgment as if he himself made it.

[30] Rule 4 of the Magistrates' Court (Civil Appeals Procedure) Rules 2001

[31] Rule 5 of the Magistrates' Court (Civil Appeals Procedure) Rules 2001 [32] Rule 11 of the Magistrates' Court (Civil Appeals Procedure) Rules 2001 [33] Rule 12 and 13 of the Magistrates' Court (Civil Appeals Procedure) Rules 2001 [34] Rule 15 of the Magistrates' Court (Civil Appeals Procedure) Rules 2001

PROCEDURE IN THE HIGH COURT

INTRODUCTION

High Court Proceedings are initiated by writ, originating summons, originating motion or petition.[35]

There are certain proceedings that **must** be initiated by a writ and these are those relating to claims for relief or remedy for any tort (other than trespass to land), relating to an allegation of fraud, claims for damages for breach of duty (whether duty exists by virtue of a contract or of a provision made by any written law), claims for breach of promise of marriage and also relating to infringement of a patent.

Any applications that are made to a High Court Judge under any written law must be initiated by originating summons. There are also some proceedings that may be begun either by writ or by originating summons where the plaintiff can choose which is more appropriate for him. Such proceedings include those where the sole or principal question at issue is the construction of any written law, of any instrument made under any written law or of any deed, will contract or other document and also where there is unlikely to be any substantial dispute of fact in those proceedings.

PRE-HEARING PROCEDURE

Writ of Summons

All writs prior to them being issued must be indorsed with a statement of the nature of the claim made or the relief or remedy required in the action begun or a statement of the amount claimed in respect of a debt demand. It should also state that further proceedings will be stayed if the defendant pays the amount claimed to the plaintiff or the Court within a certain time limit. The Plaintiff upon presenting a writ for sealing and to be served must leave with the Registrar the original writ along with as many copies of it to be served on the defendant or defendants. The Registrar shall then assign a serial number to the writ and shall sign, seal and date the writ which shall deem the writ to be issued.[36]

Originating Summons

An originating summons must include the questions the plaintiff seeks the determination or direction of the High Court or a concise statement of the relief or remedy claimed in the proceedings with sufficient particulars to identify the cause or causes of action in respect of that claim. Similar to the process in writ of summons, the Registrar will assign a serial number to the originating summons and it will be signed, sealed and dated and thereupon issued.[37]

Originating Motion and Petition No originating motion can be made *ex parte* and without previous notice to the affected parties. However if the Court is satisfied that there will be a delay in proceedings, it may make an order *ex parte* on terms such as costs or otherwise. (Any affected party may apply to the Court to set that order aside). The notice of a motion must include a concise statement of the nature of the claim made or the relief or remedy required. The plaintiff can serve a notice of motion on the defendant together with the writ of summons or originating summons or at any time after service of such writ or summons whether or not the defendant has entered on appearance in the action.[38]

Petitions must also include a concise statement on the nature of the claim sought and the names of the persons the petition should be served with. The petition should be served on the defendant not less than 7 days before the day the Registrar has fixed to be the day and time for the hearing of the petition.[39]

Similar to writ of summons and originating summons, originating motion and petitions shall also be assigned by the Registrar a serial number and be signed, sealed and dated before it is deemed to be issued.

Service of Process[40]

All writs, originating summons to which an appearance by the defendant is required, an originating summons, notices of originating motion and petitions must be served personally on each defendant.

A plaintiff must serve a statement of claim to the defendant either when the writ or notice of writ is served on the defendant or at any time after the service of the writ or notice of writ but it must be before the expiration of 14 days after the defendant enters an appearance. Thereafter, the defendant who has entered an appearance and intends to defend himself must serve a defence on the plaintiff not more than 14 days either after the time that has been limited for him to appear or after the statement of claim is served on him, whichever is the later. Next, the plaintiff who has been served the defence must serve a reply back to the defendant. If the plaintiff was also served a counter claim from the defendant and he intends to defend it, should also serve a defence on the defendant along with the reply. In each of the pleadings served, they must contain a statement setting out summarily the material facts on which the party pleading relies for his claim or defence.[41] In particular, he must plead specifically what his claim is in relation to, for instance, performance, release, statutes of limitation, fraud or any fact showing illegality and stat that the opposite party cannot claim or defend on it. This information must always be included to avoid taking the opposite party by surprise.

It is possible for the plaintiff or the defendant to apply to the Court by summons for an order that the action be tried without pleadings or further pleadings. If the Court is satisfied that the issues in dispute can be defined without pleadings or further pleadings, then it shall direct the parties to prepare a statement of the issues in dispute or if the parties are unable to agree on such a statement, the Court may settle the statement itself.

[38] Order 8 of the Supreme Court Rules [39] Order 9 of the Supreme Court Rules [40] Order 10 of the Supreme Court Rules [41] Rule 6, Order 8 of the Supreme Court Rules

Cases involving libel, slander, breach of promise of marriage and allegations of fraud does not apply in this type of action.

Where the plaintiff fails to serve a statement of claim on the defendant, the defendant may, after the expiration of the period for him to appear apply for the Court to dismiss the action.[42] If the claim relates to a liquidated demand and if the defendant fails to serve a defence, then the plaintiff may enter a final judgment against the defendant for a sum not exceeding what is claimed in the writ and also for costs.

Entering of appearance

A defendant to an action that was begun by writ may appear in the action and defend the claim either by a solicitor or by himself. Where the defendant is a body corporate, they may not enter an appearance at the action and can only be defended by a solicitor. Entering an appearance entails completing the requisite documents, namely a memorandum of appearance and sending it along with a copy of it to the Registry.[43] A memorandum of appearance basically requests the Registry to enter an appearance for the defendant or defendants specified in the memorandum. It must specify the address of the defendant's place of residence or the business address if his solicitor.

Where the defendant fails to enter an appearance, the plaintiff may after the time limited for appearing has expired, enter final judgment against that defendant for a sum not exceeding the amount claimed by the writ and for costs and proceed with the action against other defendants, if there are any.[44] He may enter an interlocutory judgment in the case of claims for unliquidated damages.

Preparing for trial[45]

A cause or matter may be tried before a Judge or the Registrar of the Supreme Court. Notice of trial may be given by the plaintiff or the other party at any time after a reply has been delivered or after the time for delivery of a reply has expired. At least 14 days before the date for trial has been fixed, the defendant shall identify to the plaintiff those documents that are central to his case that he wishes to be included in the trial bundle. At least 2 days before the trial, the plaintiff shall have 2 bundles consisting of one copy of the following documents: a) witness statements that have been exchanged including expert's reports; b) the defendant's documents that he wishes to be included in the bundle; and c) a note agreed by the parties giving a summary of the issues involved, a summary of the propositions of law, the list of authorities to be cited and a chronology of relevant events.

A pre-trial conference may also be held at any time after the commencement of proceedings, and the Court may direct the parties to attend such a conference to discuss matters relating to the action.[46] Points to consider at this pre-trial conference would

[42] Rule 1, Order 19 [43] Rule 1, Order 12 [44] Order 13 [45] Order 34 [46] Order 34A

include any possibility of settlement, the need for the parties to furnish the Court with further information as the Court would require and the Court can also give directions as it appears necessary or desirable for securing a just, expeditious and economic disposal of the action. The parties can agree to settle at any time during the pre-trial conference on all or some of the matters in dispute. The Court can then enter judgment and make an order to give effect to that settlement.

PROCEDURE AT HEARING

At the trial, the Judge will first give directions as to which party may begin the proceedings and prescribe the orders of speeches at the trial. If the defendant decides not to adduce any evidence, the plaintiff may at the close of his case make a second speech closing his case and thereafter the defendant shall make a speech in closing his case. If the defendant does decide to adduce evidence, ha may do so at the closing of the plaintiff's case. At the close of the defendant's case, the plaintiff may make a speech in reply. Rules on evidence are prescribed under Order 38 of the rules.

Where a judgment has been given for damages and there is no provision made by the judgment in how damages are to be assessed, then the damages shall be assessed by the Registrar.[47] The Court may also make an award of provisional damages if the plaintiff has made a claim for one.[48]

Every judgment after a hearing is delivered in open Court or in Chambers, either on the conclusion of the hearing or on a subsequent day of which such notice shall be given to the parties.[49] A Judge can also give judgment and his reasons, in writing at a later date by sending a copy of it to all parties to the proceedings. In this case, the original copy of the written judgment must be signed and filed. The proper officer of the Registrar must enter into the cause book a minute of every judgment or order given by the Court.

In the enforcement of a judgment for the payment of money (and not one for the payment of money into Court), it can be enforced through writ of seizure or sale, garnishee proceedings, charging orders, appointment of a receiver, and an order of committal.[50]

To avoid hearing

Payment into and out of court[51]

In any action for a debt or damages, any defendant may pay into Court a sum of money as the plaintiff claims. Within 14 days of the payment, the plaintiff may accept the money in satisfaction of that cause of action by giving such notice to the defendant.

Offer to settle[52]

Parties to any proceeding may also serve on any other person an offer to settle any one or more of the claim in the proceedings. These can be made at any time before the Court disposes of the matter.

Summary Judgment[53]

A plaintiff can apply to the Court for a summary judgment against the defendant on the ground that that defendant has no defence to the claim included in the writ. Claims relating to libel, slander, malicious prosecution, false imprisonment, seduction or breach of promise of marriage are excluded from this application.

Application for summary judgments must be made by summons supported by an affidavit verifying the facts on which the claim, or the part of the claim, to which the application relates to is based on and it should also state the plaintiff's belief that there is no defence to that claim or no defence except as to the amount of any damages. Thereafter, the Court may dismiss the plaintiff's application especially where the defendant had satisfied the Court that there is still an issue or question in dispute which ought for some reason to be tried. On the other hand, the Court may also give such judgment for the plaintiff against the defendant on that claim.

APPEALS

Any appeal from a decision of a Registrar shall lie to a Judge in Chambers.[54] The appeal shall be brought by serving a notice on every other party to the proceedings to attend an appeal hearing before a Judge on a day specified in the notice. Appeals from a Judge shall lie to the Court of Appeal.

An appeal to the Court of Appeal shall be by way of rehearing and must be brought by a notice of appeal. Every notice of appeal must be filed and served within one month from the date when such order was pronounced (in the case of an appeal from a Judge in Chambers), from the date of refusal (in the case of an appeal against the refusal of an application), and in all other cases, from the date on which the judgment or order appealed against was pronounced.

RECIPROCAL ENFORCEMENT OF FOREIGN JUDGMENTS AND FOREIGN MAINTENANCE ORDERS

Brunei Darussalam also has in force a Maintenance Orders Reciprocal Enforcement Act[55] and a Reciprocal Enforcement of Foreign Judgments Act.[56] The Maintenance Orders Act basically provides for the enforcement in Brunei Darussalam any maintenance orders made in reciprocating countries listed in the Schedule and also for maintenance order made in Brunei Darussalam to be enforced in the listed reciprocating countries. To date, the reciprocating countries are Malaysia, Singapore, Australia and Hong Kong Special

[52] Order 23 [53] Order 14 [54] Order 56 [55] CAP 175 of the Laws of Brunei [56] CAP 176 of the Laws of Brunei

Administrative Region of the People's Republic of China. Maintenance orders are those that provide for the periodical payment of money towards the maintenance of any persons the person paying is liable to maintain.

The Foreign Judgments Act makes provision for the enforcement in Brunei Darussalam any judgments given in foreign countries listed in the Schedule who will in turn also enforce judgments given in Brunei Darussalam. Judgment in this case means a judgment or order given or made by a court in any civil proceedings, judgment in any criminal proceedings for the payment of a sum of money in respect of compensation or damages to an injured party and an award in proceedings on arbitration.[57] The countries listed for the purposes of this Act as at now are only Malaysia and Singapore, through their respective High Courts.

LEGAL PROCEDURE IN THE SYARIAH COURTS

With regards to procedure in general, the Syariah Courts Act (Chapter 184) has stated that every Syariah Court in Brunei Darussalam shall have and use where necessary a seal of such form and format as may be approved by the Majlis[58]. The language that shall be used in the Syariah Courts shall be the Malay language though it may allow the use of any other language in the interest of justice[59]. However, the courts may choose for all documents or records of proceedings to be written in jawi or rumi script[60].

PROCEDURE IN CRIMINAL PROCEEDINGS

In pre-trial procedure, section 69(1) of the Religious Council and Kadis Courts Act (Chapter 77) has laid down some guidelines concerning charge. A charge shall be framed by the prosecutor or by the Court and which shall contain sufficient particulars of the offence alleged. However in practice, during the initial stage of the case, the prosecutor would normally frame the charge, whereas at the closing of the prosecution's case, it would be up to the Court (at the stage of a prima facie) to frame or amend a charge if it thinks it is not appropriate with the charge by the prosecution based on the evidence given in Court[61].

For procedure during trial, section 70 of the Religious Council and Kadis Court (Chapter 77) has outlined procedure for hearing. Section 70(1) of this Act says that any necessary sanction to prosecute shall be proved. This is in accordance with section 62 which mentioned that for any offence under section 182, 183, 185, 186, 187 or 190, no prosecution shall be instituted except by resolution of the Majlis Ugama Islam sanctioning such prosecution.

[57] Section 2 of the Reciprocal Enforcement of Foreign Judgments Act [58] Section 7(1) of the Syariah Courts Act (Chapter 184). [59] Section 7(2)(a) Ibid. [60] Section 7(2)(b) Ibid. [61] Haji Sawas Haji Jebat, *Prosedur Perbicaraan Di Mahkamah Kadi*, Jurnal Undang-Undang Syariah Brunei Darussalam, Januari-Jun 2002 Jilid 2 Bil.2, p.35.

Section 70(2) of the Act also stated that the accused shall be charged and if he pleads guilty he may be sentenced on such plea. Though it seems too simple, in practice however, the plea will only be accepted if it is made without any qualification and that the accused understood the charge made against him as well as consequences of the charge. In addition to that, section 175(1) of the Criminal Procedure Code (Chapter 7) is also practiced whereby a charge containing the particulars of the offence of which he is accused shall be framed and explained to him, and he shall be asked whether he is guilty of the offence charged or claims to be tried. And the court before recording the plea may hear the complainant and such other evidence as it considers necessary and shall ascertain that the accused understands the nature and consequences of his plea and intends to admit, without qualification, the offence alleged against him[62].

If an accused claims trial or refuses to plead, the prosecutor shall outline the facts to be proved and the relevant law and shall then call his witnesses[63]. As laid down in section 70(4), each witness shall be examined by the party calling him[64] and this shall be called his examination-in-chief[65]; be cross-examined thereafter by the party opposing him, which shall be called his cross-examination[66] and, such cross-examination may be directed to credibility[67]. Each witness may thereafter be re-examined on matters arising out of cross-examination by the party calling him[68], and such examination shall be called his re-examination[69]. Each witness have put to him at any time any question by the Court[70] and may have any further questions put to him or be recalled at any time, by leave of the Court[71]. For particulars on examination of witnesses and in ensuring the truth of syahadah syahid reference shall be made to the Syariah Courts Evidence Order, 2001[72].

After hearing the witnesses for the prosecution the Court shall either dismiss the case or call on the accused for his defence[73]. This section is to be read together with section 177(1) of the Criminal Procedure Code (Chapter 7):

"If upon taking all evidence referred to in section 176 and making such examination (if any) of the accused under section 220 as the Court considers necessary it finds that no case against the accused has been made out which, if unrebutted, would warrant his conviction, the Court may, subject to the provisions of section 186, record an order of acquittal.

If called on for his defence, the accused may address the Court and may then either give evidence or make a statement without being sworn or affirmed, in which case he shall not

[62] Section 175(2) of the Criminal Procedure Code (Chapter 7). [63] Section 70(3) of the Religious Council and Kadis Courts Act (Chapter 77). [64] Section 70(4)(a) Ibid. [65] Section 120(1) of the Syariah Courts Evidence Order, 2001(S 63/2001). [66] Section 120(2) Ibid. [67] Section 70(4)(b) of the Religious Council and Kadis Courts Act (Chapter 77). [68] Section 70(4)(c) Ibid. [69] Section 120(3) of the Syariah Courts Evidence Order, 2001(S 63/2001). [70] Section 70(4)(d) of the Religious Council and Kadis Courts Act (Chapter 77). [71] Section 70(4)(e) Ibid. [72] Chapters IX and IV respectively, (S 63/2001) [73] Section 70(5) of the Religious Council and Kadis Courts Act (Chapter 77).

be liable to be cross-examined, or may stand silent provided that if the accused gives evidence, he may be cross-examined, but not as to character or as to other offences not charged[74].

In doing so the accused may then call his witnesses[75]. He may sum up his case[76], and the prosecutor may reply generally[77]. As in any other Court, the Syariah Court, after considering the case shall then either convict or acquit the accused[78]. If the accused is convicted, the court may be informed of previous offences and shall have regard to any plea of leniency[79]. The Court shall then pass sentence according to law[80].

One important section in the Religious Council and Kadis Courts Act (Chapter 77) relating to criminal procedure is section 78 where it says that in matters of practice and procedure not expressly provided for in this Act or any rules made thereunder, the Court shall have regard to the avoidance of injustice and the convenient dispatch of business and may in criminal proceedings have regard to the practice and procedure obtaining in the civil courts.

PROCEDURE IN CIVIL PROCEEDINGS

For civil proceedings, provisions used are as mentioned in the Religious Council and Kadis Courts Act (Chapter 77) in section 80 until section 93; section 95 and section 96. In practice, the Emergency (Islamic Family Law) Order, 1999 (S 12/2000) as well as relevant provisions being used in the civil courts are also applied. This is to ensure that justice is served especially for those matters not provided for in the Act or any rules thereunder. Section 96 of the Religious Council and Kadis Courts (Chapter 77) states that:

"In matters of practice and procedure, not expressly provided for in this Act or any rules made thereunder, the Court may adopt such procedure as may seem proper for the avoidance of injustice and the disposal of the matters in issue between the parties, and may in particular, but without prejudice to the generality of the foregoing, adopt the practice and procedure for the time being in force in the Magistrates' Courts in civil proceedings."

THE LEGAL PROFESSION

LEGAL QUALIFICATIONS

A person that would qualify for admission to practise as an advocate and solicitor in Brunei Darussalam must possess one of the following requirements[1]:

i) He is a barrister-at-law of England, Northern Ireland or he must be a member of the Faculty of Advocates of Scotland; or

ii) He is a solicitor in England, Northern Ireland or a Writer to the Signet, law agent or solicitor in Scotland; or

iii) He has been in active practice as an advocate and solicitor in Singapore or in any part of Malaysia; or

iv) He possesses the Certificate of Legal Practice issued by the Qualifying Board

pursuant to section 5 of the Legal Profession Act 1976 of Malaysia; or

v) He possesses a degree in law conferred by the Universiti Islam Antarabangsa in Malaysia.

Furthermore, he must also be either a Brunei national or a person to whom a residence permit has been granted under regulations made under the Immigration Act.[2] If a person is not a Brunei national or no residence permit has been granted to him, he can only apply for admission if (along with having the academic requirements mentioned above) he has been in active practice in any part of the United Kingdom, Singapore, Malaysia, or in any other country or territory of the Commonwealth designated by the Attorney General for at least 7 years immediately preceding his application.

Admission is at the Chief Justice's discretion and he shall further take into consideration the following criteria[3]:

i) if the applicant has attained the age of 21 years;

ii) if he is of good character;

iii) if he has served satisfactorily his required period of pupilage as prescribed by the Pupillage Rules. [4]

[1] Section 3(1), Legal Profession Act (CAP 132)/Alternative Qualifications Rules 1999 [2] See Part III, Immigration Act (CAP 17) [3] Section 4, Legal Profession Act [4] Under the Pupillage Rules 2000, a pupil shall serve a period of pupilage with a qualified person who has been practicing for not less then 7 years for a period of 9 months. A qualified person can be exempted by the Chief Justice from any part of his pupilage (not more than 6 months) looking at special circumstances, if he has been a pupil of a master who is a barrister at law in England and Northern Ireland or a member of the Faculty of Advocates of Scotland or of an advocate and solicitor in Singapore or Malaysia practicing for not less than 7 years. He can also be exempted if the is or has been a solicitor in England and Northern Ireland, or a Writer of the Signet, law agent or solicitor in Scotland or he has been engaged in legal practice for not less than 6 months in any Commonwealth country or territory.

PRACTITIONERS

All advocates and solicitors that have been admitted to practise have the exclusive right to appeal and plead in all the courts of justice in Brunei Darussalam.[5]

The application process

All application for admission to become an advocate and solicitor shall be made by petition to the Chief Justice and shall be verified by affidavit.[6] The petitioner shall first file his petition at the Chief Registrar's office, accompanied by a notice intimating that he has applied. A notice shall be posted at the Supreme Court for one month before the petitioner is heard to be admitted.

A month before the petitioner is heard, he shall file an affidavit exhibiting documentary evidence which he states that he is qualified, if he has been practising law outside Brunei, evidence that there has been no disciplinary proceedings pending or contemplated against him and that his professional conduct was not under investigation. He would also need to show 2 recent certificates as to his good character and a certificate of diligence from each Master with whom he served his pupilage. The court may also request for other information or evidence as it may require.

These documents would then be filed by the Chief Registrar and within 5 days after, they shall be served on the Attorney General and upon any other relevant persons.[7]

After the application is heard and once the petitioner is admitted, his name would be entered into the roll. The Chief Registrar keeps a roll of advocates and solicitors' names with the dates of their respective admission. The name with the date of admission of every person admitted shall be entered upon the roll in order of admission.

Every advocate and solicitor is responsible for deliver to the Chief Registrar an application for a Practising Certificate every year before he does any act in the capacity of an advocate and solicitor[8]. The application shall be accompanied by a declaration in writing by the applicant stating his full name, the name under which he practices or the name of the advocate and solicitor or the firm of advocates and solicitors employing him at which he practice in Brunei Darussalam.

If he is not a Brunei Darussalam national or does not have a residence permit, he must also state that during the period in respect of which his immediately preceding practising certificate was issued, he had been in active practice in Brunei Darussalam for at least 3 months in aggregate if it was his first Practising Certificate or at least 9 months in the aggregate in any other case. All applicants are also required to pay a prescribed fee to obtain the Practising Certificate.

[5] Section 17, Legal Profession Act [6] Section 4, Legal Profession Act [7] Section 6, Legal Profession Act [8] See Part III, Legal Profession Act

Once the Chief Registrar is certain that the applicant's name is on the roll, and is satisfied with all the accompanying documents the applicant has provided, he shall issue to the applicant the practising certificate which will authorize him to practise an as advocate and solicitor in Brunei Darussalam. Every Practising Certificate shall be signed by the Chief Registrar and shall have effect from the beginning of the day of which it bears the date and shall expire at the end of the next 31st December. The Practising Certificate can however also expire once the name of the advocate and solicitor is struck off the roll or where he is adjudicated as bankrupt. In such a case, his Practising Certificate will be suspended until the Chief Justice consents to it being reinstated.

Ad- hoc admission

A judge has the discretion to admit into practice for the purpose of one case only any person who is not an ordinary resident of Brunei Darussalam but intends to come to Brunei Darussalam to appear in a case on the instructions of an Advocate and Solicitor.[9] In such cases, he must be Her Britannic Majesty's Patent as Queen's Counsel and also must possess such special skill and qualifications for the purpose of the case whether or not such special skill and qualifications are available in Brunei Darussalam.

A judge can also admit at his discretion for similar purposes, a person who is entitled to practise before the High Court in Malaysia, Singapore or Hong Kong or in any other Commonwealth country the Chief Justice may specify providing that he has not been admitted under this circumstance in respect of more than two other cases in the current calendar year.

Any person applying to be admitted on an ad hoc basis shall do so by originating motion verified by an affidavit stating the names of the parties and the brief particulars of the case he intends to appear in. The originating motion and the affidavit shall be served on the Attorney General and to the other parties to the case. The Judge prior to deciding to admit or not would usually first seek the views of each of the persons served with the application (originating motion).

The Chief Registrar shall then issue to any person admitted on an ad hoc basis a certificate to practise which would specify the case the person is to appear in. This person is deemed to be a person whose name is on the roll and to whom a practising certificate has been given to. However, his name would not be entered in the roll of names but will enter into a separate roll for such persons who are admitted on an ad-hoc basis.

Provisional admission

Advocates and solicitors can also be admitted provisionally prior to their application being heard.[10] The Chief Justice may after the petitioner has served his petition, verifying affidavit and accompanying exhibits, provisionally admit him to practise as an advocate and solicitor subject to any conditions that the Chief Justice may impose.

[9] Section 7, Legal Profession Act [10] Section 8, Legal Profession Act

Upon receiving payment of the prescribed fee, the Chief Justice will issue to every person admitted provisionally a provisional licenec to practise specifying in it any terms and conditions he has imposed. Such persons shall be entitled to practise as an advocate and solicitor as if their names were on the roll and as if a practising certificate has been issued to them. However, the Chief Justice has the discretion to revoke a provisional licence at any time. Otherwise, a provisional licence expires on the date of the final determination of admission or when a petition has been withdrawn for such person. Similar to ad-hoc cases, provisional persons' names shall be kept on a separate roll.

Other qualified practitioners

A person employed in his professional capacity as an advocate and solicitor with the Government or an approved legal department of a company incorporated in Brunei Darussalam under the Companies Act which has been designated by the Attorney General can also qualify to be practising in Brunei Darussalam providing he pays for the prescribed fee to a practising certificate.[11]

Furthermore, any person who holds the office of Attorney General, Solicitor General or Deputy Public Prosecutor also shares the rights of a qualified advocate and solicitor for as long as they continue to hold such office.[12]

To qualify to use the title of "consultant", one needs to have been either an advocate or solicitor in continuous practice for a period of not less than 10 years.[13]

Hearing and the right of appeal

All petitions and originating motions are held in open court.[14] Any appeals from any judgment or court order on any petition or originating motion lie to the Court of Appeal. The appeal can either be initiated by the petitioner himself or it could be initiated by the Attorney General or any other person that has been served with the petition or originating motion.

Miscellaneous

If the Chief Justice holds the opinion that the number of advocates practising in Brunei Darussalam is sufficient to serve the community, he shall make such a declaration to that effect in the *Government Gazette*[15]. During the period after the Declaration was made and before it is revoked, no person other than a national of Brunei shall be entitled to be admitted as an advocate or even issued a provisional licence to. His Majesty in Council can also direct at 6 months after the Declaration was made, that the name of any advocate who at that time is not an ordinary resident of Brunei Darussalam to be deleted.

It is an offence for an person who is not considered a qualified person to practise law in Brunei Darussalam, to act as an advocate and solicitor and upon conviction shall be liable

[11] Section 18, Legal Profession Act [12] Section 17(2), Legal Profession Act [13] Section 28A, Legal Profession Act [14] Section 9, Legal Profession Act [15] Section 12, Legal Profession Act

to a fine of $1,000 and to imprisonment for a term of 6 months. However, if they commit such acts which includes preparing a document involving a grant of probate or letters of administration or he acts on behalf of claimant that alleges to have a legal claim and as a result writes, publishes or sends a letter or notice threatening legal proceedings etc shall only be guilty of an offence if he can prove that the act was not done for or in expectation of any fee, gain or reward.[16]

THE LAW SOCIETY

The Law Society of Brunei Darussalam was established in 2003 in accordance with the Legal Profession (Law Society of Brunei Darussalam) Order of 2003, which is a subsidiary legislation to the Legal Profession Act.

Amongst its objectives are to maintain and improve the standards of professional conduct and learning within the legal profession, to facilitate the acquisition of legal knowledge by members of the legal profession, to assist the Government and the Courts in all matters relating to the law and to establish a library housing law books and reports to help facilitate knowledge building among the profession.[17]

Membership

The Law Society consists of all advocates and solicitors who possess a valid practising certificate and they will remain as members for as long as they hold one. The society also admit as members non-practitioners and these are advocates and solicitors who does not have a valid practising certificate but non-practitioner members are not eligible to vote and they themselves cannot be elected to the Council. Honorary members are also occasionally admitted as members to the Society as they think fit and this membership could be either for life or for such a period the Council thinks appropriate.[18]

As mentioned briefly, only practitioner members are eligible to attend and vote at any general meeting of the Society but only practitioner members who are Brunei Darussalam nationals are eligible to be elected to the Council. A practitioner member can also by resolution exclude all other members from a general meeting of the society.[19]

Any member of the society other than an honorary member may, after being given a reasonable opportunity to answer all allegations made against him, be expelled from membership or be deprived from any of the rights and privileges of the membership. A practitioner member however cannot be expelled so long as he has in force a practising certificate.[20]

[16] Section 19, Legal Profession Act [17] See Section 4, Law Society Order [18] Sections 5-8, Law Society Order [19] Section 9, Law Society Order [20] Section 10, Law Society Order

The Council

The Council of the Society is responsible for the proper management of the Society's affairs and also for the proper performance of its purposes and powers. The Council consists of statutory members and elected members.[21]

Statutory members are automatic members to the Council each time it is constituted. They comprise of the immediate past President of the Society, advocates and solicitors nominated by the Attorney General and advocates and solicitors appointed by the Council as soon as practicable after it is constituted. Elected members are members that need to be elected by the Society and they comprise of 4 practising members who have been in practice for not less than 10 years and who were elected by practicing members who have been in practice for more than 10 years, 3 practising members who have been in practice not less than 7 years and who were elected by practising members who have been in practice not less than 7 years and 3 practising members who have been in practice for not less than 5 years and who were elected by practising members who have been in practice for not less than 5 years. Every elected member holds office in the Council for two years.

It is compulsory for all members of the Society to vote.[22] If they fail to do so, they will be disqualified from applying for a practicing certificate unless they can satisfy the Chief Registrar with a reasonable excuse for not voting. He has to prove either he was not in Brunei Darussalam at the time of the election or he has a good and sufficient reason for not voting. To avoid disqualification, he can also pay a penalty of $500 which will go into the Compensation Fund.

Elections are held bi-annually in the month of September [23] and usually take place within 21 days after the annual General Meeting of the Society. Every Council constituted after an election shall take office on the next 1st January after the election and shall hold office for 2 years until the 31st December of the following year. The officers of Council are comprised of the President, Vice President, Secretary and Treasurer.[24]

Powers of the Council

The Council is mainly responsible for the management of the Society and its funds. Amongst its other powers include[25], making rules that are not already expressed by the Chief Justice, answering questions affecting the practice and etiquette of the profession, take cognizance of anything affecting the Society or the professional conduct of its members and to bring before any General Meeting, any material to the Society that would be in the profession's interests and make recommendations in relation to it. The Council may also propose legislation or report on any current legislation that has been submitted to them, create prizes and opportunity for scholarships for law students, communicate with other similar bodies and members of the profession in other places or countries to

[21] Section 13, Law Society Order [22] Section 16, Law Society Order [23] Section 17(1), Law Society) Order [24] Section 22(1) of the LP (Law Society) Order 2003 [25] Section 25, Law Society Order 2003

enable exchange of information that may be beneficial to the members of the Society. The full list of powers can be found under section 27 of the Law Society Order.

LEGAL QUALIFICATIONS FOR SYARIAH LAWYERS

Section 25 of the Syariah Courts Act (Chapter 184) has specified who may be appointed as Syar'ie Prosecutor. His Majesty the Sultan and Yang Di-Pertuan may, on the advice of the President of the Majlis Ugama Islam and after consultation with the Majlis, appoint a person who is qualified to become Syariah High Court Judge, to be the Chief Syar'ie Prosecutor[26]. The Chief Syar'ie Prosecutor shall have powers exercisable at his discretion to commence and carry out any proceedings for an offence before a Syariah Court[27]; and he shall not be subject to the direction or control of any other person or authority[28].

His Majesty the Sultan and Yang Di-Pertuan may, on the advice of the President of the Majlis and after consultation with the Chief Syar'ie Prosecutor, appoint a fit and suitable persons from members of the public service to be Syar'ie Prosecutors who shall act under the supervision and direction of the Chief Syar'ie Prosecutor and may exercise all or any right and power vested in or exercisable by the Chief Syar'ie Prosecutor himself[29].

Whereas for Syar'ie Lawyers, section 27(1) of the Syariah Courts Act (Chapter 184) says that the Chief Syar'ie Judge may, on payment of the prescribed fee, admit a person who possesses sufficient knowledge about *Hukum Syara'* and suitable to become a Syar'ie Lawyer to represent the parties in any proceedings before any Syariah Court. Subsection

(2) of section 27 also states that no person other than a Syar'ie Lawyer shall have the right to appear as a *bil-khusumah* representative in any Syariah Court on behalf of any party to any proceeding before it.

Section 28 of the Syariah Courts Act (Chapter 184), the Chief Syar'ie Judge may, with the approval of His Majesty the Sultan and Yang Di-Pertuan, make Rules of Court to provide for the procedure, qualifications and fees for admission of Syar'ie Lawyers as well as regulate, control and supervise the conduct of Syar'ie Lawyers. By virtue of that section, the Syariah Courts (Syar'ie Lawyers) Rules, 2002 has been enacted which commences on the same date as the Syariah Courts Act (Chapter 184). Part II of this Rules talks about the Establishment of Syar'ie Lawyers Committee, Part III talks about Syar'ie Lawyers, Part IV on discipline, Part V on miscellaneous provisions; whereas fees and forms under this Rules can be found in the First and Second Schedule respectively.

Rule 9 talks about admission of Syar'ie Lawyers, which shall be made by the Chief Syar'ie Judge. Rule 10 stated that a person may be admitted to be Syar'ie Lawyers if he –

(a) (i) is a Muslim and has passed the final examination which leads to a bachelor's degree in Syariah from any university or any Islamic

[26] Section 25(1) of the Syariah Courts Act (Chapter 184). [27] Section 25(2) Ibid. [28] Section 25(3) Ibid. [29] Section 25(4) Ibid.

educational institution recognized by the Government of Brunei Darussalam;

(ii) is a Muslim advocate or solicitor enrolled under the Legal Profession Act (Chapter 132) who has passed the Syar'ie Lawyer Certificate examination;

(iii) has served as a Syar'ie Judge, Kadi or Syar'ie Prosecutor for a period of not less than 3 years; or

(iv) is a Muslim who has received professional training in Islamic judicial matters which is recognized by the Government of Brunei Darussalam or who specializes in *Hukum Syara'*;

(b) has attained the age of 21 years;
(c) is of good behavior and –
(i) has never been convicted in Brunei Darussalam or in any other place of any criminal offence which makes him unfit to become a Syar'ie Lawyer;
(ii) has never been adjudged a bankrupt; and

(iii) has never been disbarred, struck off or suspended in his capacity as a legal practitioner by whatever name called in any other country.

LEGAL EDUCATION

Presently, there is no law faculty at the University of Brunei Darussalam. Most of the lawyers practicing in Brunei are either qualified in England or Malaysia.

As stated earlier in Rule 10 of the Syariah Courts (Syar'ie Lawyers) Rules, 2002, a person may be admitted as Syar'ie Lawyers if he fulfills all the necessary requirements. Therefore, in its effort to produce qualified Islamic lawyers and legal practitioners in the Syariah Court, the University of Brunei Darussalam has offered a course in Diploma In Islamic Law and Legal Practice[30], which started its first session in 2000/2001. This course stresses upon the practical aspect especially in practicality, legal administration and their executions.

Objectives of this course are, among others, to give wider opportunity for law degree holders and legal practitioners in Brunei Darussalam, in Syariah or Civil to undertake a formal program in Islamic law; to give more exposure to law graduates in Islamic law and Administration; to produce qualified Islamic lawyers; and to minimizing government expenditure on sending students abroad by providing the course locally.

Subjects offered in the program includes the Islamic Legal System, Islamic Family Law, Syariah Political Science, Islamic Judiciary and Practice, Brunei Legal System, Islamic Law and Evidence, Islamic Criminal law, Islamic Law of Contract and Trade, Procedures in Criminal and Civil and Commercial Law.

CRIMINAL PROCEDURE CODE

An Act to establish a Code of Criminal Procedure

Commencement: 1st May 1952

PART I PRELIMINARY

CHAPTER I CITATION AND APPLICATION

1.(1)This Act may be cited as the Criminal Procedure Code and is generally referred to in this Act as "this Code".

(2)*(Repealed by S 6/2016).*

(3)For the avoidance of doubt, this Code shall be read subject to Article 84C of the Constitution of Brunei Darussalam, and nothing in this Code shall be construed as conferring on any court any jurisdiction or power to entertain any proceedings referred to in Article 84C of the Constitution of Brunei Darussalam.

[S 32/2005]

Interpretation

2.(1)In this Code, unless the context otherwise requires —

"bailable offence" means an offence shown as bailable in the First Schedule to this Code or which is made bailable by any other written law for the time being in force;

"Chief Justice" means the Chief Justice of the Supreme Court for Brunei Darussalam;

"Commissioner of Police" means the Commissioner of Police, Royal Brunei Police Force;

"complaint" means the allegation made orally or in writing to a Magistrate with a view to his taking action under this Code that some person whether known or unknown has committed or is guilty of an offence;

"Court" means the High Court and a Court of a Magistrate;

"Court of Appeal" means the Court of Appeal of the Supreme Court for Brunei Darussalam;

"District Officer" includes, where the context so permits, a Dato Penghulu, a Penghulu and a Ketua;

"fine" includes any fine, pecuniary penalty or forfeiture or compensation adjudged upon any conviction of any crime or offence or for the breach of any written law for the time being in force by any Court in Brunei Darussalam;

[S 32/2005]

"High Court" means the High Court of the Supreme Court for Brunei Darussalam;

"inquiry" includes every inquiry conducted under this Code before a Magistrate;

"Judge" means a Judge of the Supreme Court and includes, where the context so permits, the Chief Justice;

"judicial proceedings" means any proceedings in the course of which evidence is or may be legally taken;

"Magistrate" means a Magistrate appointed by His Majesty the Sultan and Yang Di-Pertuan under the Subordinate Courts Act (Chapter 6) or under any written law;

[S 32/2005]

"medical officer" means a registered medical practitioner employed by Government and if no such officer is available then any other duly registered medical practitioner or any hospital assistant authorised by the Director-General of Medical Services either generally or for any specific purpose to exercise the functions of a medical officer under this Code;

[GN 273/2002]

"non-bailable offence" means an offence other than a bailable offence;

"non-seizable offence" means an offence for which and "non-seizable case" means a case in which a police officer may not ordinarily arrest without warrant according to the third column of the First Schedule or under the provisions of any other written law for the time being in force;

"offence" means any act or omission made punishable by any other written law for the time being in force;

"officer in charge of a police district or police station" means the officer appointed to perform the duties of that office and when such officer is absent therefrom or unable from illness to perform his duties, the police officer present and acting in the district or station who is next in rank below such officer;

"place" includes a house, building, tent and vessel;

"Police District" means any area which has been constituted a police district by regulations made under the Royal Brunei Police Force Act (Chapter 50), and unless and until districts are so constituted means an ordinary administrative district;

"police officer" means any member of the Royal Brunei Police Force, and includes a special police officer when mobilised or deemed to be mobilised for active service and any person vested under any written law with the powers of a police officer;

[S 4/2007]

"postal article" means any letter, postcard, book, document, pamphlet, sample parcel or package or other article whatsoever transmitted by post;

"Registrar" means the Chief Registrar, a Deputy Chief Registrar, a Senior Registrar or a Registrar of the Supreme Court and includes a Deputy or Assistant Registrar;

"seizable offence" means an offence for which, and "seizable case" means a case in which, a police officer may ordinarily arrest without warrant according to the third column of the First Schedule or under the provisions of any other written law for the time being in force;

"summons case" means a case relating to an offence not being a warrant case;

"Supreme Court" means the Supreme Court of Brunei Darussalam established by the Supreme Court Act (Chapter 5);

"warrant case" means a case relating to an offence punishable with death or with imprisonment for a term exceeding 6 months;

"youthful offender" includes any child convicted of an offence punishable by fine or imprisonment who, in the absence of legal proof to the contrary, is above the age of 7 years and under the age of 18 years in the opinion of the Court before which such child is convicted.

(2) Words which refer to acts done extend also to illegal omissions.

(3) All words and expressions used herein and defined in the Penal Code (Chapter 22) and not hereinbefore defined shall be deemed to have the meanings attributed to them by that Code.

(4) The marginal notes of this Code shall not affect the construction thereof.

Trial of offences under Penal Code and against other written laws

3. All offences under the Penal Code shall be inquired into and tried according to the provisions hereinafter contained, and all offences under any other law shall be inquired into and tried according to the same provisions, subject however to any other written law for the time being in force regulating the manner or place of inquiring into or trying such offences.

Saving of powers of Supreme Court

4. Nothing in this Code shall be construed as derogating from the powers or jurisdiction of the Supreme Court.

PART II CONSTITUTION AND POWERS OF CRIMINAL COURTS

CHAPTER II CRIMINAL COURTS GENERALLY

Classes of criminal Courts

5.(1) The Courts for the administration of criminal justice in Brunei Darussalam to which this Code applies shall be the following —

(a) High Court;

(b) Courts of Magistrates.

(2) A Judge may sit in and constitute a Court of a Magistrate.

Court to be open

6.(1) The place in which any criminal Court is held for the purpose of inquiring into or trying any offence shall be deemed an open Court, to which the public generally may have access, so far as the same can conveniently contain them.

(2) The presiding Judge or Magistrate may, if he thinks fit, on special grounds of public policy or expediency in his discretion, order at any stage of any inquiry into, or trial of, any particular case that the public

generally, or any particular person, shall not have access to, or be or remain in, the room or building used by the Court. In every such case, the grounds on which the order is made shall be recorded.

(3) This section does not apply to witnesses who shall ordinarily be excluded from the Court until they give evidence.

Section 6 read subject to other Acts *[S 62/2004]*

6A. Section 6 shall be read subject to section 15 of the Supreme Court Act (Chapter 5), section 7 of the Intermediate Courts Act (Chapter 162) and section 7 of the Subordinate Courts Act (Chapter 6).

Jurisdiction

7. Subject to the provisions of this Code, the jurisdiction of the High Court and a Court of a Magistrate in criminal matters shall extend to any offence committed —

(a) wholly or partly within Brunei Darussalam;

(b) on board any ship registered in Brunei Darussalam;

(c) on board any aircraft registered in Brunei Darussalam;

(d) on the high seas if the offence is piracy by the law of nations;

(e) by any person outside Brunei Darussalam who abets, or enters a conspiracy to commit, an offence within Brunei Darussalam, whether or not any overt act in furtherance of such conspiracy takes place within Brunei Darussalam; or

(f) by a subject of His Majesty the Sultan and Yang Di-Pertuan, whether the offence was committed within or outside Brunei Darussalam.

Powers of Courts

8. (1) Subject to the other provisions of this Code, any offence under the Penal Code may be tried by —

(a) the High Court;

(b) a Court of a Magistrate where such offence is shown in the eighth column of the First Schedule to be so triable.

(2) Where a Court of a Magistrate is given power by the eighth column of the First Schedule to try an offence for which such Court has no power to award the maximum punishment, the Court shall, if it is of the opinion that the punishment it has power to award is inadequate, commit the accused person for trial by the High Court.

Offences under other written laws

9. (1) Subject to the other provisions of this Code, any offence under any other written law shall, when any Court is mentioned in this behalf in such written law, be tried by such Court.

(2) When no Court is so mentioned, it may be tried by the High Court or any other Court to which this Code applies:

Provided that no Court of a Magistrate shall by virtue of this subsection try an offence which is punishable with imprisonment for a term which may exceed 5 years.

Sentences which High Court may pass

10. The High Court may pass any sentence authorised by law.

Sentences which Courts of Magistrates may pass

11. (1) Without prejudice to any provision of any other written law conferring special jurisdiction on Courts of Magistrates, such Courts may pass a sentence of imprisonment for a term not exceeding 3 years or a fine not exceeding $5,000 or, where the Chief Justice by notification published in the *Gazette* confers upon any Magistrate special jurisdiction, then in a Court presided over by such Magistrate, the sentence may be increased to imprisonment for a term of 7 years or a fine of $10,000.

(2) A Court of a Magistrate may pass any lawful sentence, combining any of the sentences which it is authorised by law to pass.

(3) His Majesty the Sultan and Yang Di-Pertuan may limit the jurisdiction of any Magistrate.

Power of Magistrates to sentence to imprisonment in default of fine

12. (1) A Court of a Magistrate may award such term of imprisonment in default of payment of fine as is authorised by section 254:

Provided that the term is not in excess of the Magistrate's powers under this Code.

(2) The imprisonment awarded under this section may be in addition to a substantive sentence of imprisonment for the maximum term awardable by the Magistrate under section 11.

Sentence in case of conviction of several offences at one trial

13. (1) When a person is convicted at one trial of two or more distinct offences, the Court may, subject to the provisions of section 71 of the Penal Code (Chapter 22), sentence him for such offences to the several punishments prescribed therefor which such Court is competent to inflict, such punishments to commence the one after the expiration of the other in such order as the Court may direct unless the Court directs that such punishments shall run concurrently.

(2) In the case of consecutive sentences, it shall not be necessary for the Court, by reason only of the aggregate punishment for the several offences being in excess of the punishment which it is competent to inflict on conviction of a single offence, to send the offender for trial before the High Court:

Provided that —

(a) in no case shall such person be sentenced to imprisonment for a longer period than 15 years;

(b) the aggregate punishment shall not exceed three times the amount of punishment which the Magistrate in the exercise of his ordinary jurisdiction is competent to inflict.

(3) For the purposes of appeal, aggregate sentences passed under this section in cases of convictions for several offences at one trial shall be deemed to be a single sentence.

Outstanding offences *[S 6/2016]*

13A.(1) If the accused is found guilty of an offence in any criminal proceedings begun by or on behalf of the Public Prosecutor, the Court in determining and passing sentence may with the consent of the prosecution and the accused, take into consideration any other outstanding offences that the accused admits to have committed.

(2) If the outstanding offences referred to in subsection (1) were not begun by or on behalf of the Public Prosecutor, the Court must first be satisfied that the person or authority by whom those proceedings were begun consents to that course of action.

(3) When consent is given under subsection (1) or (2) and any outstanding offences are taken into consideration in determining and passing sentence, such fact must be entered in the Court's record.

(4) After being sentenced, the accused may not, unless his conviction for the original offence under subsection (1) is set aside, be charged or tried for any such offence that the Court had taken into consideration under this section.

Criminal jurisdiction of Magistrates

14. Subject to the provisions of this Code, every Magistrate shall have cognisance of and power and authority to —

(a) hear, try, determine and dispose of in a summary way prosecutions for offences cognisable by such Magistrate;

(b) inquire into offences committed or alleged to have been committed with a view to committal for trial by the High Court;

(c) inquire into complaints of offences and summons and examine witnesses relating such offences and summons and apprehend and issue warrants for the apprehension of criminals and offenders, and deal with them according to law;

(d) issue search warrants under the provisions of this Code in that behalf, and require persons to furnish security for the peace or for their good behaviour according to law;

(e) hold inquests; and

(f) do all other matters and things which a Magistrate is empowered to do by this Code or any other Act.

Reformative training *[S 9/2006]*

14A.(1) Where a person is convicted by the Intermediate Courts or the High Court of an offence punishable with imprisonment and that person —

(a) is, on the day of his conviction, above the age of 18 years and under the age of 21 years: or

(b) is, on the day of his conviction, above the age of 14 years and under the age of 18 years, prior to his conviction, been dealt with by a Court in connection with another offence and had, in respect of that other offence, been ordered to be sent to an approved school established under section 61 of the Children and Young Persons Act (Chapter 219),

and the Court is satisfied, having regard to his character and previous conduct and to the circumstances of the offence of which he is convicted, that it is expedient with a view to his reformation and the prevention of crime that he should undergo a period of training in a reformative training centre, that Court may, *in lieu* of any other sentence, pass a sentence of reformative training.

(2) Where a person is convicted by a Court of a Magistrate of an offence punishable with imprisonment and that person —

(a) is, on the day of his conviction, above the age of 18 and under the age of 21; or

(b) is, on the day of his conviction, above the age of 14 and under the age of 18 and has, prior to his conviction, been dealt with by a Court in connection with another offence and had, in respect of that other offence, been ordered to be sent to an approved school established under section 61 of the Children and Young Persons Act (Chapter 219),

and the Court of a Magistrate is satisfied of the matters mentioned in subsection (1), the Court may commit him in custody for sentence to the High Court.

(3) Where a person is so committed for sentence, the High Court shall inquire into the circumstances of the case and may —

(a) if satisfied of the matters mentioned in subsection (1), sentence him to reformative training; or

(b) in any other case, deal with him in any manner in which the Court of a Magistrate might have dealt with him.

(4) Where a person has been ordered by a Juvenile Court under the Children and Young Persons Act (Chapter 219) to be brought before a High Court, the High Court shall inquire into the circumstances of the case and may —

(a) if satisfied that it is expedient with a view to his reformation that he should undergo a period of training in a reformative training centre, sentence him to reformative training; or

(b) in any other case, deal with him in any manner in which the Juvenile Court might have dealt with him.

(5) Before a sentence of reformative training is passed under this section, and before a person is committed for sentence under subsection (2), the Court shall consider any report or representations made by or on behalf of the Director of Prisons on the offender's physical and mental condition and his suitability for the sentence; and if the Court has not received such a report or representations it shall remand the offender in custody for such a period or periods, not exceeding 3 weeks in the case of any single period, as the Court thinks necessary to enable the report or representations to be made.

(6) A copy of any report or representation made to the Court by the Director of Prisons for the purposes of subsection (5) shall be given by the Court to the offender or his legal representative.

(7) A person sentenced to reformative training shall be detained subject to his release in accordance with the Third Schedule and while so detained shall be treated in such manner as may be prescribed by rules made under section 384.

PART III GENERAL PROVISIONS

CHAPTER III AID AND INFORMATION TO MAGISTRATES AND POLICE AND PERSONS MAKING ARRESTS

Public when to assist Magistrates and police

15.—(1) Every person is bound to assist a Magistrate, police officer or District Officer reasonably demanding his aid —

(a) in the taking or preventing the escape of any other person whom such Magistrate, police officer or District Officer is authorised to arrest;

(b) in the prevention of a breach of the peace or of any injury attempted to be committed to any railway, tramway, canal, dock, wharf, telegraph or public property;

(c) in the suppression of a riot or affray.

(2) Every person failing to give such assistance as is required by this section is guilty of an offence under section 187 of the Penal Code (Chapter 22).

Aid to persons other than police officer executing warrant

16. When a warrant is directed to a person other than a police officer, any other person may aid in the execution of such warrant if the person to whom the warrant is directed is near at hand and acting in the execution of his warrant.

Public to give information of certain matters

17. (1) Every person aware —

(a) of the commission of or the intention of any other person to commit any offence punishable under the following sections of the Penal Code (Chapter 22): 121, 121A, 122, 123, 124A, 130, 143, 144, 145, 147, 148, 194, 232, 234, 302, 304, 307, 308, 382, 392, 393, 394, 395, 396, 397, 398, 399, 402, 435, 436, 449, 450, 456, 457, 458, 459, 460, 489A, 489D;

(b) of any sudden or unnatural death or death by violence or of any death under suspicious circumstances, or of the body of any person being found dead without its being known how such person came by death,

shall in the absence of reasonable excuse, the burden of proving which shall lie upon the person so aware, forthwith give information to the officer in charge of the nearest police station or to a police officer or to the nearest District Officer of such commission or intention or of such sudden, unnatural or violent death or of the finding of such dead body, as the case may be.

(2) If any person discovers any dead body and he has reason to believe that the deceased met with his death through an unlawful act or omission, he shall not remove or in any way alter the position of the body except so far as is necessary for its safety.

(3) Every person failing to give such information as is required by this section is guilty of an offence under section 176 of the Penal Code (Chapter 22).

Police officer bound to report certain matters

18. Every police officer and every District Officer shall forthwith communicate to the nearest Magistrate or police officer in charge of a police station any information which he may have or obtain respecting —

(a) the occurrence of any sudden or unnatural death or of any death under suspicious circumstances;

(b) the finding of the dead body of any person without it being known how such person came by his death.

CHAPTER IV ARREST, ESCAPE AND RE-TAKING

Arrest, how made

19.(1) In making an arrest, the police officer or other person making the arrest shall actually touch or confine the body of the person to be arrested unless there is a submission to the custody by word or action.

(2) If such person forcibly resists the endeavour to arrest him or attempts to evade the arrest, the police officer or other person may use all means necessary to effect the arrest.

[S 32/2005]

(3) The person arrested shall not be subjected to more restraint than is necessary to prevent his escape.

(4) Nothing in this section gives a right to cause the death of a person who is not accused of an offence punishable with death or with imprisonment for 15 years.

Search of place entered by persons sought to be arrested

20.(1) If any person acting under a warrant of arrest or any police officer or District Officer having authority to arrest has reason to believe that any person to be arrested has entered into or is within any place, the person residing in or in charge of such place shall, on demand of such person acting as aforesaid or of such police officer or District Officer, allow him free ingress thereto and afford all reasonable facilities for a search therein.

(2) If ingress to such place cannot be obtained under subsection (1), it shall be lawful in any case for a person acting under a warrant, and in any case in which a warrant may be issued but cannot be obtained without affording the person to be arrested an opportunity to escape, for a police officer or District Officer —

(a) to enter such place and search therein; and

(b) in order to effect an entrance into such place, to break open any outer or inner door or window of any place whether that of the person to be arrested or of any other person if, after notification of his authority and purpose and demand of admittance duly made, he cannot otherwise obtain admittance.

(3) If any place to be searched is an apartment in the actual occupancy of a woman (not being the person to be arrested) who, according to custom, does not appear in public, such person or police officer shall before entering the apartment, give notice to the woman that she is at liberty to withdraw, and shall afford her every reasonable facility for withdrawing, and may then break open the apartment and enter it.

Search of persons in place searched under warrant

21. Whenever a search for anything is or is about to be lawfully made in any place in respect of any offence, all persons found therein may be lawfully detained until the search is completed, and they may, if the thing sought is in its nature capable of being concealed upon the person, be searched for it by or in the presence of a Magistrate or of a police officer not below the rank of Inspector or of a police officer in charge of a police station.

Power to break open any place for purposes for liberation

22. Any police officer or other person authorised to make an arrest may break open any place in order to liberate himself or any other person who having lawfully entered for the purpose of making an arrest is detained therein.

Mode of searching women

23. Whenever it is necessary to cause a woman to be searched, the search shall be made by another woman with strict regard to decency.

Search of persons arrested

24. Whenever a person is arrested —

(a) by a police officer under a warrant which does not provide for the taking of bail or under a warrant which provides for the taking of bail but the person arrested cannot furnish bail;

(b) without warrant or by a private person under a warrant and the person arrested cannot legally be admitted to bail or is unable to furnish bail,

the police officer making the arrest or, when the arrest is made by a private person, the police officer to whom such private person makes over the person arrested, may search such person and place in safe custody all articles other than necessary wearing apparel found upon him, and any of such articles which there is reason to believe were the instruments or the fruits or other evidence of the crime may be detained until his discharge or acquittal.

25. *(No section).*

Power to seize offensive weapons

26. The officer or other person making any arrest under this Code may take from the person arrested any offensive weapons which he has about his person and shall deliver all weapons so taken to the Court or officer before which or whom the officer or person making the arrest is required by law to produce the person arrested.

Search of person for name and address

27. Every person lawfully in custody, who by reason of incapacity from intoxication, illness, idiocy, mental disorder or infancy is unable to give a reasonable account of himself, may be searched for the purpose of ascertaining his name and place of abode.

[S 25/2014]

When police officer may arrest without warrant

28. (1) Any police officer or District Officer may, without an order from a Magistrate and without a warrant, arrest —

(a) any person who has been concerned in any seizable offence or against whom a reasonable complaint has been made or credible information has been received or a reasonable suspicion exists of his having been so concerned;

(b) any person having in his possession without lawful excuse, the burden of proving which shall lie on such person, any implement of house breaking;

(c) any person who has been proclaimed under section 49;

(d) any person in whose possession anything is found which may reasonably be suspected to be stolen or fraudulently obtained property and who may reasonably be suspected of having committed an offence with reference to such thing;

(e) any person who obstructs a police officer while in the execution of his duty or who has escaped or attempts to escape from lawful custody;

(f) any person reasonably suspected of being a deserter from the Royal Brunei Armed Forces or Royal Brunei Police Force or Gurkha Reserve Unit or any visiting force present for the time being in Brunei Darussalam by virtue of any written law or by virtue of any lawful arrangement made by or on behalf of Brunei Darussalam;

(g) any person taking precautions to conceal his presence under circumstances which afford reason to believe that he is taking such precautions with a view to committing a seizable offence;

(h) any person who has no ostensible means of subsistence or who cannot give a satisfactory account of himself;

(i) any person who is by repute a habitual robber, housebreaker or thief or a habitual receiver of stolen property knowing it to be stolen or who by repute, habitually commits extortion or in order to commit extortion, habitually puts or attempts to put persons in fear of injury;

(j) any person in the act of committing in his presence a breach of the peace;

(k) any person subject to the supervision of the police who fails to comply with the requirements of section 265.

(2) Nothing in this section shall be held to limit or to modify the operation of any other written law empowering a police officer or District Officer to arrest without a warrant.

Refusal to give name and residence or naming residence outside Brunei Darussalam

29. (1) When any person in the presence of a police officer or District Officer commits or is accused of committing a non-seizable offence and refuses on the demand of a police officer or District Officer to give his name and residence or gives a name or residence which such officer has reason to believe to be false, he may be arrested by such police officer or District Officer in order that his name or residence may be ascertained, and he shall, within 24 hours of the arrest, exclusive of the time necessary for the journey, be taken before the nearest Magistrate unless before that time his true name and residence are ascertained, in which case such person shall be forthwith released on his executing a bond for his appearance before a Court if so required.

(2) When any person is thus brought before a Magistrate, the Magistrate may either require him to execute a bond, with or without a surety, for his appearance before a Court if so required, or may order him to be detained in custody until he can be tried.

(3) When any person in the presence of a police officer or District Officer commits or is accused of committing a non-seizable offence and on the demand of a police officer or District Officer to give his name and residence gives as his residence a place outside Brunei Darussalam, he may be arrested by such police officer or District Officer and shall be brought forthwith either before the nearest Magistrate who may require him to execute a bond, with or without a surety, for his appearance before a Court if so required, or may order him to be detained in custody until he can be tried, or before a police officer in charge of a police station who may require him to furnish a bond, with or without a surety, for his appearance before a Court if required.

Person arrested by District Officer, how dealt with

30. A District Officer making an arrest without a warrant shall without unnecessary delay make over the person so arrested to the nearest police officer or in the absence of a police officer, take such person to the nearest police station, and a police officer shall receive every such person into custody.

Pursuit of offenders

31. For the purpose of arresting, any person whom he has power to arrest without a warrant a police officer may pursue any such person into any part of Brunei Darussalam.

Arrest by private persons

32.(1) Any private person may arrest any person who, in his view, commits a non-bailable and seizable offence or who has been proclaimed under section 49 and shall without unnecessary delay make over the person so arrested to the nearest police officer or, in the absence of a police officer, take such person to the nearest police station.

(2) If there is reason to believe that such person comes under the provisions of section 28, a police officer shall re-arrest him.

(3) If there is reason to believe that he has committed a non-seizable offence and he refuses on the demand of a police officer to give his name and residence, or gives a name or residence which the police officer has reason to believe to be false, or gives a residence which is not within Brunei Darussalam, he shall be dealt with under section 29.

(4) If there is no reason to believe that he has committed an offence, he shall be at once released.

(5) Any person who commits an offence on or with respect to the property of another may, if his name and address are unknown, be apprehended by the person injured or by any person who is using the property to which the injury is done, or by the servant of either of such persons or by any person authorised by or acting in aid of either of such persons, and may be detained until he gives his name and address and satisfies such person that the name and address so given are correct or until he can be delivered into the custody of a police officer.

(6) If any person lawfully apprehended under subsection (5) assaults or forcibly resists the person by whom he is so apprehended or any person acting in his aid he is guilty of an offence and liable on conviction to a fine of $800.

How person arrested is to be dealt with

33.(1) A police officer making an arrest without a warrant shall without unnecessary delay and subject to the provisions herein as to bail or previous release, take or send the person arrested before a Court of a Magistrate.

(2) No police officer shall detain in custody a person arrested without a warrant for a longer period than under all the circumstances of the case is reasonable.

(3) Such period should not ordinarily exceed 48 hours exclusive of the time necessary for the journey from the place of arrest to the Court, unless there are exceptional circumstances which render this not reasonably practicable.

[S 63/2002]

(4) Any police officer making an arrest under this section shall, unless the circumstances are such that the person arrested can be in no doubt with regard to the reason for his arrest, immediately upon such arrest is effected, notify to the arrested person the reason for his arrest.

Release of person arrested

34. No person who has been arrested by a police officer shall be released except on his own bond or on bail or under the order in writing of a Judge or Magistrate or officer in charge of a police station.

Offence committed in Magistrate's presence

35. When any offence is committed in the presence of a Magistrate, he may himself arrest or authorise any person to arrest the offender, and may thereupon, subject to the provisions herein as to bail, commit the offender to custody.

Arrest by or in presence of Magistrate

36. Any Magistrate may at any time arrest or authorise the arrest in his presence of any person for whose arrest he is competent at the time and in the circumstances to issue a warrant.

Power on escape to pursue and re-take

37. If a person in lawful custody escapes or is rescued, the person from whose custody he escaped or was rescued may immediately pursue and arrest him in any place and deal with such person as he might have done on the original taking.

Provisions of sections 20 and 22 to apply to arrests under section 37

38. The provisions of sections 20 and 22 apply to arrests under section 37 although the person making the arrest is not acting under a warrant and is not a police officer having authority to arrest.

CHAPTER V PROCESSES TO COMPEL APPEARANCE

Summons

Form of summons; by whom served

39. (1) Every summons to appear issued by a Court under this Code shall be in writing and signed by a Magistrate or, in the case of the Supreme Court, by the Chief Justice, a Judge or the Registrar, and it shall bear the seal of the Court.

(2) Such summons shall ordinarily be served by a police officer or if the summons is in connection with an offence under a written law which it is the duty of a Government department to enforce, by an officer of such Government department. The Court issuing the summons may if it sees fit direct it to be served by any other person.

[S 32/2005]

Service of summons

40. (1) The summons shall if practicable be served personally on the person summoned by tendering or delivering to him a copy thereof under the seal of the Court.

(2) Every person on whom a summons is so served shall, if so required by the serving officer, sign a receipt for the copy.

(3) In the case of a corporation, the summons may be served on the secretary or other like officer of the corporation.

(4) Where the person to be summoned cannot by the exercise of due diligence be found, the summons may be served by leaving a copy thereof for him with some adult member of his family or with his servant residing with him.

(5) Where the person summoned is in the service of the Government, the Court issuing the summons shall ordinarily send it in duplicate to the head of the office in which such person is employed, and such head shall thereupon cause the summons to be served in the manner provided by this section, and shall return it to the Court under his signature and duly indorsed by the person on whom it was served as required by subsection (2).

Procedure when personal service cannot be effected

41. When the person to be summoned cannot by the exercise of due diligence be found and service cannot be effected as directed by section 40(4), the serving officer shall in the presence of two witnesses affix a copy of the summons to some conspicuous part of the house or other place in which the person summoned ordinarily resides and in such case the summons, if the Court so directs either before or after such affixing, shall be deemed to have been duly served.

Proof of service

42. When a summons issued by a Court is served, an affidavit of such service purporting to be made before an officer duly authorised to administer an oath shall be admissible in evidence.

Warrant of arrest

Form of warrant of arrest

43. (1) Every warrant of arrest issued by a Court under this Code shall be in writing and signed by a Magistrate or, in the case of the Supreme Court, by the Chief Justice, a Judge or the Registrar, and it shall bear the seal of the Court.

(2) Every such warrant shall remain in force until it is cancelled by the Court which issued it or until it is executed.

Court may by indorsement on warrant direct security to be taken

44. (1) Any Court issuing a warrant for the arrest of any person may, in its discretion, direct by indorsement on the warrant that if such person execute a bond with sufficient sureties for his attendance before the Court at a specified time and thereafter until otherwise directed by the Court, the officer to whom the warrant is directed shall take such security and shall release such person from custody.

(2) The indorsement shall state —

(a) the number of sureties;

(b) the amount in which they and the person for whose arrest the warrant is issued are to be respectively bound;

(c) the time at which he is to attend before the Court.

(3) Whenever security is taken under this section, the officer to whom the warrant is directed shall forward the bond to the Court.

Warrants, to whom directed

45. (1) A warrant of arrest shall ordinarily be directed to the officer in charge of police of the District in which it is issued and to all other police officers of Brunei Darussalam, and any police officer may execute such warrant in any part of Brunei Darussalam.

(2) The Court issuing a warrant may direct it to any person or persons by name, not being police officers, and all or any one or more of such persons may execute the same.

Notification of substance of warrant

46. Any warrant of arrest lawfully issued may be executed by any police officer at any time notwithstanding that the warrant is not in his possession at the time, but a police officer or other person executing a warrant of arrest shall notify the substance thereof to the person arrested, and shall, if so required by the person arrested, show him the warrant or a copy thereof under the seal of the Court issuing the warrant as soon as practicable after the arrest.

Person arrested to be brought before Court without delay [S 32/2005]

47. The police officer or other person executing a warrant of arrest shall, subject to the provisions of section 44 as to security, without unnecessary delay bring the person arrested before the Court before which he is required by law to produce such person.

48. *(No section).*

Proclamation and attachment

Proclamation for person absconding

49. (1) If the High Court or a Court of a Magistrate has reason to believe, whether after taking evidence or not, that any person against whom a warrant has been issued by it has absconded or is concealing himself so that such warrant cannot be executed, such Court may publish a written proclamation requiring him to appear at a specified place and at a specified time.

(2) The proclamation shall be published as follows —

(a) it shall be publicly read in some conspicuous place of the town, village or kampong in or near which such person ordinarily resides;

(b) it shall be fixed to some conspicuous part of the house or other place in which such person ordinarily resides or to some conspicuous place of such town, village or kampong; and

(c) a copy thereof shall be affixed to some conspicuous part of the Court house.

(3) A statement in writing by the Court issuing the proclamation to the effect that the proclamation was duly published on a specified day shall be conclusive evidence that the requirements of this section have been complied with and that the proclamation was published on such day.

Attachment of property of person proclaimed

50. (1) The Court issuing a proclamation under section 49 may at any time order the attachment of any property movable or immovable or both belonging to the proclaimed person.

(2) If the property ordered to be attached consists of debts or other movable property, the attachment shall be made by —

(a) seizure;

(b) the appointment of a receiver;

(c) an order in writing prohibiting the delivery of such property to the proclaimed person or to any one of his behalf; or

(d) all or any two of such methods as the Court thinks fit.

(3) If the property ordered to be attached is immovable, the attachment under this section shall be made through the Land Officer of the district in which the property is situated; and upon the receipt of an order of attachment, the Land Officer shall execute the attachment by —

(a) taking possession;

(b) the appointment of a receiver;

(c) an order in writing prohibiting the payment of rent or delivery of property to the proclaimed person or to any person on his behalf; or

(d) all or any two of such methods as he thinks fit.

(4) No such attachment of any land held under a title required by law to be registered shall take effect until the order of attachment is duly registered under the law for the registration of dealings with such land for the time being in force.

(5) If the proclaimed person does not appear within the time specified in the proclamation, the property shall be at the disposal of the Government, but it shall not be sold until the expiration of 6 months from the date of the attachment unless it is subject to speedy and natural decay, or the Court considers that the sale would be for the benefit of the owner, in either of which case the Court may cause it to be sold whenever it thinks fit.

(6) Any person other than the person proclaimed may appear before the Court which made the order of attachment and claim, stating his title thereto, the property or any part thereof attached or ordered to be attached:

Provided that the claim is made within 3 months from the order of attachment.

(7) The Court shall record the claim so made and shall cause a copy thereof to be served upon the prosecutor together with a notice requiring him to attend before the Court on a day and at a time to be stated therein to show cause why the property, if attached, should not be released, or why such order of attachment should not be cancelled so far as it relates to the property so claimed.

(8) At the hearing, the Court shall proceed to inquire into the truth and justice of the claim so made and to take such evidence as may be necessary.

(9) Such inquiry shall be made, as nearly as may be practicable, in the manner prescribed by Chapter XIX for conducting trials without the aid of assessors.

(10) The Court shall, if satisfied of the truth and justice of the claim, direct the property to be released or the order to be cancelled, or is satisfied as aforesaid as to part only of the claim shall direct such part to be released or so much of the order as relates thereto to be cancelled.

(11) The Court may, in its discretion, award to the claimant costs and such expenses as it thinks proper which shall be paid by the Government.

Restoration of attached property

51. If within 2 years from the date of the attachment any person whose property is or has been at the disposal of the Government under section 50 appears voluntarily or is apprehended and brought before the Court by whose order the property was attached and proves to the satisfaction of such Court that he did not abscond or conceal himself for the purpose of avoiding execution of the warrant, and that he had no such notice of the proclamation as to enable him to attend within the time specified therein, the property or, if the property has been sold, the net proceeds of the sale or, if part only thereof has been sold, the net proceeds of the sale and the residue of the property shall after satisfying thereout all costs incurred in consequence of the attachment, be delivered to him.

Other rules regarding summonses to appear and warrants of arrest

Issue of warrant *in lieu* of or in addition to summons

52. A criminal Court may, in any case in which it is empowered to issue a summons for the appearance of any person other than an assessor, after recording its reasons in writing, issue a warrant for his arrest —

(a) if either before the issue of summons or after the issue of the summons but before the time fixed for his appearance, the Court sees reason to believe that he has absconded or will not obey the summons; or

(b) if at such time he fails to appear and the summons is proved to have been duly served in time to admit of his appearing in accordance therewith and no reasonable excuse is offered for such failure.

Service and execution in any part of Brunei Darussalam

53. All summonses to appear and warrants of arrest issued by a Magistrate may be served or executed, as the case may be, in any part of Brunei Darussalam.

Power to take bond for appearance

54. When any person for whose appearance or arrest any Court is empowered to issue a summons or warrant is present in such Court, it may require such person to execute a bond with or without sureties for his appearance in such Court.

Arrest on breach of bond appearance

55. When any person who is bound by any bond taken under this Code to appear before a Court does not so appear, such Court may issue a warrant directing that such person be arrested and produced before it.

CHAPTER VI PROCESSES TO COMPEL PRODUCTION OF DOCUMENTS AND OTHER MOVABLE PROPERTY AND FOR DISCOVERY OF PERSONS WRONGFULLY CONFINED

Summons to produce property or document

56. (1) Notwithstanding any other written law for the time being in force but subject to the provisions of the Evidence Act (Chapter 108), whenever any Court or police officer making a police investigation considers that the production of any property or document is necessary or desirable for the purposes of any investigation, inquiry, trial or other proceedings under this Code by or before such Court or police officer, such Court may issue a summons or the police officer a written order to the person in whose possession or power such property or document is believed to be, requiring him to attend and produce it or to produce it at the time and place stated in the summons or order.

[S 63/2002; S 6/2016]

(1A) In the case of banker's books, no police officer below the rank of Superintendent shall exercise any powers conferred by this section or order the production of such books unless at the place of business of the bank.

[S 63/2002]

(2) Any person required under this section merely to produce any property or document shall be deemed to have complied with the requisition if he causes such property or document to be produced instead of attending personally to produce the property or document.

(3) Nothing in this section shall be deemed to apply to any postal article, telegram or other document in the custody of the postal or telegraph authorities.

[S 63/2002]

(4) In this section, "bankers' books" include ledgers, day books, cash books, account books and all other books used in the ordinary business of a bank, whether these records are in written form or kept on microfilm, magnetic tape or any other form of mechanical or electronic data retrieval system.

[S 63/2002]

Procedure as to postal articles etc.

57. If any postal article, telegram or other document is, in the opinion of the Court of Appeal or the High Court, wanted for the purpose of any investigation, inquiry, trial or other proceedings under this Code, such Court may require the postal or telegraph authorities to deliver the postal article, telegram or other document to such person as it may direct.

Provisions of sections 39 to 42 to apply

58. The provisions of sections 39, 40, 41 and 42 apply in relation to summonses under this Chapter.

Search warrants

When search warrant may be issued

59.(1) Where —

(a) any Court has reason to believe that a person to whom a summons under section 56 or a requisition under section 57 has been or might have been addressed will not or would not produce the property or document as required by such requisition;

(b) such property or document is not known to the Court to be in the possession of any person; or

(c) the Court considers that the purposes of justice or of any inquiry, trial or other proceedings under this Code will be served by a general search or inspection,

the Court may issue a search warrant and the person to whom such warrant is directed may search and inspect in accordance therewith and with the provisions in this Chapter.

(2) Nothing in this section shall authorise any Court other than the Court of Appeal or the High Court to grant a warrant to search for a postal article, telegram or other document in the custody of the postal or telegraph authorities.

(3) A search warrant shall ordinarily be directed to the officer in charge of police of the District in which it is issued and to some other officers to be designated by name therein, and all or any of such police officers may execute such warrant.

(4) The Court issuing a search warrant may direct it to any person or persons by name, not being police officers, and all or any one or more of such persons may execute such warrant.

Power to restrict warrant

60. The Court may, if it thinks fit, specify in the warrant the particular place or part thereof to which only the search or inspection shall extend, and the person charged with the execution of such warrant shall then search or inspect only the place or part so specified.

Search of place suspected to contain stolen property, forged document etc.

61. If a Magistrate upon information and after such inquiry as he thinks necessary has reason to believe that —

(a) any place is used for the deposit or sale of stolen property, contraband goods or property unlawfully obtained;

(b) any place is used for the deposit, sale or manufacture of forged documents, false seals or counterfeit stamps or coin, or forged trade marks, instruments or materials for counterfeiting coin or stamps or for forging;

(c) any offence against any written law for the time being in force relating to gambling, pawnbrokers, opium, distillation of arrack or other spirit is being or is likely to be committed in any place;

(d) any offence against the Societies Act (Chapter 203) or any other written law relating thereto for the time being in force, or any offence against any written law relating to the protection of women and girls, is being or is likely to be committed in any place; or

(e) any stolen property, contraband goods, property unlawfully obtained, forged documents, false seals or counterfeit stamps or coin, or forged trade marks, instruments or materials for counterfeiting coin or stamps or for forging or housebreaking are concealed, kept or deposited in any place,

he may by warrant authorise the person to whom it is directed to —

(i) enter, with such assistance as may be required, such place;

(ii) search the place in the manner specified in the warrant in the presence, if practicable, of two or more inhabitants of the neighbourhood;

(iii) take possession of any property, goods, documents, seals, stamps, coins or trade marks therein found which he reasonably suspects to be stolen, contraband, unlawfully obtained, forged, false or counterfeit and also of any such instruments and materials as aforesaid;

(iv) convey such property, goods, documents, seals, stamps, coins, trade marks or materials before a Judge or Magistrate, or guard them on the spot until the offender is taken before a Judge or Magistrate or otherwise dispose thereof in some place of safety; and

(v) take into custody and bring before a Judge or Magistrate every person found in such place who appears to be guilty of any offence under paragraphs *(c)* and *(d)* or to have been privy to the deposit, sale or manufacture or keeping of any such property, goods, documents, seals, stamps, coins, trade marks, instruments or materials knowing or having reasonable cause to suspect the property or goods to have been stolen or to be contraband or otherwise unlawfully obtained, or the documents, seals, stamps, coins, trade marks, instruments or materials to have been forged, falsified or counterfeited or the instruments or materials to have been used or to be intended to be used for counterfeiting coin or stamps or for forging.

Form of search warrant

62.(1)Every search warrant issued by a Court under this Code shall be in writing and signed by a Judge or Registrar or by a Magistrate, as the case may be, and it shall bear the seal of the Court.

(2)Every such warrant shall remain in force for a reasonable number of days to be specified in the warrant.

(3)Search warrants issued under this Code may be executed in any part of Brunei Darussalam.

Search for persons wrongfully confined

63. If any Magistrate has reason to believe that any person is confined under such circumstances that the confinement amounts to an offence, he may issue a search warrant, and the person to whom the warrant is directed may search for the person confined; the search shall be made in accordance therewith and the person, if found, shall be immediately taken before a Magistrate who shall make such order as in the circumstances of the case seems proper.

Persons in charge of closed places to allow search

64.(1)Whenever any place liable to search or inspection under this Chapter is closed, any person residing in or being in charge of the place shall on demand of the officer or other person executing the warrant and on production of the warrant allow him free ingress thereto and afford all reasonable facilities for a search therein.

(2)If ingress to the place cannot be obtained, the officer or other person executing the warrant may proceed in the manner provided by section 20(2).

Magistrate issuing search warrant may attend at its execution

65. The Magistrate by whom a search warrant is issued may attend personally for the purpose of seeing that the warrant is duly exercised.

Magistrate may direct search in his presence

66. Any Magistrate may orally direct a search to be made in his presence of any place for the search of which he is competent to issue a search warrant.

Search without warrant

67.(1)If a police officer is informed that stolen property or contraband goods is or are concealed or lodged in any building or place, and that there is likelihood of the property or contraband goods being removed before a warrant under section 61 can be obtained, he may search the building or place without warrant and remove any the property or goods if —

*(a)*in the case of stolen property, the person claiming to be the owner or to be entitled to its possession, makes a declaration before him describing the property in detail and stating why he believes the property to have been stolen and to be in the building or place unlawfully, and accompanies the police officer in his search;

(b) in the case of contraband goods, he receives information from any officer of customs that certain contraband goods are believed to be in the building or place.

(2) If an officer of customs is informed and has good reason to believe such information, that contraband goods are concealed or lodged in any building or place and he has good reason to believe that such goods are likely to be removed before a warrant under section 61 can be obtained, he may search the building or place and remove any contraband goods found therein.

68. *(No section).*

List of all things seized to be made and signed

69. A list of all things seized in the course of a search made under this Chapter and of the places in which they are respectively found shall be prepared by the officer or other person making the search and signed by him.

Occupant may be present at search

70. The occupant of the place searched, or some person in his behalf, shall in every instance be permitted to attend during the search, and a copy of the list prepared and signed under section 69 shall be delivered to such occupant or person at his request.

PART IV PREVENTION OF OFFENCES

CHAPTER VII SECURITY FOR KEEPING PEACE AND FOR GOOD BEHAVIOUR

Security for keeping peace on conviction

71. (1) Whenever any person is convicted of —

(a) any offence which involves a breach of the peace or of abetting the offence;

(b) committing criminal intimidation or criminal trespass; or

(c) being a member of an unlawful assembly,

and the Court before which such person is convicted is of opinion that it is necessary to require such person to execute a bond for keeping the peace, such Court may at the time of passing sentence on such person or *in lieu* of any sentence, order him to execute a bond for a sum proportionate to his means, with or without sureties, for keeping the peace during such period in each instance as it thinks fit to fix, not exceeding 2 years if ordered by the High Court or one year if ordered by a Court of a Magistrate.

(2) If the conviction is set aside on appeal or otherwise, the bond so executed shall become void.

Security for keeping peace in other cases

72. Whenever it appears to a Magistrate that any person is likely to commit a breach of the peace or to do any wrongful act that may probably occasion a breach of the peace, the Magistrate may, in such manner as provided in section 75, require such person to show cause why he should not be ordered to execute a bond, with or without sureties, for keeping the peace for such period not exceeding one year as the Magistrate thinks fit to fix.

Security for good behaviour from suspected persons, vagrants and persons disseminating seditious matter

73. Whenever it appears to a Magistrate that —

(a) any person is behaving in a suspicious manner and that there is reason to believe such person is behaving in such manner with a view to committing an offence;

(b) any person has no ostensible means of subsistence or cannot give a satisfactory account of himself;

(c) any person either orally or in writing disseminates or attempts to disseminate or in any way abets the dissemination of —

(i) any seditious matter, that is, any matter the publication of which is punishable under the Sedition Act (Chapter 24); or

[S 32/2005]

(ii) any matter concerning a public servant which amounts to criminal intimidation or defamation under the Penal Code (Chapter 22); or

(d) any person has in his possession or custody any instrument which may be used for housebreaking or is armed with any lethal weapon and is unable to explain satisfactorily his movements or to account for the possession or custody of the housebreaking instruments or lethal weapon,

such Magistrate may, in such manner as provided in section 75, require such person to show cause why he should not be ordered to execute a bond with sureties for his good behaviour for such period not exceeding one year as the Magistrate thinks fit to fix.

Security for good behaviour from habitual offenders

74. Whenever it appears to a Magistrate that any person —

(a) is a habitual robber, housebreaker or thief, or a habitual receiver of stolen property knowing the property to have been stolen;

(b) habitually commits extortion or, in order to the committing of extortion, habitually puts or attempts to put persons in fear of injury;

(c) is a habitual protector or harbourer of thieves;

(d) is a habitual aider in the concealment or disposal of stolen property; or

(e) is a notorious bad liver or is a dangerous character,

the Magistrate may, in such manner as provided in section 75, require such person to show cause why he should not be ordered to execute a bond with sureties for his good behaviour for such period not exceeding one year as such Magistrate thinks fit to fix.

Summons or warrant if required

75.(1) When a Magistrate acting under section 72, 73 or 74 deems it necessary to require any person to show cause under such section, he shall, if such person has not been arrested without warrant and brought before the Court for the purpose of the inquiry mentioned in section 77, issue a summons requiring him to appear and show cause or, when such person is in custody but not present in Court, a warrant directing the officer in whose custody he is to produce him before the Court.

(2)Whenever it appears to the Magistrate upon the report of a police officer or upon other information, the substance of which report or information shall be recorded by the Magistrate, that there is reason to fear the commission of a breach of the peace and that such breach of the peace cannot be prevented otherwise than by the immediate arrest of such person, the Magistrate may at any time issue a warrant for his arrest.

Form of summons or warrant

76. Every summons or warrant issued under section 75 shall contain a brief statement of the substance of the information on which the summons or warrant was issued, and shall state the amount of the bond to be executed, the term for which it is to be in force and the number, character and class of sureties, if any, required.

Inquiry to be held

77.(1)When any person appears or is brought before a Magistrate in compliance with a summons or in execution of a warrant issued under section 75, the Magistrate shall proceed to inquire into the truth of the information on which he has acted and to take such further evidence as may be necessary.

(2)When any person has been arrested without warrant and brought before a Magistrate for the purpose of being bound over either to keep the peace or to be of good behaviour, the Magistrate shall, instead of requiring him to show cause, explain to such person the purport and object of the inquiry and shall take such evidence as may be produced on either part.

(3)An inquiry under this section shall be made as nearly as may be practicable in the manner hereinafter prescribed for conducting summary trials before Magistrates except that no charge need be framed.

(4)For the purposes of this section, the fact that a person is a habitual offender may be proved by evidence of general repute or otherwise.

Order to give security

78. If upon such inquiry it is proved that it is necessary for keeping the peace or maintaining good behaviour, as the case may be, that the person in respect of whom the inquiry is made should execute a bond, with or without sureties, the Magistrate shall make an order accordingly:

Provided that —

*(a)*no person shall be ordered to give security of a nature different from or for an amount larger than or for a period longer than that specified in the summons or warrant issued under section 75, if any;

*(b)*the amount of every bond shall be fixed with due regard to the circumstances of the case and shall not be excessive, but shall be such as to afford the person against whom the order is made a fair chance of complying with it;

*(c)*when the person in respect of whom the inquiry is made is not competent to contract, the bond shall be executed only by his sureties.

Discharge of persons informed against

79. If, on an inquiry under section 77, it is not proved that it is necessary for keeping the peace or maintaining good behaviour, as the case may be, that the person in respect of whom the inquiry is made should execute a bond, the Magistrate shall make an entry on the record to that effect and if such person is in custody only for the purposes of the inquiry, shall release him or, if such person is not in custody, shall discharge him.

Proceedings in all cases subsequent to order to furnish security

Commencement of period for which security is required

80. (1) If any person in respect of whom an order requiring security is made under section 71 or 78 is at the time such order is made sentenced to or undergoing a sentence of imprisonment, the period for which the security is required shall commence on the expiration of such sentence.

(2) In other cases, the period shall commence on the date of such order.

Contents of bond

81. The bond to be executed by any person shall bind him to keep the peace or to be of good behaviour, as the case may be, and in the latter case the commission or attempt to commit or the abetment of any offence punishable with imprisonment, wherever it may be committed, is a breach of the bond.

Power to reject sureties

82. A Court may in its discretion refuse to accept any particular person or persons offered as surety for good behaviour under this Chapter.

Imprisonment in default of sureties

83. (1) If any person ordered to give security under section 71 or 78 does not give such security on or before the date on which the period for which such security is to be given commences, he may be committed to prison, or if he already is in prison may be detained in prison, until such period expires or until within such period he gives such security to the Court which made the order requiring it or to the officer in charge of the prison in which he is detained.

(2) If such person is unable or unwilling to execute the bond but is willing to leave Brunei Darussalam and not return thereto for such period as the Court shall approve, the Court may, subject to the execution of any sentence of imprisonment to which he has been sentenced, order accordingly.

(3) Pending the departure of the offender from Brunei Darussalam, he may be remanded in custody.

Power to release person imprisoned for failing to give security

84. When a Court is of opinion that any person imprisoned for failing to give security under this Chapter may be released without hazard to the community or to any other person, the Court may order such person to be discharged:

Provided that a Court of a Magistrate shall not exercise this power except in cases where the imprisonment is under its own order.

Magistrate to report in cases in which security has been ordered by superior Court

85. Whenever a Magistrate is of opinion that any person imprisoned for failing to give security under this Chapter as ordered by a Court superior to his Court may be released without the hazard mentioned in

section 84, the Magistrate shall make an immediate report of the case for the orders of the superior Court, and such Court may if it thinks fit order such person to be discharged.

Discharge of security

86.(1)Any surety for the peaceable conduct or good behaviour of another person may at any time apply to a Magistrate to cancel any bond executed under this Chapter.

(2)On such application being made, the Magistrate shall issue a summons or warrant, as he thinks fit, requiring the person for whom such surety is bound to appear or be brought before him.

(3)When such person appears or is brought before the Magistrate, he shall cancel the bond and shall order such person to give for the unexpired portion of the term of the bond fresh security of the same description as the original security.

(4)Every such order shall, for the purposes of sections 81, 82, 83 and 84, be deemed to be an order made under section 71 or 78, as the case may be.

CHAPTER VIII UNLAWFUL ASSEMBLIES

Unlawful assembly may be ordered to disperse by Magistrate etc.

87.A Magistrate, the Commissioner of Police or any police officer not below the rank of Inspector or officer in charge of a police district or police station may command any unlawful assembly or any assembly of five or more persons likely to cause a disturbance of the public peace to disperse, and it shall thereupon be the duty of the members of such assembly to disperse accordingly.

When unlawful assembly may be dispersed by use of civil force

88. If upon being so commanded, any such assembly does not disperse, or if, without having been commanded to disperse, it conducts itself in such a manner as to show a determination not to disperse, a Magistrate, the Commissioner of Police or any police officer not below the rank of Inspector or officer in charge of a police district or police station may —

*(a)*proceed to disperse such assembly by force; and

*(b)*require the assistance of any male person, not being an officer, soldier, sailor or airman of the Royal Brunei Armed Forces or of any armed forces lawfully serving within Brunei Darussalam, for the purpose of dispersing such assembly,

and if necessary arresting and confining the persons who form part of it in order to disperse such assembly or that they may be punished according to law.

Use of military force

89. If any such assembly cannot be otherwise dispersed and if it is necessary for the public security that it should be dispersed, a Magistrate or a police officer may cause it to be dispersed by military force.

[S 6/2016]

Magistrate may require any officer in command of troops to disperse unlawful assembly

90.(1) When a Magistrate or a police officer determines to disperse any such assembly by military force, he may require any commissioned or non-commissioned officer in command of any soldiers, sailors or airmen of the Royal Brunei Armed Forces or of any armed forces lawfully serving within Brunei Darussalam to disperse such assembly by military force and to arrest and confine such persons forming part of it as the Magistrate or the police officer may direct or as it may be necessary to arrest and confine in order to disperse the assembly or that they may be punished according to law.

[S 6/2016]

(2) Every such officer shall obey such requisition in such manner as he thinks fit, but in so doing he shall use as little force and do as little injury to person and property as may be consistent with dispersing the assembly and arresting and detaining such persons.

When commissioned officer may disperse unlawful assembly by military force

91. When the public security is manifestly endangered by any such assembly, and when neither a Magistrate nor a police officer empowered by section 90 to require such an assembly to be dispersed by military force can be communicated with, any commissioned officer of the Royal Brunei Armed Forces or of any armed forces lawfully serving within Brunei Darussalam may disperse such assembly by military force and may arrest and confine any person forming part of it in order to disperse such assembly or that they may be punished according to law; but if while he is acting under this section it becomes practicable for him to communicate with any Magistrate or gazetted police officer, he shall do so and shall obey the instructions of such Magistrate or police officer as to whether he shall or shall not continue such action.

Protection against prosecution for acts done under this Chapter

92. No prosecution against any Magistrate or police officer or any officer, soldier, sailor or airman of any armed forces, for any act purporting to be done under this Chapter, shall be instituted in any criminal Court except with the sanction of His Majesty the Sultan and Yang Di-Pertuan in Council; and —

(a) no Magistrate or police officer acting under this Chapter in good faith;

(b) no person doing any act in good faith in compliance with a requisition under section 88 or 90;

(c) no inferior officer, soldier, sailor or airman doing any act in obedience to any order which he was bound to obey;

(d) no officer acting under section 91 in good faith,

shall be deemed to have thereby committed an offence.

CHAPTER IX PUBLIC NUISANCES

Magistrate may make conditional order for removal of nuisance

93.(1) Whenever a Magistrate considers, on receiving a report or other information and on taking such evidence, if any, as he thinks fit, that —

(a) any unlawful obstruction or nuisance should be removed from any way, harbour, lake, river or channel which is or may be lawfully used by the public or from any public place;

(b) any trade or occupation or the keeping of any goods or merchandise by reason of its being injurious to the health or physical comfort of the community should be suppressed or removed or prohibited;

*(c)*the construction of any building or the disposal of any substance likely to occasion conflagration or explosion should be prevented or stopped;

*(d)*any building or tree is in such a condition that it is likely to fall and thereby cause injury to persons living or carrying on business in the neighbourhood or passing by and that in consequence, its removal, repair or support is necessary; or

*(e)*any tank, well or excavation adjacent to any such way as aforesaid or to any public place should be fenced in such a manner as to prevent danger arising to the public,

the Magistrate may make a conditional order requiring the person causing such obstruction or nuisance, or carrying on such trade or occupation, or keeping any such goods or merchandise, or owning, possessing or controlling such building, tree, substance, tank, well or excavation, within a time to be fixed in the order to —

(i)remove such obstruction or nuisance;

(ii)supress or remove such trade or occupation;

(iii)remove such goods or merchandise;

(iv)prevent or stop the construction of such building;

(v)remove, repair or support such building;

(vi)lop or fell such tree;

(vii)alter the disposal of such substance;

(viii)fence such tank, well or excavation,

or appear before the Magistrate at a time and place to be fixed by the order and move to have the order set aside or modified in manner hereinafter provided.

(2)For the purposes of this section, a "public place" includes also property belonging to the Government and grounds left unoccupied for sanitary or recreative purposes.

Conditional order to be served or notified

94.(1)The order and any notice or order given or made under this Chapter shall, if practicable, be served on the person against whom it is made in manner in this Code provided for service of a summons.

(2)If the order cannot be served, a copy thereof shall be posted at such place as may be the fittest for conveying the information to such person.

Person against whom order is made to appear and show cause

95. The person against whom the order is made shall —

*(a)*perform within the time specified in the order that act directed thereby; or

*(b)*appear in accordance with such order and show cause against the same.

Consequence of failure to do so

96. If the person does not perform such act or appear and show cause as required by section 95, the order shall be made absolute.

Procedure on appearance to show cause

97. (1) If the person appears and shows cause against the order, the Magistrate shall take evidence in the matter.

(2) If the Magistrate is satisfied that the order is not reasonable and proper, no further proceedings shall be taken in the case.

(3) If the Magistrate is not satisfied, the order shall be made absolute.

Procedure on order being made absolute

98. When an order has been made absolute under section 96 or 97, the Magistrate shall give notice of the order to the person against whom the order was made, and shall further require him to perform the act directed by the order within a time to be fixed in the notice and inform him that, in case of disobedience, he will be liable to the penalty prescribed in that behalf in section 188 of the Penal Code (Chapter 22):

Provided that if such person is a corporation, it shall be liable only to the fine prescribed by that section.

Consequence of disobedience to order

99. (1) If the order is not performed within the time fixed, the Magistrate may cause it to be performed and may recover the costs of performing it either by sale of the buildings, goods or other property removed by order or by the distress and sale of any other movable property of such person.

(2) No suit shall lie in respect of anything done in good faith under this section.

Injunction pending final decision

100. (1) If the Magistrate making an order under section 93 considers that immediate measures should be taken to prevent imminent danger or injury of a serious kind to the public, he may issue such an injunction to the person against whom the order was made as is required to obviate or prevent such danger or injury pending the final decision of the case.

(2) In default of such person forthwith obeying the injunction, the Magistrate may use, or cause to be used, such means as he thinks fit to obviate such danger or to prevent such injury.

(3) No suit shall lie in respect of anything done in good faith by a Magistrate under this section.

Power to prohibit repetition or continuance of public nuisance

101. A Magistrate may order any person not to repeat or continue a public nuisance as defined in the Penal Code (Chapter 22) or any other written law in force for the time being.

CHAPTER X TEMPORARY ORDERS IN URGENT CASES OF NUISANCE

Power to issue order absolute at once in urgent cases

102.(1)In cases where in the opinion of a Magistrate immediate prevention or speedy remedy is desirable, the Magistrate may by a written order stating the material facts of the case and served in manner provided in section 94 direct any person —

*(a)*to abstain from a certain act; or

*(b)*to take certain order with certain property in his possession or under his management,

if the Magistrate considers that such direction is likely to prevent or tends to prevent obstruction, annoyance or injury to any persons lawfully employed, or danger to human life, health or safety, or a riot or an affray.

(2)An order under this section may in cases of emergency or in cases where the circumstances do not admit the serving in due time of notice upon the person against whom the order is made, be made *ex parte*.

(3)An order under this section may be directed to a particular person or to the public generally when frequenting or visiting a particular place.

(4)Any Magistrate may rescind or alter any order made under this section by himself or his predecessor in office.

(5)No order under this section shall remain in force for more than one month from the making thereof.

CHAPTER XI DISPUTES AS TO IMMOVABLE PROPERTY

Procedure where dispute concerning land etc. is likely to cause breach of peace

103.(1)Whenever a Magistrate is satisfied, from a police report or other information, that a dispute likely to cause a breach of the peace exists concerning any land or water or the boundaries thereof, he may make an order in writing stating the grounds of his being so satisfied and requiring the parties concerned in such dispute to attend his Court within a time to be fixed by the Magistrate and to make oral or written statements of their respective claims as respects the fact of actual possession of the subject of dispute.

(2)For the purposes of this section and of section 105, "land or water" includes buildings, markets, fisheries, crops or other produce of land and the rents or profits of any such property.

(3)A copy of the order shall be served in manner provided by this Code for the service of a summons upon such person or persons as the Magistrate directs, and at least one copy shall, if reasonably practicable, be published by being affixed to some conspicuous place at or near the subject of dispute.

(4)The Magistrate shall then, without reference to the merits of the claims of any such parties to a right to possess the subject of dispute, peruse the statements so put in, hear the parties, receive the evidence produced by them respectively, consider the effect of such evidence, take such further evidence (if any) as he thinks necessary, and if possible decide whether any and which of the parties is then in actual possession of the subject:

Provided that —

*(a)*if it appears to the Magistrate that any party has, within 2 months next before the date of such order, been forcibly and wrongfully dispossessed, he may treat the party so dispossessed as if he had been in possession at such date;

*(b)*if the Magistrate considers the case one of emergency, he may at any time attach the subject of dispute pending his decision under this section.

(5) Nothing in this section shall preclude any party so required to attend from showing that no such dispute exists or has existed, and in such case, the Magistrate shall cancel the order and all further proceedings therein shall be stayed.

(6) If the Magistrate decides that one of the parties is then in actual possession of the subject, he shall issue an order declaring such party to be entitled to retain possession thereof until evicted therefrom in due course of law, and forbidding all disturbance of the possession until the eviction.

(7) Proceedings under this section shall not abate by reason only of the death of any of the parties thereto.

Power to attach subject of dispute

104. If the Magistrate decides that none of the parties is then in actual possession or is unable to satisfy himself as to which of them is then in actual possession of the subject of dispute, he may attach it until a competent civil Court has determined the rights of the parties thereto or the persons entitled to possession thereof.

Disputes concerning rights over land or water

105. (1) Whenever a Magistrate is satisfied as aforesaid that a dispute likely to cause a breach of the peace exists concerning the right to do or prevent the doing of anything in or upon any land or water, he may —

(a) inquire into the matter; and

(b) if it appears to him that such right exists, make an order permitting such thing to be done or directing that such thing shall not be done, as the case may be, until the person objecting to such thing being done or claiming that such thing may be done obtains the decision of a competent civil Court adjudging him to be entitled to prevent the doing of or to do such thing, as the case may be.

(2) No order shall be made under this section permitting the doing of anything unless —

(a) where the right to do such thing is exercisable at all times of the year, the right has been exercised within 3 months next before the institution of the inquiry; or

(b) where the right is exercisable only at particular seasons, the right has been exercised during the season next before such institution.

Order as to costs

106. (1) When any costs have been incurred by any party to a proceeding under this Chapter for witnesses, the Magistrate giving a decision under section 103, 104 or 105 may assess such costs and direct by whom the costs shall be paid, whether by such party or by any other party to the proceeding and whether in whole or in part or proportion.

(2) All costs so directed to be paid may be recovered as if they were fines.

CHAPTER XII PREVENTIVE ACTION OF POLICE

Police to prevent offences

107. Every police officer may interpose for the purpose of preventing and shall, to the best of his ability using all lawful means, prevent the commission of any offence.

Information of design to commit offences

108. Every police officer receiving information of a design to commit any offence shall communicate such information to the police officer to whom he is subordinate and to any other officer whose duty it is to prevent or take cognisance of the commission of any such offence.

Arrest to prevent such offences

109. A police officer knowing of a design to commit any seizable offence may arrest without orders from a Magistrate and without a warrant the person so designing if it appears to such officer that the commission of the offence cannot otherwise be prevented.

Prevention of injury to public property

110. A police officer may of his own authority interpose to prevent any injury attempted to be committed in his view to any public property, movable or immovable, or the removal or injury of any public landmark or buoy or other mark used for navigation.

PART V INFORMATION TO POLICE AND THEIR POWERS TO INVESTIGATE

CHAPTER XIII DUTIES OF POLICE OFFICER ON RECEIVING INFORMATION ABOUT OFFENCES

Information of offences

111. (1) When information is received at a police station relating to the commission of an offence, being an offence of which it appears that no previous information has been received in the station, the officer in charge of the police station or a subordinate officer whose duty it is to receive reports shall proceed according to one of the subsections in this section.

(2) If the information is in writing, he shall forthwith mark on it the date and time of receipt, and, if practicable, the name and address of the person (other than a postal messenger) by whom it was delivered, and if it purports to be signed by the informant, he shall file it as a report and record the facts in a book kept for this purpose.

(3) If the information is given orally and he considers it practicable to reduce it to writing forthwith, he shall record or cause to be recorded in a book kept for this purpose a report containing the name and address of the informant, the date and time of his arrival at the station, the substance of the information and such other particulars as the nature of the case may require, and such report shall be signed by the informant, (or if he refuses to sign, a note of such refusal shall be made with any reasons given for such refusal), by the recording officer and by the interpreter, if any.

(4) If the information is given orally and it appears to him impracticable to proceed forthwith under subsection (3), he shall immediately make a note of first information in the station diary, and, if an investigation is to proceed, as soon thereafter as circumstances permit, a fuller statement by the informant shall be recorded under the provisions of subsection (3).

Duty of police to investigate offences

112. Subject to the provisions of any other written law and to any lawful order or direction given to him in that behalf, every police officer shall investigate any offence the commission of which he has reason to suspect and to take such action as he deems necessary to prevent the repetition or aggravation of any offence:

Provided that the Public Prosecutor may direct that the investigation of such non-seizable offences as may be specified in such direction need not be undertaken by the police but nothing in this Chapter shall be deemed to preclude any police officer from making such investigation as may be necessary to satisfy himself that the offence is an offence to which such direction relates.

Body samples [S 4/2007]

112A.(1)A police officer making an investigation under this Chapter may cause a body sample of a person to be obtained for forensic analysis if he has reasonable cause to believe that the body sample may confirm or disprove whether that person was involved in an offence punishable with imprisonment.

(2)If appropriate consent for a body sample to be taken is refused without good cause or cannot be obtained despite all reasonable efforts, that person may be taken before a Magistrate who may, if satisfied that there is reasonable cause to believe that the body sample may confirm or disprove whether that person was involved in an offence punishable with imprisonment, order that that person provide the body sample required.

(3)Where it is shown that the appropriate consent from a person was refused without good cause, the Court in determining whether —

*(a)*there is a case to answer against him; or

*(b)*he is guilty of the offence with which he has been charged,

may draw such inference from the refusal as it thinks proper and, based on such inference, may treat that refusal as corroboration or as amounting to corroboration of any relevant evidence against him.

Persons permitted to take body samples [S 4/2007]

112B.(1)A body sample may only be taken by —

*(a)*a person registered under the Medical Practitioners and Dentists Act (Chapter 112);

*(b)*a police officer who has received training for that purpose;

*(c)*any other suitably qualified or trained person who is authorised by the Commissioner of Police for that purpose.

(2)Before taking a body sample, the person permitted under subsection (1) to take it must satisfy himself that such taking will not endanger the person from whom it is to be taken.

(3)The fact that a body sample has been taken under this section shall be recorded by the person taking it in such form or manner as may be required by the Commissioner of Police.

(4)A person from whom a body sample is lawfully required under section 112A who —

*(a)*refuses, without reasonable excuse, to give a body sample or to allow it to be taken from him; or

*(b)*otherwise hinders or obstructs the taking of a body sample,

is guilty of an offence under section 186 of the Penal Code (Chapter 22) and the person permitted under subsection (1) to take the body sample may, with such assistance as is required, use such force as is reasonably necessary for the purpose of taking the sample.

Interpretation for sections 112A and 112B *[S 4/2007]*

112C. In sections 112A and 112B —

"appropriate consent" means —

*(a)*in relation to a person who has attained the age of 18 years, his consent in writing;

*(b)*in relation to a person who has attained the age of 14 years but has not attained the age of 18 years, the consent in writing of both that person and of his parent or guardian;

*(c)*in relation to a person who has not attained the age of 14 years, the consent in writing of his parent or guardian,

given to the police officer in charge of the case after the person concerned or his parent or guardian, as the case may be, has been informed by the police officer of the purpose for which a body sample is required and the manner by which it is to be taken;

"body sample" means —

*(a)*a sample of head hair, including the roots thereof;

*(b)*a sample taken from a nail or from under the nail;

*(c)*a swab taken from any part, other than a private part, of a person's body but not any other body orifice;

*(d)*a swab taken from a person's mouth;

*(e)*saliva;

*(f)*an impression of any part of a person's body other than an impression of a private part or an impression of the face;

*(g)*an intimate sample, being a body sample that is obtained by means of any invasive procedure;

"intimate sample" means —

*(a)*a sample of blood, semen or any other tissue fluid, urine or hair other than head hair;

*(b)*a dental impression; or

*(c)*a swab taken from a private part of a person's body or from a person's body orifice other than the mouth;

"private part" in relation to a person's body, means the genital or anal area and includes the breasts in the case of a woman.

Public not to have right to compel police officer to investigate alleged offences

113. Nothing in this Chapter shall be deemed to confer any right upon any member of the public to compel any police officer to investigate whether an offence and, if so, what offence, has been committed but it shall be the duty of any police officer making an investigation under this Chapter upon request in that behalf by the informant to inform him whether the police propose to prosecute and, if so, in respect of what offences.

Exercise of special powers

114. Every police officer making an investigation under this Chapter if in charge of a police station or not below the rank of Lance-Corporal may exercise the powers given by sections 115, 120 and 121.

Police officer's power to require attendance of witness

115.(1) A police officer making an investigation under this Chapter may by order in writing require the attendance before himself of any person who, from the information given or otherwise, appears to be acquainted with the circumstances of the case, and such person shall attend as so required.

(2) If any such person refuses to attend as so required, the police officer may report the refusal to a Magistrate who may thereupon in his discretion issue a summons or warrant to secure the attendance of such person as required by the order mentioned in subsection (1).

Examining of witnesses by police

116.(1) A police officer making a police investigation under this Chapter may examine orally any person supposed to be acquainted with the facts and circumstances of the case and shall reduce into writing any statement made by the person so examined.

(2) The person shall be bound to state truly the facts and circumstances which he is acquainted concerning the case save only that he may decline to make, with regard to any fact or circumstances, a statement which would have a tendency to expose him to a criminal charge or to a penalty or forfeiture.

(3) A statement made by any person under the provisions of this section shall be read over to him and shall, after correction if necessary, be signed by him.

Statement to police officers

117.(1) In any criminal proceedings, any statement made by any person including a person in the custody of a police officer, whether it amounts to a confession or not or is oral or in writing, made at any time, whether before or after that person is charged and whether in the course of a police investigation or not, by that person to or in the hearing of any police officer shall be admissible in evidence and, if that person tenders himself as a witness, any such statement may be used in cross-examination and for the purpose of impeaching his credit.

(2) The Court shall admit under subsection (1) a statement made by an accused, only if the prosecution satisfies the Court that the statement was voluntary, that is to say that it was not obtained by violence, inducement, threat or oppression by a person in authority.

(3) Where any person is charged with an offence or officially informed that he may be prosecuted for it, he shall be served with a notice in writing, which shall be explained to him, to the following effect —

"You have been charged with/informed that you may be prosecuted for —

(set out the charged)

Do you wish to say anything in answer to the charge? If there is any fact on which you intend to rely in your defence in court, you are advised to mention it now, if you fail to do so before your trial, the court may draw such inferences, adverse to you, as it may think proper. If you wish to mention any fact now, and you would like it written down this will be done".

(4) No statement made by an accused person in answer to a written notice served on him pursuant to subsection (3) shall be construed as a statement obtained by any violence, inducement, threat or oppression as is described in subsection (2), if it is otherwise voluntary.

(5) In subsection (3), "officially informed" means informed by a police officer or any other person charged with the duty of investigating offences or charging offenders.

(6) The Court shall admit under subsection (1) a statement made by an accused if such a statement is made after the impression caused by any such inducement, threat or promise as is referred to in subsection (2) has, in the opinion of the Court, been fully removed.

Notice of alibi

117A. (1) In any trial, the accused shall not without the leave of the Court adduce evidence in support of an alibi unless, before the end of the prescribed period, he gives notice of particulars of the alibi.

(2) Without prejudice to subsection (1), on any such trial the accused shall not without the leave of the Court call any other person to give evidence in support of an alibi unless —

(a) the notice under subsection (1) includes —

(i) the name and address of the witness; or

(ii) if the name and address is not known to the defendant at the time he gives the notice, any information in his possession which might be of material assistance in finding the witness;

(b) if the name or the address is not included in that notice, the Court is satisfied that the accused, before giving the notice, took and thereafter continued to take all reasonable steps to secure that the name or address would be ascertained;

(c) if the name or the address is not included in that notice, but the accused subsequently discovers the name or address or receives other information which might be of material assistance in finding the witness, he forthwith gives notice of the name, address or other information, as the case may be;

(d) if the accused is notified by or on behalf of the prosecutor that the witness has not been traced by the name or at the address given, he forthwith gives notice of any such information, which is then in his possession or, on subsequently receiving any such information, forthwith gives notice of it.

(3) The Court shall not refuse leave under this section if it appears to the Court that the accused was not informed of the requirement of this section.

(4) Any evidence tenders to disprove an alibi may, subject to any direction by the Court as to the time it is to be given, be given before or after evidence is given in support of the alibi.

(5) Any notice purporting to be given under this section on behalf of the accused by his advocate or solicitor shall, unless the contrary is proved, be deemed to be given with the authority of the accused.

(6) A notice under subsection (1) shall either be given in Court during, or at the end of, the committal proceedings or be given in writing to the prosecutor, and a notice under subsection (2)*(c)* or *(d)* shall be given in writing to the prosecutor.

(7) A notice required by this section to be given to the prosecutor may be given by delivering it to the Attorney General or by leaving it at the Attorney General's office, or by sending it by registered post addressed to the Attorney General at his office.

(8) In this section —

"evidence in support of an alibi" means evidence tending to show that by reason of the presence of the accused at a particular place or in a particular area at a particular time he was not, or was unlikely to have been at the place where the offence is alleged to have been committed at the time of its alleged commission;

"prescribed period" means the period expiring not less than 10 days prior to the commencement of the trial.

(9) In computing the prescribed period, there shall be disregarded any day which is a public holiday.

Proof by written statement

117B.(1) In any criminal proceedings, a written statement by any person shall, subject to the conditions mentioned in subsection (2), be admissible as evidence to the same extent as oral evidence to the same effect by that person.

(2) A statement may be tendered in evidence under subsection (1) if —

(a) the statement purports to be signed by the person who made it;

(b) the statement contains a declaration by that person to the effect that it is true to the best of his knowledge and belief; and

(c) before the hearing at which the statement is tendered in evidence, a copy of the statement is served, by or on behalf of the party proposing to tender it, on each of the other parties to the proceedings:

Provided that paragraph *(c)* does not apply if the parties agree before or during the hearing that the statement shall be so tendered.

(3) If a statement tendered in evidence under subsection (1) —

(a) is made by a person under the age of 18 years, it shall give his age;

(b) is made by a person who cannot read it, it shall be read to him before he signs it and shall be accompanied by a declaration by the person who so read the statement to the effect that it was so read;

(c) refers to any other document as an exhibit, the copy served on any other party to the proceedings under subsection (2)*(c)* shall be accompanied by a copy of that document or by such information as may be necessary in order to enable the party on whom it is served to inspect that document or a copy thereof.

(4) Notwithstanding that the written statement of a person may be admissible as evidence by virtue of this section —

(a) the party by whom or on whose behalf a copy of the statement was served may call the person making the statement to give additional evidence in the case, which may include matters which are not contained in the statement; and

(b) the maker of the statement shall attend the trial for cross-examination and re-examination.

(5) So much of any statement as is admitted in evidence by virtue of this section shall, unless the Court otherwise directs, be read aloud at the hearing and where the Court so directs an account shall be given orally of so much of any statement as is not read aloud.

(6) Any document or objects referred to as an exhibit and identified in a written statement admitted in evidence under this section shall be treated as if it had been produced as an exhibit and identified in Court by the maker of the statement.

(7) A document required by this section to be served on any person may be served —

(a) by delivering to him or to his solicitor; or

(b) in the case of a body corporate, by delivering it to the secretary or clerk of the body at its registered or principal office, or by sending it by registered post addresses to the secretary or clerk of that body at that office.

(8) In this section, "Court" includes a Magistrate.

Proof by formal admission

117C. (1) Subject to the provisions of this section, any fact of which oral evidence may be given in any criminal proceedings may be admitted for the purposes of those proceedings by or on behalf of the prosecutor or accused and the admission by any party of any such fact under this section shall as against that party be conclusive evidence in those proceedings of the fact admitted.

(2) An admission under this section —

(a) may be made before or during the proceedings;

(b) if made otherwise than in Court, shall be in writing;

(c) if made in writing by an individual, shall purport to be signed by the person making it and, if so made by a body corporate, shall purport to be signed by a director or manager, or the secretary or clerk, or some other similar officer of the body corporate;

[S 32/2005]

(d) if made on behalf of an accused who is an individual, shall be made by his advocate or solicitor;

(e) if made at any stage before the trial by an accused who is an individual, must be approved by his advocate or solicitor (whether at the time it was made or subsequently) before or during the proceedings in question.

(3) An admission under this section for the purpose of proceedings relating to any matter shall be treated as an admission for the purpose of any subsequent criminal proceedings relating to that matter (including any appeal or trial).

(4) An admission under this section may with the leave of the Court be withdrawn in the proceedings for the purpose of which it is made or any subsequent criminal proceedings relating to the same matter.

(5) In this section, "Court" includes a Magistrate.

Failure to account for objects, substances or marks

117D. (1) Where a person is arrested by a police officer and —

(a) (i) there is on his person;

(ii) in or on his clothing or footwear;

(iii) otherwise in his possession; or

(iv) in any place in which he is at the time of his arrest,

any object, substance or mark, or there is any mark on any such object;

(b) that or another police officer investigating the case reasonably believes that the presence of the object, substance or mark may be attributable to the participation of the person arrested in the commission of an offence specified by the police officer;

(c) the police officer informs the person arrested that he so believes, and requests him to account for the presence of the object, substance or mark; and

(d) the person fails or refuses to do so,

then if, in any proceedings against the person for the offence so specified, evidence of those matters is given, subsection (2) applies.

(2) Where this subsection applies, the Court —

(a) in determining whether there is a case to answer; and

(b) in determining whether the accused is guilty of the offence charged,

may draw such inferences from the failure or refusal as appear proper.

(3) Subsections (1) and (2) apply to the condition of clothing or footwear as they apply to a substance or mark thereon.

(4) Subsections (1) and (2) do not apply unless the accused was told in ordinary language by the police officer when making the request mentioned in subsection (1)(c) what the effect of this section would be if he failed or refused to comply with the request.

(5) This section applies in relation to officers of customs as it applies in relation to police officers.

(6) This section does not preclude the drawing of any inference from a failure or refusal of the accused to account for the presence of an object, substance or mark or from the condition of clothing or footwear which could properly be drawn apart from this section.

(7) This section does not apply in relation to a failure or refusal which occurred before the commencement of this section.

Failure to account for presence

117E. (1) Where —

(a) a person arrested by a police officer was found by him at a place at or about the time the offence for which he was arrested is alleged to have been committed;

(b) that or another police officer investigating the offence reasonably believes that the presence of the person at that place and at that time may be attributable to the latter's participation in the commission of the offence;

(c) the police officer informs the person that he so believes, and requests him to account for his presence; and

(d) the person fails or refuses to do so,

then if, in any proceedings against the person for the offence, evidence of those matters is given, subsection (2) applies.

(2) Where this subsection applies, the Court —

(a) in determining whether there is a case to answer; and

(b) in determining whether the accused is guilty of the offence charged,

may draw such inferences from the failure or refusal as appear proper.

(3) Subsections (1) and (2) do not apply unless the accused was told in ordinary language by the police officer when making the request mentioned in subsection (1)*(c)* what the effect of this section would be if he failed or refused to comply with the request.

(4) This section applies in relation to officers of customs as it applies in relation to police officers.

(5) This section does not preclude the drawing of any inference from a failure or refusal of the accused to account for his presence at a place which could properly be drawn apart from this section.

(6) This section does not apply in relation to a failure or refusal which occurred before the commencement of this section.

Interpretation for sections 117D and 117E and savings

117F.(1) In sections 117D and 117E —

"legal representative" means an advocate and solicitor;

"place" includes any building or part of a building, any vehicle, vessel, aircraft or hovercraft and any other place whatsoever.

(2) In sections 117D and 117E, references to an offence charged include reference to any other offence of which the accused could lawfully be convicted on that charge.

(3) A person shall not have a case to answer or be convicted of an offence solely on an inference drawn from such a failure or refusal as is mentioned in section 117D, 117E or 118.

(4) Nothing in section 117D, 117E or 118 prejudices the operation of a provision of any written law which provides (in whatever words) that any answer or evidence given by a person in specified circumstances shall not be admissible in evidence against him or some other person in any proceedings or class of proceedings (however described, and whether civil or criminal).

(5) In subsection (4), the reference to giving evidence is a reference to giving evidence in any manner, whether by furnishing information, making discovery, producing documents or otherwise.

(6) Nothing in section 117D, 117E or 118 prejudices any power of a Court, in any proceedings, to exclude evidence (whether by preventing questions being put or otherwise) at its discretion.

Circumstances in which inferences may be drawn from accused's failure to mention particular facts when charged etc.

118.(1)Where in any criminal proceedings against a person for an offence, evidence is given that the accused, on being charged with the offence or officially informed that he might be prosecuted for it, failed to mention any such fact, being a fact which in the circumstances existing at the time he could reasonably have been expected to mention when so charged or informed, as the case may be, the Court —

*(a)*in determining whether to commit the accused for trial or whether there is a case to answer; and

*(b)*in determining whether the accused is guilty of the offence charged,

may draw such inferences adverse to the accused from the failure as appear proper, and the failure may, on the basis of such inferences, be treated as, or as capable of amounting to, corroboration of any evidence given against the accused in relation to which the failure is material.

(2)In subsection (1), "officially informed" means informed by a police officer or any other person charged with the duty of investigating offences or charging offenders.

(3)Nothing in subsection (1) or (2) shall in any criminal proceedings —

*(a)*prejudice the admissibility in evidence of the silence or other reaction of the accused in the face of anything said in his presence relating to the conduct in respect of which he is charged, in so far as evidence thereof would be admissible apart from those subsections; or

*(b)*be taken to preclude the drawing of any inference from any such silence or other reaction of the accused which could be drawn apart from those subsections.

(4)Subsections (1) and (2) do not apply as regards a failure to mention a fact if the failure occurred before 1st January 1985.

Power to record statements and confessions

119.(1)Any Magistrate may record any statement or confession made to him at any time before the commencement of the inquiry or trial.

(2)Such statement or confession shall be recorded in full in writing by the Magistrate to whom it is made and shall then be forwarded to the Magistrate, if different, before whom the case is to be inquired into or tried.

(3)No Magistrate shall record any such statement or confession unless upon questioning the person making it he has reason to believe that it was made voluntarily; and when he records any confession, he shall make a memorandum at the foot of such record to the following effect —

I believe that this confession was voluntarily made. It was taken in my presence and hearing and was read over to the person making it and admitted by him to be correct and it contains a full and true account of what he said.

(Signed) *A, B.*

Magistrate

(4)The taking and recording of any statement or confession shall not disqualify a Magistrate who has so taken and recorded the statement or confession from inquiring into or trying the case.

(5) No oath or affirmation shall be administered to any person making a statement or confession as in this section provided.

Search by police officer

120. (1) Whenever an officer in charge of a police station or a police officer making an investigation has reasonable grounds for believing that any evidence or thing necessary for the purposes of an investigation into any offence which he is authorised to investigate may be found in any place and that the evidence or thing cannot in his opinion be otherwise obtained without undue delay, the officer may search or cause search to be made for such evidence or thing in any place.

(2) The officer shall, if practicable, conduct the search in person.

(3) If he is unable to conduct the search in person and there is no other person competent to make the search present at the time, he may require any officer subordinate to him to make the search, and he shall deliver to the subordinate officer an order in writing specifying the thing for which search is to be made and the place to be searched, and the subordinate officer may thereupon search for such thing in such place.

(4) The provisions of this Code as to search warrants shall, so far as may be, apply to a search made under this section.

Police officer may require bond for appearance of complainant and witnesses

121. (1) If upon a police investigation made under this Chapter it appears to the officer making such investigation that there is sufficient evidence or reasonable ground of suspicion to justify the commencement or continuance of criminal proceedings against any person, the officer may require the complainant, if any, and so many of the persons who appear to the officer to be acquainted with the circumstances of the case, as he thinks necessary, to execute a bond to appear before a Court therein named and give evidence in the matter of the charge against the accused.

(2) If any complainant or witness refuses to execute such bond, the officer shall report the refusal to the Court which may thereupon in its discretion issue a warrant or summons to secure the attendance of the complainant or witness before itself to give evidence in the matter of the charge against the accused.

Surrender of travel documents [S 6/2016]

121A. (1) A Magistrate may, on the application of a police officer not below the rank of Inspector by written notice, require a person who is the subject of an investigation in respect of an offence alleged or suspected to have been committed by him under this Code to surrender to a police officer not below the rank of Inspector any travel document in his possession.

(2) A notice under subsection (1) shall be served personally on the person to whom it is addressed.

(3) A person on whom a notice under subsection (1) is served shall comply with such notice forthwith.

(4) If a person on whom a notice under subsection (1) has been served fails to comply with the notice forthwith, he may thereupon be arrested and taken before a Magistrate.

(5) Where a person is taken before a Magistrate under subsection (4), the Magistrate shall, unless such person thereupon complies with the notice under subsection (1) or satisfies the Magistrate that he does not possess a travel document, by warrant commit him to prison there to be safely kept until —

(a) the expiry of the period of 28 days from the date of his committal to prison; or

*(b)*the person complies with the notice under subsection (1) and a Magistrate, by order, directs the Director of Prisons to discharge the person from prison (which order shall be sufficient warrant for the Director of Prisons so to do),

whichever occurs first.

(6)A travel document which is surrendered to a police officer not below the rank of Inspector under this section may be detained for 6 months from the date on which it was surrendered and may be detained for a further 3 months if a Magistrate, on application by a police officer not below the rank of Inspector, is satisfied that the investigation could not reasonably have been completed before the date of such application and authorises such further detention.

(7)All proceedings before a Magistrate under this section shall be conducted in chambers.

(8)In this section, "travel document" means a passport or other document establishing the identity or nationality of a holder.

Return of travel documents *[S 6/2016]*

121B.(1)When a travel document has been surrendered and retained by a police officer not below the rank of Inspector under section 121A, a person affected by such order may at any time make application in writing, to a Magistrate for its return, and every such application shall contain a statement of the grounds on which it is made.

(2)A Magistrate shall not consider an application made under subsection (1) unless he is satisfied that reasonable notice in writing of it has been given to the police officer not below the rank of Inspector.

(3)Before an application is granted under this section, the applicant may be required to —

*(a)*deposit such reasonable sum of cash money with the police officer not below the rank of Inspector as the Magistrate deems fit;

*(b)*provide local surety; or

*(c)*satisfy paragraphs *(a)* and *(b)*.

(4)Any such applicant or surety may be required to deposit reasonable sum of cash money with the police officer not below the rank of Inspector as the Magistrate deems fit, for retention by the police officer not below the rank of Inspector until such time when the travel document is returned to the police officer not below the rank of Inspector.

(5)Failure of the applicant to return to Brunei Darussalam or to surrender the passport to the police officer not below the rank of Inspector within the specified time will render the deposit held by the police officer not below the rank of Inspector to be forfeited to the Government and the applicant may be arrested and dealt with in the same way that a person who fails to comply with the requirement under section 121A(1) may be arrested and dealt with under section 121A(4) and (5).

(6)An application under this section may be granted subject to the conditions that —

*(a)*the applicant shall further surrender his travel document to the police officer not below the rank of Inspector at such time as may be specified; and

*(b)*the applicant shall appear at such time and place in Brunei Darussalam as may be specified.

(7) Where a travel document is returned to the applicant under this section subject to a condition imposed under subsection (6), then after the time specified under the subsection, the provisions of section 121A(6) shall continue to apply in respect of the travel document surrendered by the applicant pursuant to the condition as if no return had been made to the applicant under this section.

Diary of proceedings in police investigation *[S 6/2016]*

122. (1) Every police officer making an investigation under this Chapter shall day by day enter his proceedings in the investigation in a diary setting forth —

(a) the time at which the order for investigation, if any, reached him;

(b) the time at which he began and closed the investigation;

(c) the place or places visited by him;

(d) the person or persons questioned by him; and

(e) a statement of the circumstances ascertained through his investigation.

(2) Notwithstanding anything contained in the Evidence Act (Chapter 108), an accused person shall not be entitled, either before or in the course of any inquiry or trial, to call for or inspect the diary.

(3) If the police officer who has made the investigation refers to the diary, the entries only as the prosecutor or the police officer has referred to shall be shown to the accused and the Court shall, upon request of the prosecutor or the police officer, cause any other entry to be concealed from view or obliterated.

Report of police officer

123. Every investigation under this Chapter shall be completed without unnecessary delay and if, as a result of the investigation, it is desired to institute criminal proceedings against any person, the officer in charge of the case may, subject to any direction of the Public Prosecutor, forward to a competent Court having jurisdiction a draft charge setting out the details of the offence with which the person is to be charged.

PART VI PROCEEDINGS IN PROSECUTIONS

CHAPTER XIV JURISDICTION OF CRIMINAL COURTS IN INQUIRIES AND TRIALS

124. — 130. *(No sections).*

Conditions requisite for initiation of proceedings

Power to take cognisance of offences

131. Subject to the provisions of this Code, a Judge or Magistrate may take cognisance of an offence —

(a) upon receiving a complaint as provided by section 133;

(b) upon his own knowledge or suspicion that such offence has been committed;

(c) on any person being brought before him in custody without process and accused of having committed an offence which such Judge or Magistrate has jurisdiction either to inquire into or to try.

Sanction required for prosecution for certain offences

132.(1)No Magistrate shall take cognisance of —

*(a)*any offence punishable under section 121, 121A, 122, 123 or 505 of the Penal Code (Chapter 22), except with the previous sanction of the Public Prosecutor;

*(b)*any offence punishable under sections 172 to 188 of the Penal Code (Chapter 22), except with the previous sanction of the Public Prosecutor or on the complaint of the public servant concerned or of some public servant to whom he is subordinate;

*(c)*any offence punishable under section 193, 194, 195, 196, 199, 200, 205, 206, 207, 208, 209, 210, 211, 228 or 228A of the Penal Code (Chapter 22), except with the previous sanction of a Judge or the Public Prosecutor or, when such offence is alleged to have been committed in, or in relation to, any proceedings in any Court, except on the complaint of such Court, or of some other Court to which such Court is subordinate;

*(d)*any offence described in section 463 or punishable under section 471, 475 or 476 of the Penal Code (Chapter 22), except with the previous sanction of a Judge or the Public Prosecutor or, when such offence is alleged to have been committed by a party to any proceeding in any Court in respect of a document given in evidence in such proceedings, except on the complaint of such Court, or of some other Court to which such Court is subordinate;

*(e)*any offence punishable under section 493, 494, 495 or 496 of the Penal Code (Chapter 22), except upon a complaint made by some person aggrieved by such offence or by a Judge or the Public Prosecutor.

(2)The provisions of subsection (1) with reference to the offences named therein apply also to the abetment of such officers and to attempts to commit them.

CHAPTER XV COMPLAINTS

Examination of complainant

133.(1)When a Judge or Magistrate takes cognisance of an offence on complaint, the Judge or Magistrate shall at once examine the complainant upon oath or affirmation and the substance of the examination shall be reduced to writing and shall be signed by the complainant and also by the Judge or Magistrate.

(2)Where the complaint is made in writing by a Court or by a public servant acting or purporting to act in his official capacity, the Judge or Magistrate need not examine the complainant, but he may, if he considers it necessary, examine such public servant either on oath or affirmation or otherwise.

Postponement of issue of process

134. If the Judge or Magistrate sees reason to doubt the truth of a complaint of an offence of which he is authorised to take cognisance, he may, when the complainant has been examined, record his reason for doubting the truth of the complaint and may then postpone the issue of process for compelling the attendance of the person complained against and either inquire into the case himself or direct some police officer to make inquiries for the purpose of ascertaining the truth or falsehood of the complaint and report to him the result of the inquiries.

Dismissal of complaint

135.(1)The Judge or Magistrate before whom a complaint is made may dismiss the complaint if, after examining the complainant and recording his examination and considering the result of the inquiry, if any, made under section 134 there is in his judgment no sufficient ground for proceeding.

(2)The Judge or Magistrate, if he dismisses the complaint, shall record his reasons for doing so.

CHAPTER XVI COMMENCEMENT OF PROCEEDINGS

Issue of process

136.(1)If in the opinion of a Judge or Magistrate taking cognisance of an offence, there is sufficient ground for proceeding and the case appears to be one in которой according to the fourth column of the First Schedule a summons should issue in the first instance, he shall issue a summons for the attendance of the accused.

(2)If the case appears to be one in which according to that column a warrant should issue in the first instance, he may issue —

*(a)*a warrant; or

*(b)*if he thinks fit, a summons for causing the accused to be brought or to appear at a certain time before himself or some other Judge or Magistrate having jurisdiction.

(3)Nothing in this section shall be deemed to affect the provisions of section 52.

Personal attendance of accused may be dispensed with

137.(1)Whenever a Judge or Magistrate issues a summons he may, if he sees reason to do so, dispense with the personal attendance of the accused.

(2)The Judge or Magistrate inquiring into or trying the case may, in his discretion, at any stage of the proceedings direct the personal attendance of the accused, and if necessary enforce such attendance in the manner provided under section 136.

CHAPTER XVII PRELIMINARY INQUIRIES INTO CASES TRIABLE BY HIGH COURT

Procedure in inquiries preparatory to committal

138.(1)In the case of persons charged with any of the following offences —

*(a)*offences against the State, as defined in Chapter VI of the Penal Code (Chapter 22);

*(b)*murder;

*(c)*any offence in respect of which the punishment of death is authorised by law,

a preliminary inquiry shall be held by a Magistrate with a view to the committal of the accused person for trial before the High Court.

(2)A preliminary inquiry shall also be held unless the Public Prosecutor otherwise directs whenever a person is accused of an offence which the Public Prosecutor has by declaration published in the *Gazette*declared to be an offence to which this subsection applies or if, in the case of an offence other than the foregoing if which a person may be accused, the Public Prosecutor directs that a preliminary inquiry shall be held in respect of such offence.

(3) All other cases shall be tried summarily.

(4) The provision of section 141 shall not be deemed to authorise a Magistrate to try any charge relating to an offence in respect of which a preliminary inquiry requires to be held by virtue of this section.

Committal for trial where accused wishes to plead guilty

139. Notwithstanding section 138(1), where an accused who is brought before a Magistrate states that he wishes to plead guilty to the charge preferred against him, the Magistrate shall record the facts of the case presented by the prosecution and if the facts disclose sufficient grounds for committing the accused, he shall satisfy himself that the accused understands the nature of the charge and intends to admit without qualification the offence alleged against him and, on being so satisfied, shall commit the accused for trial for the offence.

Procedure at preliminary inquiries

Hearing and taking of evidence for prosecution

140. (1) When the accused person is brought before him, the Magistrate shall proceed to hear the case for the prosecution and to take all such evidence as may be produced in support thereof and such other evidence as the Magistrate may think fit to call for.

(2) The accused person shall be allowed to cross-examine the witnesses for the prosecution, and in such case the prosecutor may re-examine them.

(3) Nothing in this section shall prevent evidence being produced in support of the prosecution or called for by the Magistrate at any stage of the proceedings; provided that an opportunity is given to the accused to cross-examine and to answer and rebut such evidence.

(4) If the Magistrate calls for other evidence than that produced in the case for the prosecution, he shall record the fact on the depositions stating shortly the nature of the evidence he has called for.

(5) If the officer or other person conducting the prosecution applies to the Magistrate to issue process to compel the attendance of any witness or the production of any document or other thing, the Magistrate shall issue such process unless for reasons to be recorded he deems it unnecessary to do so.

When accused person to be discharged

141. (1) When the evidence referred to in section 140 has been taken and he has, if he thinks fit, examined the accused under section 220 for the purposes of enabling him to explain any circumstance appearing against him in the evidence, the Magistrate shall if he finds that there are not sufficient grounds for committing the accused person for trial discharge him, unless it appears to the Magistrate that such person should be tried before himself or before some other Magistrate in which case he shall either —

(a) forthwith frame a charge or charges in writing and call upon the accused to plead thereto; or

(b) order the accused to be tried before some other Magistrate.

(2) If the Magistrate takes action under subsection (1)*(a)* it shall not be necessary for the Magistrate to recall and re-examine the witnesses for the prosecution, but the accused may require that any witness called for the prosecution may be recalled for further cross-examination.

(3) Nothing in this section shall be deemed to prevent a Magistrate from discharging the accused at any previous stage of the case if for reasons to be recorded by such Magistrate he considers that there are not sufficient grounds for committing the accused.

(4) When the Magistrate is of opinion that there are peculiar difficulties of circumstances connected with the case or whenever he shall be so directed by a superior Court, he may remand the accused or admit him to bail and he shall forthwith send the depositions to such superior Court for instructions.

When charge to be framed

142. (1) If after taking the evidence for the prosecution the Magistrate is of opinion that on the evidence as it stands there are sufficient grounds for committing the accused for trial, he shall frame a charge under his hand declaring with what offence or offences the accused is charged.

(2) As soon as the charge has been framed, it shall be read and explained to the accused and the Magistrate shall say to him these words or words to the same effect —

"Having heard the evidence against you, do you wish to say anything in answer to the charge? You are at liberty to make your defence now or you may reserve your defence until your trial before the High Court. You are not bound to say anything unless you wish to do so, but if you elect to make your defence now, any statement you may make or evidence you may give will be taken down in writing and may be put in at your trial".

(3) A copy of the charge shall, if he so require, be given to the accused free of charge.

Committal of accused if defence reserved. Hearing and evidence for defence

143. (1) If the accused elects to reserve his defence, he shall forthwith be committed for trial before the High Court.

(2) If the accused elects to make his defence before the Magistrate, the Magistrate shall explain to him the provisions of section 221. The statement made by the accused, if any, shall be taken down in writing and read over to him and shall be signed by the Magistrate and kept with the depositions and transmitted with them as hereinafter mentioned.

(3) The evidence of the accused if he tenders himself as a witness in his own behalf *in lieu* of making a statement under subsection (2) and of any witnesses whom he may desire to call shall then be taken.

(4) The accused shall be a competent witness in his own behalf in all inquiries under this Chapter.

(5) If the accused applies to the Magistrate to issue process to compel the attendance of any witness or the production of any document or other thing, the Magistrate shall issue such process unless for reasons to be recorded he deems it unnecessary to do so.

Discharge or committal of accused

144. When the evidence referred to in section 143 has been taken, the Magistrate shall —

(a) if he finds that there are not sufficient grounds for committing him for trial, discharge the accused;

(b) if he finds that there are sufficient grounds for committing him for trial, commit the accused for trial before the High Court.

List of witnesses for defence on trial

145.(1)When the accused has been committed for trial under section 143 or 144, the Magistrate shall require him to give orally or in writing a list of the names and so far as practicable the addresses of the persons, if any, whom he wishes to be summoned to give evidence on his trial, whether such persons have given evidence before the Magistrate or not, and shall record that he has so done.

(2)If the Magistrate thinks that any witness is included in the list mentioned in subsection (1) for the purpose of vexation or delay or of defeating the ends of justice, he may require the accused to satisfy him that there are reasonable grounds for believing that the evidence of such witness is material and if he is not so satisfied may remove the name of such witness from the list, recording his reason for such action, or may require such sum to be deposited as the Magistrate thinks necessary to defray the expense of obtaining the attendance of such witness at the trial.

(3)The list of witnesses, as finally determined, shall be included in the record.

(4)The accused may at any time before his trial give to the Magistrate, or, if he is in custody, to the officer in charge of the prison for transmission to the Magistrate, a further list of persons whom he wishes to give evidence on his behalf on such trial, provided that such list be accompanied by a concise statement of the facts to be proved by such witness.

(5)The Magistrate on receiving such list and statement shall issue summonses to compel the attendance of such witnesses at the trial.

(6)The Magistrate shall also issue summonses to compel the attendance at the trial of all the witnesses included in the list framed under subsection (1).

Bond of witnesses

146.(1)Witnesses for the prosecution and defence whose attendance is necessary at the trial before the High Court and who appear before the committing Magistrate shall be bound over by him to be in attendance when called upon to give evidence at such trial and may in the discretion of the Magistrate be required to execute bonds and to find sureties for the observance of such bonds.

(2)If any witness refuses to execute the bond, the Magistrate may commit him to prison until the trial or until he gives satisfactory security that he will give evidence at the trial.

Record to be forwarded to trial Court

147.(1)When the accused is committed for trial, the committing Magistrate shall send the original record and any document, weapon or other thing which is to be produced in evidence to the Court to which the accused is committed.

(2)Any such thing which, from its bulk or otherwise, cannot conveniently be forwarded, may remain in the custody of the police.

(3)A list of all exhibits with a note of their distinguishing marks and showing which of such exhibits are forwarded with the record and which remain in the custody of the police, shall be sent with the record.

(4)The record shall comprise the following particulars —

*(a)*the serial number;

*(b)*the date of the commission of the offence;

*(c)*the date of the complaint, if any;

(d) the name, age, sex, residence and nationality (or race) of the complainant, if any;

(e) the name, age, sex, residence, if known, and nationality (or race) of the accused;

(f) the offence complained of and the offence proved, and the value of the property, if any, in respect of which the offence has been committed;

(g) the date of the summons or warrant and of the return day of the summons, if any, or on which the accused was first arrested;

(h) the date on which the accused first appeared or was brought before a Magistrate;

(i) the name and title of the officer or other person conducting the prosecution;

(j) the date of making of each adjournment or postponement, if any, and the date to which such adjournment or postponement was made and the grounds of making the adjournment or postponement;

(k) the date on which the proceedings terminated;

(l) the order made;

(m) the depositions;

(n) the statement, if any, of the accused under section 142(2);

(o) the charge;

(p) the list of witnesses given by the accused.

Power to summon supplementary witnesses

148. (1) The Magistrate may summon and examine supplementary witnesses after the committal and before the commencement of the trial and bind them over in manner provided in section 146 to appear and give evidence.

(2) Such witnesses shall be examined in the presence of the accused, who shall have the right to cross-examine them.

Custody of accused pending trial

149. The Magistrate shall, subject to the provisions of this Code regarding the taking of bail, commit the accused by warrant to custody until and during the trial.

150. *(No section).*

Addresses

151. (1) In preliminary inquiries under this Chapter —

(a) the officer or other person conducting the prosecution need not open his case but may forthwith produce his evidence;

*(b)*when the evidence for the prosecution has been taken the accused may make such comments thereon as he thinks necessary;

*(c)*if the accused elects to make his defence before the Magistrate, he may after the examination of his witnesses sum up his case.

(2)If the accused addresses the Court in accordance with subsection (1)*(b)* or *(c),* the officer or other person conducting the prosecution shall have the right to reply.

Committal for trial without consideration of evidence

151A.(1)A Magistrate holding a preliminary inquiry into an alleged offence with a view to the committal of any person for trial by the High Court may, notwithstanding the other provisions of Chapter XVII, if satisfied that all the evidence before the Court (whether for the prosecution or the defence) consists of written statements tendered to him under section 151B, commit the accused person for trial for the offence without consideration of the contents of those statements, subject to subsection (2).

(2)The accused person may request the Magistrate to consider a submission that the statements disclose insufficient evidence to put the accused person on trial for the offence, in which case the Magistrate, if he agrees with the submission after hearing the officer conducting the prosecution, shall discharge the accused person.

Written statements *in lieu* of depositions

151B.(1)In any preliminary inquiry, a written statement made by any person shall, if the conditions mentioned in subsection (2) are satisfied, be admissible to the same extent as oral evidence and to the same effect given by that person would be admissible under the Evidence Act (Chapter 108).

(2)The conditions are that —

*(a)*the statement purports to be signed by the person who made it;

*(b)*the statement contains a declaration by that person that it is true to the best of his knowledge and belief;

*(c)*not less than 7 days before the statement is tendered in evidence, a copy of it is given, by or on behalf of the party proposing to tender it, to each of the other parties to the proceedings; and

*(d)*none of the other parties, before the statement is tendered in evidence at the preliminary inquiry objects to its being so tendered under this section.

(3)Notwithstanding that a written statement made by any person may be admissible in a preliminary inquiry by virtue of this section, the Magistrate by whom the preliminary inquiry is held may, of his own motion or on the application of any party to the proceedings, require that person to attend before him and give evidence.

(4)So much of any statement as is admitted in evidence by virtue of this section shall, unless the Magistrate for reasons to be recorded by him otherwise directs, be read aloud in Court at the preliminary inquiry by the party tendering it or his representative, or by an official of the Court, as the Magistrate may direct.

(5)Any document or object referred to as an exhibit and identified in a written statement tendered in evidence under this section shall be treated as if it had been produced as an exhibit and identified in Court by the maker of the statement.

(6) So much any statement as is admitted in evidence by virtue of this section shall, if the conditions mentioned in section 33 of the Evidence Act (Chapter 108) are satisfied, be deemed to be evidence given in a judicial proceedings for the purposes of that section.

(7) Subject to the provisions of sections 151A and 151B, the provisions of Chapter XVII apply, with any necessary exceptions, qualifications or modifications, to any preliminary inquiry to which the provisions of sections 151A and 151B apply.

(8) The Magistrate may exercise the powers conferred upon him by section 145 in respect of any person whose statement has been admitted in evidence by virtue of this section as if that person had appeared before him as a witness in the preliminary inquiry, and for that purpose may summon the maker of the statement to appear before him at any time before the trial of the person or persons committed, and may issue a warrant for the arrest of the maker of the statement if he fails to appear in answer to any such summons.

CHAPTER XVIII CHARGE

Form of charge

152. (1) Every charge under this Code shall state the offence with which the accused is charged.

(2) If the law which creates the offence gives it any specific name, the offence may be described in the charge by that name only.

(3) If the law which creates the offence does not give it any specific name, so much of the definition of the offence must be stated as to give the accused notice of the matter with which he is charged.

(4) The law and section of the law against which the offence is said to have been committed shall be mentioned in the charge.

(5) The fact that the charge is made is equivalent to a statement that every legal condition required by law to constitute the offence charged was fulfilled in the particular case.

Illustrations

(a) A is charged with the murder of B. This is equivalent to a statement that A's act fell within the definition of murder given in sections 299 and 300 of the Penal Code (Chapter 22); that it did not fall within any of the general exceptions of the same Code and that it did not fall within any of the five exceptions to section 300, or that if it did fall within exception one, one or other of the three provisos to that exception applied to it.

(b) A is charged under section 326 of the Penal Code (Chapter 22) with voluntarily causing grievous hurt to B by means of an instrument for shooting. This is equivalent to a statement that the case was not provided for by section 335 of the Penal Code (Chapter 22) and that the general exceptions did not apply to it.

(c) A is accused of murder, cheating, theft, extortion, criminal intimidation, or using a false property mark. The charge may state that A committed murder cheating, theft, extortion or criminal intimidation or that he used a false property mark without reference to the definitions of those crimes contained in the Penal Code (Chapter 22); but the sections under which the offence is punishable must in each instance be referred to in the charge.

(d) A is charged under section 184 of the Penal Code (Chapter 22) with intentionally obstructing a sale of property offered for sale by the lawful authority of a public servant. The charge should be in those words.

Particulars as to time, place and person

153.(1)The charge shall contain such particulars as to the time and place of the alleged offence and the person, if any, against whom or the thing, if any, in respect of which it was committed as are reasonably sufficient to give the accused notice of the matter with which he is charged.

(2)When the accused is charged with criminal breach of trust or dishonest misappropriation of money, it shall be sufficient to specify the gross sum in respect of which the offence is alleged to have been committed and the dates between which the offence is alleged to have been committed, without specifying particular items or exact dates, and the charge so framed shall be deemed to be a charge of one offence within the meaning of section 165:

Provided that the time included between the first and last of such dates shall not exceed one year.

When manner of committing offence must be stated

154.When the nature of the case is such that the particulars mentioned in sections 152 and 153 do not give the accused sufficient notice of the matter with which he is charged, the charge shall also contain such particulars of the manner in which the alleged offence was committed as will be sufficient for that purpose.

Illustrations

*(a)*A is accused of the theft of a certain article at a certain time and place. The charge need not set out the manner in which the theft was effected.

*(b)*A is accused of cheating *B* at a given time and place. The charge must set out the manner in which *A* cheated *B*.

*(c)*A is accused of giving false evidence at a given time and place. The charge must set out that portion of the evidence given by *A* which is alleged to be false.

*(d)*A is accused of obstructing *B,* a public servant, in the discharge of his public functions at a given time and place. The charge must set out the manner in which *A* obstructed *B* in the discharge of his functions.

*(e)*A is accused of the murder of *B* at a given time and place. The charge need not state the manner in which *A* murdered *B*.

*(f)*A is accused of disobeying a direction of the law with intent to save *B* from punishment. The charge must set out the disobedience charged and the law infringed.

Sense of words used in charge to describe offence

155.In every charge, words used in describing an offence shall be deemed to have been used in the sense attached to them respectively by the law under which such offence is punishable.

Effect of errors

156.No error in stating either the offence or the particulars required to be stated in the charge, and no omission to state the offence or those particulars shall be regarded at any stage of the case as material unless the accused was in fact misled by such error or omission.

Illustrations

*(a)*A is charged under section 243 of the Penal Code (Chapter 22) with "having been in possession of counterfeit coin, having known at the time when he became possessed thereof that such coin was

counterfeit", the word "fraudulently" being omitted in the charge. Unless it appears that A was in fact misled by this omission, the error shall not be regarded as material.

[S 32/2005]

(b) A is charged with cheating B, and the manner in which he cheated B is not set out in the charge, or is set out incorrectly. A defends himself, calls witnesses, and gives his own account of the transaction. The Court may infer from this that the omission to set out the manner of the cheating is not material.

(c) A is charged with cheating B, and the manner in which he cheated B is not set out in the charge. There were many transactions between A and B, and A had no means of knowing to which of them the charge referred, and offered no defence. The Court may infer from such facts that the omission to set out the manner of the cheating was, in this case, a material error.

(d) A is charged with the murder of Johan Samad on 6th June 1984. In fact the murdered person's name was Jamil Samad and the date of the murder was 5th June 1984. A was never charged with any murder but one, and had heard the inquiry before the Magistrate which referred exclusively to the case of Jamil Samad. The Court may infer from these facts that A was not misled and that the error in the charge was immaterial.

(e) A was charged with murdering Jamil Samad on 5th June 1984 and with murdering Johan Samad (who tried to arrest him for the murder of Jamil Samad) on 6th June 1984. When charged with the murder of Jamil Samad, he was tried for the murder of Johan Samad. The witnesses present in his defence were witnesses in the case of Jamil Samad. The Court may infer from this that A was misled and that the error was material.

Procedure on arraignment on imperfect or erroneous charge

157. When any person is arraigned for trial on an imperfect or erroneous charge, the Court may frame a charge, or add to or otherwise alter the charge as the case may be, having regard to the rules contained in this Code as to the form of charges.

Illustrations

(a) A is charged with the murder of C. A charge of abetting the murder of C may be added or substituted.

(b) A is charged with forging a valuable security under section 467 of the Penal Code (Chapter 22). A charge of fabricating false evidence under section 193 of the same Code may be added.

(c) A is charged with receiving stolen property knowing it to be stolen. During the trial, it incidentally appears that he has in his possession instruments for the purpose of counterfeiting coin. A charge under section 235 of the Penal Code (Chapter 22) cannot be added.

Court may alter or add to charge

158. (1) Any Court may alter or add to any charge at any time before judgment is pronounced or, in the case of trials with the aid of assessors, before the opinions of the assessors are expressed.

(2) Every such alteration or addition shall be read and explained to the accused.

When trial may proceed immediately after alteration or addition

159. (1) If a charge is framed or an alteration or addition is made under either of section 157 or 158, the Court shall forthwith call upon the accused to plead thereto and to state whether he is ready to be tried on such charge or altered or added charge.

(2) If the accused declares that he is not ready —

(a) the Court shall duly consider the reasons he may give; and

(b) if, in the opinion of the Court, proceeding immediately with the trial is not likely to prejudice the accused in his defence or the prosecutor in the conduct of the case, the Court may, in its discretion, after such charge or alteration or addition has been framed or made, proceed with the trial as if the new or altered or added charge had been the original charge.

When new trial may be directed or trial adjourned

160. If the new or altered or added charge is such that proceeding immediately with the trial is likely, in the opinion of the Court, to prejudice the accused or the prosecutor, as mentioned in section 159, the Court may either direct a new trial or adjourn the trial for such period as may be necessary.

Stay of proceeding if prosecution of offence in altered charge requires prior sanction

161. If the offence stated in the new or altered or added charge is one for the prosecution of which prior sanction is necessary, the case shall not be proceeded with until such sanction is obtained, unless sanction has been already obtained for a prosecution on the same facts as those on which the new or altered charge is founded.

Recall of witnesses when charge altered

162. Whenever a charge is altered or added by the Court after the commencement of the trial, the prosecutor and the accused shall be allowed to recall or re-summon and examine, with reference to such alteration or addition, any witness who may have been examined, and may also call any further evidence which may be material.

Effect of material error

163. (1) If any appellate Court is of opinion that any person convicted of an offence was misled in his defence by the absence of a charge, or by an error or alteration in the charge, it may direct a new trial to be had upon a charge framed in whatever manner it thinks fit.

(2) If the Court is of opinion that the facts of the case are such that no valid charge could be preferred against the accused in respect of the facts proved, it shall quash the conviction.

Illustration

A is convicted of an offence, under section 196 of the Penal Code (Chapter 22), upon a charge which omits to state that he knew the evidence which he corruptly used or attempted to use as true or genuine, was false or fabricated. If the Court thinks it probable that *A* had such knowledge and that he was misled in his defence by the omission from the charge of the statement that he had it, it may direct a new trial upon an amended charge, but, if it appears probable from the proceedings that *A* had no such knowledge, it shall quash the conviction.

Separate charges for distinct offences

164. For every distinct offence of which any person is accused, there shall be a separate charge.

Trial of offences

165. Subject to the provisions of this Code, charges for more than one offence may be tried at one trial.

Trial for more than one offence

166.(1)A person may be charged with and tried at one trial on any number of charges which are founded on the same facts or form or are a part of a series of offences of the same or a similar character.

(2)If the acts alleged constitute an offence falling within two or more separate definitions of any law in force for the time being by which offences are defined or punished, the person accused of them may be charged with and tried at one trial for each of such offences.

(3)If several acts, of which one or more than one would by itself or themselves constitute an offence, when combined, constitute a different offence, the person accused of them may be charged with and tried at one trial for the offence constituted by such acts when combined, or for any offence constituted by any one or more of such acts.

(4)Nothing contained in this section shall affect section 71 of the Penal Code (Chapter 22).

Illustrations

To subsection (1) —

*(a)*A rescues B, a person in lawful custody, and in doing so causes grievous hurt to C,a Constable in whose custody B was. A may be charged with and tried for offences under sections 225 and 333 of the Penal Code (Chapter 22).

*(b)*A has in his possession several seals, knowing them to be counterfeit, and intending to use them for the purpose of committing several forgeries punishable under section 466 of the Penal Code (Chapter 22). A may be separately charged with and convicted for the possession of each seal under section 473 of the Penal Code (Chapter 22).

*(c)*With intent to cause injury to B, A institutes a criminal proceeding against him, knowing that there is no just or lawful ground for such proceeding; and also falsely accuses B of having committed an offence, knowing that there is no just or lawful ground for such charge. A may be separately charged with and convicted of two offences under section 211 of the Penal Code (Chapter 22).

*(d)*A, with intent to cause injury to B, falsely accuses him of having committed an offence, knowing that there is no just or lawful ground for such charge. On the trial, A gives false evidence against B, intending thereby to cause B to be convicted of a capital offence.A may be separately charged with and convicted of a capital offence. A may be separately charged with and convicted of offences under sections 211 and 194 of the Penal Code (Chapter 22).

*(e)*A with six others, commits the offences of rioting, grievous hurt and assaulting a public servant endeavouring, in the discharge of his duty as such to suppress the riot. A may be separately charged with and convicted of offences under sections 145, 325 and 152 of the Penal Code (Chapter 22).

*(f)*A threatens B, C and D at the same time with injury to their persons, with intent to cause alarm to them. A may be separately charged with and convicted of each of the three offences under section 506 of the Penal Code (Chapter 22).

The separate charges referred to in illustrations *(a)* to *(f)* respectively may be tried at the same time.

To subsection (2) —

*(g)*A wrongfully strikes B with a cane. A may be separately charged with and convicted of offences under sections 352 and 323 of the Penal Code (Chapter 22).

(h) Several stolen sacks of corn are made over to *A* and *B*, who know they are stolen property, for the purpose of concealing them. *A* and *B* thereupon voluntarily assist each other to conceal the sacks at the bottom of a grain pit. *A* and *B* may be separately charged with and convicted of offences under sections 411 and 414 of the Penal Code (Chapter 22).

(i) A exposes her child with the knowledge that she is thereby likely to cause her death. The child dies in consequence of such exposure. *A* may be separately charged with and convicted of offences under sections 317 and 304 of the Penal Code (Chapter 22).

(j) A dishonestly uses a forged document as genuine evidence, in order to convict *B*, a public servant, of an offence under section 167 of the Penal Code (Chapter 22). *A* may be separately charged with and convicted of offences under sections 471 (read with 466) and 196 of the Penal Code (Chapter 22).

To subsection (3) —

(k) A commits robbery on *B*, and in doing so voluntarily causes hurt to him. *A* may be separately charged with and convicted of offences under sections 323, 392 and 394 of the Penal Code (Chapter 22).

Where it is doubtful what offence has been committed

167. If a single act or series of acts is of such a nature that it is doubtful which of several offences the facts which can be proved will constitute, the accused may be charged with having committed all or any of such offences; and any number of such charges may be tried at once, or he may be charged in the alternative with having committed any one of those offences.

Illustrations

(a) A is accused of an act which may amount to theft, or receiving stolen property, or criminal breach of trust, or cheating. He may be charged with theft, receiving stolen property, criminal breach of trust and cheating, or he may be charged with having committed theft, or receiving stolen property, or criminal breach of trust, or cheating.

(b) A states on oath before the committing Magistrate that he saw *B* hit *C* with a club. Before the High Court Judge, *A* states on oath that *B* never hit *C*. *A* may be charged in the alternative and convicted of intentionally giving false evidence although it cannot be proved which of these contradictory statements was false.

When person charged with one offence can be convicted of another

168. If in the case mentioned in section 167 the accused is charged with one offence and it appears in evidence that he committed a different offence for which he might have been charged under the provisions of that section, he may be convicted of the offence which he is shown to have committed although he was not charged with it.

Illustration

A is charged with theft. It appears that he committed the offence of criminal breach of trust, or that of receiving stolen goods. He may be convicted of criminal breach of trust, or of receiving stolen goods (as the case may be) though he was not charged with such offence.

Person charged with offence can be convicted of attempt

169. When the accused is charged with an offence he may be convicted of having attempted to commit that offence, although the attempt is not separately charged.

Person charged with offence can be convicted of another

170. Where a person is charged with an offence and facts are proved which constitute another offence, he may be convicted of that other offence although he was not charged with it:

Provided that he may not be so convicted of any offence with a greater maximum sentence than that prescribed for the offence with which he was charged.

When persons may be charged jointly

171. When more persons than one are accused of the same offence or of different offences committed in the same transaction, or when one person is accused of committing an offence and another of abetment of or attempt to commit the same offence, they may be charged and tried together or separately as the Court thinks fit, and the provisions contained in the former part of this Chapter shall apply to all such charges.

Illustrations

(a) A and B are accused of the same murder. A and B may be charged and tried together for the murder.

(b) A and B are accused of a robbery, in the course of which A commits a murder with which B has nothing to do. A and B may be tried together on a charge of the robbery and A alone with murder.

(c) A and B are both charged with a theft, and B is charged with two other thefts committed by him in the course of the same transaction. A and B may be both tried together on a charge charging both with the one theft and B alone with the two other thefts.

(d) A and B, being members of opposing factions in a riot, should be charged and tried separately.

(e) A and B are accused of giving false evidence in the same proceedings. They should be charged and tried separately.

Withdrawal of remaining charges on conviction on one of several charges

172. (1) When more charges than one are made against the same person and when a conviction has been had on one or more of them, the officer or other person conducting the prosecution may, with the consent of the Court, withdraw the remaining charge or charges, or the Court of its own accord may stay the inquiry into or trial of such charge or charges.

(2) Such withdrawal or stay shall have the effect of an acquittal on such charge or charges, unless the conviction be set aside, in which case the said Court (subject to the order of the Court setting aside the conviction) may proceed with the inquiry into or trial of the charge or charges so withdrawn or not proceeded with.

Form of charges

173. All charges upon which persons are tried in Brunei Darussalam before the High Court shall be brought in the name of the Public Prosecutor, and be as nearly as possible in accordance with the forms in the Second Schedule.

CHAPTER XIX TRIALS WITHOUT AID OF ASSESSORS

Procedure

174. So far as practicable, the procedure laid down in this Chapter shall be observed by all Courts in trials under this Code without the aid of assessors.

Charge to be read and explained. Conviction on plea of guilty

175.(1) When the accused appears or is brought before the Court, a charge containing the particulars of the offence of which he is accused shall be framed and read and explained to him, and he shall be asked whether he is guilty of the offence charged or claims to be tried.

(2) If the accused pleads guilty to a charge whether as originally framed or as amended under section 178, the plea shall be recorded as nearly as possible in the words used by him and he may be convicted thereon:

Provided that before a plea of guilty is recorded, the Court may hear the complainant and such other evidence as it considers necessary and shall ascertain that the accused understands the nature and consequences of his plea and intends to admit, without qualification, the offence alleged against him.

Procedure when no admission is made

176.(1) If the accused refuses to plead or does not plead or claims to be tried, the Court shall proceed to hear the complainant (if any) and to take all such evidence as may be produced in support of the prosecution and such further evidence (if any) as it may, of its own motion, cause to be produced.

(2) When the Court thinks it necessary, it shall obtain from the complainant or otherwise the names of any persons likely to be acquainted with the facts of the case and to be able to give evidence for the prosecution, and shall summon to give evidence before itself such of them as it thinks necessary.

(3) The accused shall be allowed to cross-examine the complainant and all the witnesses for the prosecution, and the complainant or officer or other person conducting the prosecution may, if necessary, re-examine them.

(4) The Court may on behalf of the accused or prosecution or of its own motion put such questions to the witnesses as it considers necessary.

When no *prima facie* case

177.(1) If upon taking all the evidence referred to in section 176 and making such examination (if any) of the accused under section 220 as the Court considers necessary, it finds that no case against the accused has been made out which, if unrebutted, would warrant his conviction, the Court may, subject to the provisions of section 186, record an order of acquittal.

(2) Nothing in subsection (1) shall be deemed to prevent the Court from discharging the accused at any previous stage of the case if, for reasons to be recorded by the Court, it considers that the charge is groundless.

When *prima facie* case

178.(1) If such evidence has been taken and the Court has, if it thinks fit, examined the accused under section 220 for the purpose of enabling him to explain any circumstance appearing in the evidence against him, and the Court is of opinion that there are grounds for presuming that the accused has committed the offence charged or some other offence, which such Court is competent to try and which in its opinion it ought to try, it shall consider the charge recorded against the accused and decide whether it is sufficient and, if necessary, it shall amend the charge.

(2) The charge if amended shall be read and explained to the accused and he shall be again asked whether he is guilty or has any defence to make.

Defence

179. (1) If the accused does not plead guilty to the charge as amended or if no amendment is made, the accused shall then be called upon to enter upon his defence and to produce his evidence, and the Court shall explain to the accused the provisions of section 221, or may proceed in accordance with the provisions of section 160.

(2) If the accused elects to give evidence, his evidence shall ordinarily be taken before that of other witnesses for the defence.

(3) The complainant or officer or other person conducting the prosecution shall be allowed to cross-examine all the witnesses for the defence, and the accused may, if necessary, re-examine them.

(4) At any time when he is making his defence, the accused may be allowed to call and cross-examine any witnesses present in Court or its precincts.

(5) If the accused puts in any written statement, the Court shall file it with the record.

(6) An accused person who elects to give evidence may be cross-examined on behalf of any other accused person.

Summoning witnesses

180. (1) If the accused applies to the Court to issue any process for compelling the attendance of any witnesses (whether he has or has not been previously examined in the case) for the purpose of examination or cross-examination or the production of any document or other thing, the Court shall issue such process unless it considers that such application should be refused on the ground that it is made for the purpose of vexation, delay or for defeating the ends of justice. Such ground shall be recorded by it in writing.

(2) The Court may, before summoning any witness on such application, require that his reasonable expenses incurred in attending for the purpose of the trial be deposited in Court, or may act under the provisions of section 383.

(3) The Court may at any time adjourn the hearing of a case if satisfied that this course is in the interests of justice.

Acquittal and sentence on conviction

181. (1) If the Court finds the accused not guilty, the Court shall record an order of acquittal.

(2) If the Court finds the accused guilty or a plea of guilty is recorded against him, it shall pass sentence according to law.

Non-appearance of complainant

182. When the proceedings have been instituted upon the complaint of some person upon oath under section 131 and upon any day fixed for the hearing of the case the complainant is absent and the offence may lawfully be compounded, the Court may, in its discretion, notwithstanding anything hereinbefore contained, discharge the accused at any time before calling on him to enter upon his defence.

Non-appearance of accused

183.(1)If in a summons case the accused does not appear at the time and place mentioned in the summons and it appears to the Court that the summons was duly served a reasonable time before the time appointed for appearing and no sufficient ground is shown for an adjournment, the Court may either proceed *ex parte* to hear and determine the complaint or may adjourn the hearing to a future day.

(2)Without prejudice to the provisions of section 137, if in the case of any offence —

*(a)*which is not punishable by imprisonment except in default of payment of a fine or which if punishable by imprisonment as well as by fine is not so punishable by a term of imprisonment exceeding 6 months; and

*(b)*which shall have been declared by the written law providing for it or by resolution of His Majesty the Sultan and Yang Di-Pertuan in Council to be an offence to which the procedure provided by this subsection is applicable,

the accused pleads guilty to such offence by letter addressed to the Court, the Court may in its discretion *in lieu* of proceeding under subsection (1) deal with the case in the same manner and with the same powers as if the defendant had actually appeared before it and pleaded guilty and as if such plea had been recorded and had not been withdrawn subject nevertheless to such modifications as may be required by the physical absence of the defendant:

Provided that the Court may at any stage before sentence and shall, if it considers a sentence of imprisonment should be imposed, revoke its decision to proceed under this subsection:

Provided further that the discretion conferred on the Court to proceed under this subsection shall be exercisable only if the complainant is a public officer and so requests.

(3)Whenever the procedure provided by subsection (2) is followed —

*(a)*the complainant shall furnish the Court with a statement of facts, including matters other than previous convictions which he desires the Court to take into consideration in passing sentence;

*(b)*the complainant shall cause particulars of any previous convictions upon which it is intended to rely to be served on the defendant together with the summons or not less than 5 clear days before the date fixed by the summons for the hearing;

*(c)*matters stated in mitigation of sentence in the letter addressed by the defendant to the Court may in so far as they are not disputed by the prosecution be taken into account in passing sentence;

*(d)*the summons shall contain an endorsement or accompanying instrument under the hand of the Magistrate presiding over such Court in such terms as the Chief Justice may in pursuance of section 400 approve;

*(e)*if the Court receives a letter purporting to be signed by the complainant and has no reason to believe that it was not in fact so signed, such letter shall be deemed to have been in fact so signed until evidence to the contrary is adduced; and

*(f)*the Court shall cause the defendant to be informed of any order made by the Court and shall afford him a reasonable time to comply therewith.

(4)If after a Court has proceeded under subsection (2), that Court or any Court exercising powers of revision or appeal in respect of such proceedings is satisfied that the defendant did not plead guilty by letter in such proceedings, the Court shall have power to declare such proceedings a nullity and to make any consequential or further order.

Addresses

184. In trials under this Chapter —

(a) the officer or other person conducting the prosecution may open the case by stating shortly the nature of the offence charged and the evidence by which he proposes to prove the guilt of the accused or he may forthwith produce his evidence;

(b) when the accused is called upon to enter on his defence, he may, before producing his evidence, open his case by stating the facts or law on which he intends to rely and making such comments as he thinks necessary on the evidence for the prosecution, and if the accused gives evidence or witnesses are examined on his behalf, he may sum up his case;

(c) the officer or other person conducting the prosecution shall have the right of reply on the whole case whether the accused adduces evidence or not.

185. *(No section).*

Public Prosecutor may decline to further prosecute at any stage *[S 6/2016]*

186. (1) At any stage of any trial before the delivery of judgment, the officer or other person conducting the prosecution may, if he thinks fit, inform the Court that he does not propose further to prosecute the accused upon the charge, and thereupon all proceedings on such charge against the accused may be stayed by leave of the Court and if so stayed, the accused shall be discharged.

[S 6/2016]

(2) Such discharge shall not amount to an acquittal unless the Court so directs, except in cases covered under section 172.

(3) The Court may require a person discharged under this section to execute a bond, with or without sureties, and during such period as the Court may direct, for his reappearance before the Court on the same charge and in the meantime to keep the peace and be of good behaviour.

Power to award compensation

187. (1) If in any case the Court acquits the accused and is of opinion that the complaint, information or charge was frivolous or vexatious it may, in its discretion, either on the application of the accused or of its own motion, order the complainant or the person on whose information the complaint or charge was made, to pay to the accused or to each or any of the accused where there are more than one such compensation, not exceeding $500, as the Court thinks fit:

Provided that the Court —

(a) shall record and consider any objections which the complainant or informant may urge against the making of the order; and

(b) shall record its reasons for making such order.

(2) The sum so awarded shall be recoverable as if it were a fine; provided that if it cannot be realised the imprisonment awarded *in lieu* thereof shall not exceed 30 days.

(3) At the time of awarding compensation in any subsequent civil suit relating to the same matter, the Court shall take into account any sum paid or recovered as compensation under this subsection upon proof of the same.

Particulars to be recorded

188. In proceedings under this Chapter, the Court shall keep a record of the particulars of each case, so far as practicable, as follows —

(a) The following particulars shall be kept by the Court writer under the direction of the Judge or Magistrate —

(i) the serial number;

(ii) the date of the commission of the offence;

(iii) the date of the complaint, if any;

(iv) the name, age, sex, residence and nationality (or race) of the complainant, if any;

(v) the name, age, sex, residence and nationality (or race) of the accused;

(vi) the offence of which he is accused, the offence, if any, proved, and the value of the property in respect of which the offence has been committed;

(vii) the date of the summons or warrant and of the return day of the summons, if any, or on which the accused was first arrested;

(viii) the sentence or other final order.

(b) The following particulars shall be kept by the Judge or Magistrate —

(i) the plea of the accused and his examination, if any;

(ii) the date when the accused first appeared or was brought before the Court;

(iii) the name and title of the officer or other person conducting the prosecution;

(iv) the date of each adjournment or postponement and the date to which such adjournment or postponement was made and the grounds of making the adjournment or postponement;

(v) the date on which the proceedings terminated;

(vi) the finding;

(vii) the sentence or other final order, including the order, if any, made with regard to any exhibits or property produced in connection with the case;

(viii) the evidence of the witnesses;

(xi) a list of the exhibits;

(x) when a petition of appeal has been lodged, the grounds of the decision or the judgment if written.

Transfer of cases

189.(1) In any trial before a Magistrate in which it appears at any stage of the proceedings that from any cause any charge is one which in the opinion of such Magistrate ought to be tried by the High Court, the Magistrate shall stay proceedings in respect of such charge and transfer such charge to the High Court or if such charge relates to an offence in respect of which a preliminary inquiry requires to be held proceed under Chapter XVII with a view to the committal of the accused for trial by the High Court, and shall record the order upon the proceedings.

(2) In any trial before a Magistrate in which at any stage of the proceedings it appears to the Public Prosecutor that from any cause any charge is one which ought to be tried by the High Court, the Public Prosecutor may direct the Magistrate to stay proceedings in respect of such charge and to transfer such charge to the High Court or to proceed under Chapter XVII with a view to the committal of the accused for trial by the High Court and the Magistrate shall record the direction upon the proceedings and comply therewith.

Committal of accused to High Court for sentence

189A.(1) In any trial before a Magistrate in which it appears to the Magistrate after the conviction of the accused that a greater punishment should be inflicted in respect of the offence of which the accused has been convicted than such Magistrate has power to inflict, the Magistrate may, *in lieu* of dealing with the accused in any manner in which the Magistrate has power to deal with him, commit him to the High Court for sentence.

(2) Whenever an accused is committed to the High Court under the provisions of subsection (1), the Magistrate may remand such accused in custody to a prison or to such other place as the Magistrate deems fit pending the decision of the High Court, and the High Court shall —

(a) as respects the conviction, satisfy itself as to the correctness legality or propriety of any finding and as to regularity of any proceedings of the inferior Court, and have the powers conferred upon a Judge by section 298; and

(b) as respects the sentence, have the power to sentence the accused in accordance with the provisions of law under which he was found guilty thereof by the High Court or, if the High Court finds the accused guilty under some other provision of law, in accordance with that provisions:

Provided that an accused whom the High Court has sentenced under this paragraph may appeal to the Court of Appeal against such sentence as if he were a person convicted before the High Court appealing against sentence.

CHAPTER XX TRIALS OF CAPITAL OFFENCES

Trial of capital and certain other offences

190.(1) In all cases where the accused is charged with an offence in respect of which punishment of death is authorised by law and in any other case or class of case as the Chief Justice shall prescribe on the application of the Attorney General, the accused shall be tried by a court consisting of two Judges of the High Court, one of whom shall be the presiding Judge.

(2) The decision of the Court as to the guilt of the accused in respect of such a charge shall be arrived at unanimously and where the decision is that the accused is guilty, judgment shall be entered accordingly and the Court shall proceed to pass sentence on the convicted person according to law.

(3) Where the two Judges fail to reach an unanimous decision as to the guilt of an accused, he shall not be convicted of that offence but may, if the two Judges agree, be convicted of any lesser offence of which he could have been charged based on the same facts:

Provided that where the failure to reach an unanimous decision as to the guilt of the accused rests on the ground that one of the two Judges has made a special finding under section 320, the accused shall be dealt with in accordance with section 321.

(4) Except as provided in this section, upon all questions relating to procedure and the admission or rejection of evidence in the course of a trial under this section, the presiding Judge shall have a casting vote in the event of disagreement between the two Judges.

(5) For the purposes of this section, a Judge of the Intermediate Courts shall be deemed to be a Judge of the High Court:

Provided that —

(a) a Judge of the Intermediate Courts shall not be the presiding Judge;

(b) a Judge of the Intermediate Courts shall not sit on the trial of any particular case unless he has been directed to do so by the Chief Justice with the approval of the Permanent Secretary to the Office of the Prime Minister*.

(6) It shall not be open to the accused, either at the trial or on any appeal or other proceeding, to argue that a Judge of the Intermediate Courts is not competent to sit by reason only of the fact that such Judge has been appointed as a Deputy Public Prosecutor.

191. — 205. *(No sections).*

CHAPTER XXI ASSESSORS

206. — 215. *(No sections).*

CHAPTER XXII GENERAL PROVISIONS AS TO INQUIRIES AND TRIALS

Statement or evidence of accused

216. In cases which have been committed for trial to the High Court after a preliminary inquiry, the statement or evidence of the accused recorded by the committing Magistrate under section 143 may be put in and read as evidence.

217. — 219. *(No sections).*

Assistance to undefended accused

220. Without prejudice to section 221, if the accused is undefended, the Court may, in its discretion at the close of the evidence of any prosecution witness or at any stage prior to the closure of the case for the prosecution, question the accused as to his defence and as to whether or not he wishes to challenge or supplement any part of the prosecution evidence for the following purposes —

(a) assisting him to cross-examine the witnesses for the prosecution; or

(b) to enable the Court on behalf of the accused to put to any of such witnesses —

(i) any defence advanced by the accused;

(ii) any challenge as to the accuracy of the evidence; or

(iii) any particular modifying or supplementing the evidence adduced:

Provided that no entry shall be made in the record of any answer made by the accused and that any such answer shall be disregarded except for those purposes.

Case for prosecution to be explained by Court to accused

221. (1) At every trial or inquiry, if and when the Court calls upon the accused for his defence, it shall inform and explain to him that he may, if he wishes —

(a) make an oath or affirmation and give evidence on his own behalf in the witness box upon which he is liable to be cross-examined; or

(b) remain silent,

and that he may in any case call such witnesses on his behalf as he considers fit.

(2) The Court may also in its discretion, which shall be exercised with due regard to any previous exercise of its discretion under section 220, direct the attention of the accused to such of the evidence of the prosecution which appears to the Court to call for an explanation from the accused.

(3) *(Deleted).*

(4) The foregoing provisions of this section do not apply if the accused is defended by an advocate.

(5) The fact that the accused does not give evidence on oath or affirmation may be made the subject of any adverse comment by the prosecution, and the Court may draw such inference therefrom as it thinks just.

Procedure where accused does not understand proceedings

222. If the accused, though not insane, cannot be made to understand the proceedings, the Court may proceed with the inquiry or trial and, in cases other than cases before the High Court, if such inquiry results in a commitment, or if such trial results in a conviction, the proceedings shall be forwarded to the High Court with a report of the circumstances of the case, and the High Court shall make therein such order or pass such sentence as it thinks fit.

Power to postpone or adjourn proceedings *[S 6/2016]*

223. (1) The Court may, by order in writing, postpone or adjourn any inquiry, trial or other proceedings on such terms as it thinks fit and for as long as it considers reasonable, if the absence of a witness or any other reasonable cause makes this necessary or advisable.

(2) Subject to subsection (3), if the accused is not on bail, the Court may by a warrant remand him in custody as it thinks fit.

(3) If it appears likely that further evidence may be obtained by a remand, the Court may so remand the accused in custody for the purpose of any investigation by a law enforcement agency but not for more than 15 days at a time.

(4) If the accused is on bail, the Court may extend the bail.

(5) The Court must record in writing the reasons for the postponement or adjournment of the proceedings.

(6) Whenever a Judge or Magistrate is not available to constitute a Court of requisite jurisdiction any Magistrate may, by order in writing, notwithstanding that he has no jurisdiction in the case, if the circumstances render it necessary so to do, from time to time postpone or adjourn the trial and may remand the accused either in custody or on bail until a Judge or Magistrate is available as aforesaid.

(7) Whenever a Magistrate acts under the provisions of subsection (6) of this section, he shall report the fact forthwith to the Judge or Magistrate, as the case maybe, having jurisdiction in the case.

Compounding offences

224. (1) The offences punishable under the sections of the Penal Code (Chapter 22) described in the first two columns of Part A of the table next following may, when no prosecution for such offence is actually pending, be compounded by the person mentioned in the third column of that table; or when a prosecution for such offence is actually pending, be compounded by such person with the consent of the Court before which the case is pending.

(2) The offences punishable under the sections of the Penal Code (Chapter 22) described in Part B of the table next following may, with the consent of the Court before which the case is pending, be compounded by the person to whom the hurt has been caused.

(3) When any offence is compoundable under this section, the abetment of such offence or an attempt to commit such offence (when such attempt is itself an offence) may be compounded in like manner.

(4) When the person who would otherwise be competent to compound an offence under this section is not competent to contract, any person competent to contract on his behalf may compound such offence.

(5) The composition of an offence under this section shall have the effect of an acquittal of the accused.

(6) No offence under the Penal Code (Chapter 22) not mentioned in this section shall be compounded.

TABLE OF OFFENCES

PART A

Offence	Section of Penal Code applicable	Person by whom offence may be compounded
Uttering words etc with deliberate intent to wound the religious feelings of any person	298	The person whose religious feelings are intended to be wounded
Causing hurt	323, 334	The person to whom the hurt is caused
Wrongfully restraining or confining any person	341, 342	The person restrained or confined
Assault or use of criminal force	352, 355, 358	The person assaulted or to whom criminal force is used
Unlawful compulsory labour	347	The person compelled to labour
Mischief when the only loss or damage caused is loss or damage to a private person	426, 427	The person to whom the loss or damage is caused
Criminal trespass	447	
House trespass	448	
Criminal breach of contract of service	490, 491	The person with whom the offender has contracted

Defamation	500	
Printing or engraving matter knowing it to be defamatory	501	
Sale of printed or engraved substance containing defamatory matter knowing it to contain such matter	502	
Insult intended to provoke a breach of the peace	504	The person insulted

PART B

Offence	Section of Penal Code applicable
Voluntarily causing grievous hurt	325
Voluntarily causing grievous hurt on sudden provocation	335
Causing hurt by an act which endangers life	337
Causing grievous hurt by an act which endangers life	338

225. *(No section).*

Change of Magistrate during hearing or inquiry

226. Whenever any Magistrate after having heard and recorded the whole or any part of the evidence in an inquiry or a trial ceases to exercise jurisdiction therein and is succeeded by another Magistrate who has and who exercises such jurisdiction, the Magistrate so succeeding may act on the evidence so recorded by his predecessor, or partly recorded by his predecessor and partly recorded by himself, or he may re-summon the witnesses and recommence the inquiry or trial:

Provided that —

(a) in any trial the accused may, when the second Magistrate commences his proceedings, demand that the witnesses or any of them be re-summoned and heard;

(b) the High Court may, whether there be an appeal or not, set aside any conviction had or commitment made on evidence not wholly recorded by the Magistrate before whom the conviction was had or the commitment made, if such Court is of opinion that the accused has been materially prejudiced thereby, and may order a new inquiry or trial.

Detention of offenders attending in Court

227. (1) Any person attending a criminal Court, although not under arrest or upon a summons, may be detained by such Court for the purpose of examination for any offence of which such Court can take cognisance and which, from the evidence, he may appear to have committed, and may be proceeded against as though he had been arrested or summoned.

(2) When the detention takes place in the course of an inquiry under Chapter XVII, or after a trial has been begun, the proceedings in respect of such person shall be commenced afresh and the witnesses re-heard.

Power to view

228.(1)Any Judge or Magistrate may, at any stage of any inquiry, trial or other proceedings, after due notice to the parties, visit and inspect any place in which an offence is alleged to have been committed, or any other place which it is in his opinion necessary to view, for the purpose of properly appreciating the evidence given at such inquiry or trial, and shall without unnecessary delay record a memorandum of any relevant facts observed at such inspection:

Provided that, in the case of a trial with the aid of assessors, the Judge shall not act under this section unless an order is made under section 196 for a view by the assessors.

(2)The Judge or Magistrate may direct that the accused shall be present, and he shall take evidence at such place or places.

(3)Such memorandum shall form part of the record of the case.

Sunday or public holiday

229. No proceeding of any criminal Court shall be invalid by reason of its happening on a Sunday or public holiday.

CHAPTER XXIII MODE OF TAKING AND RECORDING EVIDENCE IN INQUIRIES AND TRIALS

Evidence to be taken in presence of accused

230. Except as otherwise expressly provided, all evidence taken under Chapters XVII, XIX, and XX shall be taken in the presence of the accused.

Manner of recording evidence

231. In inquiries and trials under this Code by or before a Magistrate, the evidence of the witnesses shall be recorded in the manner provided by this Chapter.

Record of trial

232.(1)In summons cases tried before a Magistrate, the Magistrate shall, as the examination of each witness proceeds, make a note of the substance of what such witness deposes, and such note shall be written in English or in romanised Malay by the Magistrate with his own hand in legible handwriting and shall form part of the record.

(2)In all other trials before a Magistrate and in all inquiries under Chapters XI, XVII and XXX, the evidence of each witness shall be taken down in legible handwriting in English or in romanised Malay by the Magistrate and shall form part of the record.

Mode of recording evidence

233.(1)Evidence shall not ordinarily be taken down in the form of question and answer, but in the form of a narrative.

(2)The Magistrate may, in his discretion, take down any particular question and answer.

Reading over evidence and correction

234.(1)The evidence of each witness taken in inquiries under Chapters XI and XVII shall be read over to him in the presence and hearing of the accused and shall, if necessary, be corrected.

(2)If the witness denies the correctness of any part of the evidence when the evidence is read over to him, the Magistrate may, instead of correcting the evidence, make a memorandum thereon of the objection made to it by the witness, and shall add such remarks as he thinks necessary.

(3)The evidence so taken down shall be interpreted to the witness, if necessary, in the language in which it was given or in a language which he understands.

(4)When a deposition has been read over to a witness and acknowledged to be correct, the Magistrate shall append to the evidence of the witness the letters "RA" and his initials which shall be deemed to be a certificate that the evidence has been read over and, if necessary, interpreted to the witness in the presence and hearing of the accused, and has been admitted by the witness to be correct.

(5)The absence of such a certificate in a deposition shall not be a bar to the deposition being received as evidence in any case in which it is desired to tender the deposition in evidence if it is proved by other evidence that the other requirements of this section were in fact complied with.

Interpretation of evidence to accused

235.(1)Whenever any evidence is given in a language not understood by the accused, it shall be interpreted to him in open Court in a language which he understands.

(2)When documents are put in for the purpose of formal proof, it shall be in the discretion of the Court to interpret as much thereof as appears necessary.

Remarks as to demeanour of witness

236.A Magistrate recording the evidence of a witness may, at the conclusion of such evidence and at the foot of the notes thereof, record such remarks (if any) as he thinks material respecting the demeanour of such witness whilst under examination.

Judge to take notes of evidence

236A. In all criminal cases before the High Court, the presiding Judge shall take down in writing notes of the evidence adduced.

Other persons may be authorised to take notes of evidence [S 6/2016]

236AA. Notwithstanding any provisions of this Code, a Judge or Magistrate in an inquiry or trial may cause *verbatim* notes of evidence to be taken by another person of what each witness deposes, in addition to any note of the substance of what each witness deposes which may be made or taken by the Judge or Magistrate himself, and the *verbatim* notes shall form part of the record.

Evidence through live video or live television links [S 6/2016]

236B.(1)Notwithstanding any provisions of this Code or of any other written law, but subject to the provisions of this section, a person, other than the accused, whether within or outside Brunei Darussalam, may with the leave of the Court, give evidence through a live video or live television link in any inquiry, trial, appeal or other proceedings if the Court is satisfied that it is expedient in the interests of justice to do so.

(2) Notwithstanding any provision of this Code or of any other written law, the Court may order an accused to appear before it through a live video or live television link while in remand in Brunei Darussalam in proceedings for any of the following matters —

(a) an application for bail or release on personal bond;

(b) an extension of the remand of an accused under section 223.

(3) The Court may, in exercising its powers under subsection (1) or (2), make an order on all or any of the following matters —

(a) the persons who may be present at the place where the witness is giving evidence;

(b) the persons who may be excluded from the place while the witness is giving evidence;

(c) the persons in the courtroom who must be able to be heard, or seen and heard, by the witness and by the persons with the witness;

(d) the persons in the courtroom who must not be able to be heard, or seen and heard, by the witness and by the persons with the witness;

(e) the persons in the courtroom who must be able to see and hear the witness and the persons with the witness;

(f) the stages in the proceedings during which a specified part of the order is to have effect;

(g) any other order that the Court considers necessary in the interests of justice.

(4) The Court may revoke, suspend or vary an order made under this section if —

(a) the live video or live television link system stops working and it would cause unreasonable delay to wait until a working system becomes available;

(b) it is necessary for the Court to do so to comply with its duty to ensure fairness in the proceedings;

(c) it is necessary for the Court to do so in order that the witness can identify a person or a thing or so that the witness can participate in or view a demonstration or an experiment;

(d) it is necessary for the Court to do so because part of the proceedings is being heard outside a courtroom; or

(e) there has been a material change in the circumstances after the Court has made the order.

(5) Evidence given by a witness, whether within or outside Brunei Darussalam, through a live video or live television link by virtue of this section or of any other written law is deemed for the purposes of sections 193, 194, 195, 196, 205 and 209 of the Penal Code (Chapter 22) as having been given in the proceedings in which it is given.

(6) Where a witness gives evidence in accordance with this section or any other written law, he is deemed for the purposes of this Code to be giving evidence in the presence of the Court.

(7) In subsections (3), (5) and (6), a reference to "witness" includes a reference to an accused who appears before a Court through a live video or live television link under subsection (2).

(8) Where leave is given under subsection (1) in the case of any proceedings for the evidence to be given through a television link, a Court may sit, for the purpose of the whole or part of those proceedings, at a Court or at such other place as may be determined by a Judge, Magistrate or Registrar for the purposes of this section.

Video recordings of evidence from child-witnesses

236C.(1) This section applies in relation to proceedings for an offence to which section 236B(2) applies.

(2) In such proceedings, a video recording of an interview which —

(a) is conducted between an adult and a child who is not an accused, (in this section referred to as the child-witness); and

(b) relates to any matter in issue in those proceedings,

may, with the leave of the Court, be given in evidence in so far as it is not excluded under subsection (3).

(3) Where a video recording is tendered in evidence under this section, the Court shall (subject to the exercise of any power to exclude evidence which is otherwise admissible) give leave under subsection (2), unless it is empowered to refuse such leave under subsection (4).

(4) The Court shall refuse leave under subsection (2) if —

(a) it appears that the child-witness will not be available for cross-examination, either in person or through a live television link under section 236B;

(b) any rules of court requiring disclosure of the circumstances in which the video recording was made have not been complied with to its satisfaction; or

(c) the Court is of the opinion, having regard to all the circumstances of the case, that in the interests of justice the video recording ought not to be admitted.

(5) The Court may, if it gives leave under subsection (2) and is of the opinion that in the interests of justice any part of the video recording ought not to be admitted, direct that such part shall be excluded.

(6) In considering whether any part of a video recording ought to be excluded under subsection (5), the Court shall consider whether any prejudice to an accused, which might result from the admission to that part, is outweighed by the desirability of showing the whole or substantially the whole of the video recording.

(7) Where a video recording has been admitted in evidence under this section —

(a) the child-witness shall be called by the party who tendered it in evidence, either in person or through a live television link under section 236B; and

(b) the child-witness shall not be examined-in-chief on any matter which, in the opinion of the Court, has been dealt with in his video recording evidence.

(8) Where a video recording has been given in evidence under this section, any statement made by the child-witness which is disclosed by the video recording shall be treated as if made by him in direct order evidence; and accordingly —

(a) such statement shall be admissible evidence of any fact of which such evidence from him would be admissible;

(b) no such statement shall be capable of corroborating any other evidence given by him,

and in estimating the weight, if any, to be attached to such a statement, regard shall be had to all the circumstances from which any inference can reasonably be drawn, whether as to its accuracy or otherwise.

(9) A Magistrate holding a preliminary inquiry under Chapter XVII may consider any video recording in respect of which leave under subsection (2) is to be sought at the trial, notwithstanding that the child-witness is not called at the preliminary inquiry.

(10) Nothing in this section prejudices the admissibility of any video recording which would be admissible apart from this section.

(11) In this section —

"child" means a person who is under 14 years of age when the video recording was made;

"statement" includes any representation of fact, whether made in words or otherwise;

"video recording" means any recording, on any medium, from which a moving image may by any means be produced, and includes the accompanying sound-track.

[S 32/2005]

Rules of court for sections 236B and 236C

236D. The Chief Justice may make rules of court for the purposes of sections 236B and 236C.

Cross-examination of alleged child victim

236E. Notwithstanding any provision of this Code or of any other written law, no person who is charged with an offence to which section 236B(2) applies shall in person cross-examine any witness who —

(a) is alleged —

(i) to be the person against whom the offence was committed; or

(ii) to have witnessed the commission of the offence; and

(b) (i) is under 14 years of age; or

(ii) is to be cross-examined following the admission under section 236C of a video recording of evidence from him.

CHAPTER XXIIIA RECORDING OF PROCEEDINGS BY MECHANICAL MEANS

[S 6/2016]

Application of this Chapter

236F. Notwithstanding the provisions contained in this Code or provisions of any other written law, dealing with the mode of taking andrecording of evidence, any mechanical means may be employed for the recording of any proceedings before the Court, and where mechanical means are employed, the provisions of this Chapter shall apply.

Interpretation of this Chapter

236G. In this Chapter —

"electronic record" means any digitally, electronically, magnetically or mechanically produced records stored in any equipment, device, apparatus or medium or any other form of storage such as disc, tape, film, sound track, and includes a replication of such recording to a separate storage equipment, device, apparatus or medium or any other form of storage;

"mechanical means" includes any equipment, device, apparatus or medium operated digitally, electronically, magnetically or mechanically;

"proceedings" includes any inquiry, trial, appeal, reference orrevision, or any part of it, any application, judgment, decision, ruling, direction, address, submission and any other matter done or said by or before a Court, including matters relating to procedure.

Proceedings may be recorded by mechanical means or combination of mechanical means and other modes

236H. (1) A Judge or Magistrate shall have the discretion to direct that any proceedings before any Court be recorded, in whole or in part, by any mechanical means or a combination of any mechanical means.

(2) Where any Judge or Magistrate directs that any proceedingsbe recorded by any mechanical means, the Judge or Magistrate shall satisfy himself as to the efficiency and functional capability of such mechanical means and that the mechanical means used for recording is in good working order for the purpose of ensuring that the electronic record of such proceedings is clear and accurate.

(3) Notwithstanding that any proceedings are being recorded by any mechanical means, a Judge or Magistrate may —

(a) employ any other mode of taking and recording of evidence; and

(b) at any time, direct that such recording be discontinued and that the recording of such proceedings be continued by any other mechanical means or any other mode of taking and recording of evidence.

(4) Where a Judge or Magistrate makes a ruling that any evidence adduced is inadmissible or irrelevant and shall not form part of the record of proceedings, he may direct that the electronic record of that evidence be erased or otherwise omitted from the record of proceedings.

Electronic record to be transcribed

236I. (1) Where any proceedings before any Judge or Magistrate are recorded by any mechanical means, the Judge or Magistrate shall cause the electronic record of such proceedings to be transcribed by any person authorised in writing by the Judge or Magistrate.

(2) Upon the production of the transcript by any person authorised under subsection (1), the Judge or Magistrate shall ascertain the accuracy and reliability of such transcript and where the Judge or Magistrate makes a ruling that any evidence recorded is inadmissible or irrelevant and shall not form part of the record

of proceedings, he may direct that the electronic record of that evidence be excluded from the record of proceedings.

(3) The transcript shall be authenticated by the signature of the Judge or Magistrate.

Safe custody of electronic record and transcript

236J.(1) The Judge or Magistrate shall cause any electronic record of any proceedings before the Judge or Magistrate and the authenticated copy of the transcript of that electronic record to be kept in safe custody.

(2) The electronic record shall not be erased, destroyed or otherwise disposed of —

(a) within the time allowed by law for instituting any appeal or revision in relation to the proceedings in question; or

(b) where an appeal, reference or revision in relation to the proceedings in question is instituted, until that appeal, reference or revision is finally determined or otherwise terminated.

Electronic filing, lodgement, submission and transmission of document

236K. Where any document relating to any proceedings is required to be filed, lodged with, submitted or transmitted to the Court, such filing, lodgement, submission or transmission may be done electronically as may be determined by the Court.

Issuance of Practice Direction

236L. The Chief Justice may, where necessary, issue Practice Direction relating to the use of mechanical means and any matter related to it.

CHAPTER XXIV JUDGMENT

Mode of delivering judgment

237.(1) The judgment in every trial in any criminal Court of original jurisdiction shall be pronounced in open Court, or the substance of such judgment shall be explained in open Court, either immediately or at some subsequent time of which due notice shall be given to the parties or their legal representatives, and the accused shall, if in custody, be brought up or, if not in custody, shall be required to attend to hear judgment delivered, except where his personal attendance during the trial has been dispensed with and the sentence is one of fine only or if he is acquitted in either of which cases, it may be delivered in the presence of his legal representative.

(2) Every such judgment shall be delivered in Malay or in English, and in some language understood by the accused. It shall contain the point or points for determination, the decision thereon, and the reasons for the decision. If the judgment is in writing, it shall be signed by the person delivering it and filed with the record of the proceedings. If the judgment is delivered orally, the substance of it shall be reduced to writing and filed with the record.

(3) It shall specify the offence (if any) of which, and the section of the Penal Code (Chapter 22) or other written law under which the accused is convicted, and the punishment to which he is sentenced.

(4) When the conviction is under the Penal Code (Chapter 22) and it is doubtful under which of two sections or under which of two parts of the same section of that Code the offence falls, the Court shall distinctly express the same and pass judgment in the alternative.

(5) If it is a judgment of acquittal, it shall state the offence of which the accused is acquitted, and direct that he be set at liberty.

(6) If the accused is convicted of an offence punishable with death and the Court sentences him to any punishment other than death, the Court shall in its judgment state the reason why sentence of death was not passed.

Address on sentence [S 6/2016]

237A.(1) Before a Court passes sentence on a person convicted of an offence, the officer or other person conducting the prosecution may address the Court with respect to that sentence.

(2) Without limiting the generality of subsection (1), the officer or other person conducting the prosecution may, in an address pursuant to that subsection —

(a) draw the attention of the Court to any aggravating circumstances, or the presence or absence of any extenuating circumstances, in relation to the offence;

(b) where the Court has a choice with regard to the kinds of sentence that it may impose in relation to the offence, comment on the appropriateness of those kinds of sentence; and

(c) where the Court has a choice with regard to those kinds of sentence, recommend that the Court impose one of those kinds of sentence.

(3) The failure by the officer or other person conducting the prosecution to exercise his right under subsection (1) to address the Court with respect to the sentence for the offence shall not be taken into account by the Court in determining an appeal against that sentence by the Public Prosecutor.

Effect of certain offences on persons in respect of whom committed [S 6/2016]

237B.(1) In determining the sentence to be imposed on a person for an offence to which this section applies, a Court shall take into account, and may, where necessary, receive evidence or submissions concerning any effect (whether long-term or otherwise) of the offence on the person in respect of whom the offence was committed.

(2) This section applies to —

(a) an offence which involves an assault on, or injury or threat of injury to, any person;

(b) an offence against —

(i) section 354 of the Penal Code (Chapter 22) (outraging modesty);

(ii) section 376 of the Penal Code (Chapter 22) (rape);

(iii) section 377 of the Penal Code (Chapter 22) (unnatural offences);

(iv) section 377A of the Penal Code (Chapter 22) (incest);

(v) section 2 of the Unlawful Carnal Knowledge Act (Chapter 29) (carnal knowledge);

(c) an offence which consists of attempting or conspiring to commit, or abetting the commission of, an offence referred to in paragraph (a) or (b).

(3) Where a Court is determining the sentence to be imposed on a person for an offence to which this section applies, the Court shall, upon application by the person in respect whom such offence was committed, hear the evidence of the person in respect of whom the offence was committed as to the effect of the offence on such person upon being requested to do so.

No sentence of death against person under 18 years [S 9/2006]

238.(1) Sentence of death shall not be pronounced on or recorded against a person convicted of an offence if it appears to the Court that at the time when the offence was committed he was under the age of 18 years but instead the Court shall sentence him to be detained during His Majesty the Sultan and Yang Di-Pertuan's pleasure, and, if so sentenced, he shall be liable to be detained in such place and under such conditions as the His Majesty the Sultan and Yang Di-Pertuan directs, and while so detained shall be deemed to be in legal custody.

(2) Subject to the powers of His Majesty the Sultan and Yang Di-Pertuan under this Code and any other written law, if a person is ordered to be detained under subsection (1), the Board of Visiting Justices for the prison or the board of visitors for any other place —

(a) shall review that person's case at least once a year; and

(b) may recommend to His Majesty the Sultan and Yang Di-Pertuan on the early release or further detention of that person,

and His Majesty the Sultan and Yang Di-Pertuan may thereupon order him to be released or further detained, as the case may be.

Judgment of death

239. When any person is sentenced to death, the sentence shall direct that he be hanged by the neck until he is dead, but shall not state the place where, nor the time when, the sentence is to be carried out.

Judgment not to be altered

240. No Court, other than the High Court, having once recorded its judgment, shall alter or review the judgment:

Provided that a clerical error may be rectified at any time, and that any other mistake may be rectified at any time before the Court rises for the day.

Judgment to be explained and copy supplied

241. The judgment shall be translated or explained to the accused in a language which he understands and on his application, a copy of the judgment or, when he so desires, a translation in his own language, if practicable, shall be given to him without delay. Such copy shall, in any case other than a summons case, be given free of cost.

242. — 243.(No sections).

CHAPTER XXV SUBMISSION OF SENTENCES OF DEATH TO

His Majesty the Sultan and Yang Di-Pertuan

Submission of sentence of death to His Majesty the Sultan and Yang Di-Pertuan

244. (1) In every case in which sentence of death is pronounced, the trial Judge shall forward to the Chief Justice for transmission to His Majesty the Sultan and Yang Di-Pertuan the record of the case, together with a written report under seal stating whether, in his opinion, there are any reasons, and if so what reasons, why the sentence of death should not be carried out.

(2) Upon the expiration of the time prescribed for instituting an appeal or, if an appeal has been instituted upon the dismissal of the appeal, the Chief Justice shall, as soon as conveniently may be, forward the record and the report to His Majesty the Sultan and Yang Di-Pertuan together with, if there has been an appeal, an intimation of the decision of the Court of Appeal, and such report, if any, on the case as the Court of Appeal, or if there has been no appeal, the Chief Justice, may think fit to make.

(3) His Majesty the Sultan and Yang Di-Pertuan may cause the trial Judge to be summoned to attend the meeting of the Privy Council at which the sentence of death is to be considered and to produce his notes thereat.

(4) His Majesty the Sultan and Yang Di-Pertuan, after considering the report or reports and if the trial Judge has been summoned to attend after hearing the trial Judge, shall communicate to the High Court a copy under his hand and seal of any order he makes under this Code.

CHAPTER XXVI EXECUTION OF SENTENCES

Execution of sentences of death

245. (1) If His Majesty the Sultan and Yang Di-Pertuan has ordered that the sentence of death is to be carried out, the High Court shall, on receiving a copy under His Majesty the Sultan and Yang Di-Pertuan's hand and seal of the order, issue a warrant of execution under the seal of the Court and the hand of a Judge, and shall forward the warrant to the Director of Prisons.

[GN 68/1985]

(2) The Director of Prisons on receiving the warrant of execution shall appoint an officer to carry it into effect.

[GN 68/1985]

(3) His Majesty the Sultan and Yang Di-Pertuan may order a respite of the execution of the warrant and afterwards appoint some other time or place for its execution.

Procedure where it is alleged that woman convicted of capital offence is pregnant

246. (1) Where a woman convicted of an offence punishable with death is found in accordance with the provisions of this section to be pregnant, sentence of death shall not be passed on her, and where no alternative sentence for such offence is otherwise provided for, the sentence to be passed on her shall be a sentence of imprisonment for life.

(2) Where a woman convicted of an offence punishable with death alleges that she is pregnant, or where the Court before whom she is convicted thinks fit to order so, the question whether or not the woman is pregnant shall, before sentence is passed on her, be determined by the Court.

(3) The question whether the woman is pregnant shall be determined on such evidence as may be laid before the Court on the part of the woman or the Public Prosecutor, and such woman shall not be found to be pregnant unless such pregnancy is affirmatively proved.

(4) If in proceedings under this section it is found that the woman in question is not pregnant, the woman may, as of right, appeal to the Court of Appeal.

(5) If on an appeal under subsection (4) the Court is satisfied that the finding should be set aside, it shall quash the sentence passed on the woman in question and instead pass on her a sentence of imprisonment for life.

Persons of unsound mind

247.(1) If it is made to appear to His Majesty the Sultan and Yang Di-Pertuan by a report of two of the visiting Justices of the prison in which a prisoner under sentence of death is detained or by a report of the medical officer of such prison or otherwise, that the prisoner is mentally disordered or mentally defective then, without prejudice to any powers vested in His Majesty the Sultan and Yang Di-Pertuan to grant a pardon, respite or commutation, His Majesty the Sultan and Yang Di-Pertuan shall order that the person be examined forthwith by not less than two medical officers or medical practitioners who shall examine the prisoner and inquire into his mental condition.

(2) The medical officers or medical practitioners appointed under subsection (1) may in addition to examining the prisoner, consult the prison authorities and make such other inquiries which they think may assist them in reaching conclusions about the prisoner's state of mind and they shall make a report in writing to His Majesty the Sultan and Yang Di-Pertuan and they or the majority of them may certify in writing that he is insane:

Provided that if a Commission has been appointed under subsection (3), then *in lieu* of making any report, the medical officers or medical practitioners shall give evidence as to the matters aforesaid before such Commission.

(3) Whenever His Majesty the Sultan and Yang Di-Pertuan has made an order under subsection (1), he may also in his discretion appoint a Commission consisting of a Judge or a Magistrate and such number of suitable persons as he shall think fit, or other suitable persons to inquire formally into the question whether the prisoner is mentally disordered or defective or otherwise abnormal or subnormal and whether if the sentence of death is commuted, it is desirable in all circumstances that he should be detained in a psychiatric facility, prison or in some other fit place for safe custody.

[S 25/2014]

(4) For the purposes of this Code, the chairman of the Commission shall have all the powers of a Magistrate for the summoning and examination of witnesses and the administration of oaths or affirmations and for compelling the production of documents and material objects.

(5) If after considering the report in subsection (2) of the findings and recommendations of the Commission appointed under subsection (3), it appears to His Majesty the Sultan and Yang Di-Pertuan that the prisoner is insane or that his mental condition is such that if he is detained in a prison there is a danger that he may cause physical injury to himself or others, His Majesty the Sultan and Yang Di-Pertuan may order that he be confined in such Government psychiatric facility or other suitable place for safe custody as may be specified in the order and if such an order is made, the prisoner shall be confined therein by virtue of this section.

[S 25/2014]

Procedure at execution

248.(1)*(Deleted).*

(2) There shall be present at the execution the officer whom the Director of Prisons has appointed to carry out the sentence, a medical officer or hospital assistant and such other person as the Director of Prisons may require, and there may be present any minister of religion whom the Director of Prisons thinks proper to admit.

[GN 68/1985]

(3) As soon as may be after the judgment of death has been executed, a medical officer or hospital assistant shall examine the body of the person executed and shall ascertain the fact of death and shall sign a certificate thereof on the back of the warrant of execution and deliver the same to the Director of Prisons.

[GN 68/1985]

(4) *(Deleted)*.

(5) The Director of Prisons shall return the warrant of execution duly indorsed as required by this section to the Chief Justice.

[GN 68/1985]

Escape of prisoner

249. When a sentence of death is avoided by the escape of the person sentenced to death, execution of the sentence shall be carried into effect at such other time after his recapture as a Judge shall order.

Saving for irregularity

250. No omission or error as to time and place and no defect in form in any order or warrant given under this Chapter and no omission to comply with the provisions of section 248 shall be held to render illegal any execution carried into effect under such order or warrant or intended so to have been carried into effect, or shall render any execution illegal which would otherwise have been legal.

Date of commencement of sentence *[S 63/2002]*

251. Subject to the provisions of this Code, every sentence of imprisonment to which section 252 apply shall take effect from the date on which it was passed, unless the Court passing the sentence otherwise directs.

Execution of sentences of imprisonment

252. Where the accused is sentenced to imprisonment, the Court passing the sentence shall forward a warrant to the officer in charge of the prison in which he is to be confined and, unless the accused is already confined in the prison, shall send him in the custody of the police to the prison with the warrant.

Provisions as to sentences of fine

253. (1) Whenever an offender has been sentenced to pay a fine, the Court passing the sentence may, in its discretion, make both or either of the following orders —

(a) direct by the sentence that in default of payment of the fine, the offender shall suffer imprisonment for a certain term, which imprisonment shall be in excess of any other imprisonment to which he may have been sentenced, or to which he may be liable under a commutation of a sentence;

(b) issue a warrant for the levy of the amount by distress and sale of any property belonging to the offender.

(2) A warrant for the levy of a fine may be executed at any place in Brunei Darussalam.

Imprisonment in default

254. Except in cases where the scale is specifically provided for in some other written law, the period for which the Court directs the offender to be imprisoned in default of payment of fine shall not exceed the following scale —

(a) if the offence is punishable with imprisonment —

Where the maximum term of imprisonment	The period shall not exceed
does not exceed 6 months	the maximum term or imprisonment
exceeds 6 months but does not exceed 2 years	6 months
exceeds 2 years	one-quarter of the maximum term of imprisonment;

(b) if the offence is not punishable with imprisonment —

Where the fine	The period shall not exceed
does not exceed $100	one month
exceeds $100 but does not exceed $250	2 months
exceeds $250 but does not exceed $500	4 months
exceeds $500	6 months.

Termination of imprisonment when fine paid

255. (1) The imprisonment which is imposed in default of payment of a fine shall terminate whenever that fine is either paid or levied by process of law.

(2) If, before the expiration of the time of imprisonment fixed in default of payment such a proportion of the money is paid or levied is such that the time of imprisonment suffered in default of payment is not less than proportional to the part of the fine still unpaid, the imprisonment shall terminate.

(3) The fine or any part thereof which remains unpaid may be levied at any time within 6 years after the passing of the sentence, and if under the sentence the offender is liable to imprisonment for a longer period than 6 years, then at any time prior to the expiration of that period, and the death of the offender does not discharge from liability any property which would after his death be legally liable for his debts.

Allowing time to pay fine and suspending execution of imprisonment

256.(1)When an offender has been sentenced to pay a fine, and the fine is not paid forthwith, the Court may make all or any of the following orders —

*(a)*direct that time be allowed for the payment of the fine;

*(b)*direct payment to be made of the fine by instalments;

*(c)*where the offender has been sentenced to imprisonment in default of payment of the fine under section 253, suspend the execution of the sentence of imprisonment and release the offender;

*(d)*direct that any order made under this subsection shall be conditional on the offender executing a bond with or without sureties for his appearance before the Court on the date or dates on or before which payment of the fine or the instalments thereof, as the case may be, is to be made.

(2)When a fine is directed to be paid by instalments and default is made in the payment of any instalment, the same proceedings may be taken as if default had been made in the payment of all the instalments then remaining unpaid, and in such event, or where time has been allowed for the payment of the fine and the fine has not been paid within such time, the Court may, if no such order has previously been made, make both or either of the orders specified in section 253.

(3)The provisions of this section shall be applicable also in any case in which an order for the payment of money has been made on non-recovery of which imprisonment may be awarded and the money is not paid forthwith, and if the person against whom the order has been made, on being required to enter into a bond such as is referred to in subsection (1)*(d)*, fails to do so, the Court may at once pass sentence of imprisonment.

Mode of executing sentence of whipping

257.(1)When the accused is sentenced to whipping, the instrument to be used and the number of strokes shall be specified in the sentence. In no case shall the whipping exceed 24 strokes in the case of an adult or 18 strokes in the case of a youthful offender, anything in any written law to the contrary notwithstanding.

(2)Whipping shall be inflicted on such part of the person as the Permanent Secretary to the Office of the Prime Minister* from time to time generally directs.

(3)The rattan shall be not more than half an inch in diameter.

(4)In the case of a youthful offender, whipping shall be inflicted in the way of school discipline with a light rattan.

(5)When a person is convicted at one trial of any two or more distinct offences, any two or more of which are legally punishable by whipping, the combined sentences of whipping awarded by the Court for any such offences shall not, anything in any written law to the contrary notwithstanding, exceed a total number of 24 strokes in the case of adults and 18 strokes in the case of youthful offenders.

Certain persons not punishable with whipping

258. No sentence of whipping shall be executed by instalments, and none of the following persons shall be punishable with whipping —

*(a)*females;

(b) males sentenced to death;

(c) males whom the Court considers to be more than 50 years of age.

Medical certificate required

259.(1) The punishment of whipping shall not be inflicted unless a medical officer or hospital assistant is present and certifies that the offender is in a fit state of health to undergo such punishment.

(2) If, during the execution of a sentence of whipping, a medical officer or hospital assistant certifies that the offender is not in a fit state of health to undergo the remainder of the sentence, the whipping shall be finally stopped.

Procedure if whipping cannot be inflicted

260.(1) In any case in which under section 259 a sentence of whipping is wholly or partially prevented from being executed, the offender shall be kept in custody until the Court which passed the sentence can revise it, and the Court may in its discretion either remit such sentence or sentence the offender *in lieu* of whipping, or *in lieu* of so much of the sentence of whipping as was not executed, to imprisonment for a term which may extend to 12 months, which may be in addition to any other punishment to which he has been sentenced for the same offence.

(2) Nothing in this section shall be deemed to authorise any Court to inflict imprisonment for a term exceeding that to which the accused is liable by law or which the Court is competent to inflict.

Commencement of sentence of imprisonment on prisoner already undergoing imprisonment

261.(1) When a person who is an escaped convict or is undergoing a sentence of imprisonment, is sentenced to imprisonment, such imprisonment shall commence either immediately or at the expiration of the imprisonment to which he has been previously sentenced, as the Court awarding the sentence may direct. A sentence of death shall be executed notwithstanding the pendency of any sentence of imprisonment.

(2) Nothing in subsection (1) shall be held to excuse any person from any part of the punishment to which he is liable upon his former or subsequent conviction.

Youthful offenders may be dealt with as provided by Children and Young Persons Act (Chapter 219)
[S 9/2006]

262. When a youthful offender is convicted before any criminal Court of an offence punishable by fine, imprisonment or both, and whether or not the law under which that conviction was made provides that fine, imprisonment or both shall be imposed upon the person so convicted, that court may instead of sentencing him to a fine, or to a sentence of imprisonment of any kind, deal with him as provided by the Children and Young Persons Act (Chapter 219).

Offender may be dealt with as provided by Offenders (Probation and Community Service) Act (Chapter 220) *[S 6/2006]*

263. When any person, not being a youthful offender, is convicted before any criminal Court of an offence punishable by fine, imprisonment or both, and whether or not the law under which that conviction was made provides that fine, imprisonment or both shall be imposed upon the person so convicted, the court may, instead of sentencing him to a fine or imposing any term of imprisonment in default of payment of the fine, or to a sentence of imprisonment of any kind, deal with him as provided by the Offenders (Probation and Community Service) Act (Chapter 220).

263A. *(Repealed by S 6/2006).*

Sentence of police supervision

264.(1)When a person having previously been convicted of an offence punishable with imprisonment of either description for a term of 2 years or more is convicted of any other offence, also punishable with imprisonment of either description for a term of 2 years or more, the High Court or the Court of a Magistrate may, in addition to any other punishment to which it may sentence him, direct that he be subject to the supervision of the police for a period of not more than 3 years commencing immediately after the expiration of the sentence passed on him for the last of such offences.

(2)When any person subject to the supervision of the police is, while still subject to such supervision, sentenced to a term of imprisonment within Brunei Darussalam, any term spent in prison shall be excluded from the period of supervision.

Requirements from persons subject to supervision

265.(1)Every person subject to the supervision of the police who is at large within Brunei Darussalam shall —

*(a)*notify the place of his residence to the officer in charge of the Police District in which such place is situated;

*(b)*whenever he changes his place of residence within Brunei Darussalam, notify such change of residence to the officer in charge of the Police District which he is leaving and to the officer in charge of the Police District into which he goes to reside;

*(c)*whenever he changes his place of residence to a place outside Brunei Darussalam, notify such change of residence to the officer in charge of the Police District which he is leaving.

(2)Every person subject to the supervision of the police, if a male, shall once in each month report himself at such time as is determined by the officer in charge of the Police District in which he resides either to the police officer himself or to such other person as that officer directs, and the police officer or other person may upon each occasion of the report being made, take or cause to be taken the finger prints of the person so reporting.

[S 6/2016]

Penalty for non-compliance with section 265

266. If any person subject to the supervision of the police who is at large within Brunei Darussalam —

*(a)*remains in any place for 48 hours without notifying the place of his residence to the officer in charge of the Police District in which such place is situated;

*(b)*fails to comply with the requirements of section 265 on the occasion of any change of residence; or

*(c)*fails to comply with the requirements of section 265 as to reporting himself once in each month,

he shall in every such case, unless he proves to the satisfaction of the Court before which he is tried, that he did his best to act in conformity with the law, is guilty of an offence and liable on conviction to a fine of $800 and imprisonment for a term not exceeding one year.

Warrant, by whom issuable; return of warrant

267.(1) Every warrant for the execution of any sentence may be issued either by the Judge or Magistrate who passed the sentence, or by his successor, or by another Judge or Magistrate acting in his place.

(2) When a sentence has been fully executed, the officer executing it shall return the warrant to the Court from which it was issued with an indorsement under his hand certifying the manner in which the sentence has been executed.

Saving for prerogative of mercy of His Majesty the Sultan and Yang Di-Pertuan and Constitution *[S 32/2005]*

268. Nothing in this Code shall be deemed to interfere with or derogate from the prerogative of mercy of His Majesty the Sultan and Yang Di-Pertuan and from the provisions of the Constitution of Brunei Darussalam.

CHAPTER XXVII PREVIOUS ACQUITTALS OR CONVICTIONS

Person once convicted or acquitted not to be tried again for same offence

269.(1) A person who has been tried by a Court of competent jurisdiction for an offence and convicted or acquitted of such offence shall, while the conviction or acquittal remains in force, not be liable to be tried again for the same offence nor on the same facts for any other offence for which a different charge from the one made against him might have been made under section 167 or for which he might have been convicted under section 168.

(2) A person acquitted or convicted of any offence may be afterwards tried for any distinct offence for which a separate charge might have been made against him on the former trial under of section 166(1).

(3) A person convicted of any offence constituted by any act causing consequences which, together with such act, constituted a different offence from that of which he was convicted, may be afterwards tried for such last-mentioned offence, if the consequences had not happened or were not known to the Court to have happened at the time when he was convicted.

(4) A person acquitted or convicted of any offence constituted by any acts may, notwithstanding such acquittal or conviction, be subsequently charged with and tried for any other offence constituted by the same acts which he may have committed, if the Court by which he was first tried was not competent to try the offence with which he is subsequently charged.

(5) The dismissal of a complaint or the discharge of the accused is not an acquittal for the purposes of this section.

Illustrations

(a) A is tried upon a charge of theft as a servant and acquitted. He cannot afterwards, while the acquittal remains in force, be charged upon the same facts with theft as a servant, or with theft simply, or with criminal breach of trust.

(b) A is tried upon a charge of murder and acquitted. There is no charge of robbery but it appears from the facts that A committed robbery at the time when the murder was committed; he may afterwards be charged with and tried for robbery.

(c) A is tried for causing grievous hurt and convicted. The person injured afterwards dies. A may be tried again for culpable homicide.

(d) A is tried and convicted of the culpable homicide of B. A may not afterwards be tried on the same facts for the murder of B.

(e) A is charged and convicted of voluntarily causing hurt to B. A may not afterwards be tried for voluntarily causing grievous hurt to B on the same facts unless the case comes within subsection (3).

Plea of previous acquittal or conviction

270.(1) The plea of a previous acquittal or conviction may be pleaded either orally or in writing and may be in the following form or to the following effect —

"The defendant says that by virtue of section 269 of the Criminal Procedure Code, he is not liable to be tried".

(2) Such plea may be pleaded together with any other plea, but the issue raised by such plea shall be tried and disposed of before the issues raised by the other pleas are tried.

(3) On the trial of an issue on a plea of a previous acquittal or conviction, the proceedings of the Court on the former trial, and the proceedings (if any) of any preliminary inquiry on the previous or subsequent charge, shall be admissible in evidence to prove or disprove the identity of the charges.

PART VII APPEALS, REFERENCE AND REVISION

CHAPTER XXVIII APPEALS

Dissatisfied person may appeal

271. Except as provided for in section 275, the accused person, the complainant or the Public Prosecutor, if he is dissatisfied with any judgment, sentence or order pronounced by any Magistrate in a criminal case or matter to which he is a party, may appeal to the High Court against such judgment, sentence or order for any error in law or in fact, or on the ground of the excessive severity or of the inadequacy of the sentence.

Procedure

272.(1) The appellant shall within 14 days from the time of such judgment, sentence or order being passed or made, file a petition in the Court of a Magistrate, paying at the same time the prescribed appeal fee.

(2) If the appellant is in custody, he may give notice of appeal within the said 14 days either orally or in writing to the officer in charge of the prison, and on payment of the prescribed appeal fee, the officer shall forthwith forward the notice or the purport thereof to the Court of a Magistrate.

(3) Every such petition of appeal shall be addressed to the High Court and shall state shortly the substance of the judgment appealed against and the grounds of appeal, and shall be signed by the appellant except where such notice is given orally as provided in subsection (2).

(4) No fee shall be payable when the appeal is made by a public servant acting in his official capacity.

273. — 274. *(No sections).*

Appeal against acquittal

275. When an accused person has been acquitted by a Magistrate, or where the appeal is on the ground that the sentence is insufficient, there shall be no appeal except by, or with the sanction in writing of, the Public Prosecutor:

Provided that the petition of appeal required by section 272 may be filed provisionally pending the receipt of the sanction of the Public Prosecutor under this section.

Copy of record and petition to be sent to appellate Court

276.(1)When the appellant has complied with the provisions of section 272, and subject to the provisions of section 275, the Court appealed from shall make and transmit to the High Court a certified copy of the record of the proceedings in the case together with the petition of appeal.

(2)The originals of any documents which were put in at the trial shall, together with certified copies and if necessary, translations thereof, be forwarded with the record, and the Court shall also forward any other exhibits which it considers desirable.

Summary rejection of appeal

277.(1)On receiving the documents mentioned in section 276, the Judge shall peruse the document, and if he considers that there is no sufficient ground for interfering, he may reject the appeal summarily:

Provided that no appeal shall be rejected summarily except in the case mentioned in subsection (2), unless the appellant has had a reasonable opportunity of being heard either personally or in writing in support of the appeal.

(2)Where —

*(a)*an appeal is brought on the ground that the conviction is against the weight of the evidence or that the sentence is excessive; and

*(b)*it appears to the Judge that the evidence is sufficient to support the conviction and that there is nothing in the circumstances of the case which could raise a reasonable doubt whether the conviction was right or lead him to consider that the sentence ought to be reduced,

the appeal may without being set down for hearing, be summarily rejected by an order certifying that the appeal has been lodged without any sufficient ground of complaint.

(3)If an appeal is dismissed summarily, any appeal fee paid shall be refunded to the appellant.

Appeal specially allowed in certain cases

278. The Judge may, on the application of any person desirous of appealing who may be debarred from doing so upon the ground that he has not observed some formality or requirement of this Code, permit an appeal upon such terms and with such directions to the parties as he shall consider desirable, in order that substantial justice may be done in the matter.

Stay of execution pending appeal

279. Except in the case of a sentence of whipping (the execution of which shall be stayed pending appeal), no appeal shall operate as a stay of execution, but the Court passing the sentence or the Court to which the appeal lies or the Chief Justice may stay execution on any judgment, order, conviction or sentence pending appeal, on such terms as to security for the payment of any money or the performance or non-performance of any act or the suffering of any punishment ordered by or in such judgment, order, conviction or sentence as may seem reasonable.

Setting down appeals

280. If the Judge does not reject the appeal summarily, he shall cause notice to be given to the parties that the appeal will be heard.

Procedure at hearing

281. (1) An appeal may be conducted orally or, if the appellant so desires, in writing.

(2) The appellant, if present, shall be first heard in support of the appeal, the respondent, if present, shall be heard against it, and the appellant shall be entitled to reply.

(3) If the appellant does not appear to support his appeal, the Court shall consider his appeal and may make such order thereon as it may think fit.

Non-appearance of respondent

282. (1) If at the hearing of the appeal, the respondent is not present and the Judge is not satisfied that the notice of appeal was duly served upon him, the Judge shall not make any order in the matter of the appeal adverse to or to the prejudice of the respondent, but shall adjourn the hearing of the appeal to a future day for his appearance, and shall issue the requisite notice to him for service.

(2) If the service of such last-mentioned notice cannot be effected on the respondent, the Judge shall proceed to hear the appeal in his absence.

Arrest of respondent in certain cases

283. When an appeal is presented against an acquittal, the High Court may issue a warrant directing that the accused be arrested and brought before it, and may commit him to prison pending the disposal of the appeal or admit him to bail.

Appeal from acquittal

284. In an appeal from an order of acquittal, the High Court may —

(a) dismiss the appeal;

(b) direct that further inquiry be made or order a new trial on the same or an amended charge; or

(c) find the accused guilty of any offence of which the lower Court might have convicted him and pass sentence on him according to law.

Appeal from conviction

285. In an appeal from a conviction, the High Court may —

(a) dismiss the appeal;

(b) quash the conviction and sentence and acquit or discharge the accused;

(c) direct that further inquiry be made or order a new trial on the same or an amended charge;

(d) quash the conviction and convict the accused of any offence of which the lower Court might have convicted him, and maintain, reduce or increase the sentence or alter the nature of the sentence; or

(e) uphold the conviction and maintain, reduce or increase the sentence or alter the nature of the sentence.

Appeal as to sentence

285A. In an appeal as to sentence, the High Court may reduce or increase the sentence, or alter the nature of the sentence:

Provided that when on an appeal by the Public Prosecutor on the ground of the inadequacy of sentence, the High Court increases or alters the nature of the sentence, the respondent may appeal to the Court of Appeal against such increase or alteration as if he were a person convicted before the High Court appealing against sentence.

Appeal from other order

286. In an appeal from any other order, the High Court may —

(a) dismiss the appeal;

(b) direct that further inquiry be made; or

(c) vary or reverse such order.

Order to take further evidence

287. (1) In dealing with any appeal under this Chapter, the High Court may, if it thinks additional evidence to be necessary or any witness should be recalled, either take such evidence itself or direct it to be taken by a Magistrate.

(2) When the additional evidence is taken by a Magistrate, he shall certify such evidence to the High Court which shall thereupon, as soon as may be, proceed to dispose of the appeal.

(3) Unless the High Court otherwise directs, the accused shall be present when the additional evidence is taken.

Judgment

288. (1) When the appeal has been heard, the High Court shall either at once or on some future day of which notice shall be given to the parties, deliver the judgment.

(2) The judgment shall ordinarily be delivered in open Court but in the absence of the appellant or for other just cause, the Court may deliver judgment by service of a written copy or may direct that the judgment be read out in the lower Court.

Certificate and consequence of judgment

289. (1) Whenever a case is decided on appeal by the High Court under this Chapter, it shall certify its judgment or order to the Court by which the finding, sentence or order appealed against was recorded or passed.

(2) Whenever an appeal is not dismissed, the certificate shall state the grounds upon which the appeal was allowed or the decision of the Courts of Magistrates was varied.

(3) The Court to which the High Court certifies its judgment or order shall thereupon make such orders as are conformable to the judgment or order of the High Court and, if necessary, the record shall be amended in accordance therewith.

Death of accused

290. Every appeal under section 275 shall finally abate on the death of the accused.

Grounds for reversal of judgment of Courts of Magistrates

291. No judgment or order of a Court of a Magistrate shall be reversed or set aside unless it is shown to the satisfaction of the higher Court that the judgment or order was either wrong in law or against the weight of the evidence, or, in the case of a sentence, inappropriate in the circumstances of the case.

Reference to Court of Appeal from Courts of Magistrates on grounds of public interest

291A. (1) When —

(a) an appeal from the decision of a Court of a Magistrate in a criminal matter has been heard and determined by the High Court; and

(b) the Judge who heard the appeal or the Public Prosecutor, on his own behalf or on the application of any party to the proceedings, has, within one month of such determination or within such further time as the Court of Appeal may permit, signed and filed with the Registrar a certificate that the decision of the High Court involves a point of law which it is desirable in the public interest to have determined by the Court of Appeal,

such appeal shall be re-heard by the Court of Appeal.

(2) The provisions of subsection (1) shall, *mutatis mutandis,* apply —

(a) when any order has been made by the High Court to the prejudice of an accused under section 189A(2)*(a)*;

(b) *(deleted by S 6/2016)*;

(c) when the High Court has determined a question of law reserved by a Court of a Magistrate for the consideration of the High Court under section 294; and

(d) when any order has been made by the High Court to the prejudice of the accused under section 298.

(3) Upon the filing of the certificate referred to in subsection (1), the Court of Appeal or any Judge may make such orders as it or he may see fit in respect of the arrest, custody or release on bail of any person convicted, acquitted or discharged as the result of an order of the High Court on the appeal or of the trial Court.

(4) For the purposes of the hearing before the Court of Appeal, the Judge who heard the appeal shall cause to be furnished to the Court of Appeal and to the parties to the appeal, copies of the grounds of his judgment in such appeal.

(5) The powers conferred upon the Public Prosecutor by this section shall be exercisable by the Public Prosecutor only.

Costs

292.(1)In all proceedings under this and the following Chapter, an appellate Court shall have power to award such costs or expenses as the Court thinks fit to be paid by or to the parties thereto.

(2)Costs awarded to be paid by the Public Prosecutor shall be provided out of the general revenue of Brunei Darussalam and be payable by the Permanent Secretary to the Ministry of Finance and the Public Prosecutor shall not be personally liable therefor.

(3)Costs awarded to be paid to the Public Prosecutor shall be paid by the party ordered to pay the costs to the Permanent Secretary of the Ministry of Finance.

Copies of proceedings

293.(1)If any person affected by a judgment or order passed or made by a criminal Court desires to have a copy of any order or deposition or other part of the record, he shall on applying for such copy, be furnished therewith by the Court:

Provided that he pay for the order, deposition or record such reasonable sum as the Court may direct unless the Court for some special reason thinks fit to furnish it free of cost. Such copy shall not be chargeable with stamp duty.

(2)Notwithstanding anything in subsection (1), an accused person committed for trial shall be entitled to receive on request free of charge copy of the depositions of the witnesses recorded by the Magistrate.

CHAPTER XXIX REFERENCE AND REVISION

Reservation of points of law

294.(1)Any Court may, if it thinks fit, at the conclusion of the proceedings or at any time within 7 days from the time of the judgment, acquittal, sentence or order passed or made therein, reserve for the consideration of the High Court any questions of law arising in such proceedings, setting out shortly the facts on which the law is to be applied and the questions of law to be determined thereon.

(2)Every question of law so reserved shall be submitted to such Court in the shape of a special case in the form in the Second Schedule.

(3)Every such special case shall be drawn up by the Magistrate before which the proceedings are held and shall —

*(a)*set out shortly the facts which are considered by the Magistrate to be proved;

*(b)*state the question or questions of law which has or have been reserved for the opinion of the Court;

*(c)*be sent by the Magistrate to the Registrar; and

*(d)*be set down for argument in such manner as the High Court directs.

Determination and power thereon

295.(1)The High Court shall hear and determine the question or questions of law arising on such special case and shall thereupon affirm, amend or reverse the determination in respect of which the special case has been stated or remit the matter to the Magistrate with the opinion of the Court thereon or may make such order in relation to the matter as to the Court seems fit.

(2) No Magistrate who states and delivers a special case in pursuance of this Code shall be liable to any costs in respect thereto.

Power to call for records of Court of Magistrate

296. A Judge may call for and examine the record of any proceeding before any Court of a Magistrate for the purpose of satisfying himself as to the correctness, legality or propriety of any finding, sentence or order recorded or passed and as to the regularity of any proceedings of the Court of a Magistrate.

Powers to order further inquiry

297. On examining any record under section 296 or otherwise, the revising Judge may direct the Magistrate to make, and the Magistrate shall make, further inquiry into any complaint which has been dismissed under section 135, or into the case of any accused person who has been discharged.

Powers on revision

298. (1) A revising Judge may, in any case, the record of proceedings of which has been called for by himself or which otherwise comes to his knowledge, in his discretion, exercise any of the powers conferred by sections 279, 283, 284, 285, 286, 287 and 292, or may make such other as he may deem fit.

(2) No order under this section shall be made to the prejudice of the accused unless he has had an opportunity of being heard, either personally or in writing, in his own defence.

Permission for parties to appear

299. No party has any right to be heard before a Judge when exercising his powers of revision:

Provided that the Judge may, if he thinks fit, when exercising such powers, hear any party and that nothing in this section shall be deemed to affect section 298(2).

Orders on revision

300. When a case is revised under this Chapter by a Judge, he shall certify his decision or order to the Court by which the finding, sentence or order revised was recorded or passed stating where such finding, sentence or order has been varied, and the grounds for such variation; and the Court to which the decision or order is so certified shall thereupon make such orders as are conformable to the decision so certified and, if necessary, the record shall be amended in accordance therewith.

301. *(No section).*

PART VIII SPECIAL PROCEEDINGS

CHAPTER XXX INQUESTS

Meaning of "cause of death"

302. In this Chapter, "cause of death" include not only the apparent cause of death as ascertainable by inspection or *post mortem* examination of the body of the deceased, but also all matters necessary to enable an opinion to be formed how the deceased came by his death and whether his death resulted in any way from, or was accelerated by, any unlawful act or omission on the part of any other person.

Duty of officer in charge of station

303.(1)If an officer in charge of a police station receives information that —

*(a)*a person has committed suicide;

*(b)*a person has been killed by another, or by an animal, or by machinery, or by an accident;

*(c)*a person has died under circumstances in which some other person may have committed an offence; or

*(d)*a person has died or has disappeared in circumstances which raise reasonable presumption that he has died, and the cause of such death or presumed death is not known,

he shall —

(i)immediately give information thereof to a Magistrate and himself immediately proceed or shall direct some other police officer immediately to proceed to the place where the body of such deceased person is, or, if the body has disappeared, to the place where the deceased person was last seen alive; and

(ii)there make an investigation and draw up a report of the apparent cause of death, describing, if the body is available, such wounds, fractures, bruises and other marks as may be found thereon, and stating in what manner or by what weapon or instrument (if any) the same appear to have been inflicted, and, whether the body is available or not, giving an account of such objects and circumstances as in his opinion may relate to the cause of death or the person (if any) who caused the death:

Provided that if no police officer is available to make the investigation required by this subsection, a Magistrate may direct a fit and proper person (in this section referred to as an authorised officer) to carry out such investigation and to draw up the report and forward it to the officer in charge of the police station:

Provided further that if the Magistrate is satisfied that no useful purpose would be served by any person proceeding to the place where the body is or, if the body has disappeared, to the place where the body was last seen alive, he may by order in writing under his hand dispense with such requirement.

(2)Any police or authorised officer making an investigation under this section may exercise all the powers granted to a police officer under the provisions of Chapter XIII.

(3)A report of such investigation shall be made and signed by the officer in charge of the police station and forwarded by him to the Magistrate:

Provided that if as a result of the investigation the officer drafts a charge under section 123 in respect of the death of such person, he shall forward the report to the Public Prosecutor and shall inform the Magistrate in writing of the commencement of such proceedings.

Duty of officer to arrange for *post mortem* examination in certain cases

304.(1)Every person making an investigation under section 303 shall, if there appears to him any reason to suspect that —

*(a)*the deceased came by his death in a sudden or unnatural manner or by violence; or

*(b)*his death resulted in any way from or was accelerated by any unlawful act or omission on the part of any other person,

at once inform the nearest medical officer, and shall take or send the body to the nearest Government hospital or other convenient place for the holding of a *post mortem* examination of the body by a medical officer:

Provided that if that person is satisfied as to the cause of death and that the deceased came by his death by accident, or that in all the circumstances of the case including the state of the body and the difficulties of communication, he is of the opinion that no useful purpose would be served by a further examination, he may order the body to be buried forthwith.

(2)The person making the investigation shall not remove the body if it appears to him that it should be viewed by a Magistrate in the place where it was found.

(3)Where it is not practicable to obtain the services of a medical officer, a hospital assistant may perform the duties required by this section.

Post mortem examination of body

305.(1)Upon receiving the information referred to in section 304, a medical officer or hospital assistant shall, as soon as practicable, make *post mortem* examination of the body of the deceased.

(2)The medical officer or hospital assistant, if it is necessary in order to ascertain the cause of death, shall extend the examination to the dissection of the body and an analysis of any portion thereof, and may cause any portion thereof to be transmitted to the Director-General of Medical Services.

[GN 273/2002]

Report of medical officer

306. The medical officer or hospital assistant making any such examination shall draw up a report of the appearance of the body and of the conclusion which he draws therefrom, and shall certify as to the cause of death and shall date and sign the report and transmit it to the Magistrate or officer in charge of a police station who shall attach it to the report forwarded under section 303.

Duty of Magistrate on receipt of report

307.(1)If the Magistrate shall be satisfied as to the cause of death and that the death did not result in any way from or was not accelerated by any unlawful act or omission without holding an inquest under this Chapter, he shall —

*(a)*report to the Public Prosecutor the cause of death as ascertained to his satisfaction, with his reasons for being so satisfied; and

*(b)*at the same time transmit to the Public Prosecutor all reports and documents in his possession connected with the matter.

(2)A Magistrate may in his discretion hold an inquest if there is no body available in the circumstances mentioned in section 303(1).

(3)A Magistrate shall not hold any inquest under this Chapter if he has reason to believe that criminal proceedings against any person for having caused the death of the deceased have been or are about to be commenced.

(4) In all other cases, the Magistrate shall proceed as soon as may be to hold an inquest under this Chapter.

Death of person in custody of police or in psychiatric facility [S 25/2014]

308. Notwithstanding the provisions of section 307, when any person dies while in the custody of the police or in a psychiatric facility or prison, the officer who had the custody of such person or was in charge of the psychiatric facility or prison, as the case may be, shall forthwith give intimation of the death to the nearest Magistrate, and the Magistrate or some other Magistrate shall, in the case of death in the custody of the police, and in other cases may, if he thinks expedient, hold an inquest into the cause of death and for such purpose may designate any person to make the investigation and report referred to in section 303 and that person shall for the purposes of the investigation be deemed to be a police officer.

[S 25/2014]

Powers of Magistrate

309. (1) A Magistrate holding an inquest under this Chapter shall have all the powers which he would have in holding an inquiry into an offence.

(2) A Magistrate holding an inquest under this Chapter if he considers it expedient that the body of the deceased person should be examined by a medical officer or hospital assistant in order to discover the cause of death may, whether a *post mortem* examination has been made under section 305 or not, issue his order to a medical officer or hospital assistant to make a *post mortem* examination of the body, and may for such purpose order the body to be exhumed.

(3) The Magistrate holding the inquest may, if he thinks fit, summon to assist him a jury consisting of not less than three and not more than five persons of whom at least half shall, if possible, be of the same race as the deceased.

Magistrate may view body

310. The Magistrate holding an inquest shall ordinarily view the body of the deceased and may for that purpose cause such body to be exhumed:

Provided that a Magistrate may in his discretion dispense with viewing the body if, for a reason which he shall record, he considers it to be unnecessary.

Inquiries to be made by Magistrate

311. A Magistrate holding an inquest shall inquire when, where, how and after what manner the deceased came by his death and also whether any person is criminally concerned in the cause of such death.

Evidence and finding to be recorded

312. (1) The Magistrate holding an inquest under this Chapter shall record the evidence and his finding thereon, and shall forthwith transmit to the Public Prosecutor the original of such evidence and finding duly authenticated by his signature, or a copy of such evidence and finding certified under his hand as correct.

(2) The place in which any inquest under this Chapter is held shall be a place open to the public. But a Magistrate conducting an inquest may, on special grounds of public policy or expediency, in his discretion, exclude the public or any person or persons in particular at any stage of the inquest from the place in which the inquest is being held.

Powers of Public Prosecutor and High Court as to inquests

313.(1) Notwithstanding anything in section 307, the Public Prosecutor may at any time direct a Magistrate to hold an inquest under this Chapter into the cause of, and the circumstances connected with, any death such as is referred to in sections 303 and 308, and the Magistrate to whom such direction is given shall thereupon proceed to hold an inquest and shall record his finding as to the cause of death and also as to any of the circumstances connected therewith with regard to which the Public Prosecutor may have directed him to make inquiry.

(2) When the proceedings at any inquest under this Chapter have been closed and it appears to the Public Prosecutor that further investigation is necessary, the Public Prosecutor may direct the Magistrate to reopen the inquest and to make further investigation, and thereupon the Magistrate shall have full power to reopen the inquest and make further investigation and thereafter to proceed in the same manner as if the proceedings at the inquest had not been closed:

Provided that this subsection shall not apply to any inquest at which a finding of murder or culpable homicide not amounting to murder has been returned against any person.

(3) When giving any direction under this section, the Public Prosecutor may also direct whether the body shall or shall not be exhumed.

(4) All directions given under this section shall be complied with by the Magistrate to whom they are addressed without unnecessary delay.

(5) If it is made to appear to the Public Prosecutor that it is expedient that an inquest commenced by one Magistrate should be continued by another, he may direct both Magistrates accordingly and the Magistrates shall comply with the direction.

Admissibility of medical report in certain cases

314.(1) The medical officer or hospital assistant who made the *post mortem* examination of the body of the deceased shall when possible be called as a witness but in his absence for reasonable cause, the written report of the medical officer or hospital assistant shall be admissible in evidence.

(2) The written report shall be subject to such deduction from its weight as the Court deems proper to make by reason of the report not having been made upon oath and the accused person not having any opportunity of cross-examination.

Procedure where jury has been summoned

314A.(1) If a jury has been summoned under section 309(3), the Magistrate shall not be required to arrive at or record a finding but shall direct the jury as to their verdict and shall record the verdict of such jury or, if they fail to agree, of the majority thereof which shall be deemed to be the finding and sections 312 and 313 shall in such case be construed with the modifications necessary to give effect to this section.

(2) The jury or a majority thereof, as the case may be, shall sign the verdict recorded under subsection (1).

CHAPTER XXXI PERSONS OF UNSOUND MIND

Procedure where accused is of unsound mind

315.(1) When a Court holding an inquiry or a trial has reason to suspect that the accused person is of unsound mind and consequently incapable of making his defence, it shall in the first instance inquire into the fact of such unsoundness, and if not satisfied that such person is capable of making his defence, shall postpone the inquiry or trial and shall remand him to a hospital for a period not exceeding one month.

(2)The medical officer of the hospital shall keep the person under observation during the period of his remand and before the expiry of the period, shall certify under his hand to the Court his opinion as to the state of mind of the person, and if he is unable within the period to form any definite conclusion, shall so certify to the Court and shall ask for a further remand which may extend to 2 months.

Certificate of medical officer

316.(1)If the medical officer shall certify that the accused person is of sound mind and capable of making his defence, the Court shall proceed with the inquiry or trial.

(2)If the medical officer shall certify that the person is of unsound mind and incapable of making his defence, the Court shall, if satisfied of the fact, find accordingly, and thereupon the inquiry or trial, as the case may be, shall be postponed.

(3)The certificate of the medical officer shall be receivable as evidence under this section, but the Court may require the personal attendance of the medical officer.

(4)If the accused person is certified to be of unsound mind and incapable of making his defence, it shall not be necessary for him to be present in Court during proceedings under this Chapter.

Release of person of unsound mind pending investigation or trial

317.(1)Whenever an accused person is found to be of unsound mind and incapable of making his defence, the Court, if the offence charged is bailable, may in its discretion release him on sufficient security being given that he shall be properly taken care of and shall be prevented from doing injury to himself or to any other person, and for his appearance when required before the Court or such officer as the Court appoints in that behalf or —

*(a)*in the case of a Court of a Magistrate, remand him to a prison or hospital or other suitable place of safe custody and refer the case to a Judge who may —

(i)release him on security being given as provided in this subsection;

(ii)make further enquiry or direct that further enquiry be made or order him to be tried; or

(iii)order him to be confined in a prison or hospital or other suitable place of safe custody and report the case to the Permanent Secretary to the Office of the Prime Minister*;

*(b)*in the case of the High Court, order him to be confined in a prison or hospital or other suitable place of safe custody and report the case to the Permanent Secretary to the Office of the Prime Minister* but without prejudice to the provisions of section 323.

(2)If the offence charged is non-bailable, the Court —

*(a)*in the case of a Court of a Magistrate, shall remand the accused person to a prison or hospital or other suitable place of safe custody and refer the case to a Judge who may —

(i)release him on security being given as provided in subsection (1);

(ii)make further enquiry or direct that further enquiry be made or order him to be tried; or

(iii)order him to be confined in a prison or hospital or other suitable place of safe custody and report the case to the Permanent Secretary to the Office of the Prime Minister*;

(b) in the case of the High Court —

(i) release him on security being given as provided in subsection (1); or

(ii) order him to be confined in a prison or hospital or other suitable place of safe custody and report the case to the Permanent Secretary to the Office of the Prime Minister*.

(3) Where any case is reported to the Permanent Secretary to the Office of the Prime Minister* under the provisions of subsection (1) or (2), the Permanent Secretary to the Office of the Prime Minister* shall order the accused person to be confined in a psychiatric facility, prison or other suitable place of safe custody during the pleasure of His Majesty the Sultan and Yang Di-Pertuan.

[S 25/2014]

Inquiry or trial

318. When the accused has been released under section 317, the Court may at any time require him to appear or be brought before it and may again proceed under section 315.

Defence of mental disorder at preliminary inquiry *[S 25/2014]*

319. When the accused person appears to be of sound mind at the time of a preliminary inquiry, the Magistrate, notwithstanding that it is alleged that at the time when the act was committed, in respect of which the accused person is charged, he was by reason of unsoundness of mind incapable of knowing the nature of the act or that it was wrong or contrary to law, shall proceed with the case and, if the accused person ought, in the opinion of the Magistrate to be committed for trial before the High Court, the Magistrate shall so commit him.

Defence of insanity on trial *[S 25/2014]*

320. Where —

(a) any act or omission is charged against any person as an offence; and

(b) it is given in evidence on the trial of such person for that offence that he was insane so as not to be responsible for his action at the time when the act was done or omission made,

then if it appears to the Court before which such person is tried that he did the act or made the omission charged but was insane as aforesaid at the time when he did the act or made the omission, the Court shall make a special finding to the effect that the accused was guilty of the act or omission charged but was insane as aforesaid when he did the act or made the omission.

Order for detention

321. (1) When a special finding under section 320 is made by any Court of a Magistrate, it shall report the case for the order of a Judge and shall meanwhile order the person in respect of whom it has made the finding, to be kept in custody in any prison or hospital or in such place and in such manner as the Court shall direct.

(2) If the Judge is satisfied with such special finding, he shall order that such person be confined in a psychiatric facility, prison or other suitable place of safe custody pending the order of the Permanent Secretary to the Office of the Prime Minister* under subsection (5).

[S 25/2014]

(3) If, after such inquiry as he considers necessary, the Judge is not satisfied with the special findings, he may make further inquiry or direct that further inquiry be made or order a new trial on the same or on an amended charge with such direction to the Court of a Magistrate as he shall think fit.

(4) When a special finding under section 320 is made by the High Court, it shall report the case to the Permanent Secretary to the Office of the Prime Minister* and order the person in respect of whom it has made such finding to be confined in a psychiatric facility, prison or suitable place of safe custody pending the order of the Permanent Secretary to the Office of the Prime Minister* under subsection (5).

[S 25/2014]

(5) Where any case has been reported to the Permanent Secretary to the Office of the Prime Minister* under subsection (2) or (4), the Permanent Secretary to the Office of the Prime Minister* shall order the person in respect of whom a special finding has been made to be confined in a psychiatric facility, prison or other suitable place of safe custody during the pleasure of His Majesty the Sultan and Yang Di-Pertuan.

[S 25/2014]

Visiting of prisoners of unsound mind

322. When any person is confined under the provisions of section 247, 317 or 321, two medical officers shall visit him in order to ascertain his state of mind, once at least in every 12 months, and they shall thereupon make a report to the Permanent Secretary to the Office of the Prime Minister* on the state of mind of that person.

Procedure when prisoner of unsound mind reported able to make defence

323. If the person is confined under the provision of section 317 and —

(a) the medical officers certify that in their opinion the person is capable of making his defence; and

(b) the Public Prosecutor certifies that in his opinion it is in the public interest that the trial of the person shall proceed,

he shall be taken before the Court at such time as the Court appoints, and if the Court is satisfied that such person is capable of making his defence, shall proceed with the trial.

Procedure where person of unsound mind appears to be fit for discharge

324. (1) If it is made to appear to His Majesty the Sultan and Yang Di-Pertuan by a medical report under section 322 or otherwise that a person detained or confined under the provisions of section 247, 317 or 321, in this section referred to as the patient, may have recovered his sanity and that his discharge may be warranted then, if His Majesty the Sultan and Yang Di-Pertuan is of the opinion that the discharge of the patient either unconditionally or under the provisions of sections 325 and 325A is warranted, he shall proceed to order his discharge:

Provided that if the patient is confined under the provisions of section 317, this section shall apply only if the Public Prosecutor shall have informed His Majesty the Sultan and Yang Di-Pertuan that he has declined to certify to the effect mentioned in section 323*(b)*:

Provided further that if the prisoner is confined under the provisions of section 247, His Majesty the Sultan and Yang Di-Pertuan may, *in lieu* of discharging the prisoner, order that he be transferred to a prison to serve the remainder of any sentence of imprisonment remaining unexpired and that it shall be a condition of any discharge under this subsection that the balance of any sentence of imprisonment shall have been remitted or shall be remitted from a date not later than the date as from which the discharge is to take effect.

(2) For the purposes of assisting him in forming an opinion under subsection (1), His Majesty the Sultan and Yang Di-Pertuan may in his discretion appoint a Commission consisting of a Judge or a Magistrate and such number of suitable persons or other suitable persons, as he shall deem fit, to inquire formally into the question whether the discharge of the patient is warranted.

(3) A Commission appointed under subsection (2) shall sit in camera:

Provided that the patient or his representative and the Attorney General or his representative shall have the right without leave to appear and be heard by the Commission.

Delivery of person of unsound mind to care of relative

325.(1) Whenever any relative or friend of any person confined under the provisions of section 247, 317 or 321 desires that he be delivered over to his care and custody, the Permanent Secretary to the Office of the Prime Minister*, upon the application of the relative or friend and on his giving security to the satisfaction of the Permanent Secretary to the Office of the Prime Minister*, that the person delivered shall be properly taken care of and shall be prevented from doing injury to himself or to any other person, may, in his discretion, order the person to be delivered to the relative or friend.

(2) Whenever the person is so delivered, it shall be upon condition that he shall be produced for the inspection of such officer and at such times as the Permanent Secretary to the Office of the Prime Minister* directs.

(3) The provisions of section 322 or 324 shall, *mutatis mutandis,* apply to persons delivered under the provisions of this section, and the certificate of the inspecting officer appointed under this section shall be receivable as evidence.

Conditional discharge of person who has been of unsound mind

325A.(1) Whenever the Permanent Secretary to the Office of the Prime Minister* orders the discharge of a person confined under the provisions of section 247, 317, 321 or under the provisions of this section, it shall be lawful for him to make the discharge conditional upon the compliance by the person with such conditions relating to the further medical observation, care, control or supervision of that person as he may consider desirable in the interest of that person or in the public interest and the contravention of any such condition by that person shall constitute an offence punishable with a fine of $8,000.

(2) Upon conviction of that person of an offence under subsection (1), the Magistrate may, if he has any reason to believe that there has been a relapse in the mental condition of that person, *in lieu* of or in addition to any penalty under subsection (1), order that person to be confined in prison, hospital or in such place as the Magistrate shall think fit.

(3) When any person is confined under the provisions of subsection (2), he shall be visited by two medical officers who shall make a report to the Permanent Secretary to the Office of the Prime Minister* on the state of mind of that person.

(4) Upon the receipt of a report under subsection (3), the Permanent Secretary to the Office of the Prime Minister* may, if the medical officers so recommend, revoke the order by which that person was discharged whereupon that person shall be liable to be dealt with in like manner as if he had never been discharged or shall order that person be discharged.

CHAPTER XXXII PROCEEDINGS IN CASE OF CERTAIN OFFENCES AFFECTING ADMINISTRATION OF JUSTICE

Procedure in certain cases mentioned in section 132

326. When any civil or criminal Court is of opinion that there is ground for inquiring into any offence referred to in section 132(1)*(b)*, *(c)*, *(d)* or *(f)* and committed before it or brought under its notice in the course of a judicial

proceeding, such Court, after making any preliminary inquiry that may be necessary, may send the case for inquiry or trial to a Court having jurisdiction and may send the accused in custody, or take sufficient security for his appearance, before such Court, and may bind over any person to appear and give evidence on such inquiry or trial.

Power of Courts in certain offences committed before themselves

327. The High Court or a Court of a Magistrate may charge a person for any offence referred to in section 132(1)*(b)*, *(c)*, *(d)* or *(e)* and committed before it or brought under its notice in the course of a judicial proceeding, and may commit for trial to a Court having jurisdiction, or admit to bail and itself try such person upon its own charge.

Summary procedure for offences committed in Court

328. Where any such offence as is described in section 175, 178, 179, 180 or 228 of the Penal Code (Chapter 22) is committed in the view or presence of any Court of a Magistrate whether civil or criminal, the Court may cause the offender to be detained in custody, and at any time before the rising of the Court on the same day the Court may, if it thinks fit, take cognisance of the offence and sentence the offender to imprisonment for 14 days or to a fine of $400, and in default of payment to imprisonment for one month.

Record of facts constituting offence

329. (1) In every such case, the Court shall record the facts constituting the offence, with the statement (if any) made by the offender as well as the finding and sentence.

(2) If the offence is an offence punishable under section 228 of the Penal Code (Chapter 22), the record must show the nature and stage of the judicial proceedings in which the Court interrupted or insulted was sitting, and the nature of the interruption or insult

Alternative procedure

330. If the Court, in any case, considers that a person accused of any of the offences referred to in section 328 and committed in its view or presence may be better dealt with by ordinary process of law, the Court, after recording the facts constituting the offence and the statement of the accused as provided under section 329, may —

(a) direct the accused to be prosecuted; and

(b) require security to be given for the appearance of such accused person before a Magistrate or, if sufficient security is not given, forward such person, under custody, to a Magistrate.

Power to remit punishment

331. When any Court has, under section 328, adjudged an offender to punishment for refusing or omitting to do anything which he was lawfully required to do or for any intentional insult or interruption, the Court may, in its discretion, discharge the offender or remit the punishment on his submission to the order or requisition of the Court or on apology being made to its satisfaction.

Refusal to give evidence

332. If any witness before a Court of a Magistrate —

(a) refuses to answer such questions as are put to him or to produce any document in his possession or power which the Court requires him to produce; and

(b) does not offer any reasonable excuse for such refusal,

the Court may for reasons to be recorded in writing, sentence him to imprisonment for 14 days, unless in the meantime such person consents to be examined and to answer or to produce the document. In the event of his persisting in this refusal, he may be dealt with according to the provisions of section 328 or 330, notwithstanding any sentence he may have undergone under this section.

Appeal

333. (1) Any person sentenced by any lower Court under the provisions of this Chapter may appeal to the Court to which an appeal ordinarily lies.

(2) The provisions of Chapter XXVIII shall, so far as they are applicable, apply to appeals under this section.

(3) The provisions of Chapter XXIX shall also apply to all proceedings by a Magistrate under this Chapter.

334. *(No section).*

CHAPTER XXXIII MAINTENANCE OF WIVES AND CHILDREN

335. — 340A. *(No sections).*

CHAPTER XXXIV DIRECTIONS OF NATURE OF HABEAS CORPUS

Power of Court to make certain orders

341. The High Court may, whenever it thinks fit, direct that —

(a) any person be set at liberty who —

(i) is detained in any prison within Brunei Darussalam or a warrant of extradition; or

(ii) is alleged to be illegally or improperly detained in public or private custody within Brunei Darussalam;

(b) any defendant in custody under a writ of attachment be brought before the Court to be dealt with according to law.

Form of application

342. Every application to bring up before the Court a person detained on a warrant of extradition or alleged to be illegally or improperly detained in custody shall be supported by oral evidence or affidavit stating where and by whom the person is detained and, so far as they are known, the facts relating to such detention, with the object of satisfying the Court that there is probable ground for supposing that the person is detained against his will and without just cause.

Warrant

343.(1) In any case in which the Court orders a person in custody to be brought before it, a warrant in writing shall be prepared and signed by the Judge or Registrar and sealed with the seal of the Court.

(2) Such warrant shall, unless otherwise ordered, be delivered to the applicant who shall cause it to be served personally upon the person to whom it is directed or otherwise as the Court shall direct.

Attendance of prisoner in criminal case

344.(1) Whenever the presence of any person detained in a prison situate within Brunei Darussalam is required in any criminal Court, the Court may issue a warrant addressed to the officer in charge of the prison requiring the production of such person before the Court in proper custody at a time and place to be named in the warrant.

(2) The officer in charge of the prison shall cause the person named in the warrant to be brought as directed and shall provide for his safe custody during his absence from prison.

(3) Every such Court may, by indorsement on the warrant, require the person named in the warrant to be brought up at any time to which the matter wherein such person is required, is adjourned.

(4) Every warrant shall be sealed with the seal of the Court and signed by the Judge, Registrar or Magistrate, as the case may be.

Appeal

345. Any person aggrieved by any decision or direction of the Court under this Chapter may appeal to the Court to which an appeal ordinarily lies.

PART IX SUPPLEMENTARY PROVISIONS

CHAPTER XXXV BAIL

Bail may be discretionary or obligatory

346. Bail shall be discretionary for the purposes of this Chapter when —

(a) it is declared by any written law to be discretionary in respect of any offence;

(b) the offence is declared by the First Schedule to be non-bailable; or

(c) the offence alleged against the person arrested or detained is punishable by imprisonment for a term of 2 years or more, whether or not it is also punishable by fine.

Bail shall be obligatory in any case in which it is not discretionary.

Duty and discretion to admit bail

347.(1) When any person other than a person accused of an offence punishable with death, imprisonment for life or imprisonment for 15 years or more is arrested or detained without warrant by a police officer or upon a warrant under which there is no endorsement under section 44 that a security may be taken for his appearance or appears or is brought before a Magistrate or Court, and is prepared at any time while in the custody of such officer or at any state of the proceedings before such Court to give bail, such person —

(a) shall, if the case is one in which bail is obligatory, be entitled subject to the provisions of this Chapter to be admitted to bail by a Magistrate or Court or any police officer not below the rank of Inspector; and

(b) may, if the case is one in which bail is discretionary, be admitted to bail in the discretion of such Magistrate or Court or any police officer not below the rank of Inspector:

Provided that it shall be lawful for any such officer in exercising this discretion to have regard to any instructions in connection therewith which may be issued by the Public Prosecutor for the guidance of police officers:

Provided further that such officer or Court may instead of taking bail from such person, release him on his executing a bond without sureties for his appearance as provided under subsections (2) and (3).

(2) Notwithstanding anything contained in subsection (1), the High Court may in any case direct that any person be admitted to bail irrespective of the offence of which he is accused.

(3) Any Court may at any subsequent stage of any proceedings under this Code —

(a) cause any person who has been released under this section to be arrested and may commit him to custody; or

(b) direct that any bail required by any police officer or any Court of a Magistrate be reduced or increased:

Provided that the Court of Appeal may exercise the power hereby conferred as if the words "of a Magistrate" in paragraph *(b)* had been deleted.

(4) Where any police officer exercises the power of granting bail under this section he shall immediately report the complaint and details of the bail allowed to a Magistrate.

Amount of bond

348. The amount of every bond executed under this Chapter shall be fixed with due regard to the circumstances of the case as being sufficient to secure the attendance of the person arrested but shall not be excessive.

Bond to be executed

349. Before any person is released on bail, or released on his own bond, a bond for such sum of money as the police officer or Court, as the case may be, thinks sufficient shall be executed by that person, and when he is released on bail a bond shall also be executed by one or more sufficient sureties, conditioned that that person shall attend at the time and place mentioned in the bond, and shall continue so to attend until otherwise directed by the police officer or Court, as the case may be.

Person to be released

350. (1) As soon as the bond has been executed, the person for whose appearance it has been executed shall be released and when he is in prison the Court admitting him to bail shall issue an order of release to the officer in charge of the prison, and such officer, on receipt of the order, shall release him.

(2) Nothing in this section or in section 346 or 347 shall be deemed to require the release of any person liable to be detained for some matter other than that in respect of which the bond was executed.

When warrant of arrest may be issued against person bailed

351. If, through mistake, fraud or otherwise, insufficient sureties have been accepted, or if they afterwards become insufficient, the Court admitting him to bail may issue a warrant of arrest directing that the person released on bail be brought before it, and may order him to find sufficient sureties, and on his failing so to do may commit him to prison.

Sureties may apply to have bond discharged. Procedure subsequent thereto

352. (1) All or any sureties for the attendance and appearance of a person released on bail may at any time apply to a Magistrate to discharge the bond either wholly or so far as relates to the applicants.

(2) On such application being made, the Magistrate shall issue his warrant of arrest directing that the person so released be brought before him.

(3) On the appearance of such person pursuant to the warrant, or on his voluntary surrender, the Magistrate shall direct the bond to be discharged, either wholly or so far as relates to the applicants, and shall call upon that person to find other sufficient sureties, and if he fails to do so may commit him to custody.

(4) A surety may at any time arrest the person for whose attendance and appearance he is a surety and forthwith bring him before a Magistrate, who shall thereupon discharge such surety's bond and shall call upon that person to find other sufficient surety, and if he fails to do so shall commit him to custody.

Appeal

353. Any person aggrieved by any order or refusal of any lower Court made under this Chapter may appeal to the Court to which an appeal ordinarily lies.

CHAPTER XXXVI BONDS

Deposit instead of bond

354. When any person is required by any Court or officer to execute a bond, with or without sureties, such Court or officer may permit or require him to deposit a sum of money to such amount as the Court or officer may fix, *in lieu* of the penalty in the bond.

Procedure on forfeiture of bond

355. (1) Whenever it is proved to the satisfaction of the Court by which a bond under this Code has been taken or, when the bond is for appearance before a Court, whenever it is proved to the satisfaction of such Court that the bond has been forfeited, the Court shall record the grounds of such proof and may call upon any person bound by such bond to pay the penalty thereof or to show cause why it should not be paid.

(2) If sufficient cause is not shown and the penalty is not paid, the Court may proceed to recover the bond by issuing a warrant for the attachment and sale of the property belonging to the person.

(3) If the penalty is not paid and cannot be recovered by such attachment and sale, the person so bound shall be liable, by order of the Court which issued the warrant, to imprisonment for a term which may extend to 6 months.

(4) The Court may, in its discretion, remit any portion of the penalty mentioned and enforce payment in part only.

Appeal

356. Any person aggrieved by any order of any lower Court made under this Chapter may appeal to the Court to which an appeal ordinarily lies.

CHAPTER XXXVII DISPOSAL OF PROPERTY SUBJECT OF OFFENCES

Order for custody and disposal of property in certain cases

357.(1) When any property regarding which any offence appears to have been committed, or which appears to have been used for the commission of any offence, is produced before any criminal Court during any inquiry or trial, the Court may —

(a) make such order as it thinks fit for the proper custody of such property pending the conclusion of the inquiry or trial; and

(b) if the property is subject to speedy or natural decay, after recording such evidence as it thinks necessary, order it to be sold or otherwise disposed of.

(2) When an inquiry or a trial in any criminal Court is concluded, the Court may make such order as it thinks fit for the disposal by destruction, confiscation, or delivery to any person claiming to be entitled to possession thereof, or otherwise of any property or document produced before it or in its custody or regarding which any offence appears to have been committed, or which has been used for the commission of any offence.

(3) When the High Court makes such order and cannot through its own officers conveniently deliver the property to the person entitled thereto, such Court may direct that the order be carried into effect by a Magistrate.

(4) Nothing in this section shall be deemed to prohibit any Court from delivering any property under the provisions of subsection (2) to any person claiming to be entitled to the possession thereof, on his executing a bond with or without sureties to the satisfaction of the Court, engaging to restore such property to the Court if the order made under this section is modified or set aside on appeal.

Explanation — In this section, "property" includes, in the case of property regarding which an offence appears to have been committed, not only such property as has been originally in the possession or under the control of any party, but also any property into or for which the same may have been converted or exchanged, and anything acquired by the conversion or exchange, whether immediately or otherwise.

Direction *in lieu* of order

358. *In lieu* of itself making an order under section 357, the Court may direct the property to be delivered to a Magistrate, who shall, in such cases, deal with it as if it had been seized by the police and the seizure had been reported to him in the manner mentioned in this Chapter.

Payment to innocent person of money found on accused

359. When any person is convicted of any offence which includes or amounts to theft or receiving stolen property and it is proved that another person has bought the stolen property from him without knowing or having reason to believe that the property was stolen and that any money has, on his arrest, been taken out of the possession of the convicted person, the Court may, on the application of the purchaser and on the restitution of the stolen property to the person entitled to the possession thereof, order that out of such money a sum not exceeding the price paid by the purchaser be delivered to him.

Stay of order

360. The High Court may direct any order under section 357 or 359 made by a Court of a Magistrate to be stayed pending consideration by the High Court and may modify, alter or annul such order.

Destruction of libellous and other matter

361.(1) On a conviction under section 292, 293, 501 or 502 of the Penal Code (Chapter 22), the Court may order the destruction of all the copies of the thing in respect of which the conviction was had and which are in the custody of the Court or remain in the possession of the person convicted.

(2) The Court may, in the same manner, on a conviction under section 272, 273, 274 or 275 of the Penal Code (Chapter 22), order the food, drink, drug or medical preparation in respect of which the conviction was had to be destroyed.

Restoration of possession of immovable property

362.(1) Whenever a person is convicted of an offence attended by criminal force and it appears to the Court that by such force any person has been dispossessed of any immovable property, the Court may, if it thinks fit, order the property to be restored to the possession of the person who has been dispossessed.

(2) No such order shall prejudice any right or interest to or in the immovable property which any person may be able to establish in a civil suit.

Procedure by police on seizure of property

363.(1) The seizure or finding by any police officer of property taken under section 24 or alleged or suspected to have been stolen or found under circumstances which create suspicion of the commission of any offence shall be forthwith reported to a Magistrate, who shall make such order as he thinks fit respecting the delivery of such property to the person entitled to the possession thereof, or, if such person cannot be ascertained, respecting the custody and production of the property.

(2) If the person so entitled is known, the Magistrate may order the property to be delivered to him on such conditions (if any) as the Magistrate thinks fit. If such person is unknown, the Magistrate may detain it, and shall in such case issue a public notification specifying the articles of which such property consists and requiring any person who may have a claim thereto to appear before him and establish his claim within 6 months from the date of the notification.

(3) The notification shall, if the value of the property exceeds $500, be published in the *Gazette*.

Procedure where no claim established

364.(1) If no person within such period establishes his claim to the property and if the person in whose possession the property was found is unable to show that it was legally acquired by him, the property shall be at the disposal of the Government and may be sold under the order of a Magistrate.

(2) In the case of an order made under this section, an appeal shall lie to the Court to which an appeal ordinarily lies.

Procedure where owner unknown

365. If the person entitled to the possession of the property is unknown or absent and the property is subject to speedy and natural decay, or the Magistrate to whom its seizure or finding is reported is of opinion that its sale would be for the benefit of the owner, the Magistrate may at any time direct it to be sold, and the

provisions of sections 363 and 364 shall, as nearly as may be practicable, apply to the net proceeds of the sale.

Order suspended pending appeal

365A. No order made under this Chapter shall come into force until after the expiration of the time prescribed for instituting an appeal or, if an appeal has been instituted, until the dismissal of the appeal, in the proceedings in respect of which such order was made unless the property is subject to speedy or natural decay in which case a Judge or Magistrate may, after recording such evidence as he thinks necessary, order its disposal immediately.

CHAPTER XXXVIII TRANSFER OF CRIMINAL CASES

Power to transfer cases

366.(1)Whenever it is made to appear to the High Court that —

*(a)*a fair and impartial inquiry or trial cannot otherwise be had;

*(b)*some question of law of unusual difficulty is likely to arise;

*(c)*a view of the place in or near which any offence has been committed may be required for the satisfactory inquiry into or trial of the offence;

*(d)*an order under this section will tend to the general convenience of the parties or witnesses; or

*(e)*such an order is expedient for the ends of justice, or is required by any provision of this Code,

the High Court may order that any offence be inquired into or tried by any specified Court of a Magistrate competent to inquire into or try such offence, or that any particular criminal case be transferred to and tried before the High Court, or that a person committed for trial in one place be tried in another place.

(2)The High Court may exercise any of its powers under this section either on the report of the lower Court, or on the application of a party interested, or on its own initiative.

Application for transfer

367.(1)Every application for the exercise of the power conferred by section 366 may be made personally or in writing and when required shall be supported by affidavit.

(2)When an accused person makes an application under this section, the High Court may, if it thinks fit, direct him to execute a bond, with or without sureties, on condition that he will, if convicted, pay the expenses of the prosecution.

CHAPTER XXXIX IRREGULARITIES IN PROCEEDINGS

368.(*No section*).

Procedure when confession irregularly taken

369. If any Court before which a confession or other statement of an accused person recorded under section 119 or 220 is tendered or has been received in evidence finds that any of the provisions of such section have not been complied with by the Magistrate recording the statement, it shall take evidence that the person duly made the statement recorded and, if it is satisfied of the same, the statement shall be admitted if the error has not injured the accused as to his defence on the merits.

Omission to frame charge

370.(1)No finding or sentence pronounced or passed shall be deemed invalid merely on the ground that no charge was framed unless, in the opinion of the Court of Appeal or revision, a failure of justice has been occasioned thereby.

(2)If the appellate or revising Court thinks that a failure of justice has been occasioned by the omission to frame a charge, it shall order that a charge be framed and that a new trial be held.

Irregularities not to vitiate proceedings

371.(1)Subject to the provisions of sections 369 and 370, no finding, sentence or order passed or made by a Court of competent jurisdiction shall be reversed or altered on account of —

*(a)*any error, omission or irregularity in the complaint, summons, warrant, charge, judgment or other proceedings before or during trial, or in any inquiry or other proceedings under this Code;

*(b)*the want of any sanction required by section 132;

*(c)*the omission to inform an accused person of his rights under section 221;

*(d)*the want of qualification of any assessor;

*(e)*the improper admission or rejection of any evidence; or

*(f)*any misdirection in any charge to assessors,

unless such error, omission, improper admission or rejection of evidence, irregularity, want or misdirection has occasioned a failure of justice.

(2)In determining whether any error, omission or irregularity in any proceedings under this Code has occasioned a failure of justice, the Court shall have regard to the fact whether the objection could and should have been raised at an earlier stage in the proceedings.

Power of Chief Justice to dispense with provisions of Code

372. Where owing to the illiteracy or lack of understanding of any person against whom any proceedings under this Code are being taken, or for other valid reason, it is not in the opinion of the Chief Justice reasonably necessary or practicable to carry out any provision of this Code, the Chief Justice may —

*(a)*authorise any Court or Magistrate to dispense with such provision; and

*(b)*direct either generally or in any particular case or class of case that any Court or Magistrate shall, notwithstanding any of the provisions of this Code, proceed in such manner as the Chief Justice shall direct.

Unlawful distress; irregularity no trespass

373. No distress made under this Code shall be deemed unlawful, nor shall any person making the distress be deemed a trespasser, on account of any defect or want of form in the summons, conviction, writ of distress or other proceedings relating thereto, but all persons aggrieved by such irregularity may recover full satisfaction for the special damage caused thereby in any Court of competent jurisdiction.

CHAPTER XL PUBLIC PROSECUTOR

Public Prosecutor and Deputies

374.(1)The Attorney General shall be the Public Prosecutor and shall have the general direction and control of criminal prosecutions and proceedings under this Code or under any other written law.

(2)His Majesty the Sultan and Yang Di-Pertuan may appoint fit and proper persons to be Deputy Public Prosecutors who shall be under the general control and direction of the Public Prosecutor and may exercise any or all of the powers under this Code as may be delegated to him by the Public Prosecutor.

(3)The Public Prosecutor may, by notification published in the *Gazette,* delegate all or any of the powers vested in him by this Code to any Deputy Public Prosecutor and the exercise of these powers by such Deputy Public Prosecutor shall then operate as if they had been exercised by the Public Prosecutor, provided that the Public Prosecutor may in like manner revoke any delegation made by him under this section.

Conduct of prosecutions

375.(1)Every criminal prosecution and every inquiry shall be conducted —

*(a)*by the Public Prosecutor or a Deputy Public Prosecutor, or by some person expressly authorised in writing by the Public Prosecutor or His Majesty the Sultan and Yang Di-Pertuan;

*(b)*by a police officer; or

*(c)*by an officer of a Government department or of any public utility company in matters which concern his department or company.

(2)In cases where no such officer is available, the prosecution shall be conducted as the Public Prosecutor or the Court shall direct.

(3)In non-seizable cases, any private person may appear in person to prosecute for an offence against his own person or property.

(4)In any case in which a private person is appearing in person under subsection (3), the Public Prosecutor may at any stage of the proceedings by notice in writing or by oral intimation to the Court, given by a person or officer authorised to conduct the case under the provisions of subsection (1) or (2), intervene and assume the conduct of such proceedings; and as from the date of any such intervention, shall be deemed to be a party to the proceedings *in lieu* of such private person.

(5)The provisions of subsection (4) shall apply to any appeal in a criminal prosecution to which the Public Prosecutor is not a party and, subject to the provisions of section 299, shall apply to proceedings by way of revision under Chapter XXIX.

(6)In any case not falling within subsection (3), the proceedings shall be deemed to be conducted by the Public Prosecutor and he shall for all purposes be deemed to be party thereto.

Public Prosecutor may call for police report of record of preliminary inquiry

376.(1)The Public Prosecutor may —

*(a)*at any time call for a copy of the report of any police investigation or for a copy of the record of any preliminary inquiry that has been held under Chapter XVII; or

*(b)*may direct generally that in any specified offence or offences such report or record shall be sent to him,

and the officer or Magistrate shall send such report or record accordingly.

(2)Notwithstanding that the Public Prosecutor has not called for such report or record, the officer making such report or the Magistrate holding such inquiry, if he is in doubt whether a charge can properly be made, or what charge ought to be made against the accused, or what evidence or further evidence ought to be taken, may send a copy of the report or record to the Public Prosecutor.

(3)Pending the instructions of the Public Prosecutor, the inquiry, trial or further consideration of the case shall be adjourned, unless the Public Prosecutor shall otherwise direct.

Power of Public Prosecutor to enter *nolle prosequi*

377.(1)In any criminal case and at any stage thereof before judgment, the Public Prosecutor may, either personally or in writing, inform the Court that he intends that the proceedings shall not continue, and thereupon the accused shall be at once discharged in respect of such charges as may be specified, and if he has been committed to prison shall be released or, if on bail, his bond and that of his sureties, if any, shall be discharged.

(2)Such discharge shall not operate as a bar to any subsequent proceedings against him on account of the same facts.

When Public Prosecutor may direct Magistrate to take further evidence

378.(1)If the Public Prosecutor is of opinion that a criminal offence is disclosed and that further proceedings should be taken against the accused but that the evidence already obtained or taken is in any particular or respect defective and is not sufficient to afford a foundation for a full and proper trial, he may by an order in writing signed by himself require the police to make further investigation or require the Magistrate to hold an inquiry or, if an inquiry has been held, to take such further evidence as may be specified or indicated in the order either by way of examining any witnesses who have already given their testimony, or otherwise to continue the inquiry.

(2)Upon the order of the Public Prosecutor being received by the Magistrate he shall cause the accused person to appear before him and shall hold or shall resume and proceed with the inquiry in pursuance of such order.

(3)If an inquiry or supplemental inquiry is directed to be held the accused person, if at large on bail, shall be called upon by written notice to appear before a Court of a Magistrate, and if in prison shall by an order of the Magistrate be brought before the Court on a day appointed therefor.

(4)All the provisions in respect of the original inquiry shall be applicable, so far as may be, to the supplemental inquiry.

(5)The Magistrate shall at the termination of the inquiry or supplemental inquiry forthwith transmit a copy of the record to the Public Prosecutor.

(6)A supplemental inquiry may be continued by a Magistrate other than the Magistrate who conducted the original inquiry.

(7)The Public Prosecutor may, *in lieu* of or in addition to requiring the Magistrate to take further evidence under subsection (1), give notice to the accused that the prosecution intends to call further evidence at the trial and indicating the nature thereof:

Provided that failure to give such notice or that the notice does not indicate with sufficient clarity the nature of the evidence to be called shall not render the evidence inadmissible but shall entitle the accused to such adjournment, if any, as the Court shall consider may in the interests of justice be required.

Public Prosecutor may alter charge and give instructions

379.In addition to the powers conferred on him by sections 375, 377 and 378, the Public Prosecutor upon receiving a copy of the report of a police investigation or the record of an inquiry may —

*(a)*frame, alter or re-draw the charge or charges against the accused or frame an additional charge or charges against the accused having regard to the provisions of this Code as to the form of charges; and

*(b)*give such instructions with regard to the inquiry as he may consider desirable and the Magistrate shall, subject to this Code, carry into effect the instructions and shall conduct the inquiry accordingly.

CHAPTER XLI GENERAL

Affidavits, before whom sworn

380.(1)Any affidavit if otherwise admissible may be used in a criminal Court if it is sworn or affirmed —

*(a)*in Brunei Darussalam, before any Judge, Registrar, Deputy Registrar, Magistrate or other person lawfully authorised to administer oaths;

*(b)*elsewhere in the Commonwealth, before any Judge, Court, Notary Public or person lawfully authorised to administer oaths;

*(c)*in any other place, before any Consul or Vice-Consul of Brunei Darussalam.

(2)The Court shall take judicial notice of the seal or signature (as the case may be) of any Judge, Court, Notary Public, Consul, Vice-Consul or other person appended or subscribed to any affidavit.

When witness not required to attend

380A.(1)Any document purporting to be a report under the hand of any of the persons mentioned in subsection (2) upon any person, matter or thing examined or analysed by him may be given in evidence in any enquiry, trial or other proceedings under the Supreme Court Act (Chapter 5), the Subordinate Courts Act (Chapter 6), or the Code, unless such person shall be required to attend as witness —

*(a)*by the Court; or

*(b)*by an accused upon giving notice in writing to the prosecution not less than 7 clear days before the commencement of the trial:

Provided always that in any case in which the prosecution intends to give in evidence any such report, a copy thereof shall be delivered to the accused not less than 14 clear days before the commencement of the trial, unless the Court otherwise allows.

(2)The following are persons to whom the provision of subsection (1) applies —

(a) Government medical officers;

(b) any person employed for the time being wholly or partly on analytical work in any department of the Government;

(c) any chemist or any person employed for the time being on analytical work by the Government of the Federation of Malaysia or Singapore;

(d) *(deleted by S 6/2016)*;

(e) any inspector of weights and measures duly appointed as such under the provisions of any written law;

(f) any person or class of persons to whom the Permanent Secretary to the Office of the Prime Minister, notification published in *Gazette*, declares that the provisions of this section shall apply.

[S 6/2016]

(3) Persons referred to in subsection (2) shall by this Code be bound to state the truth in reports made under their hands.

Power of Court to summon and examine persons

381. Any Court may at any stage of any inquiry, trial or other proceedings under this Code summon any person as a witness, or examine any person in attendance though not summoned as a witness, or recall and re-examine any person already examined, and the Court shall summon and examine or recall and re-examine any such person if his evidence appears to it essential to the just decision of the case.

Order for payment of costs of prosecution and compensation

382. (1) When a person is convicted of any crime or offence, the Court may, in its discretion, make either or both of the following orders against him in addition to any other punishment —

(a) an order for the payment by him of the costs of his prosecution or such part thereof as the Court directs;

(b) an order for the payment by him of a sum to be fixed by the Court by way of compensation to any person, or the representatives of any person, injured in respect of his person, character or property by the crime or offence for which the sentence is passed.

(2) The Court shall specify the person to whom any sum in respect of costs or compensation as mentioned in subsection (1), is to be paid, and payment thereof may be enforced in the same manner as if the amount thereof were a fine, or in such other manner as the law for the time being directs.

(3) The Court may direct that an order for payment of costs, or an order for payment of compensation, shall have priority, and, if no direction be given, an order for payment of costs shall have priority over an order for payment of compensation.

(4) An order for payment under this section shall not prejudice any right to a civil remedy for the recovery of any property or for the recovery of damages but the Court shall take into account the amount of compensation paid under the order.

(5) Every order made under this section by a Magistrate shall be appealable to the Court to which an appeal ordinarily lies.

(6) The powers conferred by this section may be exercised on appeal, reference or revision.

Payment of expenses of prosecutors and witnesses

383. In every criminal case, the Court may in its discretion order payment by Government to the prosecutor and to the witnesses both for the prosecution and for the defence, or to such of them as it thinks fit, of the expenses incurred by them severally in and about attending the Court, and also compensation for their trouble and loss of time, subject to such rules as are prescribed.

Rules as to rates etc. *[S 9/2006]*

384. His Majesty the Sultan and Yang Di-Pertuan may make rules for the following matters —

[S 6/2016]

(a) the rates or scales of payment of the expenses and compensation to be ordered;

(b) the form of the certificates mentioned in section 385 and the details to be inserted therein;

(c) the treatment, training and detention of persons sentences to reformative training.

Certificate of Magistrate

385. (1) The Magistrate who commits a case for trial shall certify under his hand in the prescribed form the amount of expenses and compensation allowable to each prosecutor and witness in respect of his attendance before him.

(2) The amount of any other expenses and compensation to the prosecutors and witnesses to whom the High Court orders payment shall be ascertained by the Registrar.

[S 6/2016]

Reward for unusual exertion

386. Whenever it appears to any Court that a private person has shown unusual courage, diligence or exertion in the apprehension of a person accused of having committed, attempted to commit or abetted an offence punishable with death or rigorous imprisonment, such Court may order payment to him by Government of any sum not exceeding $500.

Compensation for family of person killed in arresting

387. If any person is killed in endeavouring to arrest or to keep in lawful custody a person accused as mentioned in section 386, the Minister of Finance, with the approval of His Majesty the Sultan and Yang Di-Pertuan, may order payment by Government to the wife, husband, parent or child of the deceased of such sum or sums as appear reasonable in compensation for the loss sustained.

[S 6/2016]

Recovery of money payable under order

388. Any money (other than a fine) payable by virtue of any order made under this Code shall be recoverable as if it were a fine.

Superior police officer may exercise powers of subordinate officers

389. Any police officer to whom an officer in charge of a police station is subordinate may exercise the same powers as may be exercised by the officer in charge of the police station and any police officer to whom an officer in charge of a Police District is subordinate may exercise the same powers as may be exercised by the officer in charge of the Police District.

Power of police to seize property suspected of being stolen

390. Any member of the Royal Brunei Police Force may seize any property which is alleged or may be suspected to have been stolen, or which is found under circumstances which create suspicion that an offence has been committed, and such member, if subordinate to the officer in charge of the nearest police station, shall forthwith report the seizure to such officer.

Person released on bail to give address for service

391. When any person is released on bail, or on his own bond, he shall give to the Court or officer taking such bail or bond an address at which service upon him of all notices and process may be made; and in any case where such person cannot be found, or for other reasons such service on him cannot be effected, any notice or process left for such person at such address shall be deemed to have been duly served upon him.

Power to compel restoration of abducted persons

392. Upon complaint made to a Magistrate on oath of the abduction or unlawful detention of a woman or of a female child under the age of 14 years for any unlawful purpose, he may make an order for the immediate restoration of the woman to her liberty, or of such female child to her husband, parent, guardian or other person having the lawful charge of such child, and may compel compliance with such order, using such force as may be necessary.

Compensation for giving in charge groundlessly

393. (1) Whenever any person causes a police officer to arrest another person if it appears to the Judge or Magistrate who takes cognisance of the case that there was no sufficient ground for causing such arrest, the Judge or Magistrate may award such compensation, not exceeding $500, to be paid by the person so causing the arrest of each person so arrested for his loss of time and any expenses incurred by him in the matter as the Judge or Magistrate shall think fit.

(2) All compensation awarded under this section may be recovered as if it were a fine.

(3) Such compensation shall be no bar to an action for false imprisonment.

Magistrate not to act where interested

394. No Magistrate shall, except with the permission of the High Court, try or commit for trial any case in which he is a party or personally interested.

Explanation — A Magistrate shall not be deemed to be a party or personally interested within the meaning of this section in any case by reason only that he is concerned therein in a public capacity, or by reason only that he has viewed the place in which any transaction material to the case is alleged to have occurred, and made an inquiry in connection with the case.

Public servants not to bid at sales under this Code

395. A public servant, having any duty to perform in connection with the sale of any property under this Code, shall not purchase or bid for the property.

When receivers etc. charged evidence of other cases allowed

396. Where proceedings are taken against any person for having received goods knowing them to be stolen or for having in his possession stolen property, evidence may be given at any stage of the proceedings that there was found in the possession of such person other property stolen within the preceding period of 12 months, and such evidence may be taken into consideration for the purpose of proving that such person knew the property to be stolen which forms the subject of the proceedings taken against him.

When evidence of previous conviction may be given

397. Where proceedings are taken against any person for having received goods knowing them to be stolen or for having in his possession stolen property and evidence has been given that the stolen property has been found in his possession, then if such person has within 5 years immediately preceding been convicted of any offence involving fraud or dishonesty, evidence of such previous conviction may be given at any stage of the proceedings and may be taken into consideration for the purpose of proving that the accused knew the property which was proved to be in his possession to have been stolen.

Forms

398. The forms in the Second Schedule, with such variation as the circumstances of each case may require, may be used for the respective purposes therein mentioned.

Application of fines

399. Any Court imposing any fines under the authority of any law for the time being in force may award any portion thereof not exceeding half to an informer.

Power to make rules and frame forms

400. The Chief Justice may —

(a) make rules for the preparation and transmission of returns and statements to be prepared and submitted by Courts of Magistrates;

(b) frame forms for every proceeding, in those Courts for which he thinks a form should be provided;

(c) amend or alter the forms in the Second Schedule.

PART X JURISDICTION OF COURT OF APPEAL

CHAPTER XLII (REPEALED BY S 63/2002)

401. — 404. *(Repealed by S 63/2002)*

CHAPTER XLIII REFERENCE

Interpretation of Chapter XLIII

405. In this Chapter, unless the context otherwise requires, "reference" means a reference of a point of law to the Court of Appeal under this Chapter.

Reference to Court of Appeal

406.(1) If a person (in this Chapter referred to as the respondent) has been acquitted of any charge in a trial before the High Court in the exercise of its original criminal jurisdiction, the Public Prosecutor may, if he desires the opinion of the Court of Appeal on a point of law which has arisen in the case, refer the point to the Court of Appeal which shall, in accordance with this Chapter, consider the point and give its opinion on it.

(2) A reference shall —

(a) be in writing signed by the Public Prosecutor;

(b) specify the point of law referred and, where appropriate, such facts of the case as are necessary for the proper consideration of the point of law;

(c) summarise the arguments intended to be put to the Court of Appeal;

(d) specify the authorities intended to be cited;

(e) be entitled "Reference under the Criminal Procedure Code (Chapter 7)" together with the year and number of the reference; and

(f) be filed with the Registrar within 21 days, or within such further time as the Court of Appeal may allow, after the date on which the respondent was acquitted.

(3) No mention shall be made in the reference of the proper name of any person or place which is likely to lead to the identification of the respondent.

Notice of reference to be served on respondent

407.(1) The Registrar shall cause to be served on the respondent notice of the reference which shall also —

(a) inform the respondent that the reference will not affect the trial in relation to which it is made or any acquittal in that trial;

(b) invite the respondent, within such period as may be specified in the notice (being not less than 28 days from the date of service of the notice), to inform the Registrar if he wishes to present any argument to the Court of Appeal and, if so, whether he wishes to present such argument in person or by advocate on his behalf.

(2) The Court of Appeal shall not hear argument by the Public Prosecutor until the period specified in the notice has expired, unless the respondent agrees or has indicated that he does not wish to present any argument to the Court of Appeal.

Withdrawal or amendment of reference

408.(1) The Public Prosecutor may withdraw or amend the reference at any time before the Court of Appeal has begun the hearing. After that, the Public Prosecutor may withdraw or amend the reference by leave of the Court of Appeal.

(2) The Public Prosecutor shall cause notice of such withdrawal or amendment to be served on the respondent.

Hearing

409. For the purposes of its consideration of a point referred to it under this Chapter, the Court of Appeal shall hear argument —

(a) by the Public Prosecutor;

(b) if the respondent desires to present any argument, by an advocate on his behalf or by the respondent himself; and

(c) if the Court of Appeal so directs, by an advocate appointed as *amicus curiae* by the Registrar.

Costs

410. Where, on a point being referred to the Court of Appeal under this Chapter, the respondent appears by an advocate for the purpose of presenting any argument to the Court of Appeal, he shall be entitled to his costs of such sums as are reasonably sufficient to compensate him for any expenses properly incurred by him for the purpose of being represented on the reference; and any amount recoverable under this section shall be ascertained as soon as practicable by the Registrar.

Reference not to affect trial

411. A reference shall not affect the trial in relation to which the reference is made or any acquittal in that trial.

Reservation by Judge

412. (1) A Judge of the High Court may reserve for the consideration of the Court of Appeal any question of law which may arise on the trial of any charge.

(2) In exercising his power under subsection (1), the Judge may act either of his own motion or on the application of the Public Prosecutor or the defence.

(3) A Judge may, if he reserves a question of law under subsection (1) and the accused person has been convicted —

(a) postpone judgment until the question has been considered and decided; and

(b) commit the person convicted to prison or admit him to bail, with or without one or more sufficient sureties, and in such sum as he may think fit, on condition that he is to appear at such time or times as the Judge may direct and receive judgment.

(4) Upon consideration of a question reserved under subsection (1), the Court of Appeal may —

(a) affirm or quash the conviction or order a new trial; and

(b) make such other orders as may be necessary to give effect to its decision:

Provided that the Court of Appeal may, notwithstanding that it is of the opinion that the question so reserved might be decided in favour of the convicted person, affirm the conviction if it considers that no miscarriage of justice has actually occurred.

Conviction or not guilty by reason of insanity or disability

413.(1)Where a person has been convicted by any court or has been found not guilty by reason of insanity, or has been found to be under disability, His Majesty the Sultan and Yang Di-Pertuan may, at any time either —

*(a)*refer to the Court of Appeal the whole case, which shall then be treated for all purposes as an appeal to the Court of Appeal by the person; or

*(b)*refer to the Court of Appeal for its opinion any point arising in the case, and the Court of Appeal shall consider the point so referred and furnish His Majesty the Sultan and Yang Di-Pertuan with its opinion thereon.

(2)A reference by His Majesty the Sultan and Yang Di-Pertuan under this section may be made by him either on an application by the person referred to in subsection (1) or without any such application.

CHAPTER XLIV APPEALS BY PERSONS CONVICTED

[S 63/2002]

General right of appeal against conviction

414.A person convicted of any offence after trial in the High Court may appeal to the Court of Appeal against his conviction.

Appeal against conviction allowed

415.(1)Except as provided by this Code, the Court of Appeal shall allow an appeal against conviction if it thinks that —

*(a)*the conviction should be set aside on the ground that it is unsafe or unsatisfactory;

*(b)*the conviction should be set aside on the ground of a wrong decision on any question of law; or

*(c)*there was a material irregularity in the course of the trial,

and in any other case shall dismiss the appeal.

(2)The Court of Appeal may, notwithstanding that it is of the opinion that the point raised in the appeal might be decided in favour of the appellant, dismiss the appeal if it considers that no miscarriage of justice has actually occurred.

(3)The Court of Appeal shall, if it allows the appeal, quash the conviction.

SECOND SCHEDULE

(sections 173, 294(2), 398 and 400)

FORMS

I — Summons to an accused person

(section 39)

of   To

Whereas your attendance is necessary to answer to a charge of

you are hereby required to appear on the   day of

at before   Court at .   the

Dated this   day of ,   20 .

(Seal)

(Signature and title of office)

II — Warrant of arrest

(section 43)

To the Commissioner of Police and all other police officers

Whereas stands charged with the offence of   of

you and to produce   are directed to arrest the said

him ,   , 20   day of   on the   at

before Court at .   the

Dated this   , 20 .   day of

(Signature and title of office)

(Seal)

(section 44)

This Warrant may be indorsed as follows —

If dollars,   shall give bail himself in the sum of   the said

with   dollars, [or 2 sureties each in the sum of   one surety in the sum of day   dollars] to attend before the Court on the of and to continue so to attend until directed by me, he may be released.

Dated this   day of ,   20 .

(Signature and title of office)

III — Bond and bail-bond after arrest under a warrant

(section 54)

I   , of   being brought before the Court at   under a warrant issued to compel my appearance to answer to a charge of   do hearby bind myself to attend in theCourt at   on the   day next, to answer to the said charge, and to continue so to attend   of until otherwise directed by the Court; and, in case of my making default herein, I bind myself to forfeit to His Majesty the Sultan and Yang Di-Pertuan the sum of

dollars [which I hereby deposit].

Dated this   day of ,   20 .

(Signature)

I [*or* We] do hereby declare myself [*or* ourselves] surety [*or* sureties] for the abovenamed   of   , that he shall attend before the   Court at   , on the   day of   next, to answer to the charge on which he has been   arrested, and shall continue so to attend until otherwise directed by the Court; and, in case of his making default therein, I [*or* we] hereby bind myself [*or*ourselves, jointly and severally] to forfeit to His Majesty the Sultan and Yang Di-Pertuan the sum of   dollars [which I [*or* we] hereby deposit].

Dated this   day of ,   20 .

(Signature)

IV — Proclamation requiring the appearance of a person accused

(section 49)

Whereas complaint has been made before me that   of

has committed [*or* is suspected to have committed] the offence of   punishable under section of the

Penal Code (Chapter 22), and it has been returned to a warrant of arrest thereupon issued that the said cannot be found; and whereas it has been shown to my satisfaction that the said has absconded

[*or* is concealing himself to avoid the service of the said warrant, *as the case*

may be]:

Proclamation is hereby made that the said   of   is required to appear before the Court at   to answer the said complaint within   days from this date.

Dated this   day of ,   20 .

(Signature and title of office)

(Seal)

V — Proclamation requiring the attendance of a witness

(section 49)

Whereas complaint has been made before me that   of   has committed [or is suspected to have committed] the offence of   and a warrant has been issued to compel the attendance of   of   before the Court at   to be examined touching the matter of the said complaint; and whereas it has been returned to the said warrant that the said   cannot be served, and it has been shown to my satisfaction that he has absconded [or is concealing himself to avoid the service of the said warrant]:

Proclamation is hereby made that the said   is required to appear before the Court at   on the   day of   , 20 next, at o'clock, to be examined touching the offence complained of.

Dated this   day of ,   20 .

(Signature and title of office)

(Seal)

VI — Order of attachment to compel the attendance of a witness

(section 50)

To the Police Officer in charge of the Police District of

Whereas a warrant has been duly issued to compel the attendance of   of   to testify concerning a complaint pending before this Court, and it has been returned to the said warrant that it cannot be served; and whereas it has been shown to the satisfaction of the Court that he has absconded [or is concealing himself to avoid the service of the said warrant]; and thereupon a Proclamation was duly issued and published requiring the said   to appear and give evidence at the time and place mentioned therein, and he had failed to appear.

This is to authorise and require you to attach by seizure the movable property belonging to the said   to the value of   dollars which you may find within Brunei Darussalam and to hold the said property under attachment pending the further order of this Court, and to return this warrant with an indorsement certifying the manner of its execution.

Dated this   day of ,   20 .

(Signature and title of office)

(Seal)

VII — Warrant in the first instance to bring up a witness

(section 52)

To [*name and description of the Police Officer or other person or persons who is or are to execute the warrant*].

Whereas complaint has been made before me that   of

has [*or* is suspected to have] committed the offence of   and it appears likely that   of can give evidence concerning the said complaint; and whereas the Court has good and sufficient reason to believe that he will not attend as a witness on the hearing of the said complaint unless compelled to do so:

This is to authorise and require you to arrest the said   of

and on the   day of   , to bring him before   , 20   the   Court at to be examined touching the offence complained of.

Given under my hand and the seal of the Court, this   day of   , 20

(Signature and title of office)

(Seal)

VIII — Warrant to Search after Information of a Particular Offence

(section 59)

To [*name and description of the Police Officer or other person or persons who is or are to execute the warrant*].

Whereas information has been laid [*or* complaint has been made] before me of the commission [*or* suspected commission] of the offence of

and it has been made to appear to me that the production of the articles specified in the schedule below is essential to the inquiry now being made [*or* about to be made] into the said offence [*or* suspected offence]:

This days from the date   is to authorise and require you within the space of hereof to search for the said articles specified in the schedule below in the   [*describe the house or place, or part thereof, to which the search is to be confined*], and, if found, to produce the same forthwith before the Court; returning this warrant, with an indorsement certifying what you have done under it, immediately upon its execution.

Given under my hand and the seal of the Court, this   day of   , .   20

(Signature and title of office)

(Seal)

IX — Warrant to search suspected place of deposit

(section 61)

To [*name and description of the Police Officer or other person or persons who is or are to execute the warrant*].

Whereas information has been laid before me, and on due inquiry there- upon I have been led to believe that the [*describe the house or other place*] is used as a place for the deposit [*or* sale] of stolen property [*or if for either of the other purposes expressed in the section, state the purpose in the words of the section*]:

This is to authorise and require you within the space of   days from the date hereof to enter the said house [*or other place*] with such assistance as shall be required, and to use, if necessary, reasonable force for that purpose, and to search every part of the said house [*or other place, or if the search is to be confined to a part, specify the part clearly*] and to seize and take possession of any property [*or document, or* stamps, *or* seals, or coins, *or* trade marks, *as the case may be*] — [*Add (when the case requires it)* and also of any instruments and materials which you may reasonably believe to be kept for the manufacture of forged documents, *or* trade marks, *or* counterfeit stamps, *or* false seals, *or* counterfeit coin, *as the case may be*] and forthwith to bring before this Court such of the said things as may be taken possession of; returning this warrant, with an indorsement certifying what you have done under it, immediately upon its execution.

Given under my hand and the seal of the Court, this   day of   , .   20

(Signature and title of office)

(Seal)

X — Bond to Keep the Peace

(section 72)

Whereas I,   inhabitant of   have been called upon to enter into a bond to keep the peace for the term of   I hereby bind myself not to commit a breach of the peace, or do any act that may probably occasion a breach of the peace, during the said term; and, in case of my making default therein, I hereby bind myself to forfeit to His Majesty the Sultan and Yang Di-Pertuan the sum of   dollars [which I hereby deposit].

Dated this   day of ,   20 .

(Signature)

XI — Bond for good behaviour

(sections 73 and 74)

Whereas I   inhabitant of,   have been called upon to enter into bond to be of good behaviour to His Majesty the Sultan and Yang Di-Pertuan and to all his subjects for the term of I hereby bind myself to be of good behaviour to His Majesty the Sultan and Yang Di-Pertuan and to all his subjects during the aid term; and, in case of my making default therein, I hereby bind myself to forfeit to His Majesty the Sultan and Yang Di-Pertuan the sum of   dollars [which I hereby deposit].

(Signature)

Where a Bond with Sureties is to be executed, add — We do hereby declare ourselves sureties for the abovenamed   that he will be of good behaviour to His Majesty the Sultan and Yang Di-Pertuan and to all his subjects during the said term; and, in case of his making default therein, we hereby bind ourselves, jointly and severally, to forfeit to His Majesty the Sultan and Yang Di-Pertuan the sum of dollars [which we hereby deposit].

Dated this   day of ,   20 .

(Signature)

XII — Order to show cause

(section 75)

Whereas information has been received by me that [*here set out the substance of the information received*].

It is hereby ordered that   do attend at the   Court at   on the day of   ,   20 at   o'clock to show cause why he should not be ordered to execute a bond for his good behaviour in the sum of   dollars to be in force for the term of months with   sufficient sureties being [*here state character and class of sureties required*].

Given under my hand and the seal of the Court, this   day of   .   , 20

(Signature and title of office)

XIII — Summons on information of a probable breach of the peace

(section 75)

of   To

Whereas it has been made to appear to me by credible information that [*state the substance of the information*], and that you are likely to commit a breach of the peace [*or by which act a breach of the peace will probably be occasioned*], you are hereby required to attend at the   Court at   on the day of   , at   , 20   o'clock in the forenoon, to show cause why you should not be required to enter into a bond for   dollars [*when sureties are required, add* — and also to give security by the bond of one (*or two, as the case may be*) surety (*or* sureties) in the sum of dollars (*each, if more than one*), that you will keep the peace for the term of   ].

Given under my hand and the seal of the Court, this   day

of   , 20

(Signature and title of office)

(Seal)

XIV — Warrant of commitment on failure to find security

to keep the peace

(section 83)

To the Officer in charge of the Prison at

Whereas   of   appeared before me on the

day of   in obedience to a summons calling upon him to show cause why   he should not enter into a bond for   dollar with one surety [or a bond with two sureties each in   dollars], that he the said would keep the peace for the period of   . And whereas an order was then made requiring the said   to enter into and find such security [state the security ordered when it differs from that mentioned in the summons], and he has failed to comply with the said order:

This is to authorise and require you to receive the said   into your custody, together with this warrant, and to keep him safely in prison for the said period of   unless he shall, in the meantime, comply with the said order by himself and his surety [or sureties] entering into the said bond, in which case the same shall be received, and the said

released; and to return this warrant with an indorsement certifying the manner of its execution.

Given under my hand and the seal of the Court, this   day of   , 20

(Signature and title of office)

(Seal)

XV — Warrant of commitment on failure to find security for

good behaviour

(section 83)

To the Officer in charge of the Prison at

Whereas it has been made to appear to me that   of

has been and is lurking within the District of   having no ostensible means of subsistence [*or* and that he is unable to give any satisfactory account of himself]:

Whereas evidence of the general character of   of

has been adduced before me and recorded, from which it appears that he is a habitual robber [*or* house-breaker etc. *as the case may be*].

And whereas an order has been recorded stating the same and requiring the said   to furnish security for his behaviour for the term of   by entering into a bond with one surety [*or* two or more sureties, *as the case may be*], himself for   dollars, and the said surety [*or* each of the said sureties] for   dollars, and the said   has failed to comply with the said order, and for such default has been adjudged imprisonment for   unless the said security be sooner furnished:

This is to authorise and require you to receive the said   into your custody, together with this warrant, and to keep him safely in prison for the said period of   unless he shall, in the meantime, comply with the said order by himself and his surety [*or* sureties] entering into the said bond, in which case the same shall be received, and the said

released; and to return this warrant with an indorsement certifying the manner of its execution.

Given under my hand and the seal of the Court, this   day of   .   , 20

(Signature and title of office)

(Seal)

XIV — Warrant to discharge a person imprisoned on failure to give security

(section 79)

To the Officer in charge of the Prison at   (or other officer in whose custody the person is)

Whereas   of   was committed to your custody under warrant of this Court dated the day of   ,   , 20

and of the Criminal   has since duly given security under section Procedure Code,

or

and there have appeared to me sufficient grounds for the opinion that he can be released without hazard to the community:

This is to authorise and require you forthwith to discharge the said from your custody, unless he is liable to be detained for some other cause.

Given under my hand and the seal of the Court, this   day of   .   , 20

(Signature and title of office)

(Seal)

XVII — Order for the removal of nuisance

(section 93)

of   To

Whereas it has been made to appear to me that you have caused an obstruction [*or* nuisance] to persons using the public roadway [*or other public place*] which etc. *(describe the road or public place)*, by etc. *(state what it is that causes the obstruction or nuisance)* and that such obstruction [*or nuisance*] still exists:

or

Whereas it has been made to appear to me that you are carrying on as owner, or manager, the trade or occupation of   at

and that the same is injurious to the public health [*or* comfort] by reason *(state briefly in what manner the injurious effects are caused)*, and should be suppressed or removed to a different place:

or

Whereas it has been made to appear to me that you are the owner [*or are in possession of, or have the control over*] a certain tank [*or* well, *or*excavation] being without a fence [*or* insecurely fenced]:

or

Whereas etc., etc. *(as the case may be)*:

I do hereby direct and require you within   to [*state what is to be done*] or to appear at in the   Court of   on the   day of   next,   , 20 and to show cause why this order should not be enforced:

or

I do hereby direct and require you within   to cease carrying on the said trade or occupation at the said place, and not again to carry on the same, or to remove the said trade from the place where it is now carried on, or to appear etc.:

or

I do hereby direct and require you within   to put up a   sufficient fence [*state the kind of fence and the part to be fenced*] or to appear etc.

or

I do hereby direct and require you etc. [*as the case may be*].

Given under my hand and the seal of the Court, this   day of   .   , 20

(Signature and title of office)

(Seal)

XVIII — Notice and peremptory order by Magistrate after

order absolute

(section 96)

of   To

Notice is hereby given that an order absolute has been made against you requiring you   and you are hereby directed and required to obey the said order within   on peril of the penalty provided by section 188 of the Penal Code for disobedience thereto.

Given under my hand and the seal of the Court, this   day of   .   , 20

(Signature and title of office)

(Seal)

XIX — Injunction to provide against imminent danger

pending decision

(section 100)

of   To

Whereas a conditional order was made by this Court on the   day of   , requiring you , 20   and it has been made to appear to this Court that the nuisance mentioned in the said order is attended with so imminent serious danger to the public as to render necessary immediate measures to prevent such danger: You are hereby under the provisions of section 100 of the Criminal Procedure Code, directed and enjoined forthwith to *(state plainly what is required to be done as a temporary safeguard)* pending the final decision of the case.

Given under my hand and the seal of the Court, this   day of   .   , 20

(Signature and Title of Office)

(Seal)

XX — Order of Magistrate prohibiting the repetition etc.

of a nuisance

(section 101)

of   To

Whereas it has been made to appear to this Court that etc. [*state the proper recital, guided* by Form No. XVII or Form No. XXI, *as the case may be*]:

You are hereby ordered and enjoined not to repeat the said nuisance by again placing, or causing, or permitting to be placed etc. [*as the case may be*].

(Signature and title of office)

(Seal)

XXI — Order of Magistrate to prevent obstruction, riot etc.

(section 102)

of   To

Whereas it has been made to appear to this Court that you are in possession [*or* have the management] of and that, in digging a drain on the said land, you are about to throw or place a portion of the earth and stones dug up upon the adjoining public road, so as to occasion risk of obstruction to persons using the road:

or

Whereas it has been made to appear to this Court that you and a number of other person [*mention the class of persons*] are about to meet and proceed in a religious procession along the public street etc. [*as the case may be*] and that such

or

procession is likely to lead to a riot or an affray:

Whereas etc. etc. [*as the case may be*]:

You are hereby ordered not to place or permit to be placed any of the earth or stones dug from your land in any part of the said road.

or

The procession passing along the said street is hereby prohibited, and you are warned and enjoined not to take any part in such procession [*or, as the case recited may require*].

Given under my hand and the seal of the Court, this   day of   .   , 20

(Signature and title of office)

(Seal)

XXII — Order of Magistrate declaring party entitled to retain possession of land etc. in dispute

(section 103)

Whereas it appears to the undersigned Magistrate on the grounds duly recorded, that a dispute, likely to induce a breach of the peace, existed between [*describe the parties by name and residence, or residence only if the dispute be between bodies of villagers*] concerning certain

situate at   the parties were called upon to give in to this Court a written statement of their respective claims as to the fact of actual possession of the said [*the subject of dispute*], and this Court being satisfied by due inquiry had thereupon, without reference to the merits of the claim of either of the said parties to the legal right of possession, that the claim of actual possession by the said   is true:

It is hereby decided and declared that he is [*or* they are] in possession of the said   and entitled to retain such possession until ousted by due course of law, and any disturbance of his [*or* their] possession in the meantime is forbidden.

Given under my hand and the seal of the Court, this   day of   .   , 20

(Signature and title of office)

(Seal)

XXIII — Warrant of attachment in the case of a dispute as to the possession of land etc.

(section 104)

To   the Police Officer in charge at [*or*, To the

Collector   of Land Revenue].

Whereas it having been made to appear to the undersigned Magistrate that a dispute likely to induce a breach of the peace existed between

of   and   of   concerning certain   situate at   , the said parties were thereupon duly called upon to state to this Court in writing their respective claims as to the fact of actual possession of the said   . And whereas, upon due inquiry into the said claims, this Court has decided that neither of the said parties was in possession of the said   [*or* this Court unable to satisfy itself as to which of the said parties was in possession as aforesaid]:

This is to authorise and require you to attach the said *(the subject of dispute)* by taking and keeping possession thereof, and to hold the same under attachment until the decree or order of a competent Court determining the rights of the parties, or the claim to possession, shall have been obtained; and to return his warrant with an indorsement certifying the manner of its execution.

Given under my hand and the seal of the Court, this   day of   .   , 20

(Signature and title of office)

(Seal)

XXIV — Order of Magistrate prohibiting the doing of anything on land or water
(section 105)

A dispute having arisen concerning the right of use of
situate at   possession of which land [*or* water] is claimed exclusively by   and it appearing to this Court, on due inquiry into the same, that the said land [*or* water] has been open to the enjoyment of such use by the public [*or if by any individual or a class of persons, describe him or them*], and [*if the use can be enjoyed throughout the year* — that the said use has been enjoyed within 3 months of the institution of the said inquiry, *or if the use is enjoyable only at particular seasons, say* during the last of the seasons at which the same is capable of being enjoyed]:
It is hereby ordered that the said   or any one in their interest, shall not take [*or* retain] possession of the said land [*or* water] to the exclusion of the enjoyment of the right of use aforesaid, until he [*or* they] shall obtain the decree or order of a competent Court adjudging him [*or*them] to be entitled to exclusive possession.
Given under my hand and the seal of the Court, this   day of   .   , 20

(Signature and title of office)

(Seal)

XXIV(A) — Application for approval for the taking [S 4/2007] of body sample
(section 112A(2))

TO A MAGISTRATE IN THE MAGISTRATES COURT AT ....
I, ... [name and post of the applicant], apply for an order of a Magistrate to the taking of a body sample, namely ...., from .... [name of the suspect] on the following grounds —
(i) the said person is suspected of having committed an offence punishable with imprisonment contrary to section .... of the ....; and
(ii) it is believed that the sample may confirm or disprove the commission of the offence by the said person.
Dated this   day of ,   .   20
....
Applicant
(name, post and signature)

XXIV(B) — Approval for the taking of body sample [S 4/2007]

(section 112A(2))

To: ....

An application has been made to the undersigned, a Magistrate, by .... [name of the applicant] on .... [date] and the undersigned Magistrate, is satisfied that there are reasonable grounds —

(i) for suspecting that the said person has committed an offence punishable with imprisonment contrary to section .... of the ....; and
(ii) for believing that the sample may confirm or disprove the commission of the offence by the said person.
I hereby order that the suspect provide the body sample required, namely .... [description of sample] to ....
Dated this   day of ,   .   20
....
Magistrate

XXV — Bond to prosecute or give evidence

(section 121)

I,   of   do hereby bind myself to attend at the Court at   , at   o'clock on the   day of   next,   and then and there to give evidence in the matter of a charge of   against one *A.B*: and in case of my making default herein, I bind myself to forfeit to His Majesty the Sultan and Yang Di-Pertuan the sum of   dollars [which I hereby deposit].
Dated this   day of ,   .   20

(Signature)

XXVI — Remand warrant

(sections 149 and 223)

In the Magistrate's Court at   Case No.   to the   of Prisons: / O.C.P.D.

Whereas   was this day brought before this Court suspected of/accused of/charged with having committed an offence under section   of   and it is necessary to remand the accused:

This is to authorise you and require you to receive the accused into your custody together with this Warrant and him safely to keep until the   day of   , when you shall cause him to be brought before   , 20 this Court at   o'clock in the fore/afternoon, unless you shall be otherwise ordered in the meantime.

Dated at this   day of   ,   .   20

Magistrate

XXVII — Charges
(sections 152, 153 and 154)
(I) — Charges with One Head

On Penal Code (Chapter 22) section 121.

1. That you, on or about the   day of   , at   , 20   , waged war against His Majesty the Sultan and Yang Di-Pertuan and thereby committed an offence punishable under section 121 of the Penal Code (Chapter 22).

On section 161.

2. That you, being a public servant in the   Department directly   accepted from [*state the name*], for another party [*state the name*] a gratification other than legal remuneration as a motive for forbearing to do an official act, and thereby committed an offence punishable under section 161 of the Penal Code (Chapter 22).

On section 166.

3. That you, on or about the   day of   , at   , 20   , did [*or omitted to do, as the case may be*]   such   conduct being contrary to the provisions of the   Act, section

and known by you to be prejudicial to   and thereby   committed an offence punishable under section 166 of the Penal Code (Chapter 22).

On section 193.

4.That you, on or about the   day of   , at   , 20   , in the course of the trial of   before   , stated   in evidence that   which statement you either knew or   believed to be false, or did not believe to be true, and thereby committed an offence punishable under section 193 of the Penal Code (Chapter 22).

On section 304.

5.That you, on or about the   day of   , a   , 20   t   , committed culpable homicide not amounting to murder, by causing the death of and thereby committed an offence punishable under section 304 of the Penal Code (Chapter 22).

On section 306.

6.That you, on or about the   day of   , at   , 20   , abetted the commission of suicide by   A,B, a person in a state of intoxication, and thereby committed an offence punishable under section 306 of the Penal Code (Chapter 22).

On section 325.

7.That you, on or about the   day of   , at   , 20   , voluntarily caused grievous hurt to , and thereby committed an offence   punishable under section 325 of the Penal Code (Chapter 22).

On section 392.

8.That you, on or about the   day of   , at   , 20   , robbed and thereby committed an offence punishable under section 392 of the Penal Code (Chapter 22).

On section 395.

9.That you, on or about the   day of   , at   , 20   , committed gang-robbery, an offence punishable under section 395 of the Penal Code (Chapter 22).

(II) — Charges with two or More Heads

On section 241.

1.*First* — That you, on or about the   day of   , at   , 20   , knowing a coin to be counterfeit, delivered the same to another person, by name A,B, as genuine, and thereby committed an offence punishable under section 241 of the Penal Code (Chapter 22).

Secondly — That you, on or about the   day of   , at   , 20   , knowing a coin to be counterfeit attempted to induce another person, by name A,B, to receive it as genuine, and thereby committed an offence punishable under section 241 of the Penal Code (Chapter 22).

On sections 302 and 304.

2.*First* — That you, on or about the   day of   , at   , 20   , committed murder by causing the death of   , and thereby committed an offence punishable under section 202 of the Penal Code (Chapter 22).

Secondly — That you, on or about the   day of   , at   , 20   , committed culpable homicide not amounting to murder by causing the   death of and thereby committed an offence punishable under section 304 of the Penal Code (Chapter 22).

On sections 379 and 382.

3.*First* — That you, on or about the   day of   ,   , 20   at   , committed theft, and there by committed an offence   punishable under section 379 of the Penal Code (Chapter 22).

Secondly — That you, on or about the   day of   , at   , 20   , committed theft, having made preparations for causing death to a   person in order to the committing of such theft, and thereby committed an offence punishable under section 382 of the Penal Code (Chapter 22).

Thirdly — That you, on or about the   day of   , at   , 20   , committed theft, having made preparation for causing restraint to a person in order to the effecting of your escape after the committing of such theft, and thereby committed an offence punishable under section 382 of the Penal Code (Chapter 22).

Fourthly — That you, on or about the   day of   , at   , 20   , committed theft, having made preparation for causing fear or hurt to a   person in order to the retaining of property taken by such theft, and thereby committed an offence punishable under section 382 of the Penal Code (Chapter 22).

Alternative charges on section 193.

4.That you, on or about the   day of   , at   , 20   , in the course of the inquiry into   stated in evidence   before that   and that you, on or about the   day of ,   ,   20 at   , in the course of the trial of   , before,   stated in evidence that   one of which statements you either knew or believed to be false, did not believe to be true, and thereby committed an offence punishable under section 193 of the Penal Code (Chapter 22).

(III) — Charges for Theft after a Previous Conviction

That you, on or about the   day of   , at   , 20   , committed theft, and thereby committed an offence punishable under section 379 of the Penal Code (Chapter 22).

And further that you, before the committing of the said offence, that is to say, on the   day of , had been convicted by   , 20   the   Court at   of an offence punishable under   Chapter XVII of the Penal Code (Chapter 22) with imprisonment for a term of 3 years, that is to say, the offence of house-breaking by night [*describe the offence in the words used in the section under which the accused was convicted*] which conviction is still in full force and effect, and that you are thereby liable to enhanced punishment under section 75 of the Penal Code (Chapter 22).

XXVIII — Warrant of commitment on a sentence of imprisonment or fine

(sections 175 and 181)

To the Officer in charge of the Prison of

Whereas on the   day of   , [, 20 *name of prisoner*] was convicted in the
Court, , of the offence of   under section   [*or* sections   ] of the Penal Code
(Chapter 22) [*or* of the   Act], and was sentenced to   .

This is to authorise and require you, the said Officer, to receive the said
into your custody, together with this warrant, and carry the aforesaid sentence into execution according to law.

Given under my hand and the seal of the Court, this   day of   .   , 20
                                                                              (Signature and Title of Office)

(Seal)

XXIX — Warrant of imprisonment on failure to recover amends

by distress

(section 187)

To the Officer in charge of the Prison at

Whereas   of   has brought against   of
           the complaint that   , and the same has been dismissed as frivolous [*or* vexatious],
and the order of dismissal awards payment by the said   of   of the sum of
dollars as amends; and whereas the said sum has not been paid and cannot be recovered by distress of the
movable property of the said   and an order has been made for his imprisonment for the period
of   days, unless the aforesaid sum be sooner paid:

This is to authorise and require you, the said Officer, to receive the said

into your custody, together with this warrant, and to keep him safely in prison for the said period of
subject to the provisions of section 69 of the Penal Code (Chapter 22), unless the said sum be sooner paid;
and on the receipt thereof forthwith to set him at liberty, returning this warrant with an indorsement certifying
the manner of its execution.

Given under my hand and the seal of the Court, this   day of   .   , 20
                                                                              (Signature and title of office)

(Seal)

XXX — Summons to a witness

(sections 39 and 176)

In the   Court

v

of   To

Whereas your attendance is required in Court as it is understood that you are likely to be able to give material evidence in the above case:

You are hereby summoned to appear before the   Court

on   the   day of   ,   , 20 at   m., to testify what you know concerning the matter of the said case, and not to depart thence without leave of the Court; and you are hereby warned that if you shall, without just excuse, neglect or refuse to appear on the said date, a warrant will be issued to compel your attendance.

And you are further required to bring with you and produce to the Court the following documents which are believed to be in your possession, viz. —

Given under my hand and the seal of the Court, this   day of   . , 20

Fees $

(Signature and title of office)

(Seal)

XXXI — Summons to assessors

(Repealed)

XXXII — Warrant of commitment under sentence of death

(section 242)

To the Officer in charge of the Prison at
Whereas   on the   day of   , was duly convicted in the   , 20 Court,   , of the offence of murder under section 302 of the Penal Code (Chapter 22), and sentenced to suffer death.
This is to authorise and require into your custody,   you, the said Officer, to receive the said together with this warrant and to keep him safely in prison until you shall receive the further warrant or order.
Dated this   day of ,   20 .

(Signature and title of office)

XXXIII — Warrant of execution on a sentence of death

(section 245)

In the High Court of the Supreme Court of Brunei Darussalam

To the Superintendent of Prisons:

Whereas in the High Court, holden at   on the

was found guilty of the murder of   and was sentenced to death [and whereas an appeal to the Court of Appeal was dismissed on the day of   ,], and whereas His Majesty the Sultan and Yang Di-Pertuan has not   20 seen fit to exercise the Prerogative of Mercy.

This is to authorise and require you, the Superintendent of Prisons, to carry the said sentence of death into execution by causing the said   to be hanged by the neck till he is dead, at such time as you, acting under the powers of your said appointment as Superintendent of Prisons, shall appoint, and to return this Warrant to the Court with an indorsement certifying that the sentence has been carried into effect, together with a Certificate of Death under the hand of a Medical Officer.

Given under my hand and the seal of the Court, this   day of   .   , 20

(Chief Justice/Judge)

(Seal)

XXXIV — Warrant to levy a fine by distress and sale

(section 253)

of   To

Whereas   of   was on the   day of   ,   , 20 convicted before me of the offence of   and sentenced to pay a fine of   dollars, and whereas the said although   required to pay the said fine, has not paid the same or any part thereof:

This is to authorise and require you to make distress by seizure of any property belonging to the said which may be found within the District   of   and, if within   next after such distress the said sum shall not be paid [*or* forthwith], to sell the property distrained, or so much thereof as shall be sufficient to satisfy the said fine, returning this warrant, with an indorsement certifying what you have done under it, immediately upon its execution.

Given under my hand and the seal of the Court, this   day of   .   , 20

(Signature and title of office)

(Seal)

Form of Indorsement

Whereas it has been proved to me that the signature *T.S,* to the within warrant is that of *T,S,* a Magistrate , I do hereby authorise the execution in the District of   .   of the said warrant by

(Magistrate)

XXXV — Bond to appear and receive judgment

(sections 263 and 264)

Whereas I   inhabitant of   have been called upon to enter   into a bond to appear before the Court of   at   if and when called upon to receive the judgment of the said Court for the offence of   whereof I have been convicted, and in the meantime to keep the peace and to be of good behaviour: I hereby bind myself to appear on the   day of   , in the said Court or whenever I shall be   , 20 thereto required, and in the meantime to be of good behaviour and to keep the peace towards His Majesty the Sultan and Yang Di-Pertuan and to all his subjects; and in case I make default in any of the conditions herein I bind myself to forfeit to His Majesty the Sultan and Yang Di-Pertuan the sum of   dollars [which I hereby deposit].

Dated this   day of ,   20 .

(Signature)

Where a Bond with Sureties is to be executed, add — We do hereby declare ourselves sureties for the abovenamed   that he will appear in the Court of   at   on the day   of   , or whenever he shall be thereto required, and   , 20   that he will in the meantime be of good behaviour and keep the peace towards His Majesty the Sultan and Yang Di-Pertuan and towards all his subjects; and in case of his making default in any of the conditions herein, we bind ourselves, jointly and severally, to forfeit to His Majesty the Sultan and Yang Di-Pertuan the sum of   dollars [which we hereby deposit].

Dated this   day of ,   20 .

(Signature)

XXXVI — Form of petition of appeal

(section 272)

To *Chief Justice and Justices of the High Court of the Supreme Court of Brunei Darussalam:* [or as the case may require].

The petition of *A.B.*

Showeth as follows:

1. Your petitioner the abovenamed *A.B.* was charged with

and convicted at the   Court held at   on the day of   , and the following order was made thereon   , 20

[*here state shortly the substance of the judgment or sentence*].

2. Your petitioner is dissatisfied with the said judgment on the grounds following: [*here state the particular grounds of appeal on which the appellant relies*].

3. Your petitioner prays that such judgment or sentence may be reversed or that such order may be thereon as justice may require.

(Appellant)

XXXVII — Form of special case

(section 294)

In the High Court of the Supreme Court of Brunei Darussalam

In the matter of a complaint in which *A.B.* was complainant and *G.H.* accused.

Case stated by the undersigned under the provisions of section 294 of the Criminal Procedure Code (Chapter 7).

At before the undersigned on the   a Court held at

day of   , one   , 20 *G.H.* the abovenamed accused was charged as follows:

At the hearing of the said charge it was proved before me that [*here set out so much of evidence and admitted facts of the case as is necessary to raise the question or questions of law intended to be submitted*].

It was thereupon contended on the part of the accused [or complainant as the case may be]. [*Here state the legal objection taken*].

But [*or* And] I being of opinion that [*here state the ground on which the Court decided the case*] held that [*here state the decision and judgment of the Court*].

The question for the opinion of the High Court is whether the said determination was correct in point of law and what should be done in the premises.
Dated this   day of ,   20 .

(Signature)
(Magistrate)

(Seal)

XXXVIII — Warrant of commitment in certain cases of contempt

when a fine is imposed

(section 328)

To the Officer in charge of the Prison at

Whereas at a Court holden before me on this   , in the presence [day of 20*or* view] of the Court committed wilful contempt:

And whereas for such contempt the said   has been adjudged by the   Court to pay a fine of   dollars, or in default to suffer   .   simple imprisonment for the space of

This is to authorise and require you to receive the said   into your custody, together with this warrant, and to keep him safely in prison for the said period of   unless   the said fine be sooner paid; and, on the receipt thereof, forthwith to set him at liberty, returning this warrant with an indorsement certifying the manner of its execution.
Given under my hand and the seal of the Court, this   day of   .   , 20

(Signature and title of office)

(Seal)

XXXIX — Warrant of commitment of witness refusing to answer

(section 332)

To the Officer in charge of the Prison at

Whereas   of   being summoned [*or* brought before this Court] as a witness and this day required to give evidence on an inquiry into an alleged offence, refused to answer a certain question [*or* certain questions] put to him touching the said alleged offence, and duly recorded, without alleging any just excuse for such refusal, and for this contempt has been adjudged detention in   custody for

This is to authorise and require the said   into custody, and to keep him safely in your custody for the space of   days, unless in   the meantime he shall consent to be examined and to answer the questions asked of him, and on the last of the said days, or forthwith on such consent being known, to bring him before this Court to be dealt with according to law; returning this warrant with an indorsement certifying the manner of its execution.

Given under my hand and the seal of the Court, this   day of   , 20

(Signature and title of office)

(Seal)

XL — Form of warrant

(section 341)

To or Officer in charge of the   the Officer in charge of the Prison at [name of asylum] or *to* [name of officer] *in charge of*

You are hereby required to produce   now a prisoner in the [*name of prison*] *or* now in custody at the [*name of asylum*] *or* now in your charge, before the   Court at   on the day of , at   , 20   of the same day, there to be dealt with according to law; and unless the said   shall then and there by the said Court be   ordered to be discharged, cause him, after the said Court shall have dispensed with his further attendance, to be conveyed back to the said prison [*or asylum or other custody*].

Dated this   day of ,   20 .

(Signature and title of office)

(Seal)

XLI — Form of warrant

(section 341)

To the Officer in charge of the Prison at

You are hereby required to produce   now a prisoner in your custody   under a warrant of attachment before the   Court on the   day of   , at   , 20 to be dealt   with according to law; and you shall then and there abide by such order as shall be made by the said Court. And unless the said

shall then and there by the said Court be ordered to be released you shall, after the said Court shall have dispensed with his further attendance, cause him to be conveyed back to the said prison [*or other place of custody*].

Dated this   day of ,   20 .

(Signature and title of office)

(Seal)

XLII — Warrant to bring up prisoner to give evidence

(section 344)

To the Officer in charge of the Prison at

You are hereby required to produce   now a prisoner in your custody before this Court on the day of   , at   , 20   there to give evidence in   a certain charge or prosecution now pending before this Court against   and after the said   shall have given his testimony before this Court or this Court shall have dispensed with his further attendance cause him to be conveyed back to the prison.

Given under my hand and the seal of the Court, this   day of   .   , 20

(Signature and title of office)

(Seal)

XLIII — Bond and bail bond on a preliminary inquiry before

a Magistrate

(section 346)

I   of   being in custody [*or* brought before the   Court at] charged with the offence of   , and required to give security for my attendance in that Court [and in the High Court if required], do bind myself to attend at the said Court on every day of the preliminary inquiry into the said charge, and should the case be sent for trial by the High Court to be and appear before the said Court when called upon to answer the charge against me; and, in case of my making default herein, I bind myself to forfeit to His Majesty the Sultan and Yang Di-Pertuan the sum of   dollars [which I hereby deposit].

Dated this   day of ,   20 .

(Signature)

I hereby declare myself [*or* we jointly and severally declare ourselves and each of us] surety [*or* sureties] for the said   that he shall attend at the   Court at   on every day of the preliminary inquiry into the offence charged against him and, should the case be sent for trial by the High Court, that he shall be and appear before the said Court to answer the charge against him; and, in case of his making default therein, I bind myself [*or* we bind ourselves, jointly and severally] to forfeit to His Majesty the Sultan dollars [which we hereby deposit].   and Yang Di-Pertuan the sum of

Dated this   day of ,   20 .

(Signature)

XLIV — Warrant to discharge a person imprisoned on failure

to give security

(section 350)

To the Officer in charge of the Prison at

Whereas   of   was committed to your custody under warrant of this Court, dated the day of   , and has since with his surety [, 20 or sureties] duly executed a bond under the Criminal Procedure Code (Chapter 7):

This is to authorise and require you forthwith to discharge the said from your custody, unless he is liable to be detained for some other matter.
Given under my hand and the seal of the Court, this   day of   .   , 20
(Signature and title of office)

(Seal)

XLV — Warrant of attachment to enforce a bond

(section 335)

To

Whereas   of   has failed to appear on pursuant to his recognisance, and has by such default forfeited to His Majesty the Sultan and Yang Di-Pertuan the sum of   dollars   and whereas the said   has, on due notice to him, failed to pay the said sum or   show any sufficient cause why payment should not be enforced against him:

This is to authorise and require you to attach any movable property of the said   that you may find within Brunei Darussalam by seizure and detention; and if the said amount be not paid within 3 days, to sell the property so attached or so much of it as may be sufficient to realise the amount aforesaid, and to make return of what you have done under this warrant immediately upon its execution.
Given under my hand and the seal of the Court, this   day of   .   , 20
(Signature and title of office)

(Seal)

XLVI — Notice to surety on breach of a bond

(section 355)

of   To

Whereas on the   day of   , you became surety for   , 20   of   that he should appear before this Court on the   day of   , and bound yourself in default thereof to   , 20 forfeit the sum of   dollars to His Majesty the Sultan and Yang Di-Pertuan and whereas the said   has failed to appear before this Court, and by reason of such default you have forfeited the aforesaid sum of   dollars:
You are hereby required to pay the days from this date, why payment of the   said penalty or show cause, within said sum should not be enforced against you.
Given under my hand and the seal of the Court, this   day of   .   , 20
(Signature and title of office)

(Seal)

XLVII — Notice to surety of forfeiture of bond for good behaviour

(section 355)

of   To

Whereas on the   day of   of   , you became surety by a bond for   , 20   that he would be of good behaviour for the period of   and   bound yourself in default thereof to forfeit the sum of   dollars   to His Majesty the Sultan and Yang Di-Pertuan and whereas the said   has been convicted of the offence of   committed since you became such surety, whereby your security bond has become forfeited:

You are hereby required to pay the said penalty of   dollars, or to show cause within   days why it should not be paid.

Given under my hand and the seal of the Court, this   day of   .   , 20

(Signature and title of office)

(Seal)

XLVIII — Warrant of attachment against a surety

(section 355)

To

Whereas   of   has bound himself as surety for the appearance of   [*state the condition of the bond*], and the said   has made   default, and thereby forfeited to His Majesty the Sultan and Yang Di-Pertuan the sum of   dollars.

This is to authorise and require you to attach any movable property of the said   which you may find by seizure and detention; and, if the said amount be not paid within 3 days, to sell the property so attached, or so much of it as may be sufficient to realise the amount aforesaid, and make return of what you have done under this warrant immediately upon its execution.

Given under my hand and the seal of the Court, this   day of   .   , 20

(Signature and title of office)

(Seal)

XLIX — Warrant of commitment of the surety of an accused

person admitted to bail

(section 355)

To the Officer in charge of the Prison at

Whereas   of   has bound himself as a surety for the appearance of   [*state the condition of the bond*] and the said has therein made default whereby the penalty mentioned in the said bond has been forfeited to His Majesty the Sultan and Yang Di-Pertuan and whereas the said   has, on due   notice to him, failed to pay the said sum or show any sufficient cause why payment should not be enforced against him, and the same cannot be recovered by attachment and sale of movable property of his, and an order has been made for his imprisonment for [*specify the period*]:

This is to authorise and require you,   into your custody with   , to receive the said   this warrant, and to keep him safely in prison for the said [*term of imprisonment*] and to return this warrant with an indorsement certifying the manner of its execution.

Given under my hand and the seal of the Court, this   day of   .   , 20

(Signature and title of office)

(Seal)

L — Notice to the principal of forfeiture of a bond to keep

the peace

(section 355)

of   To

Whereas on the   day of   , you entered into a bond not to commit etc. [, 20 *as in the bond*], and proof of the forfeiture of the same has been given before me and duly recorded:
You are hereby called upon to pay the said penalty of   dollars or to show cause before me within   days why payment of the same should not be enforced against you.
Dated this   day of ,   20 .

(Signature and title of office)

(Seal)

LI — Warrant to attach the property of the principal on breach

of a bond to keep the peace

(section 335)

To

Whereas   of   did on the   day of   ,   , 20 enter into a bond for the sum of   dollars, binding himself not to commit a breach of the peace etc. [*as in the bond*], and proof of the forfeiture of the said bond has been given before me and duly recorded; and whereas notice has been given to the said   calling upon him to show cause why the said sum should not be paid, and he has failed to do so or to pay the said sum:

This is to authorise and require you to attach by seizure the property belonging to the said   to the value of   dollars which you may find; and if the said sum be not paid within   , to sell the property so attached or so   much of it as may be sufficient to realise the same, and to make return of what you have done under this warrant immediately upon its execution.
Given under my hand and the seal of the Court, this   day of   .   , 20

(Signature and title of office)

(Seal)

LII — Warrant of imprisonment on breach of a bond to

keep the peace

(section 355)

To the Officer in charge of the Prison at

Whereas proof has been given before me and duly recorded that

of   has committed a breach of the bond entered into by him to keep the peace, whereby he has forfeited to His Majesty the Sultan and Yang Di-Pertuan the sum of   dollars; and whereas the said   has failed to pay the said sum or to show cause why the said sum should not be paid, although duly called upon to do so, and payment thereof cannot be enforced by attachment of his movable property,

and an order has been made for the imprisonment of the said   for the period of .

This is to authorise and require you, the said Officer of the said prison to receive the said   into your custody, together with this warrant, and to keep him safely in the said prison for the said period of ; and to return this warrant with an indorsement certifying the manner of its execution.

Given under my hand and the seal of the Court, this   day of   .   , 20

(Signature and title of office)

(Seal)

LIII — Warrant of attachment and sale on forfeiture of bond

for good behaviour

(section 355)

To

Whereas   of   did on the   day of   ,   , 20 give security by bond in the sum of   dollars for the good   behaviour of   , and proof has been given before me duly   recorded of the commission by the said   of the offence of   whereby the said bond has been forfeited; and whereas notice has been given to the said   calling upon him to show cause why the said   sum should not be paid, and he has failed to do or to pay the said sum:

This is to authorise and require you to attach by seizure the property belonging to the said   to the value of   dollars, which you may find, and if the said   sum be not paid within   to sell the property so attached, or   so much of it as may be sufficient to realise the same, and to make return of what you have done under this warrant immediately upon its execution.

Given under my hand and the seal of the Court, this   day of   .   , 20

(Signature and Title of Office)

(Seal)

LIV — Warrant for imprisonment on forfeiture of bond

for good behaviour
(section 355)

To the Officer in charge of the Prison at

Whereas   of   did on the   day of   , give security by bond   , 20 in the sum of   dollars for the good behaviour of   and proof of the breach of the said bond has been given before me and duly   recorded   , whereby the said   has forfeited to His Majesty the Sultan and Yang Di-Pertuan the sum of dollars; and whereas he has failed to pay the said sum or to show cause why the said sum should not be paid, although duly called upon to do so, and payment thereof cannot be enforced by attachment of his property, and an order has been made for the imprisonment of the said   .   for the period of

This is to authorise and require you   , to receive the said   into your custody; together with this warrant, and to keep him safely in prison for the said period of   ; returning this warrant with an indorsement certifying the manner of its execution.

Given under my hand and the seal of the Court, this   day of   .   , 20

(Signature and title of office)

(Seal)

THIRD SCHEDULE RELEASE OF PERSONS SENTENCED TO REFORMATIVE TRAINING

[S 9/2006]

(section 14A(7))

1. A person sentenced to reformative training shall be detained in a reformative training centre for such period, not extending beyond 3 years after the date of his sentence, as the Visiting Justices may determine, and shall then be released:

Provided that no person shall be released from a reformative training centre before the expiration of 18 months from the date of his sentence except by direction of the Minister.

2. A person shall, after his release from a reformative training centre and until the expiration of 4 years from the date of his sentence, be under the supervision of such person as may be specified in a notice to be given to him by the Visiting Justices on his release, and shall, while under that supervision, comply with such requirements as may be so specified:

Provided that the Visiting Justices may at any time modify or cancel any of the requirements or order that the person who is under supervision shall cease to be under supervision.

3. If before the expiration of 4 years from the date of his sentence the Visiting Justices are satisfied that a person who is under supervision after his release from a reformative training centre under paragraph 1 has failed to comply with any requirement for the time being specified in the notice given to him under paragraph 2, they may by order recall him to a reformative training centre, and thereupon he shall be liable to be detained in the reformative training centre until the expiration of 3 years from the date of his sentence, or until the expiration of 6 months from the date of his being taken into custody under the order whichever is the later and, if at large, shall be deemed to be unlawfully at large:

Provided that —

(a) any such order shall, at the expiration of 4 years from the date of the sentence, cease to have effect unless the person to whom it relates is then in custody thereunder; and

THIRD SCHEDULE — *(continued)*

(b) the Visiting Justices may at any time release a person who is detained in a reformative training centre under this paragraph; and paragraphs 1 and 2 shall apply in the case of a person so released as they apply in the case of a person released under paragraph 1.

4. If any person while under supervision, or after his recall to a reformative training centre, is sentenced to corrective training or reformative training his original sentence of reformative training shall cease to have effect; and if he is so sentenced to imprisonment, any period for which he is imprisoned under that sentence shall count as part of the period for which he is liable to detention in a reformative training centre under his original sentence.

5. (1) Notwithstanding paragraph 1, the Minister may on the recommendation of the Visiting Justices, direct that a detainee shall be released daily engage in such employment (including self-employment) as the Minister may specify.

(2) Any direction made under sub-paragraph (1) shall have effect for a period to be fixed by the Minister and may be subject to such conditions as he may imposed.

(3) The Minister may at any time revoke any direction made under sub-paragraph (1).

(4) The Minister may, subject to such conditions as he thinks fit, grant leave to a detainee in respect of whom a direction has been made under sub-paragraph (1) to spend his leave at such place as he may specify.

(5) The Minister may at any time revoke any leave granted to a detainee under sub-paragraph (4).

(6) Where any direction made under sub-paragraph (1) is in force in respect of a detainee or any leave is granted under sub-paragraph (4) to a detainee, the superintendent of the reformative training centre shall release him at such times and for such periods as are necessary to give effect to the direction or grant of leave.

THIRD SCHEDULE — (continued)

(7) If any detainee in respect of whom a direction has been made under sub-paragraph (1) or to whom leave has been granted under sub-paragraph (4) remains at large without lawful excuse or fails to return to his place of detention after such direction or leave has been revoked, he shall be deemed to be unlawfully at large and to have escaped from lawful custody.

(8) Every person released under this paragraph shall continue to be in the legal custody of the superintendent of the reformative training centre from which he is released during every period for which he is so released.

(9) In this paragraph, "detainee" means any person who is detained in a reformative training centre in pursuance of a sentence passed under section 14A.

5. The Visiting Justices in exercising their functions under this Schedule shall act in accordance with any general or special directions of the Minister, and shall consider any report made to them by the superintendent of a reformative training centre on the advisability of releasing a person.

6. In this Schedule —

"Minister" means the Minister of Home Affairs;

"Visiting Justices" means The Board of Visiting Justices appointed under section 60(1) of the Prisons Act (Chapter 51), and includes any committee thereof as the Minister may direct.

(a) the proper verdict would have been one of not guilty by reason of insanity; or

(b) the case is not one where there should have been a verdict of acquittal, but that there should have been a finding that the accused person was under disability,

the Court of Appeal shall make an order that the appellant be admitted to a prison or hospital as the Court of Appeal may direct.

(2) On making an order under this section, the Court of Appeal may give such directions as it thinks fit for his detention pending his admission to a prison or hospital.

Retrial

420. (1) Where the Court of Appeal allows an appeal against conviction and it appears to the Court of Appeal that the interests of justice so require, it may order the appellant to be retried.

(2) A person shall not under this section be ordered to be retried for any offence other than —

(a) the offence of which he was convicted at the original trial and in respect of which his appeal is allowed as mentioned in subsection (1);

(b) an offence of which he could have been convicted at the original trial on a charge for the first mentioned offence;

(c) an offence charged in an alternative count in respect of which the Judge did not give a verdict in consequence of convicting him of the first mentioned offence; and

(d) any other offence which may have been disclosed by evidence adduced at the original trial.

Supplementary provisions as to retrial

421. (1) A person who is to be retried for an offence in pursuance of an order under section 420 shall be tried on a fresh charge preferred by the Public Prosecutor before the High Court.

(2) The Court of Appeal may, on ordering a retrial make such orders as appear to it to be necessary or expedient —

(a) for the custody or admission to bail of the person ordered to be retried pending his retrial; or

(b) for the retention pending retrial of any property or money forfeited, restored or paid by virtue of the original conviction or any order made on that conviction.

(3) If the person ordered to be retried was, immediately before the determination of his appeal, liable to be detained in pursuance of an order made under Chapter XXXI —

(a) that order shall continue in force pending the retrial as if the appeal had not been allowed; and

(b) any order made by the Court of Appeal under this section for his custody or admission to bail shall have effect subject to that order.

Appeal against sentence

422. (1) A person convicted of any offence after trial in the High Court may appeal to the Court of Appeal against any sentence (not being a sentence fixed by law) passed on him for the offence.

(2) This section shall also provide rights of appeal against sentence when a person is dealt with by the High Court (otherwise than on appeal from a Magistrate) for an offence of which he was not convicted by the High Court.

(3) An appeal against sentence lies under this section if an offender is committed for sentence by a Magistrate under this Code or any other written law.

Supplementary provisions as to appeal against sentence

423. (1) Where the High Court has passed on an appellant two or more sentences in the same proceedings, an appeal against any one of those sentences shall be treated as an appeal in respect of both or all of them.

(2) On an appeal against sentence, the Court of Appeal, if it considers that the appellant should be sentenced differently for an offence for which he was dealt with by the lower Court, may —

(a) quash any sentence or order which is the subject of the appeal; and

(b) in place of it, pass such sentence or make such order as it thinks appropriate for the case (whether more or less severe) and as the lower Court had power to pass or make when dealing with him for the offence.

Appeal against finding of insanity

424. A person in whose case there is returned a finding of not guilty by reason of insanity may appeal to the Court of Appeal against the finding.

Appeal under section 424

425. (1) Subject to the provisions of this section, the Court of Appeal shall allow an appeal under section 424 if it is of opinion that —

(a) the verdict should be set aside on the ground that it is unsafe or unsatisfactory;

(b) the order of the court giving effect to the verdict should be set aside on the ground of a wrong decision of any question of law; or

(c) there was a material irregularity in the course of the trial,

and in any other case shall dismiss the appeal.

(2) Notwithstanding subsection (1), the Court of Appeal may dismiss an appeal under section 424 if it is of opinion that, notwithstanding the point raised in the appeal might be decided in favour of the appellant, no miscarriage of justice has actually occurred.

(3) Where apart from this subsection —

(a) an appeal under section 424 would be allowed; and

(b) none of the grounds for allowing it relates to the question of the insanity of the appellant,

the Court of Appeal may dismiss the appeal if it is of opinion that, but for the insanity of the appellant, the proper verdict would have been that he was guilty of an offence other than the offence charged.

(4) Where an appeal under section 424 is allowed, the following provisions apply —

(a) if the ground or one of the grounds for allowing the appeal is that the finding as to the insanity of the appellant ought not to stand and the Court of Appeal is of opinion that the proper verdict would have been that he was guilty of an offence (whether the offence charged or any other offence of which the Judge could have found him guilty), the Court of Appeal shall —

(i) substitute for the verdict of not guilty by reason of insanity, a verdict of guilty of that offence; and

(ii) have the same powers of punishing or otherwise dealing with the appellant, and other powers, as the trial Court would have had if the Judge had come to the substituted verdict; and

(b) in any other case, the Court of Appeal shall substitute for the verdict of not guilty by reason of insanity, a verdict of acquittal.

Order on disposal of appeal under section 424

426. (1) Where, on an appeal under section 424, the Court of Appeal is of opinion that the case is not one where there should have been a verdict of acquittal but that there should have been a finding that the accused person was under disability, the Court of Appeal shall make an order that the appellant be admitted to a prison or hospital as the Court of Appeal may direct.

(2) Where in accordance with section 425(4)*(b)* the Court of Appeal substitutes a verdict of acquittal and it is of opinion that —

(a) the appellant is suffering from mental disorder of a nature or degree which warrants his detention in a hospital (with or without medical treatment); and

[S 25/2014]

(b) he ought to be so detained in the interests of his own health or safety or with a view to the protection of other persons,

the Court of Appeal shall make an order that the appellant be admitted to such prison or hospital as may be specified.

(3) On making an order under this section, the Court of Appeal may give such directions as it thinks fit for his detention pending his admission to a prison or hospital.

Right of appeal if person found incapable of making defence

427. Where there has been a determination under Chapter XXXI of the question of a person's fitness to make his defence by a Judge of the High Court, the person may appeal to the Court of Appeal against the finding.

Disposal of appeal under section 427

428. (1) The Court of Appeal shall allow an appeal under section 427 if it is of opinion that —

(a) the finding should be set aside on the ground that it is unsafe or unsatisfactory;

(b) the order giving effect to the finding should be set aside on the ground of a wrong decision on any question of law; or

(c) there was a material irregularity in the course of the determination of the question of fitness to be tried,

and in any other case (except one to which subsection (3) applies) shall dismiss the appeal.

(2) Notwithstanding subsection (1), the Court of Appeal may dismiss the appeal if it is of opinion that, notwithstanding that the point raised in the appeal might be decided in favour of the appellant, no miscarriage of justice has actually occurred.

(3) An appeal under section 427 may, where the question of fitness to be tried was determined later than on the accused being charged, be allowed by the Court of Appeal (notwithstanding that the finding was properly come to) if the Court of Appeal is of opinion that the case is one in which the accused person should have been acquitted before the question of fitness to be tried was considered; and, if an appeal is allowed under this subsection, the Court of Appeal shall, in addition to quashing the finding, direct a verdict of acquittal to be recorded (but not a verdict of not guilty by reason of insanity).

(4) Subject to subsection (3), where an appeal under section 427 is allowed, the appellant may be tried for the offence with which he was charged, and the Court of Appeal may make such orders as appear to it to be necessary or expedient pending any such trial for his custody or admission to bail.

Appeal not to be allowed on certain grounds

429. Except where, in the opinion of the Court of Appeal, a miscarriage of justice has actually occurred, no appeal shall be allowed because of —

(a) any defect which, if pointed out during the progress of the trial, might have been amended by the trial Court; or

(b) any informality in the swearing of a witness.

Procedure for appeal

430.(1) A person who wishes to appeal to the Court of Appeal shall give notice of appeal in such manner as may be provided by rules and orders made under section 441.

(2) Notice of appeal shall be given within 28 days —

(a) from the date of the conviction, verdict or finding appealed against;

(b) in the case of appeal against sentence, from the date on which sentence was passed; or

(c) in the case of an order made or treated as made on conviction, from the date of the making of the order.

(3) If sentence was passed more than 7 days after the date of conviction, verdict or finding, notice of appeal against the conviction, verdict or finding may be given within 28 days from the date on which sentence was passed.

(4) The time for giving notice under this section may be extended, either before or after it expires, by the Court of Appeal.

(5) In the case of a conviction involving a sentence of death or corporal punishment —

(a) the sentence shall not be executed until after the expiration of the time within which notice of appeal may be given; and

(b) if notice is so given, the appeal shall be heard and determined with as much expedition as is practicable, and the sentence shall not be executed until after the determination of the appeal.

Bail

431. The Court of Appeal may, if it thinks fit on the application of an appellant, admit him to bail pending the determination of his appeal.

Groundless appeals

432.(1) If it appears to the Registrar that a notice of an appeal does not show any substantial ground of appeal, he may refer the appeal to the Court of Appeal for summary determination.

(2) If a case is referred to it under subsection (1), the Court of Appeal may, if it considers that the appeal is frivolous or vexatious and can be determined without any full hearing, dismiss the appeal summarily, without calling on anyone to attend the hearing or to appear for the prosecution thereon.

Preparation of case

433.(1) The Registrar shall —

(a) take all necessary steps for obtaining a hearing of any appeal of which notice is given to him and which is not dismissed summarily under section 432; and

(b) obtain and lay before the Court of Appeal in proper form all documents, exhibits and other things which appear necessary for the proper determination of the appeal.

(2) Rules and orders made under section 441 may enable an appellant to obtain from the Registrar any documents or things, including copies or reproductions of documents, required for his appeal.

Appellant may be present

434. (1) Except as provided by this section, an appellant shall be entitled to be present, if he wishes it, on the hearing of his appeal, although he may be in custody.

(2) A person in custody shall not be entitled to be present —

(a) on any proceedings preliminary or incidental to an appeal; or

(b) where he is in custody in consequence of a verdict of not guilty by reason of insanity or of a finding of disability,

unless the Court of Appeal gives him leave to be present.

(3) The power of the Court of Appeal to pass sentence on a person may be exercised although he is for any reason not present.

Evidence

435. (1) For the purposes of this Chapter, the Court of Appeal may —

(a) order the production of any document, exhibit or other thing connected with the proceedings, the production of which appears to it to be necessary for the determination of the case;

(b) order any witness who would have been a compellable witness in the proceedings from which the appeal lies to attend for examination and be examined before the Court of Appeal, whether or not he was called in those proceedings; and

(c) subject to subsection (3), receive the evidence, if tendered, of any witness.

(2) Without prejudice to subsection (1), where evidence is tendered to the Court of Appeal thereunder it shall, unless it is satisfied that the evidence, if received, would not afford any ground for allowing the appeal, exercise its powers of receiving it if —

(a) it appears to it that the evidence is likely to be credible and would have been admissible in the proceedings from which the appeal lies on an issue which is the subject of the appeal; and

(b) it is satisfied that it was not adduced in those proceedings but that there is a reasonable explanation for the failure to adduce it.

(3) Subsection (1)*(c)* applies to any witness (including the appellant) who is competent but not compellable, and applies also to the appellant's husband or wife where the appellant makes an application for that purpose and the evidence of the husband or wife could not have been given in the proceedings from which the appeal lies except on such an application.

(4) For the purposes of this Chapter, the Court of Appeal may order the examination of any witness whose attendance might be required under subsection (1)*(b)* to be conducted, in manner provided by rules and orders made under section 441, before any Judge or other person appointed by the Court of Appeal for the purpose, and allow the admission of any depositions so taken as evidence before the Court of Appeal.

Effect of appeal on sentence

436.(1) The time during which an appellant is in custody pending the determination of his appeal shall, subject to any direction which the Court of Appeal may give to the contrary, be reckoned as part of the term of any sentence to which he is for the time being subject.

(2) Where the Court of Appeal gives a contrary direction under subsection (1), it shall state its reasons for doing so.

(3) Where an appellant is admitted to bail under section 431, the time during which he is at large after being admitted to bail shall be disregarded in computing the term of any sentence to which he is for the time being subject.

(4) The term of any sentence passed by the Court of Appeal shall, unless the Court of Appeal otherwise directs, begin to run from the time when it would have begun to run if passed in the proceedings from which the appeal lies.

Restitution

437.(1) The operation of an order for the restitution of property to a person made on a conviction by the High Court shall (unless the trial Court directs to the contrary in any case in which, in its opinion, the title to the property is not in dispute) be suspended —

(a) in any case, until the expiration of 28 days from the date of conviction; and

(b) where notice of appeal is given within 28 days from the date of conviction, until the determination of the appeal.

(2) In cases where the operation of such an order is suspended until the determination of the appeal, the order shall not take effect as to the property in question if the conviction is quashed on appeal.

(3) Provision may be made by rules and orders made under section 441 for securing the safe custody of any property pending the suspension of the operation of any such order.

(4) The Court of Appeal may by order annul or vary any order made by the trial Court for the restitution of property to any person, although the conviction is not quashed; and the order, if annulled, shall not take effect and, if varied, shall take effect as so varied.

Costs

438.(1) This section applies to any appeal —

(a) under section 414 against conviction;

(b) under section 412 against a verdict of not guilty by reason of insanity;

(c) under section 426 against a finding that the appellant is under disability.

(2) Where an appeal to which this section applies is allowed, the Court of Appeal may, subject to subsection (3), order the payment out of the public revenue of the costs of the appellant.

(3) No order shall be made under this section where —

(a) in the case of an appeal referred to in subsection (1)(a), the appellant is ordered under section 420 to be retried;

(b) in the case of an appeal referred to in subsection (1)(b), the provisions of section 425(4)(a) apply; or

(c) in the case of an appeal referred to in subsection (1)(c) the provisions of section 428(4) apply.

(4) The costs payable under this section shall be such sums as appear to the Court of Appeal reasonably sufficient to compensate the appellant for any expenses properly incurred by him in the appeal, including any proceedings preliminary or incidental thereto or in the trial Court or before a Magistrate.

(5) The amount of costs ordered to be paid under this section shall, except where the amount is fixed by the Court of Appeal, be ascertained by the Registrar.

CHAPTER XLIVA APPEALS BY PUBLIC PROSECUTOR

[S 63/2002]

Appeal by Public Prosecutor against acquittal *[S 63/2002]*

438A. Notwithstanding any other provisions of this Code or of any other written law, the Public Prosecutor may appeal to the Court of Appeal against any acquittal of any person by the High Court in the exercise of its original criminal jurisdiction.

Arrest of respondent *[S 63/2002]*

438B. When there is an appeal by the Public Prosecutor under section 438A, the Court of Appeal may issue a warrant directing that the accused be arrested and brought before it, and may commit him to prison pending the determination of the appeal or admit him to bail.

Respondent not present *[S 63/2002]*

438C. Where, at the hearing of the appeal, the respondent is not present and the Court of Appeal is not satisfied that the notice of appeal was duly served upon him, the Court of Appeal shall not make any order in the matter of the appeal adverse to or to the prejudice of the respondent, but shall adjourn the hearing of the appeal to a future day for his appearance, and shall issue the requisite notice to him to service.

Grounds for allowing appeal *[S 63/2002]*

438D. (1) Except as provided by this Code, the Court of Appeal shall allow an appeal by the Public Prosecutor under section 438A if it thinks that —

(a) the acquittal should be set aside on the ground that it is unsafe or unsatisfactory;

(b) the acquittal should be set aside on the ground of a wrong decision on any question of law; or

(c) there was a material irregularity in the course of the trial, and in any other case shall dismiss the appeal.

(2) Notwithstanding subsection (1), the Court of Appeal may dismiss the appeal if it considers that, notwithstanding that the point raised in the appeal might be decided in favour of the Public Prosecutor, no miscarriage of justice has actually occurred.

(3)The Court of Appeal shall, if it allows the appeal, quash the acquittal.

(4)An order of the Court of Appeal quashing an acquittal shall, except when under section 438H the respondent is ordered to be retired, operate as a direction to the trial Court to enter, instead of the record of acquittal, a judgment and verdict of conviction.

Where appeal allowed [S 63/2002]

438E.(1)This section applies where on an appeal by the Public Prosecutor against an acquittal after trial on two or more charges, the Court of Appeal allows the appeal in respect of one or some of the charges only.

(2) The Court of Appeal may in respect of any charge on which the respondent remains convicted pass such sentence, in substitution for any sentence passed thereon at the trial, as it thinks proper and which is authorised by law for the offence of which he remains convicted on that charge (whether the sentence so substituted is more or less severe).

Special finding [S 63/2002]

438F.(1)This section applies on an appeal by the Public Prosecutor against an acquittal of a person in whose case the Judge has made a special finding.

(2) If the Court of Appeal considers that a wrong conclusion had been arrived at by the Judge, it may, instead of allowing the appeal, order such conclusion to be recorded as appears to it to be in law required and pass such sentence in substitution for the sentence passed at the trial as may be authorised by law.

Finding of insanity or unfitness to plead [S 63/2002]

438G.(1)Where, on an appeal against an acquittal by the Public Prosecutor, the Court of Appeal is of the opinion that —

*(a)*the proper verdict would have been one of not guilty by reason of insanity; or

*(b)*the case is not one where there should have been a verdict of acquittal but that there should have been a finding that the respondent was under disability,

the Court of Appeal shall make an order that the respondent be admitted to a prison or hospital as the Court of Appeal may direct.

(2)On making an order under this section, the Court of Appeal may give such directions as it thinks fit for the detention of the respondent pending his admission to a prison or hospital.

Retrial [S 63/2002]

438H.(1)Where the Court of Appeal allows an appeal by the Public Prosecutor against an acquittal and it appears to the Court of Appeal that the interests of justice so require, it may order the respondent to be retried.

(2)The respondent shall not under this section be ordered to be retried for any offence other than —

*(a)*the offence in respect of which he was acquitted and in respect of which the appeal is allowed as mentioned in subsection (1);

*(b)*an offence of which he could have been convicted at the original trial on a charge for the first mentioned offence;

*(c)*an offence charged in an alternative count in respect of which the Judge did not give a verdict; and

*(d)*any other offence which may have been disclosed by evidence adduced at the original trial.

Supplementary provisions as to retrial *[S 63/2002]*

438I.(1) A person who is to be retried for an offence in pursuance of an order under section 438H shall be tried on a fresh charge preferred by the Public Prosecutor.

[S 32/2005]

(2)The Court of Appeal may, on ordering a retrial, make such orders as appear to it to be necessary or expedient for —

*(a)*the detention in custody or admission to bail of the person ordered to be retried, pending his retrial; or

*(b)*the retention pending the retrial of any property or money howsoever paid by virtue of the original acquittal or of any order made on that acquittal.

(3)If the person ordered to be retried was, immediately before the determination of the appeal by the Public Prosecutor, liable to be detained in pursuance of a finding made under Chapter XXXI —

*(a)*that finding shall continue in force pending the retrial as if the appeal of the Public Prosecutor had not been allowed; and

*(b)*any order made by the Court of Appeal under this section for his detention in custody or admission to bail shall have effect subject to that finding.

Appeal by Public Prosecutor against sentence *[S 63/2002]*

438J. Notwithstanding any other provision of this Code or of any other written law, the Public Prosecutor may appeal to the Court of Appeal against any sentence passed on any person by the High Court (not being a sentence fixed by law) in the exercise of its original criminal jurisdiction.

Supplementary provisions as to appeal against sentence *[S 63/2002]*

438K.(1)Where the High Court has passed on an accused two or more sentences in the same proceeding, an appeal by the Public Prosecutor against any one of those sentences shall be treated as an appeal in respect of both or all of them.

(2)On an appeal against sentence by the Public Prosecutor, the Court of Appeal, if it considers that the respondent should be sentenced differently for an offence for which he was dealt with, may —

*(a)*quash any sentence or order which is the subject of the appeal; and

(b) in place of it pass such sentence or make such order as it thinks appropriate for the case (whether such sentence or order is more or less severe) and as the lower Court had power to pass or make when dealing with him for the offence.

Right of appeal by Public Prosecutor if person found incapable of making defence *[S 63/2002]*

438L. Where there has been a finding by a Judge of the High Court under Chapter XXXI of the question of a person's fitness to make his defence, the Public Prosecutor may appeal to the Court of Appeal against that finding.

Disposal of appeal under section 438K *[S 63/2002]*

438M.(1) The Court of Appeal shall allow an appeal by the Public Prosecutor under section 438L if it thinks that —

(a) the finding should be set aside on the ground that it is unsafe or unsatisfactory;

(b) the order giving effect to the finding should be set aside on the ground of a wrong decision on any question of law; or

(c) these was a material irregularity in the course of the finding of the question of fitness to be tried,

and in any other case (except one to which subsection (3) applies) shall dismiss the appeal.

(2) Notwithstanding subsection (1), the Court of Appeal may dismiss the appeal if it considers that, notwithstanding that the point raised in the appeal might be decided in favour of the Public Prosecutor, no miscarriage of justice has actually occurred.

(3) An appeal by the Public Prosecutor under section 438L may, where the question of fitness to be tried was determined later than on the respondent being charged, be allowed by the Court of Appeal (notwithstanding that the finding was properly come to) if the Court of Appeal is of the opinion that the case is one in which the respondent should have not been acquitted before the question of fitness to be tried was considered; and, if an appeal is allowed under this subsection, the Court of Appeal shall, in addition to quashing the finding, direct that a new trial be ordered.

(4) Subject to subsection (3), where appeal under section 438L is allowed, the respondent may be tried for the offence with which he was charged, and the Court of Appeal may make such order as appear to it to be necessary or expedient pending any such trial for his detention in custody or admission to bail.

Appeal of Public Prosecutor not to be allowed on certain grounds *[S 63/2002]*

438N. Except where, in the opinion of the Court of Appeal, a miscarriage of justice has actually occurred, no appeal by the Public Prosecutor shall be allowed under this Chapter because of —

(a) any defect which, if pointed out during the progress of the trial, might have been amended by the trial Court; or

(b) any informality in the swearing of a witness.

Procedure for appeal by Public Prosecutor *[S 63/2002]*

438O.(1) The Public Prosecutor, in any appeal under this Chapter, shall give notice of appeal in such manner as may be provided by rules and orders made under section 441.

(2) Notice of appeal shall be given within 28 days from the date of the acquittal or finding appealed against or, in the case of an appeal against sentence, from the date on which the sentence was passed or, in the case of an order made or treated as made on conviction, from the date of the making of the order.

(3) If sentence was passed more than 7 days after the date of the acquittal or finding, notice of appeal against the acquittal or finding may be given within 28 days from the date on which the sentence was passed.

(4) The time for giving notice under this section may be extended, either before or after it expires, by the Court of Appeal.

Groundless appeals by Public Prosecutor *[S 63/2002]*

438P.(1) If it appears to the Registrar that a notice of appeal by the Public Prosecutor under this Chapter does not show any substantial ground of appeal, he may refer the appeal to the Court of Appeal for summary determination.

(2) If a case is referred to it under subsection (1), the Court of Appeal may, if it considers that the appeal is frivolous or vexatious and can be determined without a full hearing, dismiss the appeal summarily without calling on any person to attend the hearing.

Preparation of case *[S 63/2002]*

438Q.(1) The Registrar shall —

(a) take all necessary steps for obtaining a hearing of any appeal by the Public Prosecutor of which notice has been given to him and which is not dismissed summarily under section 438O; and

(b) obtain and lay before the Court of Appeal in proper form all documents, exhibits and other things which appear necessary for the proper determination of the appeal.

(2) Rules and orders made under section 441 may enable the Public Prosecutor to obtain from the Registrar any documents or things, including copies or reproductions of documents, required for his appeal.

Evidence *[S 63/2002]*

438R.(1) For the purposes of this Chapter, the Court of Appeal may —

(a) order the production of any document, exhibit or other thing connected with the proceedings, the production of which appears to it to be necessary for the determination of the appeal by the Public Prosecutor;

(b) order any witness who would have been a compellable witness in the proceedings from which the appeal lies to attend for examination and be examined before the Court of Appeal, whether or not he was called in those proceedings; and

(c) subject to subsection (3), receive the evidence, if tendered, of any witness.

(2) Without prejudice to subsection (1), where the evidence is tendered to the Court of Appeal, it shall, unless it is satisfied that the evidence, if received would not afford any ground for allowing the appeal, exercise its powers of receiving it if —

(a) it appears to it that the evidence is likely to be credible and would have been admissible in the proceedings from which the appeal lies on an issue which is the subject of the appeal; and

*(b)*it is satisfied that it was not adduced in those proceedings but that there is a reasonable explanation for the failure to adduce it.

(3)Subsection (1)*(c)* applies to any witness who is competent but not compellable, and applies also to the respondent's husband or wife where the Public Prosecutor makes an application for that purpose and the evidence of the husband or wife could not have been given in the proceedings from which the appeal lies except on such an application.

(4)For the purposes of this Chapter, the Court of Appeal may order the examination of any witness whose attendance might be required under subsection (1)*(b)* to be conducted, in manner provided by rules and orders made under section 441, before any Judge or other person appointed by the Court of Appeal for that purpose, and allow the admission of any depositions so taken as evidence before the Court of Appeal.

Effect of appeal on sentence *[S 63/2002]*

438S.(1)The time during which a respondent is detained in custody pending the determination of an appeal by the Public Prosecutor shall, subject to any direction which the Court of Appeal may give to the contrary, be reckoned as part of the term of any sentence of imprisonment which the Court of Appeal may impose.

(2)Where the Court of Appeal gives a contrary direction under subsection (1), it shall state its reasons for doing so.

(3)The term of any sentence passed by the Court of Appeal shall, unless the Court of Appeal otherwise directs, begin to run from the time when it would have begun to run if passed in the proceedings from which the appeal lies.

Restitution *[S 63/2002]*

438T.(1)The operation of an order for the restitution of property to any person made on an acquittal by the High Court shall (unless the trial Court directs to the contrary in any case in which, in its opinion, the title to the property is not in dispute) be suspended —

*(a)*in any case, until the expiration of 28 days from the date of the acquittal; and

*(b)*where notice of appeal is given by the Public Prosecutor within 28 days from the date of the acquittal, until the determination of the appeal.

(2)In cases where the operation of such an order is suspended until the determination of the appeal, the order shall not take effect as to the property in question if the acquittal is quashed on appeal.

(3)Provision may be made by rules and orders made under section 441 for securing the safe custody of any property, pending the suspension of the operation of any such order.

(4)The Court of Appeal may by order annul or vary any order made by the trial Court for the restitution of property to any person, although the conviction is not quashed; and the order, if annulled, shall not take effect and, if varied, shall take effect as so varied.

CHAPTER LXV GENERAL

Powers of single Judge

439.(1)The powers of the Court of Appeal under this Part which are specified in subsection (2) may be exercised by a single Judge of the High Court or of the Court of Appeal in the same manner as they may be exercised by the Court of Appeal and subject to the same provision.

(2) The powers are the following —

(a) to extend the time within which notice of appeal may be given;

(b) to allow an appellant to be present at any proceedings;

(c) to order a witness to attend for examination;

(d) to admit an appellant to bail;

(e) to make orders under sections 421(2) and 438I(2) and to discharge or vary such orders;

[S 63/2002]

(f) to give directions under sections 436(1) and 438S(1);

[S 63/2002]

(g) to make order under section 438 for the payment of costs;

(h) to order a respondent to be committed to prison or admitted to bail under section 438B.

[S 63/2002; S 32/2005]

(3) If the single Judge refuses an application by an appellant or applicant to exercise in his favour any of the powers above specified, the appellant or applicant shall be entitled to have the application determined by the Court of Appeal.

Practice and procedure

440. Subject to this Code and to any other written law, the practice and procedure to be followed in the Court of Appeal shall be that which is from time to time in force in England for similar matters, so far as this may be possible.

Rules and orders

441. (1) The Chief Justice may make rules and orders governing the practice and procedure to be followed under this Part.

(2) Such rules and orders may provide for —

(a) regulating and prescribing forms to be used in the Court of Appeal;

(b) the times within which documents must be filed or notice given;

(c) the duties of the officers of the Court of Appeal;

(d) the manner in which cases and arguments are to be presented;

(e) generally for the better carrying out of the provisions of this Code in relation to criminal matters in the Court of Appeal.

FIRST SCHEDULE TABULAR STATEMENT OF OFFENCES UNDER THE PENAL CODE

(sections 8(1)(b), 136(1) and 346(b))

Explanatory Note —

1. The entries in the Second and Seventh columns of this Schedule, headed respectively "Offence" and "Maximum Punishment under the Penal Code", are not intended as definitions of the offences and punishment described in the several corresponding sections of the Penal Code, or even as abstracts of those sections, but merely as references to the subject of the section, the number of which is given in the first column.

2. The entries in the Third column of this Schedule are not intended in any way to restrict the powers of arrest without warrant which may be lawfully exercised by Police Officers.

3. The Eighth column must be read in conjunction with sections 8 and 9 of the Code. All cases under the Penal Code may be tried by the High Court and when a Court of a Magistrate is mentioned it implies not that the High Court has no jurisdiction but that the Court of a Magistrate has concurrent jurisdiction with the High Court to try the case. Where the maximum punishment prescribed may be awarded by the Court of a Magistrate the case should ordinarily be tried by that Court, but where the maximum punishment is greater than that which the Court of a Magistrate may award it is a matter of discretion which Court should try the case. (See section 189 of the Code).

4. In the Seventh column the word "imprisonment," except where otherwise stated, means imprisonment of either description.

CHAPTER V — ABETMENT

1	2	3	4	5	6	7	8
Penal Code Section	Offence	Whether the police may ordinarily arrest without warrant or not	Whether a warrant or a summons shall ordinarily issue in the first instance	Whether bailable or not	Whether compoundable or not	Maximum punishment under the Penal Code	By what Court triable
109	Abetment of any offence, if the act abetted is committed in conse-quence, and where no express provision is made for its punishment	May arrest without warrant if arrest for the offence abetted may be made without warrant, but not otherwise	According as a warrant or summons may issue for the offence abetted	According as the offence abetted is bailable or not	According as the offence abetted is compoundable or not	The same punishment as for the offence abetted	The Court by which the offence abetted is triable
110	Abetment of	May arrest	According	According	According as the	The same	The

1	2	3	4	5	6	7	8
	any offence, if the person abetted does the act with a different intention from that of the abettor	without warrant if arrest for the offence abetted may be made without warrant, but not otherwise	as a warrant or summons may issue for the offence abetted	as the offence abetted is bailable or not	offence abetted is compoundable or not	punishment as for the offence abetted	Court by which the offence abetted is triable
111	Abetment of any offence, when one act is abetted and a different act is done; subject to the proviso	May arrest without warrant if arrest for the offence abetted may be made without warrant, but not otherwise	According as a warrant or summons may issue for the offence abetted	According as the offence abetted is bailable or not	According as the offence abetted is compoundable or not	The same punishment as for the offence intended to be abetted	The Court by which the offence abetted is triable
113	Abetment of any offence, when an effect is caused by the act abetted different from that intended by the abettor	May arrest without warrant if arrest for the offence abetted may be made without warrant, but not otherwise	According as a warrant or summons may issue for the offence abetted	According as the offence abetted is bailable or not	According as the offence abetted is compoundable or not	The same punishment as for the offence committed	The Court by which the offence abetted is triable
114	Abetment of any offence, if abettor is present when offence is committed	May arrest without warrant if arrest for the offence abetted may be made without warrant, but not otherwise	According as a warrant or summons may issue for the offence abetted	According as the offence abetted is bailable or not	According as the offence abetted is compoundable or not	The same punishment as for the offence committed	The Court by which the offence abetted is triable

CHAPTER V — ABETMENT — (continued)

1	2	3	4	5	6	7	8
Penal Code Section	Offence	Whether the police may	Whether a warrant or a summons shall	Whether bailable or not	Whether compoundable or not	Maximum punishment under the Penal Code	By what Court triable

		ordinarily arrest without warrant or not	ordinarily issue in the first instance				
115	Abetment of any offence, punishable with death or with imprisonment for 15 years, if the offence be not committed in consequence of the abetment	May arrest without warrant if arrest for the offence abetted may be made without warrant, but not otherwise	According as a warrant or summons may issue for the offence abetted	Not bailable	According as the offence abetted is compoundable or not	Imprisonment for 7 years and fine	The Court by which the offence abetted is triable
115	If an act which causes harm is done in consequence of the abetment	May arrest without warrant if arrest for the offence abetted may be made without warrant, but not otherwise	According as a warrant or summons may issue for the offence abetted	Not bailable	According as the offence abetted is compoundable or not	Imprisonment for 14 years and fine	The Court by which the offence abetted is triable
116	Abetment of an offence, punishable with impri-sonment, if the offence be not committed in consequence of the abetment	May arrest without warrant if arrest for the offence abetted may be made without warrant, but not otherwise	According as a warrant or summons may issue for the offence abetted	According as the offence abetted is bailable or not	According as the offence abetted is compoundable or not	Imprisonment extending to a quarter part of the longest term and of any description provided for the offence, fine or both	The Court by which the offence abetted is triable
116	If the abettor or the person abetted be a public servant whose duty it is to prevent the offence	May arrest without warrant if arrest for the offence abetted may be made without warrant, but not otherwise	According as a warrant or summons may issue for the offence abetted	According as the offence abetted is bailable or not	According as the offence abetted is compoundable or not	Imprisonment extending to half of the longest term and of any description provided for the offence, fine or both	The Court by which the offence abetted is triable
117	Abetting the commission of offence by public, or by more than ten persons	May arrest without warrant if arrest for the offence abetted may be made	According as a warrant or summons may issue for the offence	According as the offence abetted is bailable or not	According as the offence abetted is compoundable or not	Imprisonment for 3 years, fine or both	The Court by which the offence abetted is triable

| | | without warrant, but not otherwise | abetted | | | | |

CHAPTER V — ABETMENT

1	2	3	4	5	6	7	8
Penal Code Section	Offence	Whether the police may ordinarily arrest without warrant or not	Whether a warrant or a summons shall ordinarily issue in the first instance	Whether bailable or not	Whether compoundable or not	Maximum punishment under the Penal Code	By what Court triable
118	Concealing a design to commit an offence punishable with death or imprisonment for 15 years if the offence be committed	May arrest without warrant if arrest for the offence abetted may be made without warrant, but not otherwise	According as a warrant or summons may issue for the offence abetted	Not bailable	According as the abetted is compoundable or not	Imprisonment for 7 years and fine	The Court by which the offence abetted is triable
118	If the offence be not committed	May arrest without warrant if arrest for the offence abetted may be made without warrant, but not otherwise	According as a warrant or summons may issue for the offence abetted	Not bailable	According as the abetted is compoundable or not	Imprisonment for 3 years and fine	The Court by which the offence abetted is triable
119	A public servant concealing a design to commit an offence which it is his duty to prevent, if the offence be committed	May arrest without warrant if arrest for the offence abetted may be made without warrant, but not otherwise	According as a warrant or summons may issue for the offence abetted	According as the offence abetted is bailable or not	According as the abetted is compoundable or not	Imprisonment extending to half of the longest term and of any description provided for the offence, fine or both	The Court by which the offence abetted is triable
119	If the offence be punishable with death or	May arrest without warrant if	According as a warrant or	Not bailable	According as the abetted is compoundable	Imprisonment for 10 years	The Court by which

		imprisonment for 15 years	arrest for the offence abetted may be made without warrant, but not otherwise	summons may issue for the offence abetted		or not		the offence abetted is triable
119	If the offence be not committed	May arrest without warrant if arrest for the offence abetted may be made without warrant, but not otherwise	According as a warrant or summons may issue for the offence abetted	According as the offence abetted is bailable or not	According as the abetted is compoundable or not	Imprisonment extending to a quarter part of the longest term and of any description provided for the offence, fine or both	The Court by which the offence abetted is triable

CHAPTER V — ABETMENT — (continued)

1	2	3	4	5	6	7	8
Penal Code Section	Offence	Whether the police may ordinarily arrest without warrant or not	Whether a warrant or a summons shall ordinarily issue in the first instance	Whether bailable or not	Whether compoundable or not	Maximum punishment under the Penal Code	By what Court triable
120	Concealing a design to commit an offence punishable with imprisonment, if the offence be committed	May arrest without warrant if arrest for the offence abetted may be made without warrant, but not otherwise	According as a warrant or summons may issue for the offence abetted	According as the offence abetted is bailable or not	According as the abetted is compoundable or not	Imprisonment extending to a quarter part of the longest term and of any description provided for the offence, fine or both	The Court by which the offence abetted is triable
120	If the offence be not committed	May arrest without warrant if arrest for the offence abetted may be made without warrant, but not	According as a warrant or summons may issue for the offence abetted	According as the offence abetted is bailable or not	According as the abetted is compoundable or not	Imprisonment extending to one-eighth part of the longest term and of the description provided for the offence, fine or both	The Court by which the offence abetted is triable

| | otherwise | | | | | |

CHAPTER VA — CRIMINAL CONSPIRACY

120B	Criminal conspiracy to commit an offence punishable with death or imprisonment for 2 years or upwards	May arrest without warrant if arrest for the offence which is the object of the conspiracy may be made without warrant, but not otherwise	According as a warrant or summons may issue for the offence which is the object of the conspiracy	According as the offence which is the object of the conspiracy is bailable or not	Not compoundable	The same punishment as for the abetment of the offence	High Court where the offence which is the object of the conspiracy is triable exclusively by such Court In all other cases High Court or Court of a Magistrate
	Criminal conspiracy in any other case	Shall not arrest without warrant	Summons	Bailable	Not compoundable	Imprisonment for 10 years and fine	High Court where the offence which is the object of the conspiracy is triable exclusively by such Court In all other cases High Court or Court of a Magistrate

CHAPTER VI — OFFENCES AGAINST THE STATE

1	2	3	4	5	6	7	8
Penal Code Section	Offence	Whether the police may ordinarily arrest without warrant or not	Whether a warrant or a summons shall ordinarily issue in the first instance	Whether bailable or not	Whether compoundable or not	Maximum punishment under the Penal Code	By what Court triable
121	Waging war against His Majesty the Sultan and Yang Di-Pertuan	Shall not arrest without warrant	Warrant	Not bailable	Not compoundable	Death or imprisonment for life	High Court
121A	Conspiracy to commit offences punishable by section 121	Shall not arrest without warrant	Warrant	Not bailable	Not compoundable	Imprisonment for life	High Court
122	Collecting, men, arms, or ammunition or otherwise preparing to	Shall not arrest without	Warrant	Not bailable	Not compoundable	Imprisonment for 15 years and fine	High Court

	wage war against His Majesty the Sultan and Yang Di-Pertuan	warrant					
123	Concealing the existence of a design to wage war	Shall not arrest without warrant	Warrant	Not bailable	Not compoundable	Imprisonment for 10 years and fine	High Court

CHAPTER VII — OFFENCES RELATING TO ARMY, NAVY, AIR FORCE AND POLICE

131	Abetting mutiny, or attempting to seduce an officer, soldier or sailor from his allegiance or duty	May arrest without warrant	Warrant	Not bailable	Not compoundable	Imprisonment for 15 years and fine	High Court
132	Abetment of mutiny, if mutiny is committed in consequence thereof	May arrest without warrant	Warrant	Not bailable	Not compoundable	Death or imprisonment for 15 years and fine	High Court

CHAPTER VII — OFFENCES RELATING TO ARMY, NAVY, AIR FORCE AND POLICE — (continued)

1	2	3	4	5	6	7	8
Penal Code Section	Offence	Whether the police may ordinarily arrest without warrant or not	Whether a warrant or a summons shall ordinarily issue in the first instance	Whether bailable or not	Whether compoundable or not	Maximum punishment under the Penal Code	By what Court triable
133	Abetment of an assault by an officer, soldier or sailor on his superior officer, when in execution of his office	May arrest without warrant	Warrant	Not bailable	Not compoundable	Imprisonment for 3 years and fine	Court of a Magistrate
134	Abetment of such assault, if the assault is committed	May arrest without warrant	Warrant	Not bailable	Not compoundable	Imprisonment for 7 years and fine	High Court
135	Abetment of the desertion of an officer, soldier or sailor	May arrest without warrant	Warrant	Bailable	Not compoundable	Imprisonment for 2 years, fine or both	Court of a Magistrate
136	Harbouring such an officer, soldier or sailor who has deserted	May arrest without warrant	Warrant	Bailable	Not compoundable	Imprisonment for 2 years, fine or both	Court of a Magistrate
137	Deserter concealed on board merchant vessel, through negligence of master or person in thereof	Shall not arrest without warrant	Summons	Bailable	Not compoundable	Fine of $4,000	Court of a Magistrate
138	Abetment of act of insubordination by an officer, soldier or sailor, if the offence be committed in consequence	May arrest without warrant	Warrant	Bailable	Not compoundable	Imprisonment for 6 months, fine or both	Court of a Magistrate

CHAPTER VII — OFFENCES RELATING TO THE ARMY, NAVY, AIR FORCE AND POLICE — (continued)

1	2	3	4	5	6	7	8
Penal Code Section	Offence	Whether the police may ordinarily arrest without warrant or not	Whether a warrant or a summons shall ordinarily issue in the first instance	Whether bailable or not	Whether compoundable or not	Maximum punishment under the Penal Code	By what Court triable
140	Wearing the dress or carrying any token used by a soldier, with intent that it may be believed that he is such a soldier	May arrest without warrant	Summons	Bailable	Not compoundable	Imprisonment for 3 months, fine of $4,000 or both	Court of a Magistrate

CHAPTER VIII — OFFENCES AGAINST THE PUBLIC TRANQUILLITY

143	Being member of an unlawful assembly	May arrest without warrant	Summons	Bailable	Not compoundable	Imprisonment for one year and fine	Court of a Magistrate
144	Joining an unlawful assembly armed with any deadly weapon	May arrest without warrant	Warrant	Bailable	Not compoundable	Imprisonment for 5 years and fine	Court of a Magistrate
145	Joining or continuing in an unlawful assembly, knowing that it has been commanded to disperse	May arrest without warrant	Warrant	Bailable	Not compoundable	Imprisonment for 5 years and fine	Court of a Magistrate
147	Rioting	May arrest without warrant	Warrant	Bailable	Not compoundable	Imprisonment for 5 years and fine	Court of a Magistrate
148	Rioting, armed with any deadly weapon	May arrest without warrant	Warrant	Bailable	Not compoundable	Imprisonment for 10 years and fine	Court of a Magistrate
149	If an offence be committed by any member of an unlawful assembly, every other member of such assembly shall be guilty of the offence	According as arrest may be made without warrant for the offence or not	According as a warrant or summons may issue for the offence abetted	According as the offence is bailable or not	Not compoundable	The same as for the offence	The Court by which the offence is triable

CHAPTER VIII — OFFENCES AGAINST THE PUBLIC TRANQUILLITY — (continued)

1	2	3	4	5	6	7	8
Penal Code Section	Offence	Whether the police may	Whether a warrant or a summons	Whether bailable or not	Whether compoundable or not	Maximum punishment under the Penal Code	By what Court triable

1	2	3	4	5	6	7	8
		ordinarily arrest without warrant or not	shall ordinarily issue in the first instance				
150	Hiring, engaging or employing persons to take part in an unlawful assembly	May arrest without warrant	According to the offence committed by the person hired, engaged or employed	According as the offence is bailable or not	Not compoundable	The same as for a member of such assembly, and for any offence committed by any member of such assembly	The Court by which the offence is triable
151	Knowingly joining or continuing in any assembly of 5 or more persons after it has been commanded to disperse	May arrest without warrant	Summons	Bailable	Not compoundable	Imprisonment for 6 months, fine or both	Court of a Magistrate
152	Assaulting or obstructing public servant when suppressing riot etc	May arrest without warrant	Warrant	Bailable	Not compoundable	Imprisonment for 3 years, fine or both	Court of a Magistrate
153	Wantonly giving provoca-tion with intent to cause riot if rioting be committed	May arrest without warrant	Warrant	Bailable	Not compoundable	Imprisonment for 3 years, fine or both	Court of a Magistrate
153	If not committed	May arrest without warrant	Summons	Bailable	Not compoundable	Imprisonment for one year, fine or both	Court of a Magistrate
153A	Promoting enmity between classes	Shall not arrest without warrant	Warrant	Bailable	Not compoundable	Imprisonment for 5 years and fine	Court of a Magistrate
154	Owner or occupier of land not giving information of riot etc	Shall not arrest without warrant	Summons	Bailable	Not compoundable	Fine of $4,000	Court of a Magistrate

CHAPTER VIII — OFFENCES AGAINST THE PUBLIC TRANQUILLITY — (continued)

1	2	3	4	5	6	7	8
Penal Code Section	Offence	Whether the police may ordinarily arrest without warrant or not	Whether a warrant or a summons shall ordinarily issue in the first instance	Whether bailable or not	Whether compoundable or not	Maximum punishment under the Penal Code	By what Court triable
155	Person for whose benefit or on whose behalf a riot takes place not using all lawful means to prevent it	Shall not arrest without	Summons	Bailable	Not compoundable	Fine	Court of a Magistrate

156	Agent of owner or occupier for whose benefit a riot is committed not using all lawful means to prevent it	Shall not arrest without warrant	Summons	Bailable	Not compoundable	Fine	Court of a Magistrate
157	Harbouring persons hired for an unlawful assembly	May arrest without warrant	Summons	Bailable	Not compoundable	Imprisonment for 6 months, fine or both	Court of a Magistrate
158(1)	Being hired to take part in an unlawful assembly or riot	May arrest without warrant	Summons	Bailable	Not compoundable	Imprisonment for 6 months, fine or both	Court of a Magistrate
158(2)	Or to go armed	May arrest without warrant	Warrant	Bailable	Not compoundable	Imprisonment for 5 years and fine	Court of a Magistrate
160	Committing affray	Shall not arrest without warrant	Summons	Bailable	Not compoundable	Imprisonment for 3 years and fine	Court of a Magistrate

CHAPTER IX — OFFENCES BY OR RELATING TO PUBLIC SERVANTS

1	2	3	4	5	6	7	8
Penal Code Section	Offence	Whether the police may ordinarily arrest without warrant or not	Whether a warrant or a summons shall ordinarily issue in the first instance	Whether bailable or not	Whether compoundable or not	Maximum punishment under the Penal Code	By what Court triable
161	Being or expecting to be a public servant, and taking a gratification other than legal remuneration in respect of an official act	May arrest without warrant	Warrant	Bailable	Not compoundable	Imprisonment for 7 years and fine	Court of a Magistrate
162	Taking a gratification in order by corrupt or illegal means to influence a public servant	Shall not arrest without warrant	Summons	Bailable	Not compoundable	Imprisonment for 7 years and fine	Court of a Magistrate
163	Taking a gratification for the exercise of personal influence a public servant	Shall not arrest without warrant	Summons	Bailable	Not compoundable	Imprisonment for 7 years and fine	Court of a Magistrate
164	Abetment by a public servant of the offences defined in the last 2 preceding clauses with reference to himself	Shall not arrest without warrant	Summons	Bailable	Not compoundable	Imprisonment for 7 years and fine	Court of a Magistrate
165	Public servant obtaining any valuable thing, without consideration, from a person concerned in any proceeding or business transacted by such public servant	Shall not arrest without warrant	Summons	Bailable	Not compoundable	Imprisonment for 7 years and fine	Court of a Magistrate

CHAPTER IX — OFFENCES BY OR RELATING TO PUBLIC SERVANTS — (continued)

1	2	3	4	5	6	7	8
Penal Code Section	Offence	Whether the police may ordinarily arrest without warrant or not	Whether a warrant or a summons shall ordinarily issue in the first instance	Whether bailable or not	Whether compoundable or not	Maximum punishment under the Penal Code	By what Court triable
166	Public servant disobeying a direction of the law with intent to cause injury to any person	Shall not arrest without warrant	Summons	Bailable	Not compoundable	Imprisonment for 3 years and fine	Court of a Magistrate
167	Public servant framing an incorrect document with intent to cause injury	Shall not arrest without warrant	Summons	Bailable	Not compoundable	Imprisonment for 7 years and fine	Court of a Magistrate
168	Public servant unlawfully engaging in trade	Shall not arrest without warrant	Summons	Bailable	Not compoundable	Imprisonment for 3 years and fine	Court of a Magistrate
169	Public servant unlawfully buying or bidding for property	Shall not arrest without warrant	Summons	Bailable	Not compoundable	Imprisonment for 7 years and fine, and confiscation of property if purchased	Court of a Magistrate
170	Personating a public servant	May arrest without warrant	Warrant	Bailable	Not compoundable	Imprisonment for 7 years and fine	Court of a Magistrate
171	Wearing garb or carrying token used by public servant with fraudulent intent	May arrest without warrant	Summons	Bailable	Not compoundable	Imprisonment for 3 years and fine	Court of a Magistrate

CHAPTER X — CONTEMPTS OF LAWFUL AUTHORITY OF PUBLIC SERVANTS

1	2	3	4	5	6	7	8
Penal Code Section	Offence	Whether the police may ordinarily arrest without warrant or not	Whether a warrant or a summons shall ordinarily issue in the first instance	Whether bailable or not	Whether compoundable or not	Maximum punishment under the Penal Code	By what Court triable
172	Absconding to avoid service of summons or other proceeding from a public servant	Shall not arrest without	Summons	Bailable	Not compoundable	Imprisonment for one year and fine	Court of a Magistrate

1	2	3	4	5	6	7	8
		warrant					
172	If summons or notice require attendance in person etc in a Court of Justice	Shall not arrest without warrant	Summons	Bailable	Not compoundable	Imprisonment for 3 years and fine	Court of a Magistrate
173	Preventing the service or the affixing of any summons or notice, or the removal of it when it has been affixed, or preventing a proclamation	Shall not arrest without warrant	Summons	Bailable	Not compoundable	Imprisonment for one year and fine	Court of a Magistrate
173	If summons or notice requires attendance in person etc in a Court of Justice	Shall not arrest without warrant	Summons	Bailable	Not compoundable	Imprisonment for 3 years and fine	Court of a Magistrate
174	Not obeying a legal order to attend at a certain place in person or by agent, or departing therefrom without authority	Shall not arrest without warrant	Summons	Bailable	Not compoundable	Imprisonment for one year and fine	Court of a Magistrate

CHAPTER X — CONTEMPTS OF LAWFUL AUTHORITY OF PUBLIC SERVANTS — (continued)

1	2	3	4	5	6	7	8
Penal Code Section	Offence	Whether the police may ordinarily arrest without warrant or not	Whether a warrant or a summons shall ordinarily issue in the first instance	Whether bailable or not	Whether compoundable or not	Maximum punishment under the Penal Code	By what Court triable
174	If the order requires personal attendance etc in a Court of Justice	Shall not arrest without warrant	Summons	Bailable	Not compoundable	Imprisonment for 3 years and fine	Court of a Magistrate
175	Intentionally omitting to produce a document to a public servant by a person legally bound to produce or deliver such document	Shall not arrest without warrant	Summons	Bailable	Not compoundable	Imprisonment for one month, fine of $2,000 or both	Court of a Magistrate
175	If the document is required to be produced in or delivered to a Court of Justice	Shall not arrest without warrant	Summons	Bailable	Not compoundable	Imprisonment for 6 months, fine of $4,000 or both	Court of a Magistrate
176	Intentionally omitting to give notice or information to a public servant by a person legally bound to give such notice or information	Shall not arrest without warrant	Summons	Bailable	Not compoundable	Imprisonment for one month, fine of $2,000 or both	Court of a Magistrate
176	If the notice or information required respects the commission of an offence etc	Shall not arrest without warrant	Summons	Bailable	Not compoundable	Imprisonment for 6 months, fine of $4,000 or both	Court of a Magistrate
177	Knowingly furnishing false	Shall not	Summons	Bailable	Not	Imprisonment for 6	Court of a

	information to a public servant	arrest without warrant			compoundable	months, fine of $4,000 or both	Magistrate

CHAPTER X — CONTEMPTS OF THE LAWFUL AUTHORITY OF PUBLIC SERVANTS — (continued)

1	2	3	4	5	6	7	8
Penal Code Section	Offence	Whether the police may ordinarily arrest without warrant or not	Whether a warrant or a summons shall ordinarily issue in the first instance	Whether bailable or not	Whether compoundable or not	Maximum punishment under the Penal Code	By what Court triable
177	If the information required respects the commission of an offence etc	Shall not arrest without warrant	Summons	Bailable	Not compoundable	Imprisonment for 2 years, fine or both	Court of a Magistrate
178	Refusing oath when duly required to take oath by a public servant	Shall not arrest without warrant	Summons	Bailable	Not compoundable	Imprisonment for 6 months, fine of $4,000 or both	Court in which the offence is committed
179	Being legally bound to state truth, and refusing to answer questions	Shall not arrest without warrant	Summons	Bailable	Not compoundable	Imprisonment for 6 months, fine of $4,000 or both	Court in which the offence is committed
180	Refusing to sign a statement made to a public servant when legally required to do so	Shall not arrest without warrant	Summons	Bailable	Not compoundable	Imprisonment for 3 months, fine of $2,000 or both	Court in which the offence is committed
181	Knowingly stating to a public servant on oath as true that which is false	Shall not arrest without warrant	Summons	Bailable	Not compoundable	Imprisonment for 3 years and fine	Court of a Magistrate
182	Giving false information to a public servant in order to cause him to use his lawful power to the injury or annoyance of any person	Shall not arrest without warrant	Summons	Bailable	Not compoundable	Imprisonment for 6 months, fine of $4,000 or both	Court of a Magistrate
183	Resistance to the taking of property by the lawful authority of a public servant	Shall not arrest without warrant	Summons	Bailable	Not compoundable	Imprisonment for 6 months, fine of $4,000 or both	Court of a Magistrate

CHAPTER X — CONTEMPTS OF THE LAWFUL AUTHORITY OF PUBLIC SERVANTS — (continued)

1	2	3	4	5	6	7	8
Penal Code	Offence	Whether the	Whether a	Whether bailable or	Whether compoundable	Maximum punishment under	By what Court

Section		police may ordinarily arrest without warrant or not	warrant or a summons shall ordinarily issue in the first instance	not	or not	the Penal Code	Court triable
184	Obstructing sale of property offered for sale by authority of a public servant	Shall not arrest without warrant	Summons	Bailable	Not compoundable	Imprisonment for one month, fine of $2,000 or both	Court of a Magistrate
185	Bidding, by a person under a legal incapacity to purchase it, for property at a lawfully authorised sale, or bidding without intending to perform the obligations incurred thereby	Shall not arrest without warrant	Summons	Bailable	Not compoundable	Imprisonment for one month, fine of $800 or both	Court of a Magistrate
186	Obstructing public servant in discharge of his public functions	Shall not arrest without warrant	Summons	Bailable	Not compoundable	Imprisonment for 3 months, fine of $2,000 or both	Court of a Magistrate
187	Omission to assist public servant when bound by law to give such assistance	Shall not arrest without warrant	Summons	Bailable	Not compoundable	Imprisonment for one month, fine of $800 or both	Court of a Magistrate
187	Wilfully neglecting to aid a public servant who demands aid in the execution of process, the prevention of offences etc	Shall not arrest without warrant	Summons	Bailable	Not compoundable	Imprisonment for 6 months, fine of $4,000 or both	Court of a Magistrate

CHAPTER X — CONTEMPTS OF THE LAWFUL AUTHORITY OF PUBLIC SERVANTS — (continued)

1	2	3	4	5	6	7	8
Penal Code Section	Offence	Whether the police may ordinarily arrest without warrant or not	Whether a warrant or a summons shall ordinarily issue in the first instance	Whether bailable or not	Whether compoundable or not	Maximum punishment under the Penal Code	By what Court triable
188	Disobedience to an order lawfully promulgated by a public servant, if such disobedience causes obstruction, annoyance or injury to persons lawfully employed	Shall not arrest without warrant	Summons	Bailable	Not compoundable	Imprisonment for one month, fine of $800 or both	Court of a Magistrate
188	If such disobedience causes danger to human life, health or safety etc	Shall not arrest	Summons	Bailable	Not compoundable	Imprisonment for 6 months, fine of	Court of a Magistrate

						$4,000 or both	
189	Threatening a public servant with injury to him, or one in whom he is interested, to induce him to do any official act	Shall not arrest without warrant	Summons	Bailable	Not compoundable	Imprisonment for 5 years and fine	Court of a Magistrate
190	Threatening any person to induce him to refrain from making a legal application for protection from injury	Shall not arrest without warrant	Summons	Bailable	Not compoundable	Imprisonment for 3 years and fine	Court of a Magistrate

CHAPTER XI — FALSE EVIDENCE AND OFFENCES AGAINST PUBLIC JUSTICE

1	2	3	4	5	6	7	8
Penal Code Section	Offence	Whether the police may ordinarily arrest without warrant or not	Whether a warrant or a summons shall ordinarily issue in the first instance	Whether bailable or not	Whether compoundable or not	Maximum punishment under the Penal Code	By what Court triable
193	Giving or fabricating false evidence in a judicial proceeding	Shall not arrest without warrant	Warrant	Bailable	Not compoundable	Imprisonment for 7 years and fine	High Court
193	Giving or fabricating false evidence in any other case	Shall not arrest without warrant	Warrant	Bailable	Not compoundable	Imprisonment for 3 years and fine	Court of a Magistrate
194	Giving or fabricating false evidence with intent to cause any person to be convicted of a capital offence	Shall not arrest without warrant	Warrant	Bailable	Not compoundable	Imprisonment for 15 years and fine	High Court
194	If innocent person be thereby convicted and executed	Shall not arrest without warrant	Warrant	Bailable	Not compoundable	Death or as above	High Court
195	Giving or fabricating false evidence with intent to procure conviction of an offence punishable with imprisonment for 7 years upwards	Shall not arrest without warrant	Warrant	Bailable	Not compoundable	The same as for the offence	The Court by which the offence is triable
196	Using in a judicial proceeding evidence known to be false or fabricated	Shall not arrest without warrant	Warrant	According as the offence of giving such evidence is bailable or not	Not compoundable	The same as for giving or fabricating false evidence	High Court

CHAPTER XI — FALSE EVIDENCE AND OFFENCES AGAINST PUBLIC JUSTICE — (continued)

1	2	3	4	5	6	7	8
Penal Code Section	Offence	Whether the police may ordinarily arrest without warrant or not	Whether a warrant or a summons shall ordinarily issue in the first instance	Whether bailable or not	Whether compoundable or not	Maximum punishment under the Penal Code	By what Court triable
197	Knowingly issuing or signing a false certificate relating to any fact of which such certificate is by law admissible in evidence	Shall not arrest without warrant	Warrant	Bailable	Not compoundable	The same as for giving false evidence	Court of a Magistrate
198	Using as a true certificate one known to be false in a material point	Shall not arrest without warrant	Warrant	Bailable	Not compoundable	The same as for giving false evidence	Court of a Magistrate
199	False statement made in any declaration which is by law receivable as evidence	Shall not arrest without warrant	Warrant	Bailable	Not compoundable	The same as for giving false evidence	Court of a Magistrate
200	Using as true any such declaration known to be false	Shall not arrest without warrant	Warrant	Bailable	Not compoundable	The same as for giving false evidence	Court of a Magistrate
201	Causing disappearance of evidence of an offence committed, or giving false information touching it, to screen the offender, if a capital offence	Shall not arrest without warrant	Warrant	Bailable	Not compoundable	Imprisonment for 7 years and fine	High Court
201	If punishable with impri-sonment for 10 years	Shall not arrest without warrant	Warrant	Bailable	Not compoundable	Imprisonment for 3 years and fine	High Court

CHAPTER XI — FALSE EVIDENCE AND OFFENCES AGAINST PUBLIC JUSTICE — (continued)

1	2	3	4	5	6	7	8
Penal Code Section	Offence	Whether the police may ordinarily arrest without warrant or not	Whether a warrant or a summons shall ordinarily issue in the first	Whether bailable or not	Whether compoundable or not	Maximum punishment under the Penal Code	By what Court triable

201	If punishable with less than 10 years imprisonment	Shall not arrest without warrant	Warrant	Bailable	Not compoundable	Imprisonment for a quarter of the longest term, and of the description provided for the offence, fine or both	High Court or Court of a Magistrate
202	Intentional omission to give information of an offence by a person legally bound to inform	Shall not arrest without warrant	Warrant	Bailable	Not compoundable	Imprisonment for 6 months, fine or both	Court of a Magistrate
203	Giving false information respecting an offence committed	Shall not arrest without warrant	Warrant	Bailable	Not compoundable	Imprisonment for 2 years, fine or both	Court of a Magistrate
204	Secreting or destroying any document to prevent its production as evidence	Shall not arrest without warrant	Warrant	Bailable	Not compoundable	Imprisonment for 2 years, fine or both	Court of a Magistrate
205	False personation for the purpose of any act or proceeding in a suit or criminal prosecution, or for becoming bail or security	Shall not arrest without warrant	Warrant	Bailable	Not compoundable	Imprisonment for 3 years, fine or both	Court of a Magistrate
206	Fraudulent removal or concealment etc of property to prevent its seizure as a forfeiture, or in satisfaction of a fine under sentence, or in execution of a decree	Shall not arrest without warrant	Warrant	Bailable	Not compoundable	Imprisonment for 2 years, fine or both	Court of a Magistrate

CHAPTER XI — FALSE EVIDENCE AND OFFENCES AGAINST PUBLIC JUSTICE — (continued)

1	2	3	4	5	6	7	8
Penal Code Section	Offence	Whether the police may ordinarily arrest without warrant or not	Whether a warrant or a summons shall ordinarily issue in the first instance	Whether bailable or not	Whether compoundable or not	Maximum punishment under the Penal Code	By what Court triable
207	Claiming, property without right or practising deception touching any right to it, to prevent its being taken as a forfeiture, or in satisfaction of a fine under sentence, or in execution of a decree	Shall not arrest without warrant	Warrant	Bailable	Not compoundable	Imprisonment for 2 years, fine or both	Court of a Magistrate
208	Fraudulently suffering a decree to pass for a sum not due, or suffering decree to be executed after it has been	Shall not arrest without	Warrant	Bailable	Not compoundable	Imprisonment for 2 years, fine or both	Court of a Magistrate

209	False claim in a Court of Justice	Shall not arrest without warrant	Warrant	Bailable	Not compoundable	Imprisonment for 2 years and fine	Court of a Magistrate
210	Fraudulently obtaining a decree for a sum not due, or causing a decree to be executed after it has been satisfied	Shall not arrest without warrant	Warrant	Bailable	Not compoundable	Imprisonment for 2 years, fine or both	Court of a Magistrate
211	False charge of offence made with intent to injure	Shall not arrest without warrant	Warrant	Bailable	Not compoundable	Imprisonment for 2 years, fine or both	Court of a Magistrate
211	If offences charged be punishable with death or imprisonment for 7 years and upwards	Shall not arrest without warrant	Warrant	Bailable	Not compoundable	Imprisonment for 7 years and fine	High Court

CHAPTER XI — FALSE EVIDENCE AND OFFENCES AGAINST PUBLIC JUSTICE — (continued)

1	2	3	4	5	6	7	8
Penal Code Section	Offence	Whether the police may ordinarily arrest without warrant or not	Whether a warrant or a summons shall ordinarily issue in the first instance	Whether bailable or not	Whether compoundable or not	Maximum punishment under the Penal Code	By what Court triable
212	Harbouring an offender, if the offence be capital	May arrest without warrant	Warrant	Bailable	Not compoundable	Imprisonment for 5 years and fine	High Court
212	If punishable with imprisonment for 10 years	May arrest without warrant	Warrant	Bailable	Not compoundable	Imprisonment for 3 years and fine	Court of a Magistrate
212	If punishable with imprisonment for one year and not for 10 years	May arrest without warrant	Warrant	Bailable	Not compoundable	Imprisonment for a quarter of the longest term, and of the description provided for the offence, fine or both	Court of a Magistrate
213	Taking gift etc to screen an offender from punishment, if the offence be capital	Shall not arrest without warrant	Warrant	Bailable	Not compoundable	Imprisonment for 7 years and fine	High Court
213	If punishable with imprisonment for 10 years	Shall not arrest without warrant	Warrant	Bailable	Not compoundable	Imprisonment for 3 years and fine	Court of a Magistrate
213	If punishable with imprisonment for less than 10	Shall not arrest	Warrant	Bailable	Not compoundable	Imprisonment for a quarter of the longest term, and of	Court of a Magistrate

214	years	without warrant				the description provided for the offence, fine or both	
214	Offering gift or restoration of property in consideration of screening offender, if the offence be capital	May arrest without warrant	Warrant	Bailable	Not compoundable	Imprisonment for 7 years and fine	High Court
214	If punishable with imprisonment for 10 years	May arrest without warrant	Warrant	Bailable	Not compoundable	Imprisonment for 3 years and fine	Court of a Magistrate

CHAPTER XI — FALSE EVIDENCE AND OFFENCES AGAINST PUBLIC JUSTICE — (continued)

1	2	3	4	5	6	7	8
Penal Code Section	Offence	Whether the police may ordinarily arrest without warrant or not	Whether a warrant or a summons shall ordinarily issue in the first instance	Whether bailable or not	Whether compoundable or not	Maximum punishment under the Penal Code	By what Court triable
214	If with imprisonment for less than 10 years	May arrest without warrant	Warrant	Bailable	Not compoundable	Imprisonment for a quarter of the longest term, and of the description provided for the offence, fine or both	Court of a Magistrate
215	Taking gift to help to recover movable property of which a person has been deprived by an offence, without causing apprehension of offender	May arrest without warrant	Warrant	Bailable	Not compoundable	Imprisonment for 2 years, fine or both	Court of a Magistrate
216	Harbouring an offender who has escaped from custody, or whose apprehension has been ordered, if the offence be capital	May arrest without warrant	Warrant	Bailable	Not compoundable	Imprisonment for 7 years and fine	High Court
216	If punishable with imprisonment for 10 years	May arrest without warrant	Warrant	Bailable	Not compoundable	Imprisonment for 3 years, with or without fine	Court of a Magistrate
216	If with imprisonment one year and not for 10 years	May arrest without warrant	Warrant	Bailable	Not compoundable	Imprisonment for a quarter of the longest term, and of the description provided for the offence, fine or both	Court of a Magistrate
216A	Harbouring gang-robbers	May arrest without warrant	Warrant	Bailable	Not compoundable	Imprisonment for 7 years and fine	High Court

CHAPTER XI — FALSE EVIDENCE AND OFFENCES AGAINST PUBLIC JUSTICE — (continued)

1	2	3	4	5	6	7	8

Penal Code Section	Offence	Whether the police may ordinarily arrest without warrant or not	Whether a warrant or a summons shall ordinarily issue in the first instance	Whether bailable or not	Whether compoundable or not	Maximum punishment under the Penal Code	By what Court triable
216B	Harbouring suspected bad characters	May arrest without warrant	Warrant	Bailable	Not compoundable	Imprisonment for 3 years and fine and cancellation of any licence for sale of intoxicating liquors etc	Court of a Magistrate
217	Public servant disobeying a direction of law with intent to save person from punishment, or property from forfeiture	Shall not arrest without warrant	Summons	Bailable	Not compoundable	Imprisonment for 2 years, fine or both	Court of a Magistrate
218	Public servant framing an incorrect record or writing with intent to save person from punishment, or property from forfeiture	Shall not arrest without warrant	Warrant	Bailable	Not compoundable	Imprisonment for 3 years, fine or both	Court of a Magistrate
219	Public servant in a judicial proceeding corruptly making and pronouncing an order, report, verdict or decision which he knows to be contrary to law	Shall not arrest without warrant	Warrant	Bailable	Not compoundable	Imprisonment for 7 years, fine or both	High Court
220	Commitment for trial or confinement by any person having authority who knows that he is acting contrary to law	Shall not arrest without warrant	Warrant	Bailable	Not compoundable	Imprisonment for 7 years, fine or both	High Court

CHAPTER XI — FALSE EVIDENCE AND OFFENCES AGAINST PUBLIC JUSTICE — (continued)

1	2	3	4	5	6	7	8
Penal Code Section	Offence	Whether the police may ordinarily arrest without warrant or not	Whether a warrant or a summons shall ordinarily issue in the first instance	Whether bailable or not	Whether compoundable or not	Maximum punishment under the Penal Code	By what Court triable
221	Intentional omission to apprehend on the part of a public servant bound by law to apprehend an offender, if the offence be capital	Shall not arrest without warrant	Warrant	Bailable	Not compoundable	Imprisonment for 7 years, with or without fine	High Court

221	If punishable with impri-sonment for 10 years	Shall not arrest without warrant	Warrant	Bailable	Not compoundable	Imprisonment for 3 years, with or without fine	Court of a Magistrate
221	If punishable with impri-sonment for less than 10 years	Shall not arrest without warrant	Warrant	Bailable	Not compoundable	Imprisonment for 2 years, with or without fine	Court of a Magistrate
222	Intentional omission to apprehend on the part of a public servant bound by law to apprehend person under sentence of a Court of Justice, if under sentence of death	Shall not arrest without warrant	Warrant	Not bailable	Not compoundable	Imprisonment for 15 years, with or without fine	High Court
222	If under sentence of imprisonment for 10 years or upwards	Shall not arrest without warrant	Warrant	Not bailable	Not compoundable	Imprisonment for 7 years, with or without fine	High Court
222	If under sentence of imprisonment for less than 10 years, or lawfully committed to custody	Shall not arrest without warrant	Warrant	Bailable	Not compoundable	Imprisonment for 3 years, fine or both	Court of a Magistrate

CHAPTER XI — FALSE EVIDENCE AND OFFENCES AGAINST PUBLIC JUSTICE — (continued)

1	2	3	4	5	6	7	8
Penal Code Section	Offence	Whether the police may ordinarily arrest without warrant or not	Whether a warrant or a summons shall ordinarily issue in the first instance	Whether bailable or not	Whether compoundable or not	Maximum punishment under the Penal Code	By what Court triable
223	Escape from confinement negligently suffered by a public servant	Shall not arrest without warrant	Summons	Bailable	Not compoundable	Imprisonment for 2 years, fine or both	Court of a Magistrate
224	Resistance or obstruction by a person to his lawful apprehension or escaping from custody	May arrest without warrant	Warrant	Bailable	Not compoundable	Imprisonment for 2 years, fine or both	Court of a Magistrate
225	Resistance or obstruction to the lawful apprehension of another person, or rescuing him from lawful custody	May arrest without warrant	Warrant	Bailable	Not compoundable	Imprisonment for 2 years, fine or both	Court of a Magistrate
225	If charged with an offence punishable with impri-sonment for 10 years	May arrest without warrant	Warrant	Not bailable	Not compoundable	Imprisonment for 3 years and fine	Court of a Magistrate
225	If charged with a capital offence	May arrest without warrant	Warrant	Not bailable	Not compoundable	Imprisonment for 7 years and fine	High Court
225	If the person is sentenced to imprisonment for 10 years or	May arrest without	Warrant	Not bailable	Not compoundable	Imprisonment for 7 years and fine	High Court

	upwards	warrant					
225	If under sentence of death	May arrest without warrant	Warrant	Not bailable	Not compoundable	Imprisonment for 15 years and fine	High Court
225A	Intentional omission to apprehend, or sufferance of escape, on part of public servant	Shall not arrest without warrant	Warrant	Bailable	Not compoundable	Imprisonment for 3 years, fine or both	Court of a Magistrate

CHAPTER XI — FALSE EVIDENCE AND OFFENCES AGAINST PUBLIC JUSTICE — (continued)

1	2	3	4	5	6	7	8
Penal Code Section	Offence	Whether the police may ordinarily arrest without warrant or not	Whether a warrant or a summons shall ordinarily issue in the first instance	Whether bailable or not	Whether compoundable or not	Maximum punishment under the Penal Code	By what Court triable
225A	Negligent omission to do same	Shall not arrest without warrant	Summons	Bailable	Not compoundable	Imprisonment for 2 years, fine or both	Court of a Magistrate
225B	Resistance or obstruction to lawful apprehension, or escape or rescue, in cases not otherwise provided for	May arrest without warrant	Warrant	Bailable	Not compoundable	Imprisonment for 6 months, fine or both	Court of a Magistrate
226	Unlawful return from deportation	May arrest without warrant	Warrant	Not bailable	Not compoundable	Imprisonment for 7 years and fine	High Court
227	Violation of condition of remission of punishment	Shall not arrest without warrant	Summons	Not bailable	Not compoundable	Punishment of original sentence; or, if part of the punishment has been undergone, the residue	The Court by which the original offence was triable
228	Intentional insult or interruption to a public servant sitting in any stage of a judicial proceeding	Shall not arrest without warrant	Summons	Bailable	Not compoundable	Imprisonment for 3 years and fine	Court of a Magistrate
228A	Contempt of Court not otherwise provided for	Shall not arrest without warrant	Summons	Bailable	Not compoundable	Imprisonment for 3 years and fine	Court of a Magistrate
229	Personation of an assessor	Shall not arrest without warrant	Summons	Bailable	Not compoundable	Imprisonment for 2 years, fine or both	Court of a Magistrate
229A	Offences for which no special punishment is provided	Shall not arrest without warrant	Summons	Bailable	Not compoundable	Fine of $5,000	Court of a Magistrate

CHAPTER XII — OFFENCES RELATING TO COIN AND GOVERNMENT STAMPS

1	2	3	4	5	6	7	8
Penal Code Section	Offence	Whether the police may ordinarily arrest without warrant or not	Whether a warrant or a summons shall ordinarily issue in the first instance	Whether bailable or not	Whether compoundable or not	Maximum punishment under the Penal Code	By what Court triable
232	Counterfeiting or per-forming any part of the process of counterfeiting coin	May arrest without warrant	Warrant	Not bailable	Not compoundable	Imprisonment for 15 years and fine	High Court
234	Making, buying or selling instrument for the purpose of counter-feiting coin	May arrest without warrant	Warrant	Not bailable	Not compoundable	Imprisonment for 7 years and fine	High Court
235	Possession of instrument or material for the purpose of using the same for counterfeiting coin	May arrest without warrant	Warrant	Not bailable	Not compoundable	Imprisonment for 10 years and fine	High Court
236	Abetting in Brunei Darussalam the counter-feiting out of Brunei Darussalam of coin	May arrest without warrant	Warrant	Not bailable	Not compoundable	The punishment provided for abetting the counterfeiting of such coin within Brunei Darussalam	High Court
238	Import or export of counterfeiting coin, knowing the same to be counterfeit	May arrest without warrant	Warrant	Not bailable	Not compoundable	Imprisonment for 10 years and fine	High Court
240	Delivery of coin proccessed with know-ledge that it is counterfeit	May arrest without warrant	Warrant	Not bailable	Not compoundable	Imprisonment for 10 years and fine	High Court

CHAPTER XII — OFFENCES RELATING TO COIN AND GOVERNMENT STAMPS — (continued)

1	2	3	4	5	6	7	8
Penal Code Section	Offence	Whether the police may ordinarily arrest without warrant or not	Whether a warrant or a summons shall ordinarily issue in the first instance	Whether bailable or not	Whether compoundable or not	Maximum punishment under the Penal Code	By what Court triable

241	Delivery of coins as genuine, which, when first possessed, the deliverer did not know to be counterfeit	May arrest without warrant	Warrant	Not bailable	Not compoundable	Imprisonment for 2 years and fine of ten times the value of the coin	Court of a Magistrate
243	Possession of counterfeit coin by person who knew it to be counterfeit when he became possessed thereof	May arrest without warrant	Warrant	Not bailable	Not compoundable	Imprisonment for 7 years and fine	High Court
247	Fraudulently or dishonestly diminishing weight or altering the composition of coin	May arrest without warrant	Warrant	Not bailable	Not compoundable	Imprisonment for 7 years and fine	High Court
249	Altering appearance of coin with intent that it shall pass as coin of a different description	May arrest without warrant	Warrant	Not bailable	Not compoundable	Imprisonment for 7 years and fine	High Court
251	Delivery of coin possessed with the knowledge that it is altered	May arrest without warrant	Warrant	Not bailable	Not compoundable	Imprisonment for 10 years and fine	High Court
253	Possession of coin by person who knew it to be altered when he became possessed thereof	May arrest without warrant	Warrant	Not bailable	Not compoundable	Imprisonment for 5 years and fine	Court of a Magistrate

CHAPTER XII — OFFENCES RELATING TO COIN AND GOVERNMENT STAMPS — (continued)

1	2	3	4	5	6	7	8
Penal Code Section	Offence	Whether the police may ordinarily arrest without warrant or not	Whether a warrant or a summons shall ordinarily issue in the first instance	Whether bailable or not	Whether compoundable or not	Maximum punishment under the Penal Code	By what Court triable
254	Delivery to another of coin as genuine which, when first possessed the deliverer did not know to be altered	May arrest without warrant	Warrant	Bailable	Not compoundable	Imprisonment for 2 years and fine of ten times the value of the	Court of a Magistrate

1	2	3	4	5	6	7	8
255	Counterfeiting a Government stamp	May arrest without warrant	Warrant	Bailable	Not compoundable	Imprisonment for 10 years and fine	High Court
256	Having possession of an instrument or material for the purpose of counterfeiting a stamp	May arrest without warrant	Warrant	Bailable	Not compoundable	Imprisonment for 7 years and fine	High Court
257	Making, buying or selling instrument for the purpose of counterfeiting a Government stamp	May arrest without warrant	Warrant	Bailable	Not compoundable	Imprisonment for 7 years and fine	High Court
258	Sale of counterfeit Government stamp	May arrest without warrant	Warrant	Bailable	Not compoundable	Imprisonment for 7 years and fine	High Court
259	Having possession of a counterfeit Government stamp	May arrest without warrant	Warrant	Bailable	Not compoundable	Imprisonment for 7 years and fine	High Court
260	Using as genuine a Government stamp, known to be counterfeit	May arrest without warrant	Warrant	Bailable	Not compoundable	Imprisonment for 7 years and fine	High Court

CHAPTER XII — OFFENCES RELATING TO COIN AND GOVERNMENT STAMPS — (continued)

1	2	3	4	5	6	7	8
Penal Code Section	Offence	Whether the police may ordinarily arrest without warrant or not	Whether a warrant or a summons shall ordinarily issue in the first instance	Whether bailable or not	Whether compoundable or not	Maximum punishment under the Penal Code	By what Court triable
261	Effacing any writing from a substance bearing a Government stamp, or removing from a document a stamp used for it with intent to cause loss to Government	May arrest without warrant	Warrant	Bailable	Not compoundable	Imprisonment for 3 years, fine or both	Court of a Magistrate
262	Using a Government stamp known to have been used before	May arrest without warrant	Warrant	Bailable	Not compoundable	Imprisonment for 2 years, fine or both	Court of a Magistrate
263	Erasure of mark denoting that stamp has been used	May arrest without warrant	Warrant	Bailable	Not compoundable	Imprisonment for 3 years, fine or both	Court of a Magistrate

263A	Making, using etc fictitious stamp	May arrest without warrant	Warrant	Bailable	Not compoundable	Fine of $5,000 and confiscation of material	Court of a Magistrate
263B	Selling articles bearing designs resembling currency	May arrest without warrant	Warrant	Bailable	Not compoundable	Imprisonment for 6 months, fine of $4,000 or both	Court of a Magistrate

CHAPTER XIII — OFFENCES RELATING TO WEIGHTS AND MEASURES

264	Fraudulent use of false instrument for weighing	Shall not arrest without warrant	Summons	Bailable	Not compoundable	Imprisonment for 3 years, fine or both	Court of a Magistrate
265	Fraudulent use of false weight or measure	Shall not arrest without warrant	Summons	Bailable	Not compoundable	Imprisonment for 3 years, fine or both	Court of a Magistrate
266	Being in possession of false weights or measures for fraudulent use	Shall not arrest without warrant	Summons	Bailable	Not compoundable	Imprisonment for 3 years, fine or both	Court of a Magistrate

CHAPTER XIII — OFFENCES RELATING TO WEIGHTS AND MEASURES — (continued)

1	2	3	4	5	6	7	8
Penal Code Section	Offence	Whether the police may ordinarily arrest without warrant or not	Whether a warrant or a summons shall ordinarily issue in the first instance	Whether bailable or not	Whether compoundable or not	Maximum punishment under the Penal Code	By what Court triable
267	Making or selling false weights or measures for fraudulent use	Shall not arrest without warrant	Summons	Bailable	Not compoundable	Imprisonment for 3 years, fine or both	Court of a Magistrate

CHAPTER XIV — OFFENCES AFFECTING PUBLIC HEALTH, SAFETY, CONVENIENCE, DECENCY AND MORALS

269	Negligently doing any act known to be likely to spread infection of any disease dangerous to life	May arrest without warrant	Summons	Bailable	Not compoundable	Imprisonment for 5 years and fine	Court of a Magistrate

270	Malignantly doing any act known to be likely to spread infection of any disease dangerous to life	May arrest without warrant	Summons	Bailable	Ditto	Imprisonment for 7 years and fine	Court of a Magistrate
271	Knowingly disobeying any quarantine rule	Shall not arrest without warrant	Summons	Bailable	Not compoundable	Imprisonment for one year and fine	Court of a Magistrate
272	Adulterating food or drink intended for sale, so as to make the same noxious	Shall not arrest without warrant	Summons	Bailable	Not compoundable	Imprisonment for 2 years and fine	Court of a Magistrate
273	Selling any food or drink as food and drink, knowing the same to be noxious	Shall not arrest without warrant	Summons	Bailable	Not compoundable	Imprisonment for 2 years and fine	Court of a Magistrate

CHAPTER XIV — OFFENCES AFFECTING THE PUBLIC HEALTH, SAFETY, CONVENIENCE, DECENCY AND MORALS — (continued)

1	2	3	4	5	6	7	8
Penal Code Section	Offence	Whether the police may ordinarily arrest without warrant or not	Whether a warrant or a summons shall ordinarily issue in the first instance	Whether bailable or not	Whether compoundable or not	Maximum punishment under the Penal Code	By what Court triable
274	Adulterating any drug or medical preparation intended for sale so as to lessen its efficiency, or to change its operation, or to make it noxious	Shall not arrest without warrant	Summons	Bailable	Not compoundable	Imprisonment for 2 years and fine	Court of a Magistrate
275	Offering for sale or issuing from a dispensary any drug or medical preparation known to have been adulterated	Shall not arrest without warrant	Summons	Bailable	Not compoundable	Imprisonment for 2 years and fine	Court of a Magistrate
276	Knowingly selling or issuing from a dispensary any drug or medical preparation as a different drug or medical preparation	Shall not arrest without warrant	Summons	Bailable	Not compoundable	Imprisonment for 2 years, fine of $4,000 or both	Court of a Magistrate
276A	Not being a medical practitioner, using forceps in the delivery of a child	May arrest without warrant	Summons	Bailable	Not compoundable	Imprisonment for 2 years, fine of $8,000 or both	Court of a Magistrate

277	Fouling the water of a public spring or reservoir	May arrest without warrant	Summons	Bailable	Not compoundable	Imprisonment for one year and fine	Court of a Magistrate
277A(1)	Offences caused by fire	May arrest without warrant	Summons	Bailable	Not compoundable	Fine of $100,000	Court of a Magistrate
277A(2)	Offences caused by fire	May arrest without warrant	Summons	Bailable	Not compoundable	Imprisonment for 5 years, fine or both	Court of a Magistrate

CHAPTER XIV — OFFENCES AFFECTING THE PUBLIC HEALTH, SAFETY, CONVENIENCE, DECENCY AND MORALS — (continued)

1	2	3	4	5	6	7	8
Penal Code Section	Offence	Whether the police may ordinarily arrest without warrant or not	Whether a warrant or a summons shall ordinarily issue in the first instance	Whether bailable or not	Whether compoundable or not	Maximum punishment under the Penal Code	By what Court triable
278	Making atmosphere noxious to health	Shall not arrest without warrant	Summons	Bailable	Not compoundable	Fine of $100,000	Court of a Magistrate
279	Driving or riding on a public way so rashly or negligently as to endanger human life etc	May arrest without warrant	Summons	Bailable	Not compoundable	Imprisonment for 3 years and fine	Court of a Magistrate
280	Navigating any vessel so rashly or negligently as to endanger human life etc	May arrest without warrant	Summons	Bailable	Not compoundable	Imprisonment for 5 years and fine of $10,000	Court of a Magistrate
281	Exhibition of a false light, mark or buoy	May arrest without warrant	Warrant	Bailable	Not compoundable	Imprisonment for 7 years, fine or both	High Court
282	Conveying for hire any person by water in a vessel in such a state, or so loaded, as to endanger his life	May arrest without warrant	Summons	Bailable	Not compoundable	Imprisonment for 5 years and fine	Court of a Magistrate
283	Causing danger, obstruction or injury in any public way or line of navigation	May arrest without warrant	Summons	Bailable	Not compoundable	Fine	Court of a Magistrate
284	Dealing with any poisonous substance so as to endanger human life etc	Shall not arrest without warrant	Summons	Bailable	Not compoundable	Imprisonment for 5 years and fine	Court of a Magistrate

CHAPTER XIV — OFFENCES AFFECTING THE PUBLIC HEALTH, SAFETY, CONVENIENCE,

DECENCY AND MORALS — (continued)

1	2	3	4	5	6	7	8
Penal Code Section	Offence	Whether the police may ordinarily arrest without warrant or not	Whether a warrant or a summons shall ordinarily issue in the first instance	Whether bailable or not	Whether compoundable or not	Maximum punishment under the Penal Code	By what Court triable
285	Dealing with fire or any combustible matter so as to endanger human life etc	May arrest without warrant	Summons	Bailable	Not compoundable	Imprisonment for 6 months, fine or both	Court of a Magistrate
286	So dealing with any explosive substance	May arrest without warrant	Summons	Bailable	Not compoundable	Imprisonment for 5 years and fine	Court of a Magistrate
287	So dealing with any machinery	Shall not arrest without warrant	Summons	Bailable	Not compoundable	Imprisonment for 5 years and fine	Court of a Magistrate
288	A person omitting to guard against probable danger to human life by the fall of any building over which he has a right entitling him to pull it down or repair it	Shall not arrest without warrant	Summons	Bailable	Not compoundable	Imprisonment for 5 years and fine	Court of a Magistrate
289	A person omitting to take order with any animal in his possession, so as to guard against danger to human life, or of grievous hurt from such animal	May arrest without warrant	Summons	Bailable	Not compoundable	Imprisonment for 5 years and fine	Court of a Magistrate
290	Committing a public nuisance	Shall not arrest without warrant	Summons	Bailable	Not compoundable	Fine	Court of a Magistrate
291	Continuance of nuisance after injunction to discontinue	May arrest without warrant	Summons	Bailable	Not compoundable	Imprisonment for 3 years and fine	Court of a Magistrate

CHAPTER XIV — OFFENCES AFFECTING THE PUBLIC HEALTH, SAFETY, CONVENIENCE,

DECENCY AND MORALS — (continued)

1	2	3	4	5	6	7	8

Penal Code Section	Offence	Whether the police may ordinarily arrest without warrant or not	Whether a warrant or a summons shall ordinarily issue in the first instance	Whether bailable or not	Whether compoundable or not	Maximum punishment under the Penal Code	By what Court triable
292	Sale etc of obscene books	May arrest without warrant	Warrant	Bailable	Not compoundable	Imprisonment for 2 years and fine not less than $500 and not more than $5,000	Court of a Magistrate
292	In case of second or subsequent conviction	May arrest without warrant	Warrant	Bailable	Not compoundable	Imprisonment for 5 years and fine not less than $1,000 and not more than $30,000	Court of a Magistrate
293	Having in possession obscene books etc for sale or exhibition	May arrest without warrant	Warrant	Bailable	Not compoundable	Imprisonment for 3 years and fine not less than $1,000 not more than $10,000	Court of a Magistrate
293	In case of second or subsequent conviction	May arrest without warrant	Warrant	Bailable	Not compoundable	Imprisonment for 5 years and fine not less than $3,000 and not more than $50,000	Court of a Magistrate
293A	Possession of indecent photograph of child	May arrest without warrant	Warrant	Not bailable	Not compoundable	Imprisonment for 5 years, fine or both	Court of Magistrate
293B	Taking, distribution, showing, advertisement, access of indecent photograph of child	May arrest without warrant	Warrant	Not bailable	Not compoundable	Imprisonment for 10 years, fine or both	High Court
294	Obscene songs	May arrest without warrant	Warrant	Not bailable	Not compoundable	Imprisonment for 3 years and fine not less than $500 and not more than $5,000	Court of a Magistrate
294	In case of second or subsequent conviction	May arrest without warrant	Warrant	Not bailable	Not compoundable	Imprisonment for 5 years and fine not less than $1,000 and not more than $30,000	Court of a Magistrate

CHAPTER XIV — OFFENCES AFFECTING THE PUBLIC HEALTH, SAFETY, CONVENIENCE, DECENCY AND MORALS — (continued)

1	2	3	4	5	6	7	8
Penal Code Section	Offence	Whether the police may ordinarily arrest without warrant or not	Whether a warrant or a summons shall ordinarily issue in the first instance	Whether bailable or not	Whether compoundable or not	Maximum punishment under the Penal Code	By what Court triable
294A	Prostitution	May arrest without warrant	Warrant	Not bailable	Not compoundable	Imprisonment for one year and fine not less than $500 and not more than $5,000	Court of a Magistrate
294A	In the case of second or subsequent conviction	May arrest without warrant	Warrant	Not bailable	Not compoundable	Imprisonment for 3 years and fine not less than $1,000 and not more than $10,000	Court of a Magistrate
294B	Paying for sexual service	May arrest without warrant	Warrant	Not bailable	Not compoundable	Imprisonment for one year and fine not less than $1,000 and not more than $5,000	Court of a Magistrate
294B	In the case of second or subsequent conviction	May arrest without warrant	Warrant	Not bailable	Not compoundable	Imprisonment for 3 years and fine not less than $2,000 and not more than $10,000	Court of a Magistrate

CHAPTER XV — OFFENCES RELATING TO RELIGION

1	2	3	4	5	6	7	8
295	Destroying, damaging or defiling a place of worship or sacred object with intent to insult the religion of any class or persons	May arrest without warrant	Summons	Bailable	Compoundable	Imprisonment for 5 years and fine	Court of a Magistrate
296	Causing a disturbance to an assembly engaged in religious worship	May arrest without warrant	Summons	Bailable	Compoundable	Imprisonment for 3 years and fine	Court of a Magistrate

CHAPTER XV — OFFENCES RELATING TO RELIGION — (continued)

1	2	3	4	5	6	7	8
Penal Code Section	Offence	Whether the police may ordinarily arrest without warrant or not	Whether a warrant or a summons shall ordinarily issue in the first instance	Whether bailable or not	Whether compoundable or not	Maximum punishment under the Penal Code	By what Court triable
297	Trespassing in place of worship or sepulchre, disturbing funeral with intention to wound the feelings or to insult the religion of any person, or offering indignity to a human corpse	May arrest without warrant	Summons	Bailable	Compoundable	Imprisonment for one year and fine	Court of a Magistrate
297A	Interference with grave or human remains	May arrest without warrant	Warrant	Not bailable	Not compoundable	Imprisonment for 7 years, fine or both	High Court
298	Uttering any word or making any sound in the hearing, or making any gesture or placing any object in the sight of any person, with intention to wound his religious feelings	Shall not arrest without warrant	Summons	Bailable	Compoundable	Imprisonment for one year, fine or both	Court of a Magistrate

CHAPTER XVI — OFFENCES AFFECTING THE HUMAN BODY

Offences affecting life

302	Murder	May arrest without warrant	Warrant	Not bailable	Not compoundable	Death	High Court
304	Culpable homicide not amounting to murder, if act by which the death is caused is done with the intention of causing death, etc	May arrest without warrant	Warrant	Not bailable	Not compoundable	Imprisonment for life	High Court

CHAPTER XVI — OFFENCES AFFECTING THE HUMAN BODY — (continued)

Offences affecting life

1	2	3	4	5	6	7	8
Penal Code Section	Offence	Whether the	Whether a	Whether bailable or not	Whether compoundable	Maximum punishment	By what Court

Penal Code Section	Offence	Whether the police may ordinarily arrest without warrant or not	Whether a warrant or a summons shall ordinarily issue in the first instance	Whether bailable or not	Whether compoundable or not	Maximum punishment under the Penal Code	By what Court triable
304	If act is done with know-ledge that it is likely to cause death, but without any intention to cause death etc	May arrest without warrant	Warrant	Not bailable	Not compoundable	Imprisonment for 15 years, fine or both	High Court
304A(1)	Causing death by rash or negligent driving of motor vehicles or rash or negligent use of firearms or explosive	May arrest without warrant	Warrant	Not bailable	Not compoundable	Imprisonment for 10 years and fine	Court of a Magistrate
304A(2)	Causing death by rash or negligent act	May arrest without warrant	Warrant	Bailable	Not compoundable	Imprisonment for 5 years and fine	Court of a Magistrate
305	Abetment of suicide committed by a child, or insane or delirious person or an idiot, or a person intoxicated	May arrest without warrant	Warrant	Bailable	Not compoundable	Death or imprisonment for life	High Court
306	Abetting the commission of suicide	May arrest without warrant	Warrant	Bailable	Not compoundable	Imprisonment for 10 years and fine	High Court
307	Attempting to murder	May arrest without warrant	Warrant	Bailable	Not compoundable	Imprisonment for 20 years and fine	High Court
307	If such act cause hurt to any person	May arrest without warrant	Warrant	Bailable	Not compoundable	Imprisonment for life	High Court

CHAPTER XVI — OFFENCES AFFECTING THE HUMAN BODY — (continued)

Offences affecting life

1	2	3	4	5	6	7	8
Penal Code Section	Offence	Whether the police may ordinarily arrest without warrant	Whether a warrant or a summons shall ordinarily issue in the	Whether bailable or not	Whether compoundable or not	Maximum punishment under the Penal Code	By what Court triable

1	2	3	4	5	6	7	8
		or not	the first instance				
307	Attempt to murder by convict undergoing sentence of 15 years' imprisonment, if hurt is caused	May arrest without warrant	Warrant	Bailable	Not compoundable	Death or as above	High Court
308	Attempt to commit culpable homicide (Where hurt not caused to any person)	May arrest without warrant	Warrant	Bailable	Not compoundable	Imprisonment for 5 years and fine	Court of a Magistrate
308	If such act cause hurt to any person	May arrest without warrant	Warrant	Bailable	Not compoundable	Imprisonment for 10 years and fine	High Court
309	Attempt to commit suicide	May arrest without warrant	Warrant	Bailable	Not compoundable	Imprisonment for one year, fine or both	Court of a Magistrate
Causing of miscarriage; injuries to unborn children; exposure of infants; and concealment of births							
312	Causing miscarriage (Where woman not quick with child)	May arrest without warrant	Warrant	Bailable	Not compoundable	Imprisonment for 3 years, fine or both	Court of a Magistrate
312	If woman be quick with child	May arrest without warrant	Warrant	Bailable	Not compoundable	Imprisonment for 7 years and fine	High Court
313	Causing miscarriage without woman's consent	May arrest without warrant	Warrant	Not bailable	Not compoundable	Imprisonment for 10 years and fine	High Court
314	Death caused by an act done with intent to cause miscarriage	May arrest without warrant	Warrant	Not bailable	Not compoundable	Imprisonment for 10 years and fine	High Court

CHAPTER XVI — OFFENCES AFFECTING THE HUMAN BODY — (continued)

Causing of miscarriage; injuries to unborn children; exposure of infants; and concealment of births

1	2	3	4	5	6	7	8
Penal Code Section	Offence	Whether the police may ordinarily arrest without warrant or not	Whether a warrant or a summons shall ordinarily issue in the	Whether bailable or not	Whether compoundable or not	Maximum punishment under the Penal Code	By what Court triable

			first instance				
314	If act done without woman's consent	May arrest without warrant	Warrant	Not bailable	Not compoundable	Imprisonment for 15 years and fine	High Court
315	Act done with intent to prevent a child being born alive, or to cause it to die after its birth	May arrest without warrant	Warrant	Not bailable	Not compoundable	Imprisonment for 10 years, fine or both	High Court
316	Causing death of a quick unborn child by an act amounting to culpable homicide	May arrest without warrant	Warrant	Not bailable	Not compoundable	Imprisonment for 10 years and fine	High Court
317	Exposure of a child under 12 years of age by parent or person having care of it with intention of wholly abandoning it	May arrest without warrant Act, No 2/57	Warrant	Bailable	Not compoundable	Imprisonment for 7 years, fine or both	High Court
318	Concealment of birth by secret disposal of dead	May arrest without warrant Act, No 2/57	Warrant	Bailable	Not compoundable	Imprisonment for 2 years, fine or both	Court of a Magistrate
Hurt							
323	Voluntarily causing hurt	Shall not arrest without warrant	Summons	Bailable	Compoundable	Imprisonment for 3 years and fine	Court of a Magistrate
324	Voluntarily causing hurt by dangerous weapons or means	May arrest without warrant	Summons	Bailable	Not compoundable	Imprisonment for 7 years and whipping	Court of a Magistrate

CHAPTER XVI — OFFENCES AFFECTING THE HUMAN BODY — (continued)

Hurt

1	2	3	4	5	6	7	8
Penal Code Section	Offence	Whether the police may ordinarily arrest without warrant or not	Whether a warrant or a summons shall ordinarily issue in the first instance	Whether bailable or not	Whether compoundable or not	Maximum punishment under the Penal Code	By what Court triable
325	Voluntarily causing grievous hurt	May arrest without warrant	Summons	Bailable	Compoundable when permission is given	Imprisonment for 10 years and whipping	High Court

326	Voluntarily causing grievous hurt by dangerous weapons or means	May arrest without warrant	Summons	Not bailable	Not compoundable	Imprisonment for 15 years and whipping	High Court
327	Voluntarily causing hurt to extort property or a valuable security, or to constrain to do anything which is illegal or which may facilitate the commission of an offence	May arrest without warrant	Warrant	Not bailable	Not compoundable	Imprisonment for 10 years and whipping	High Court
328	Administering stupefying drug with intent to cause hurt etc	May arrest without warrant	Warrant	Not bailable	Not compoundable	Imprisonment for 10 years and whipping	High Court
329	Voluntarily causing grievous hurt to extort property or a valuable security, or to constrain to do anything which is illegal, or which may facilitate the commission of an offence	May arrest without warrant	Warrant	Not bailable	Not compoundable	Imprisonment for 15 years and whipping	High Court

CHAPTER XVI — OFFENCES AFFECTING THE HUMAN BODY — (continued)

Hurt

1	2	3	4	5	6	7	8
Penal Code Section	Offence	Whether the police may ordinarily arrest without warrant or not	Whether a warrant or a summons shall ordinarily issue in the first instance	Whether bailable or not	Whether compoundable or not	Maximum punishment under the Penal Code	By what Court triable
330	Voluntarily causing hurt to extort confession or information or to compel restoration of property etc	May arrest without warrant	Warrant	Bailable	Not compoundable	Imprisonment for 7 years and whipping	High Court
331	Voluntarily causing grievous hurt to extort confession or information or compel restoration of property etc	May arrest without warrant	Warrant	Not bailable	Not compoundable	Imprisonment for 10 years and whipping	High Court
332	Voluntarily causing hurt to deter public servant from his duty	May arrest without warrant	Warrant	Bailable	Not compoundable	Imprisonment for 5 years and whipping	Court of a Magistrate
333	Voluntarily causing grievous hurt to deter public servant from his duty	May arrest without warrant	Warrant	Not bailable	Not compoundable	Imprisonment for 10 years and whipping	High Court
334	Voluntarily causing hurt on grave and sudden	Shall not arrest	Summons	Bailable	Compoundable	Imprisonment for 6 months	Court of a Magistrate

	provocation not in- tending to hurt any other than the person who gave the provocation	without warrant				and fine	
335	Causing grievous hurt on grave and sudden pro- vocation not intending to hurt any other than the person who gave the provocation	May arrest without warrant	Summons	Bailable	Compoundable when permission is given	Imprisonment for 5 years and fine	Court of a Magistrate

CHAPTER XVI — OFFENCES AFFECTING THE HUMAN BODY — (continued)

Hurt

1	2	3	4	5	6	7	8
Penal Code Section	Offence	Whether the police may ordinarily arrest without warrant or not	Whether a warrant or a summons shall ordinarily issue in the first instance	Whether bailable or not	Whether compoundable or not	Maximum punishment under the Penal Code	By what Court triable
336	Doing any act which endangers human life or the personal safety of others	May arrest without warrant	Summons	Bailable	Not compoundable	Imprisonment for one year, fine of $1,000 or both	Court of a Magistrate
337	Causing hurt by an act which endangers human life etc	May arrest without warrant	Summons	Bailable	Compoundable when permission is given	Imprisonment for 2 years and fine	Court of a Magistrate
338	Causing grievous hurt by an act which endangers human life etc	May arrest without warrant	Summons	Bailable	Compoundable when permission is given	Imprisonment for 5 years and fine	Court of a Magistrate
Wrongful restraint and wrongful confinement							
341	Wrongfully restraining any person	May arrest without warrant	Summons	Bailable	Compoundable	Imprisonment for one year and fine	Court of a Magistrate
342	Wrongfully confining any person	May arrest without warrant	Summons	Bailable	Compoundable	Imprisonment for 3 years and fine	Court of a Magistrate
343	Wrongfully confining for 3 or more days	May arrest without warrant	Summons	Bailable	Not compoundable	Imprisonment for 5 years and fine	Court of a Magistrate
344	Wrongfully confining for 10 or more days	May arrest without warrant	Summons	Bailable	Not compoundable	Imprisonment for 7 years and whipping with	Court of a Magistrate

| 345 | Keeping any person in wrongful confinement, knowing that a writ has been issued for his liberation | Shall not arrest without warrant | Summons | Bailable | Not compoundable | not less than 3 strokes Imprisonment for 5 years, in addition to imprisonment under any other section | Court of a Magistrate |

CHAPTER XVI — OFFENCES AFFECTING THE HUMAN BODY — (continued)

Wrongful restraint and wrongful confinement

1	2	3	4	5	6	7	8
Penal Code Section	Offence	Whether the police may ordinarily arrest without warrant or not	Whether a warrant or a summons shall ordinarily issue in the first instance	Whether bailable or not	Whether compoundable or not	Maximum punishment under the Penal Code	By what Court triable
346	Wrongful confinement in secret	May arrest without warrant	Summons	Bailable	Not compoundable	Imprisonment for 5 years, in addition to imprisonment under any other section	Court of a Magistrate
347	Wrongful confinement for the purpose of extorting property or constraining to an illegal act etc	May arrest without warrant	Summons	Bailable	Not compoundable	Imprisonment for 10 years and whipping with not less than 3 strokes	Court of a Magistrate
348	Wrongful confinement for the purpose of extorting confession or information, or of compelling restoration of property etc	May arrest without warrant	Summons	Bailable	Not compoundable	Imprisonment for 7 years and whipping with not less than 3 strokes	Court of a Magistrate
Criminal force and assault							
352	Assault or use of criminal force otherwise than on grave provocation	Shall not arrest without warrant	Summons	Bailable	Compoundable	Imprisonment for one year and fine	Court of a Magistrate
353	Assault or use of criminal force to deter a public servant from discharge of his duty	May arrest without warrant	Warrant	Bailable	Not compoundable	Imprisonment for 5 years and fine	Court of a Magistrate
354	Assault or use of criminal	May arrest	Warrant	Bailable	Not	Imprisonment	Court of a

		force to a person with intent to outrage the modesty of that person	without warrant			compoundable	for 5 years and whipping	Magistrate

CHAPTER XVI — OFFENCES AFFECTING THE HUMAN BODY — (continued)

Criminal force and assault

1	2	3	4	5	6	7	8
Penal Code Section	Offence	Whether the police may ordinarily arrest without warrant or not	Whether a warrant or a summons shall ordinarily issue in the first instance	Whether bailable or not	Whether compoundable or not	Maximum punishment under the Penal Code	By what Court triable
354A	Aggravated outraging modesty	May arrest without warrant	Warrant	Non-bailable	Not compoundable	Imprisonment for 7 years and whipping	Court of a Magistrate
354B	Outraging modesty by person in position of trust or authority	May arrest without warrant	Warrant	Non- bailable	Not compoundable	Imprisonment for 10 years and whipping	High Court
355	Assault or criminal force with intent to dishonour a person, otherwise than on grave and sudden provocation	Shall not arrest without warrant	Summons	Bailable	Compoundable	Imprisonment for 5 years and whipping	Court of a Magistrate
356	Assault or criminal force in attempt to commit theft of property worn or carried by a person	May arrest without warrant	Warrant	Not bailable	Not compoundable	Imprisonment for 5 years and whipping	Court of a Magistrate
357	Assault or use of criminal force in attempt wrongfully to confine a person	May arrest without warrant	Warrant	Bailable	Not compoundable	Imprisonment for 3 years and whipping	Court of a Magistrate
358	Assault or use of criminal force on grave and sudden provocation	Shall not arrest without warrant	Summons	Bailable	Compoundable	Imprisonment for 6 months and fine of $2,000	Court of a Magistrate

CHAPTER XVI — OFFENCES AFFECTING THE HUMAN BODY — (continued)

Kidnapping, abduction, slavery and forced labour

1	2	3	4	5	6	7	8
Penal Code Section	Offence	Whether the warrant or	Whether a	Whether bailable or not	Whether compoundable or not	Maximum punishment under the Penal Code	By what Court

		police may ordinarily arrest without warrant or not	a summons shall ordinarily issue in the first instance				triable
363	Kidnapping	May arrest without warrant	Warrant	Not bailable	Not compoundable	Imprisonment for 10 years and fine	High Court
364	Kidnapping or abducting in order to murder	May arrest without warrant	Warrant	Not bailable	Not compoundable	Death	High Court
365	Kidnapping or abducting with intent secretly and wrongfully to confine a person	May arrest without warrant	Warrant	Not bailable	Not compoundable	Imprisonment for 30 years and whipping with not less than 12 strokes	High Court
366	Kidnapping or abducting a woman to compel her marriage or to cause her defilement etc	May arrest without warrant	Warrant	Not bailable	Not compoundable	Imprisonment for 30 years and whipping with not less than 12 strokes	High Court
366A	Procuration of minor girl	May arrest without warrant	Warrant	Not bailable	Not compoundable	Imprisonment for 30 years and whipping with not less than 12 strokes	High Court
366B	Importation of girl from foreign country	May arrest without warrant	Warrant	Not bailable	Not compoundable	Imprisonment for 30 years and whipping with not less than 12 strokes	High Court
367	Kidnapping or abducting in order to subject a person to grievous hurt, slavery etc	May arrest without warrant	Warrant	Not bailable	Not compoundable	Imprisonment for 30 years and whipping with not less than 12 strokes	High Court
368	Concealing or keeping in confinement a kidnapped person	May arrest without warrant	Warrant	Not bailable	Not compoundable	Punishment for kidnapping or abduction	High Court

CHAPTER XVI — OFFENCES AFFECTING THE HUMAN BODY — (continued)

Kidnapping, abduction, slavery and forced labour

1	2	3	4	5	6	7	8
Penal Code Section	Offence	Whether the police may ordinarily arrest without warrant or not	Whether a warrant or a summons shall ordinarily issue in the first instance	Whether bailable or not	Whether compoundable or not	Maximum punishment under the Penal Code	By what Court triable
369	Kidnapping or abducting a child with intent to take property from the person of such child	May arrest without warrant	Warrant	Not bailable	Not compoundable	Imprisonment for 30 years and whipping with not less than 12 strokes	High Court
370	Buying or disposing of any person as a slave	Shall not arrest without warrant	Warrant	Bailable	Not compoundable	Imprisonment for 30 years and whipping with not less than 12 strokes	High Court
371	Habitual dealing in slaves	May arrest without warrant	Warrant	Not bailable	Not compoundable	Imprisonment for 30 years and whipping with not less than 12 strokes	High Court
372	Selling or letting to hire a minor for purposes of prostitution etc	May arrest without warrant	Warrant	Not bailable	Not compoundable	Imprisonment for 30 years and whipping with not less than 12 strokes	High Court
373	Buying or obtaining possession of a minor for the same purposes	May arrest without warrant	Warrant	Not bailable	Not compoundable	Imprisonment for 30 years and whipping with not less than 12 strokes	High Court
373A	Importing women by fraud with intent etc	May arrest without warrant	Warrant	Not bailable	Not compoundable	Imprisonment for 30 years and whipping with not less than 12 strokes	High Court
374	Unlawful compulsory labour	May arrest without warrant	Warrant	Bailable	Compoundable	Imprisonment for 3 years and fine	High Court

CHAPTER XVI — OFFENCES AFFECTING THE HUMAN BODY — (continued)

Rape, unnatural offences and incest

1	2	3	4	5	6	7	8
Penal Code Section	Offence	Whether the police may ordinarily arrest without warrant or not	Whether a warrant or a summons shall ordinarily issue in the first instance	Whether bailable or not	Whether compoundable or not	Maximum punishment under the Penal Code	By what Court triable
376	Rape	May arrest without warrant	Warrant	Not bailable	Not compoundable	Imprisonment for 30 years and whipping with not less than 12 strokes	High Court
377	Unnatural offences	May arrest without warrant	Warrant	Not bailable	Not compoundable	Imprisonment for 10 years and fine	High Court
377A	Incest	May arrest without warrant	Warrant	Not bailable	Not compoundable	Imprisonment for 10 years and fine	Court of a Magistrate
377B	Engaging in sexual activity in the presence of person under 16	May arrest without warrant	Warrant	Not bailable	Not compoundable	Imprisonment for 5 years, fine or both	Court of a Magistrate
377C	Causing a person under 16 to watch sexual act	May arrest without warrant	Warrant	Not bailable	Not compoundable	Imprisonment for 5 years, fine or both	Court of a Magistrate
377D(1)	Obtaining consideration for sexual services with person under 18	May arrest without warrant	Warrant	Not bailable	Not compoundable	Imprisonment for 7 years and whipping	Court of a Magistrate
377D(2)	Communicating with another to obtain consideration for sexual services with person under 18	May arrest without warrant	Warrant	Not bailable	Not compoundable	Imprisonment for 3 years, fine or both	Court of a Magistrate
377E	Commercial sex with person under 18 outside Brunei Darussalam	May arrest without warrant	Warrant	Not bailable	Not compoundable	Imprisonment for 7 years and whipping	Court of a Magistrate

CHAPTER XVI — OFFENCES AFFECTING THE HUMAN BODY — (continued)

Rape, unnatural offences and incest

1	2	3	4	5	6	7	8
Penal Code Section	Offence	Whether the	Whether a warrant or	Whether bailable or not	Whether compoundable or not	Maximum punishment under the	By what Court

		police may ordinarily arrest without warrant or not	a summons shall ordinarily issue in the first instance			Penal Code	triable
377F	Tour outside Brunei Darussalam for commercial sex with person under 18	May arrest without warrant	Warrant	Not bailable	Not compoundable	Imprisonment for 10 years, fine or both	High Court
377G	Sexual grooming of person under 16	May arrest without warrant	Warrant	Not bailable	Not compoundable	Imprisonment for 3 years, fine or both	Court of a Magistrate
377H	Voyeurism	May arrest without warrant	Warrant	Not bailable	Not compoundable	Imprisonment for 3 years, fine or both	Court of a Magistrate
377I	Printing, publication of voyeuristic recordings	May arrest without warrant	Warrant	Not bailable	Not compoundable	Imprisonment for 5 years, fine or both	Court of a Magistrate

CHAPTER XVII — OFFENCES AGAINST PROPERTY

Theft

379	Theft	May arrest without warrant	Warrant	Not bailable	Not compoundable	Imprisonment for 3 years, fine or both	Any magistrate
380	Theft in a building, tent or vessel	May arrest without warrant	Warrant	Not bailable	Not compoundable	Imprisonment for 7 years and fine	Any magistrate
380A	Theft in protected place or place of worship	May arrest without warrant	Warrant	Not bailable	Not compoundable	Imprisonment for 10 years and whipping	High Court
381	Theft by clerk or servant of property in possession of master or employer	May arrest without warrant	Warrant	Not bailable	Not compoundable	Imprisonment for 7 years and fine	Court of a Magistrate

CHAPTER XVII — OFFENCES AGAINST PROPERTY — (continued)

Theft

1	2	3	4	5	6	7	8
Penal Code Section	Offence	Whether the police may ordinarily	Whether a warrant or a summons shall	Whether bailable or not	Whether compoundable or not	Maximum punishment under the Penal Code	By what Court triable

1	2	3	4	5	6	7	8
		arrest without warrant or not	ordinarily issue in the first instance				
382	Theft, preparation having been made for causing death or hurt, or restraint, or fear of death or of hurt or of restraint, in order to the committing of such theft or to retiring after committing it, or to retaining property taken by it	May arrest without warrant	Warrant	Not bailable	Not compoundable	Imprisonment for 15 years and whipping	High Court
Extortion							
384	Extortion	May arrest without warrant	Warrant	Not bailable	Not compoundable	Imprisonment for 7 years and whipping	Court of a Magistrate
385	Putting or attempting to put in fear or injury, in order to commit extortion	May arrest without warrant	Warrant	Not bailable	Not compoundable	Imprisonment for 10 years and whipping	Court of a Magistrate
386	Extortion by putting a person in fear of death or grievous hurt	May arrest without warrant	Warrant	Not bailable	Not compoundable	Imprisonment for 15 years and whipping	High Court
387	Putting or attempting to put a person in fear of death or grievous hurt, in order to commit extortion	May arrest without warrant	Warrant	Not bailable	Not compoundable	Imprisonment for 15 years and whipping	High Court

CHAPTER XVII — OFFENCES AGAINST PROPERTY — (continued)

Extortion

1	2	3	4	5	6	7	8
Penal Code Section	Offence	Whether the police may ordinarily arrest without warrant or not	Whether a warrant or a summons shall ordinarily issue in the first instance	Whether bailable or not	Whether compoundable or not	Maximum punishment under the Penal Code	By what Court triable
388	Extortion by threat of accusation of an offence punishable with death, or imprisonment for 10 years	May arrest without warrant	Warrant	Not bailable	Not compoundable	Imprisonment for 10 years and whipping	High Court

388	If the offence threatened be an unnatural offence	May arrest without warrant	Warrant	Not bailable	Not compoundable	Imprisonment for 15 years	High Court
389	Putting a person in fear of accusation of offence punishable with death, or with imprisonment for 10 years, in order to commit extortion	May arrest without warrant	Warrant	Not bailable	Not compoundable	Imprisonment for 10 years and whipping	High Court
389	If the offence be an unnatural offence	May arrest without warrant	Warrant	Not bailable	Not compoundable	Imprisonment for 15 years	High Court
Robbery and gang-robbery							
392	Robbery	May arrest without warrant	Warrant	Not bailable	Not compoundable	Imprisonment for 30 years and whipping with not less than 12 strokes	High Court
392	If committed between sunset and sunrise	May arrest without warrant	Warrant	Not bailable	Not compoundable	Imprisonment for 30 years and whipping with not less than 12 strokes	High Court
393	Attempt to commit robbery	May arrest without warrant	Warrant	Not bailable	Not compoundable	Imprisonment for 30 years and whipping with not less than 12 strokes	High Court

CHAPTER XVII — OFFENCES AGAINST PROPERTY — (continued)

Robbery and gang-robbery

1	2	3	4	5	6	7	8
Penal Code Section	Offence	Whether the police may ordinarily arrest without warrant or not	Whether a warrant or a summons shall ordinarily issue in the first instance	Whether bailable or not	Whether compoundable or not	Maximum punishment under the Penal Code	By what Court triable
394	Person voluntarily causing hurt in committing or attempting to commit	May arrest without warrant	Warrant	Not bailable	Not compoundable	Imprisonment for 30 years and whipping	High Court

	robbery, or any other person jointly concerned in such robbery					with not less than 12 strokes	
395	Gang-robbery	May arrest without warrant	Warrant	Not bailable	Not compoundable	Imprisonment for 30 years and whipping with not less than 12 strokes	High Court
396	Gang-robbery with murder	May arrest without warrant	Warrant	Not bailable	Not compoundable	Death	High Court
397	Robbery or gang-robbery or attempted robbery or gang-robbery with attempt to cause death or grievous hurt	May arrest without warrant	Warrant	Not bailable	Not compoundable	Imprisonment for not less than 7 years and whipping with not less than 12 strokes	High Court
398	Robbery or gang-robbery or attempted robbery or gang-robbery when armed with deadly weapon	May arrest without warrant	Warrant	Not bailable	Not compoundable	Imprisonment for not less than 7 years and whipping with not less than 12 strokes	High Court
399	Making preparation to commit gang-robbery	May arrest without warrant	Warrant	Not bailable	Not compoundable	Imprisonment for 10 years and whipping with not less than 12 strokes	High Court

CHAPTER XVII — OFFENCES AGAINST PROPERTY — (continued)

Robbery and gang-robbery

1	2	3	4	5	6	7	8
Penal Code Section	Offence	Whether the police may ordinarily arrest without warrant or not	Whether a warrant or a summons shall ordinarily issue in the first instance	Whether bailable or not	Whether compoundable or not	Maximum punishment under the Penal Code	By what Court triable
400	Belonging to a gang of persons associated for the purpose of habitually	May arrest without warrant	Warrant	Not bailable	Not compoundable	Imprisonment for 15 years and whipping	High Court

1	2	3	4	5	6	7	8
	committing gang-robbery					with not less than 6 strokes	
401	Belonging to a wandering gang of persons associated for the purpose of habitually committing theft	May arrest without warrant	Warrant	Not bailable	Not compoundable	Imprisonment for 7 years and whipping with not less than 6 strokes	High Court
402	Being one of two or more persons assembled for the purpose of committing gang-robbery	May arrest without warrant	Warrant	Not bailable	Not compoundable	Imprisonment for 7 years and whipping with not less than 6 strokes	High Court
Criminal misappropriation of property							
403	Dishonest misappropriate of movable property, or converting it to one's own use	May arrest without warrant	Warrant	Bailable	Not compoundable	Imprisonment for 2 years, fine or both	Court of a Magistrate
404	Dishonest misappropria-tion of property, knowing that it was in possession of a deceased person at his death and that it has not since been in the possession of any person legally entitled to it	May arrest without warrant	Warrant	Bailable	Not compoundable	Imprisonment for 3 years and fine	High Court

CHAPTER XVII — OFFENCES AGAINST PROPERTY — (continued)

Criminal misappropriation of property

1	2	3	4	5	6	7	8
Penal Code Section	Offence	Whether the police may ordinarily arrest without warrant or not	Whether a warrant or a summons shall ordinarily issue in the first instance	Whether bailable or not	Whether compoundable or not	Maximum punishment under the Penal Code	By what Court triable
404	If by clerk or person employed by deceased	May arrest without warrant	Warrant	Bailable	Not compoundable	Imprisonment for 7 years and fine	Court of a Magistrate
Criminal breach of trust							
406	Criminal breach of trust	May arrest without warrant	Warrant	Not bailable	Not compoundable	Imprisonment for 5 years and fine	Court of a Magistrate

407	Criminal breach of trust by a carrier, wharfinger etc	May arrest without warrant	Warrant	Not bailable	Not compoundable	Imprisonment for 10 years and fine	High Court
408	Criminal breach of trust by a clerk or servant	May arrest without warrant	Warrant	Not bailable	Not compoundable	Imprisonment for 10 years and fine	High Court
409	Criminal breach of trust by a public servant or by a banker, merchant or agent etc	May arrest without warrant	Warrant	Not bailable	Not compoundable	Imprisonment for 10 years and fine	High Court
Receiving of stolen property							
410	Suspected stolen property	May arrest without warrant	Warrant	Bailable	Not compoundable	Imprisonment for 3 months and fine of $1,600, or if previous conviction under Chapter XVII, imprisonment for one year and fine	Court of a Magistrate
411	Dishonestly receiving stolen property, knowing it to be stolen	May arrest without warrant	Warrant	Not bailable	Not compoundable	Imprisonment for 3 years, fine or both	Court of a Magistrate

CHAPTER XVII — OFFENCES AGAINST PROPERTY — (continued)

Receiving of stolen property

1	2	3	4	5	6	7	8
Penal Code Section	Offence	Whether the police may ordinarily arrest without warrant or not	Whether a warrant or a summons shall ordinarily issue in the first instance	Whether bailable or not	Whether compoundable or not	Maximum punishment under the Penal Code	By what Court triable
412	Dishonestly receiving stolen property knowing that it was obtained by gang-robbery	May arrest without warrant	Warrant	Not bailable	Not compoundable	Imprisonment for 15 years and fine	High Court
413	Habitually dealing in stolen property	May arrest without warrant	Warrant	Not bailable	Not compoundable	Imprisonment for 10 years and fine	High Court
414	Assisting in concealment or disposal of stolen property, knowing it to be stolen	May arrest without warrant	Warrant	Not bailable	Not compoundable	Imprisonment for 5 years and fine	Court of a Magistrate

Cheating							
417	Cheating	Shall not arrest without warrant	Warrant	Bailable	Not compoundable	Imprisonment for 3 years and fine	Court of a Magistrate
418	Cheating a person whose interest the offender was bound, either by law or by legal contract, to protect	Shall not arrest without warrant	Warrant	Bailable	Not compoundable	Imprisonment for 7 years and fine	Court of a Magistrate
419	Cheating by personation	May arrest without warrant	Warrant	Bailable	Not compoundable	Imprisonment for 7 years and fine	Court of a Magistrate
420	Cheating and thereby dishonestly inducing delivery of property or the making, alteration of a valuable security	May arrest without warrant	Warrant	Bailable	Not compoundable	Imprisonment for 7 years and fine	Court of a Magistrate

CHAPTER XVII — OFFENCES AGAINST PROPERTY — (continued)

Fraudulent deeds and dispositions of property

1	2	3	4	5	6	7	8
Penal Code Section	Offence	Whether the police may ordinarily arrest without warrant or not	Whether a warrant or a summons shall ordinarily issue in the first instance	Whether bailable or not	Whether compoundable or not	Maximum punishment under the Penal Code	By what Court triable
421	Fraudulent removal or concealment of property etc to prevent distribution among creditors	Shall not arrest without warrant	Warrant	Bailable	Not compoundable	Imprisonment for 5 years, fine or both	Court of a Magistrate
422	Fraudulently preventing from being made available for his creditors a debt or demand due to the offender	Shall not arrest without warrant	Warrant	Bailable	Not compoundable	Imprisonment for 5 years, fine or both	Court of a Magistrate
423	Fraudulent execution of deed of transfer containing a false statement of consideration	Shall not arrest without warrant	Warrant	Bailable	Not compoundable	Imprisonment for 5 years, fine or both	Court of a Magistrate
424	Fraudulent removal or concealment of property of himself, or any other person, or assisting in the doing thereof, or dishonestly releasing any demand or	Shall not arrest without warrant	Warrant	Bailable	Not compoundable	Imprisonment for 5 years, fine or both	Court of a Magistrate

	claim to which he entitled						
Mischief							
426	Mischief	Shall not arrest without warrant	Summons	Bailable	Compoundable when the only loss or damage caused is loss or damage to a private person	Imprisonment for 2 years, fine or both	Court of a Magistrate

CHAPTER XVII — OFFENCES AGAINST PROPERTY — (continued)

Mischief

1	2	3	4	5	6	7	8
Penal Code Section	Offence	Whether the police may ordinarily arrest without warrant or not	Whether a warrant or a summons shall ordinarily issue in the first instance	Whether bailable or not	Whether compoundable or not	Maximum punishment under the Penal Code	By what Court triable
427	Mischief, and thereby causing damage to the amount of $500 or upwards	Shall not arrest without warrant	Warrant	Bailable	Compoundable when the only loss or damage caused is loss or damage to a private person	Imprisonment for 5 years and whipping with not less than 2 strokes	Court of a Magistrate
427A	Mischief, and thereby causing damage in protected place or place of worship	May arrest without warrant	Warrant	Bailable	Not compoundable	Imprisonment for 5 years and whipping with not less than 4 strokes	Court of a Magistrate
428	Mischief by killing, poisoning, maiming, or rendering useless an animal	May not arrest without warrant	Warrant	Bailable	Not compoundable	Imprisonment for 5 years and whipping with not less than 2 strokes	Court of a Magistrate
430	Mischief by causing diminution of supply of water for agricultural purposes etc	May arrest without warrant	Warrant	Bailable	Not compoundable	Imprisonment for 5 years and whipping with not less than 4 strokes	Court of a Magistrate
431	Mischief by injury to public road, bridge, navigable river or channel and rendering it impassable or less safe for travelling or conveying property	May arrest without warrant	Warrant	Bailable	Not compoundable	Imprisonment for 5 years and whipping with not less than 4 strokes	Court of a Magistrate

CHAPTER XVII — OFFENCES AGAINST PROPERTY — (continued)

Mischief

1	2	3	4	5	6	7	8
Penal Code Section	Offence	Whether the police may ordinarily arrest without warrant or not	Whether a warrant or a summons shall ordinarily issue in the first instance	Whether bailable or not	Whether compoundable or not	Maximum punishment under the Penal Code	By what Court triable
432	Mischief by causing inundation or obstruc-tion to public drainage, attended with damage	May arrest without warrant	Warrant	Bailable	Not compoundable	Imprisonment for 5 years and whipping with not less than 4 strokes	Court of a Magistrate
433	Mischief by destroying or moving or rendering less useful a light-house or seamark, or by exhibiting false lights	May arrest without warrant	Warrant	Bailable	Not compoundable	Imprisonment for 7 years and whipping with not less than 4 strokes	High Court
434	Mischief by destroying or moving etc a landmark fixed by public authority	Shall not arrest without warrant	Warrant	Bailable	Not compoundable	Imprisonment for 5 years and whipping with not less than 4 strokes	Court of a Magistrate
435	Mischief by fire or explosive substance with intent to cause damage	May arrest without warrant	Warrant	Bailable	Not compoundable	Imprisonment for 15 years and whipping with not less than 6 strokes	High Court
436	Mischief by fire or explosive substance with intent to destroy a house etc	May arrest without warrant	Warrant	Not bailable	Not compoundable	Imprisonment for life	High Court
437	Mischief with intent to destroy or make unsafe a decked vessel or vessel of 20 tons burden	May arrest without warrant	Warrant	Not bailable	Not compoundable	Imprisonment for 15 years and whipping with not less than 6 strokes	High Court
438	The mischief described in the last section when committed by fire or explosive substance	May arrest without warrant	Warrant	Not bailable	Not compoundable	Imprisonment for life	High Court

CHAPTER XVII — OFFENCES AGAINST PROPERTY — (continued)

Mischief

1	2	3	4	5	6	7	8
Penal Code Section	Offence	Whether the police may ordinarily arrest without warrant or not	Whether a warrant or a summons shall ordinarily issue in the first instance	Whether bailable or not	Whether compoundable or not	Maximum punishment under the Penal Code	By what Court triable
439	Running vessel ashore with intent to commit theft etc	May arrest without warrant	Warrant	Not bailable	Not compoundable	Imprisonment for 10 years and whipping with not less than 6 strokes	High Court
440	Mischief committed after preparation made for causing death, or hurt etc	May arrest without warrant	Warrant	Not bailable	Not compoundable	Imprisonment for 10 years and whipping with not less than 6 strokes	Court of a Magistrate
Criminal trespass							
447	Criminal trespass	May arrest without warrant	Summons	Bailable	Compoundable	Imprisonment for one year and fine	Court of a Magistrate
448	House-trespass	May arrest without warrant	Warrant	Bailable	Compoundable	Imprisonment for 3 years and fine	Court of a Magistrate
448A	Punishment for house-trespass in protected place or place of worship	May arrest without warrant	Warrant	Warrant	Not compoundable	Imprisonment of not less than 2 years and not more than 7 years and whipping with not less than 2 strokes	Court of a Magistrate
449	House-trespass in order to the commission of an offence punishable with death	May arrest without warrant	Warrant	Not bailable	Not compoundable	Imprisonment for life and fine	High Court
450	House-trespass in order to the commission of an offence punishable with imprisonment for 15 years	May arrest without warrant	Warrant	Not bailable	Not compoundable	Imprisonment for 10 years and whipping	High Court

CHAPTER XVII — OFFENCES AGAINST PROPERTY — (continued)

Criminal trespass

1	2	3	4	5	6	7	8

Penal Code Section	Offence	Whether the police may ordinarily arrest without warrant or not	Whether a warrant or a summons shall ordinarily issue in the first instance	Whether bailable or not	Whether compoundable or not	Maximum punishment under the Penal Code	By what Court triable
451	House-trespass in order to the commission of an offence punishable with imprisonment	May arrest without warrant	Warrant	Bailable	Not compoundable	Imprisonment for 5 years and fine	Court of a Magistrate
451	If the offence is theft	May arrest without warrant	Warrant	Not bailable	Not compoundable	Imprisonment for 10 years and fine	High Court
452	House-trespass, having made preparation for causing hurt, assault etc	May arrest without warrant	Warrant	Not bailable	Not compoundable	Imprisonment for 10 years and whipping	High Court
453	Lurking house-trespass, or house-breaking	May arrest without warrant	Warrant	Not bailable	Not compoundable	Imprisonment for 5 years and whipping	Court of a Magistrate
453A	Punishment for lurking house-trespass or house-breaking in protected place or place of worship	May arrest without warrant	Warrant	Not bailable	Not compoundable	Imprisonment of not less than 3 years and not more than 10 years and whipping with not less than 3 strokes	High Court
454	Lurking house-trespass, or house-breaking in order to the commission of an offence punishable with imprisonment	May arrest without warrant	Warrant	Not bailable	Not compoundable	Imprisonment for 5 years and whipping	Court of a Magistrate
454	If the offence is theft	May arrest without warrant	Warrant	Not bailable	Not compoundable	Imprisonment for 10 years and whipping	High Court

CHAPTER XVII — OFFENCES AGAINST PROPERTY — (continued)

Criminal trespass

1	2	3	4	5	6	7	8
Penal Code Section	Offence	Whether the police may	Whether a warrant or a summons	Whether bailable or not	Whether compoundable or not	Maximum punishment under the Penal Code	By what Court triable

		ordinarily arrest without warrant or not	summons shall ordinarily issue in the first instance				
455	Lurking house-trespass or house-breaking after preparation made for causing hurt assault etc	May arrest without warrant	Warrant	Not bailable	Not compoundable	Imprisonment for 10 years and whipping	High Court
456	Lurking house-trespass or house-breaking by night	May arrest without warrant	Warrant	Not bailable	Not compoundable	Imprisonment for 5 years and whipping	Court of a Magistrate
456A	Punishment for lurking house-trespass or house-breaking by night in protected place or place of worship	May arrest without warrant	Warrant	Not bailable	Not compoundable	Imprisonment of not less than 3 years and not more than 10 years and whipping with not less than 3 strokes	High Court
457	Lurking house-trespass or house-breaking by night in order to the commission of an offence punishable with imprisonment	May arrest without warrant	Warrant	Not bailable	Not compoundable	Imprisonment for 5 years and whipping	Court of a Magistrate
457	If the offence is theft	May arrest without warrant	Warrant	Not bailable	Not compoundable	Imprisonment for 15 years and whipping	High Court
458	Lurking house-trespass or house-breaking by night, after preparation for causing hurt etc	May arrest without warrant	Warrant	Not bailable	Not compoundable	Imprisonment for 30 years and whipping with not less than 6 strokes	High Court

CHAPTER XVII — OFFENCES AGAINST PROPERTY — (continued)

Criminal trespass

1	2	3	4	5	6	7	8
Penal Code Section	Offence	Whether the police may ordinarily arrest without warrant	Whether a warrant or a summons shall ordinarily issue in	Whether bailable or not	Whether compoundable or not	Maximum punishment under the Penal Code	By what Court triable

		warrant or not	the first instance				
459	Grievous hurt caused whilst committing lurking house-trespass or house-breaking	May arrest without warrant	Warrant	Not bailable	Not compoundable	Imprisonment for 30 years and whipping with not less than 6 strokes	High Court
460	Death or grievous hurt caused by one of several persons jointly concerned in house-breaking by night etc	May arrest without warrant	Warrant	Not bailable	Not compoundable	Imprisonment for life	High Court
461	Dishonestly breaking open or unfastening any closed receptacle containing or supposed to contain property	May arrest without warrant	Warrant	Bailable	Not compoundable	Imprisonment for 5 years and whipping	Court of a Magistrate
462	Being entrusted with any closed receptacle containing or supposed to contain any property and fraudulently opening the same	May arrest without warrant	Warrant	Ditto	Not compoundable	Imprisonment for 5 years and whipping	Court of a Magistrate

CHAPTER XVIII — OFFENCES RELATING TO DOCUMENTS, FALSE DOCUMENTS AND CURRENCY NOTES AND BANK NOTES

1	2	3	4	5	6	7	8
Penal Code Section	Offence	Whether the police may ordinarily arrest without warrant or not	Whether a warrant or a summons shall ordinarily issue in the first instance	Whether bailable or not	Whether compoundable or not	Maximum punishment under the Penal Code	By what Court triable
465	Forgery	May arrest without warrant	Warrant	Bailable	Not compoundable	Imprisonment for 5 years and fine	Court of a Magistrate
466	Forgery of a record of a Court of Justice or of a Register of Births etc kept by a public servant	May arrest without warrant	Warrant	Not bailable	Not compoundable	Imprisonment for 7 years and fine	High Court
467	Forgery of a valuable security, will, or authority to make or transfer any valuable security, or to receive any money etc	May arrest without warrant	Warrant	Not bailable	Not compoundable	Imprisonment for 10 years and fine	High Court
468	Forgery for the purpose of cheating	May arrest without	Warrant	Not bailable	Not compoundable	Imprisonment for 10 years	High Court

			warrant			and fine	
469	Forgery for the purpose of harming the reputation of any person, or knowing that it is likely to be used for the purpose	May arrest without warrant	Warrant	Not bailable	Not compoundable	Imprisonment for 5 years and fine	Court of a Magistrate
471	Using as genuine a forged document which is known to be forged	May arrest without warrant	Warrant	Not bailable	Not compoundable	Punishment for forgery	Court of a Magistrate

CHAPTER XVIII — OFFENCES RELATING TO DOCUMENTS, FALSE DOCUMENTS AND CURRENCY NOTES AND BANK NOTES — (continued)

1	2	3	4	5	6	7	8
Penal Code Section	Offence	Whether the police may ordinarily arrest without warrant or not	Whether a warrant or a summons shall ordinarily issue in the first instance	Whether bailable or not	Whether compoundable or not	Maximum punishment under the Penal Code	By what Court triable
472	Making or counterfeiting a seal, plate etc with intent to commit a forgery punishable under section 467, or possessing with like intent any such seal, plate etc knowing the same to be counterfeit	May arrest without warrant	Warrant	Not bailable	Not compoundable	Imprisonment for 10 years and fine	High Court
473	Making or counterfeiting a seal, plate etc with intent to commit a forgery punishable otherwise than under section 467, or possessing with like intent any such seal, plate etc knowing the same to be counterfeit	May arrest without warrant	Warrant	Not bailable	Not compoundable	Imprisonment for 10 years and fine	High Court
474	Having possession of a document, knowing it to be forged, with intent to use it as genuine; if the document is one of the description mentioned in section 466	May arrest without warrant	Warrant	Not bailable	Not compoundable	Imprisonment for 10 years and fine	High Court

CHAPTER XVIII — OFFENCES RELATING TO DOCUMENTS, FALSE DOCUMENTS AND CURRENCY NOTES AND BANK NOTES — (continued)

1	2	3	4	5	6	7	8

Penal Code Section	Offence	Whether the police may ordinarily arrest without warrant or not	Whether a warrant or a summons shall ordinarily issue in the first instance	Whether bailable or not	Whether compoundable or not	Maximum punishment under the Penal Code	By what Court triable
474	If the document is one of the description mentioned in section 467	May arrest without warrant	Warrant	Not bailable	Not compoundable	Imprisonment for 15 years and fine	High Court
475	Counterfeiting a device or mark used for authenticating documents described in section 467 or possessing counterfeit marked material	May arrest without warrant	Warrant	Not bailable	Not compoundable	Imprisonment for 10 years and fine	High Court
476	Counterfeiting a device or mark used for authenticating documents other than those described in section 467 or possessing counterfeit marked material	May arrest without warrant	Warrant	Not bailable	Not compoundable	Imprisonment for 10 years and fine	High Court
477	Fraudulently destroying or defacing, or attempting to destroy or deface, or secreting a will etc	Shall not arrest without warrant	Warrant	Not bailable	Not compoundable	Imprisonment for 10 years and fine	High Court
477A	Falsification of accounts	Shall not arrest without warrant	Warrant	Not bailable	Not compoundable	Imprisonment for 10 years and fine	High Court
489A	Counterfeiting currency notes or bank notes	May arrest without warrant	Summons	Bailable	Not compoundable	Imprisonment for 15 years and fine	High Court
489B	Using as genuine forged or counterfeit currency notes or bank notes	May arrest without warrant	Summons	Bailable	Not compoundable	Imprisonment for 15 years and fine	High Court

CHAPTER XVIII — OFFENCES RELATING TO DOCUMENTS, FALSE DOCUMENTS AND CURRENCY NOTES AND BANK NOTES — (continued)

1	2	3	4	5	6	7	8
Penal Code Section	Offence	Whether the police may ordinarily	Whether a warrant or a summons shall	Whether bailable or not	Whether compoundable or not	Maximum punishment under the Penal Code	By what Court triable

1	2	3	4	5	6	7	8
		arrest without warrant or not	ordinarily issue in the first instance				
489C	Possession of forged or counterfeit currency notes or bank notes	May arrest without warrant	Warrant	Not bailable	Not compoundable	Imprisonment for 10 years and fine	High Court
489D	Making or possessing instruments or materials for forging for counterfeiting currency notes or bank notes	May arrest without warrant	Warrant	Not bailable	Not compoundable	Imprisonment for 10 years and fine	High Court

CHAPTER XX — OFFENCES RELATING TO MARRIAGE

493	Cohabitation caused by a man deceitfully inducing a belief of lawful marriage	Shall not arrest without warrant	Warrant	Not bailable	Not compoundable	Imprisonment for 10 years and fine	High Court
494	Marrying again during the lifetime of a husband or wife	Shall not arrest without warrant	Warrant	Bailable	Not compoundable	Imprisonment for 7 years and fine	High Court
495	Same offence with concealment of the former marriage from the person with whom subsequent marriage is contracted	Shall not arrest without warrant	Warrant	Not bailable	Not compoundable	Imprisonment for 10 years and fine	High Court

CHAPTER XX — OFFENCES RELATING TO MARRIAGE — (continued)

1	2	3	4	5	6	7	8
Penal Code Section	Offence	Whether the police may ordinarily arrest without warrant or not	Whether a warrant or a summons shall ordinarily issue in the first instance	Whether bailable or not	Whether compoundable or not	Maximum punishment under the Penal Code	By what Court triable
496	Marriage ceremony fraudulently gone through without lawful marriage	Shall not arrest without warrant	Warrant	Not bailable	Not compoundable	Imprisonment for 7 years and fine	High Court
498	Enticing or taking away or detaining with a criminal intent a married woman	Shall not arrest without	Warrant	Not bailable	Compoundable	Imprisonment for 2 years, fine or both	Court of a Magistrate

| | | | warrant | | | | |

CHAPTER XXI — DEFAMATION

500	Defamation	Shall not arrest without warrant	Warrant	Bailable	Compoundable	Imprisonment for 5 years and fine	Court of a Magistrate
501	Printing or engraving matter knowing it to be defamatory	Shall not arrest without warrant	Warrant	Bailable	Compoundable	Imprisonment for 5 years and fine	Court of a Magistrate
502	Sale of printed or engraved substance containing defamatory matter, knowing it to contain such matter	Shall not arrest without warrant	Warrant	Bailable	Compoundable	Imprisonment for 5 years and fine	Court of a Magistrate

CHAPTER XXII — CRIMINAL INTIMIDATION, INSULT AND ANNOYANCE

| 504 | Insult intended to provoke a breach of the peace | Shall not arrest without warrant | Warrant | Bailable | Compoundable | Imprisonment for 3 years and fine | Court of a Magistrate |
| 505 | False statement, rumour etc circulated with intent to cause mutiny or offence against the public peace | Shall not arrest without warrant | Warrant | Not bailable | Not compoundable | Imprisonment for 5 years and fine | Court of a Magistrate |

CHAPTER XXII — CRIMINAL INTIMIDATION, INSULT AND ANNOYANCE — (continued)

1	2	3	4	5	6	7	8
Penal Code Section	Offence	Whether the police may ordinarily arrest without warrant or not	Whether a warrant or a summons shall ordinarily issue in the first instance	Whether bailable or not	Whether compoundable or not	Maximum punishment under the Penal Code	By what Court triable
506	Criminal intimidation	May arrest without warrant	Warrant	Bailable	Not compoundable	Imprisonment for 3 years, fine or both	Court of a Magistrate
506	If threat be to cause death or grievous hurt	May arrest without warrant	Warrant	Bailable	Not compoundable	Imprisonment for 7 years, fine or both	High Court
507	Criminal intimidation by anonymous communication or having taken precaution to conceal whence the threat	May arrest without warrant	Warrant	Bailable	Not compoundable	Imprisonment for 3 years, in addition to the punishment	Court of a Magistrate

	comes					under section 506	
508	Act caused by inducing a person to believe that he will be rendered an object of Divine displeasure	May arrest without warrant	Warrant	Bailable	Not compoundable	Imprisonment for 3 years, fine or both	Court of a Magistrate
509	Uttering any word or making any gesture intended to insult the modesty of a woman etc	Shall not arrest without warrant	Warrant	Bailable	Not compoundable	Imprisonment for 3 years and fine	Court of a Magistrate
510	Appearing in a public place etc in a state of intoxication, an causing annoyance to any person	May arrest without warrant	Warrant	Bailable	Not compoundable	Imprisonment for 6 months and fine	Court of a Magistrate

CHAPTER XXIII — ATTEMPTS TO COMMIT OFFENCES

1	2	3	4	5	6	7	8
Penal Code Section	Offence	Whether the police may ordinarily arrest without warrant or not	Whether a warrant or a summons shall ordinarily issue in the first instance	Whether bailable or not	Whether compoundable or not	Maximum punishment under the Penal Code	By what Court triable
511	Attempting to commit offences punishable with imprisonment, fine or whipping or with a combination of such punishments and in such attempt doing any act toward the commission of the offence	According as the offence is one in respect of which the Police may arrest without warrant or not	According as the offence is one in respect of which a summons or warrant shall ordinarily issue	According as the offence contemplated by the offender is bailable or not	Compoundable when offence attempted is compoundable	Imprisonment not exceeding one half the term provided for the offence and fine and whipping	The Court by which the offence itself is triable

OFFENCES AGAINST OTHER LAWS

	If punishable with death or imprisonment for 3 years or upwards	May arrest without warrant	Warrant	Not bailable	Not compoundable		
	If punishable with imprisonment for less than 3 years or with fine only	Shall not arrest without warrant	Summons	Bailable	Not compoundable		

TRAVEL TO BRUNEI

US STATE DEPARTMENT SUGGESTIONS

COUNTRY DESCRIPTION: Brunei (known formally as the State of Brunei Darussalam) is a small Islamic Sultanate on the north coast of the island of Borneo. The capital, Bandar Seri Begawan, is the only major city. Tourist facilities are good, and generally available.

ENTRY REQUIREMENTS: For information about entry requirements, travelers may consult the Consular Section of the Embassy of the State of Brunei Darussalam, Suite 300, 2600 Virginia Ave., N.W. Washington, D.C. 20037; tel. (202) 342-0159.

MEDICAL FACILITIES: Adequate public and private hospitals and medical services are available in Brunei. Medical care clinics do not require deposits usually, but insist upon payment in full at time of treatment, and may require proof of ability to pay prior to treating or discharging a foreigner. U.S. medical insurance is not always valid outside the United States, and may not be accepted by health providers in Brunei. Travelers may wish to check with their health insurance providers regarding whether their U.S. policy applies overseas. The Medicare/ Medicaid program does not provide payment of medical services outside the United States. Supplemental medical insurance with specific overseas coverage, including provision for medical evacuation may be useful. Travel agents or insurance providers often have information about such programs. Useful information on medical emergencies abroad is provided in the Department of State, Bureau of Consular Affairs' brochure *Medical Information for Americans Traveling Abroad*, available via our home page and autofax service. For additional health information, the international travelers hotline of the Centers for Disease Control and Prevention may be reached at 1-877-FYI-TRIP (1-877-394-8747), via the CDC autofax service at 1-888-CDC-FAXX (1-888-232-3299), or via the CDC home page on the Internet: http://www.cdc.gov.

INFORMATION ON CRIME: The crime rate in Brunei is low, and violent crime is rare. The loss or theft abroad of a U.S. passport should be reported immediately to the local police and to the U.S. Embassy. Useful information on guarding valuables and protecting personal security while traveling abroad is provided in the Department of State pamphlet, *A Safe Trip Abroad*. It is available from the Superintendent of Documents, U.S. Government Printing Office, Washington, D.C. 20402 or via the Internet at http://www.access.gpo.gov /su_docs.

CRIMINAL PENALTIES: While in a foreign country, a U.S. citizen is subject to that country's laws and regulations, which sometimes differ significantly from those in the United States and do not afford the protections available to the individual under U.S. law. Penalties for breaking the law can be more severe than in the United States for similar offenses. Persons violating the law, even unknowingly, may be expelled, arrested or imprisoned. The trafficking in and the illegal importation of controlled drugs are very serious offenses in Brunei. Brunei has a mandatory death penalty for many narcotics offenses. Under the current law, possession of heroin and morphine derivatives of more than 15 grams, and cannabis of more than 20 grams, carries the death sentence. Possession of lesser amounts carries a minimum twenty-year jail term and caning.

AVIATION OVERSIGHT: The U.S. Federal Aviation Administration (FAA) has assessed the Government of Brunei's Civil Aviation Authority as Category 1 - in compliance with international aviation safety standards for oversight of Brunei's air carrier operations. For further information, travelers may contact the Department of Transportation within the U.S. at 1-800-322-7873, or visit the FAA's Internet website at http://www.faa.gov/avr/iasa/index.htm. The U.S. Department of Defense (DOD) separately assesses some foreign air carriers for suitability as official providers of air services. For information regarding the DOD policy on specific carriers, travelers may contact DOD at 618-256-4801.

ROAD SAFETY: Roads are generally good and most vehicles are new and well-maintained. However, vehicular accidents are now one of the leading causes of death in Brunei. Possibly due to excessive speed, tropical torrential rains, or driver carelessness, Brunei suffers a very high traffic accident rate.

CUSTOMS INFORMATION: More detailed information concerning regulations and procedures governing items that may be brought into Brunei is available from the Embassy of the State of Brunei Darussalam in the United States.

Registration/Embassy Location: U.S. citizens living in or visiting Brunei are encouraged to register in person or via telephone with the U.S. Embassy in Bandar Seri Begawan and to obtain updated information on travel and security within the country. The U.S Embassy is located on the third floor, Teck Guan Plaza, Jalan Sultan, in the capital city of Bandar Seri Begawan. The mailing address is American Embassy PSC 470 (BSB), FPO AP, 96534; the telephone number is (673)(2) 229-670; the fax number is (673) (2) 225-293.

Brunei-Muara

On her state visit to Brunei in September of 1998, Her Majesty Queen Elizabeth II of Britain made a tour of the Kampung Ayer in the capital a part of her busy itinerary. Made up of numerous communities, and home to some 30,000 people, the Kampung Ayer ("Villages on Water") is certainly the most well-known of all attractions in the country.

Kampung Ayer has been around for a very long time. When Antonio Pigafetta visited the country in the mid-16th century; Kampung Ayer was already a well-established, "home to some 25,000 families," according to Pigafetta. It was the hub for governance, business and social life in Brunei at that time.

The Kampung Ayer of today retains many of its old-world features described by Pigafetta. Only now, its daily well being is overlooked by the chiefs of the many villages in the area. The Kampung has almost all the amenities available in other communities, such as schools, shops and mosques. The houses there are usually well equipped with the latest in modern technology.

For as low as $1, boatmen will ferry passengers along the breadth and length of the Brunei river.

River cruises aboard ferryboats can start at both ends of the Brunei river, one at the Muara side, at the Queen Elizabeth jetty (named after the reigning British queen after her first Brunei visit in 1972), and others at the various river boat taxi stations in the heart of town.

The journey from the other end of the river starts at Kota Batu, the 16th century capital. The upstream journey during the 10 miles per hour cruise passes an ancient landmark, the tomb of Brunei's fifth ruler, Sultan Bolkiah, the Singing Captain, under whose reign Brunei was a dominant power in the 15th century.

On one bank of the Brunei river is a newer relic, a British warship used dur-ing World War II, sheltered from the elements.

The ferry moves on to Kampong Ayer, the Venice of the East. During the 18th century, here lived the fishermen, blacksmiths, kris (native sword) makers, brass artisans, nipa palm mat makers, pearl and oyster collectors, traders and goldsmiths.

A new Kampong Ayer has risen, settlements of concrete houses with glass windowpanes, and connected by cement bridges instead of the rickety, wooden catwalks.

Overlooking the old Kampong Ayer is the House of Twelve Roofs (Bum-bungan Dua Belas), built in 1906 and formerly the official home of the British resident. In the Kota Batu area on Jalan Residency is the Arts and Handicrafts Centre, where traditional arts and crafts have been revived.

But Kampung Ayer is only one of the many charms of Brunei that intrigue visitors to the country.

The Sultan Omar Ali Saifuddien Mosque in the heart of Bandar Seri Begawan continues to attract visitors fascinated by its majestic presence, and its role in the spiritual development of the Muslim citizens of the country. The mosque is practically synonymous with Brunei in general, and with the capital in particular.

Situated very close to the mosque is the public library with its attractive mural depicting Brunei's lifestyles in the 60s. The mural was done by one of Brunei's foremost artist, Pg Dato Hj Asmalee, formerly the director of Welfare, Youth and Sports, but now the country's ambassador to a neighbour-ing country.

Another landmark of the capital is the Yayasan Sultan Hj Hassanal Bolkiah commercial complex, across the road from the Sultan Omar Ah Saifuddien mosque. The newly estab-lished complex is the prime shopping centre in Brunei - four storeys of some of the premier big-name retailers in the region! There're outlets brandishing branded clothing, fast food, video games, books and many more. There's a supermarket in the Yayasan's west wing, and a food court on the east.

The Royal Regalia Building is a new addition to the attractions found in the capital. Within easy walking distance of all the hotels in the capital centre, the Royal Regalia Building houses artifacts used in royal ceremonies in the country. Foremost among the displays are the Royal Chariot, the gold and silver ceremonial armoury and the jewel-encrusted crowns used in coronation ceremonies.

Entrance is free, and visitors are expected to take off their shoes before entering. Opening hours are from 8.30am to 5.00pm daily except for Fridays, the Building opens from 9.00am until II.30am, and in the afternoon, from 2.30pm till 5.00pm.

Located next to the Royal Regalia Building is the Brunei History Centre. Drop by the centre and learn all about the genealogy and history of the sultans of Brunei, and members of the royal family. There is an exhibition area open to the public from 7.45 am to 12.15pm, and I.30pm to 4.3Opm daily except for Fridays.

Across the road from the Brunei Hotel, is what is known throughout Borneo as the 'tamu.' A 'tamu' is a congregation of vendors selling farm produce and general items. If you are lucky, you can find valuable bargains among the potpourri of metalware and handicraft hawked by some peddlers.

The main Chinese temple in the country lies within sight of the 'tamu.' Its elaborately designed roof and loud red color of its outer walls make the temple stand out from among the more staid schemes of nearby buildings.

A visit during one of the many festivals that is observed at this sanctum of Taoist beliefs would be a celebration of colors, spectacle and smell. Another place of worship that should not be missed by visitors to Brunei is the Church of St Andrew's. The church, possibly the oldest in Brunei, is designed like an English country parish, complete with bells in the let fry. It lies within walking distance of the Royal Regalia Building.

If you are staying in a hotel or Bandar Seri Begawan, why not pay the nightly foodstalls a visit? The stalls are located at a site in front of Sheraton Hotel, and serve a wide variety of hawker fare cheap! A dollar worth of the fried noodles is enough to fill you up.

Check out the local burgers. They're as delicious as those you'll find in established fast food outlets. Or try out 'Roti John'-the Malay version of the Big Mac. Ask for 'goreng pisang' (banana fritters), 'begedil' (potato balls), or 'popiah' (meat rolls), in your jaunts to the sweetmeat stalls.

Outside the capital center, a worthwhile place to visit is the Jame' Asr Hassanil Bolkiah Mosque in Kiarong, about six kilometers away. This is a beautiful sanctuary for communication with God, a personal bequest from His Majesty the Sultan of Brunei himself for the people of the country.

More than just a place of worship, the Jame' Asr is also a center for learning. Classes teaching Islamic religious principles and practices are held there regularly, as do religious lectures. And every Friday morning, the lobbies of its vast edifice are filled with children studying the Quran.

A visit to the mosque is usually part of the itinerary of package tours to Brunei, but if not, visitors can make the necessary arrangement with local tour operators. Visitors wishing to come inside the mosque need to report to the officers on duty, at the security counter on the ground floor.

Further on, you will find the Jerudong Park Playground. Situated some 20 kms to the west of the capital, JP as it is popularly called, is a must-go place for visitors to the country. It has been described as "Brunei's first high-tech wonderland for people of all ages."

There are many amusement rides at the Jerudong Park Playground to cater to everyone's need.

For those who like to live life on the edge, you would be pleased to know that JP has THREE (that's right, three) roller coasters, each with different degrees of thrills (or insanity factors if you want).

'Pusing Lagi' takes riders up a crest almost six storeys high, and then takes them down a steep incline, before twisting and turning at breakneck speed, so much so you will regret the 'Roti John' you just had.

'Boomerang' is for people who would rather go for diabolical twists and turns, while 'Pony Express' is a ride for those newly-initiated to roller-coasters.

Other popular rides include the 'Condor', a very fast merry-go-round that takes you up some five stores high, the 'Aladdin' (a mechanical 'flying carpet'), 'Flashdance' (no dancing experience required), and the wildly swinging 'Pirate Ship'.

There is also a bumper car arena, only for children and youngsters though, a video arcade and tracks for skateboarding and carting. For those who prefer something more sedate, also available are a 'Merry-Go-Round', certainly the most beautiful this side of London, and the 'Simulator Tour' (virtual reality rides into the fantastic and the exotic). Try the up-tower rides, where you are taken up a tower 15 stores high, and given a superb view of the park, and the surrounding area.

Situated next to the playground is the 20-acre Jerudong Park Gardens, which is well-known for its concert class auditorium. This was where Michael Jackson had his performances some years back, drawing a record 60,000 people to a colorful extravaganza the first time he performed.

Whitney Houston was another megastar who has had performed here, as well as Stevie ("I Just Called To Say I Love You) Wonder and the wonderful Seal ("Kissed By A Rose").

And if all that running and riding gives you an appetite, there's good food to be found in the eating area next to the parking lot. Almost anything you could crave for is available, ranging from the local hawker spreads to international fast food fare. If you're not doing anything on a Friday morning or late afternoon, take the no.55 purple bus to the end of its line at Jerudong Beach. Jerudong Beach on Fridays, especially around 9.00-10.00am, is a hive of activity as fishermen start landing their catch and customers rush to avail themselves of the freshest fish possible. The people you'll get to meet there are among the friendliest in the country, easy with the smile and always ready for the idle chatter.

But the place is more than just an informal fish market. Local fruits hang prominently from many of the stalls, and food stalls sell take-outs to cater to hungry visitors. Swim in the calm, waveless waters of the man-made cove, or try your luck fishing, if that is what you want to do. Just go around people watching.

 And if you need to go back to town, just board the purple bus to make the return journey.

The Bukit Shabbandar Forest Park is just the place to put those hiking legs to use. About ten minutes drive from the Jerudong Park Playground, the park is hectares upon hectares of greenery, dissected by tracks and paths for hiking, jogging and biking. While hiking, you can partake the wonders of the local forests - the rich diversity of its plant life, the exquisite charms and colors of the insects and reptiles that live within, and the symphony in the singing of the birds. Bukit Shahbandar Forest Park is just one of the 11 forest reserves in the country. To the east of Bandar Seri Begawan, about 6 kms into the Kota Batu area, visitors will find the Brunei Museum exhibits artifacts that archive the history of Negara Brunei Darussalam, both ancient and the relatively recent.

Well made cannons and kettles with their dragon motifs and elaborate patterns recall the glory days of the country -when Brunei was an important political and mercantile power in the region with territories that stretched that stretched all the way from Luzon Island in the Philippines to the whole western Borneo island.

There are exhibits which depict the traditional lifestyles of the various communities in the country, plus displays on the local flora and fauna. The exhibit by the local petroleum company Brunei Shell, illustrates the history on the discovery of oil in the country, and the commodity's significant role in economy of Brunei.

The Museum is open every day except Mondays from 9.00am till 5.00pm. On Fridays however, there is a scheduled prayer break from 11.30am until 2.30pm.

And situated downhill of the Brunei Museum is the Malay Technology Museum, which, as its name implies, houses the technological tools utilised by the Malays in ancient times.

A government booklet describes it as offering the "the visitor an intriguing insight into the lifestyle of the people of Brunei in by-gone eras". The Technology Museum is open daily, except Tuesdays, from 9.00 am till 5.00 pm. with a 3-hour midday prayer break on Fridays. Entrance is free.

There is an "Asean Square" in Persiaran Damuan which is located on a stretch between Jalan Tutong and the bank of the Brunei River about 4.5km from the capital. The "Asean Square" has on permanent display the work of a chosen sculptor themed Harmony in Diversity from each of the Asean member countries.

HOLIDAYS

Brunei Darussalam's vision is to promote the country as a unique tourist destination and gateway to tourism excellence in South East Asia. The objectives are to create international awareness of Brunei Darussalam as a holiday destination; to maximize earings of foreign exchange and make tourism as one of the main contributor to GDP. In addition, it will create employment opportunities.

The country offers a wide variety of attractive places to be visited and experienced. The rainforest and National Parks are rich in flora and fauna. Its most magnificent mosques, water village (traditional and historic houses on stilts), rich culture and Jerudong Theme Park are among the uniqueness of Brunei Darussalam.

The government is now actively promoting tourism as an important part of its economic diversification. It would like to see a target of 1 million-visitor arrival by the year 2000. From January to August 1999, the statistic recorded 405,532 visitors visited Brunei Darussalam.

National Day Celebration

The nation celebrates this joyous occasion on the 23rd of February and the people usually prepare themselves two months beforehand. Schoolchildren, private sector representatives and civil servants work hand-in-hand rehearsing their part in flash card displays and other colourful crowd formations. In addition mass prayers and reading of Surah Yaasin are held at mosques throughout the country.

Fasting Month (Ramadhan)

Ramadhan is a holy month for all Muslims. This marks the beginning of the period of fasting - abstinence from food, drink and other material comforts from dawn to dusk. During this month, religious activities are held at mosques and *suraus* throughout the country

Hari Raya Aidilfitri

Hari Raya is a time for celebration after the end of the fasting month of Ramadhan. In the early part of the first day, prayers are held at every mosque in the country. Families get together to seek forgiveness from the elders and loved ones. You will see Bruneians decked-out in their traditional garb visiting relatives and friends.

Special festive dishes are made especially for Hari Raya including satay (beef, chicken or mutton kebabs), ketupat or lontong (rice cakes in coconut or banana leaves), rendang (spicy marinated beef) and other tantalizing cuisines. In these auspicious occassion Istana Nurul Iman was open to the public as well as to visitors for 3 days. This provides the nation and other visitors the opportunity to meet His Majesty and other members of the Royal Family, in order to wish them a Selamat Hari Raya Aidilfitri.

Royal Brunei Armed Forces Day

31st of May marks the commemoration of the Royal Brunei Armed Forces formation day. The occassion is celebrated with military parades, artillery displays, parachuting and exhibitions.

Hari Raya Aidiladha

This is also known as Hari Raya Korban. Sacrifices of goats and cows are practiced to commemorate the Islamic historical event of Prophet Ibrahim S.A.W. The meat is then distributed among relatives, friends and the less fortunates.

His Majesty the Sultan's Birthday

This is one of the most important events in the national calendar with activities and festivities taking place nationwide. Celebrated on 15th July, this event begins with mass prayer throughout the country. On this occassion, His Majesty the Sultan delivers a 'titah' or royal address followed by investiture ceremony held at the Istana Nurul Iman. The event is also marked with gatherings at the four districts where His Majesty meets and gets together with his subjects.

Birthday of the Prophet Muhammad

In Brunei Darussalam, this occasion is known as the Mauludin Nabi S.A.W. Muslims throughout the country honour this event. Readings from the Holy Koran - the Muslim Holy Book, and an address on Islam from officials of the Ministry of Religious Affairs marks the beginning of this auspicious occasion. His Majesty the Sultan also gives a royal address and with other members of the Royal family, leads a procession on foot through the main streets of Bandar Seri Begawan. Religious functions, lectures and other activities are also held to celebrate this important occasion nationwide.

Chinese New Year

Celebrated by the Chinese community, this festival lasts for two weeks. It begins with a reunion dinner on the eve of the Lunar New Year to encourage closer rapport between family members. For the next two week, families visit one another bringing with them oranges to symbolize longevity and good fortune. Traditional cookies and food are aplenty during this festivity. Unmarried young people and children will receive 'angpow' or little red packets with money inside, a symbolic gesture of good luck, wealth and health.

Christmas Day

Throughout the world, 25th of December marks Christmas day, a significant day for all Christians. Christmas is nevertheless a joyous and colourful celebration enjoyed by Christians throughout the country.

Teachers' Day

Teachers' Day is celebrated on every 23rd September in recognition of the good deeds of the teachers to the community, religion and the country. It is celebrated in commemoration of the birthday of the late Sultan Haji Omar 'Ali Saifuddien Saadul Khairi Waddien, the 28th Sultan of Brunei for his contribution in the field of education including religious education. On this occassion, three awards are given away namely, Meritorious Teacher's Award, Outstanding Teacher's Award and "Guru Tua" Award.

Public Service Day

The date 29th September is observed as the Public Service Day with the objective to uphold the aspiration of the Government of His Majesty the Sultan and Yang Di-Pertuan of Brunei Darussalam towards creating an efficient, clean, sincere and honest public service. The Public Service Day commemorates the promulgation of the first written Constitution in Brunei Darussalam. The Public Service Day is celebrated with the presentation of the meritorious service award to Ministries and Government Departments.

PUBLIC HOLIDAYS

1 January	New Year's Day
8 January	* Hari Raya Aidilfitri
5 February	Chinese New Year
23 February	National Day
16 Mac	* Hari Raya Aidiladha
6 April	Muslim Holy Month of Hijiriah
31 May	Royal Brunei Armed Forces Day
15 Jun	The Birthday of Prophet Muhammad S.A.W.
15 July	The Birthday of His Majesty Sultan Haji Hassanal Bolkiah Mu'izzaddin Waddaulah, Sultan and Yang Di-Pertuan of Brunei Darussalam
25 October	* Israk Mikraj
27 November	* First Day of Ramadhan (Muslim fasting month)
13 December	Anniversary of The Revelation of the Quran
25 December	Christmas
27 December	* Hari Raya Aidilfitri

BUSINESS CUSTOMS

Customs & Traditions:	Brunei Darussalam possess a long heritage of traditions and customs, behavioural traits and forms of address. Muslims observe religious rites and rituals, which is woven into the lifestyle of Bruneian Malays. Breach of Malay conduct can be liable to prosecution in Islamic courts.
Social Protocol for non-Muslims:	It is customary for Bruneians to eat with their fingers rather than use forks and spoons. Always use the right hand when eating. It is polite to accept even just a little food and drink when offered. When refusing anything that is being offered, it is polite to touch the plate lightly with the right hand. As the left hand is considered unclean, one should use one's right hand to give and receive things. Bruneians sit on the floor, especially when there's a fairly large gathering of people. It is considered feminine to sit on the floor with a woman's legs tucked to one side, and equally

polite for men to sit with folded legs crossed at the ankles.

It's rude for anyone to sit on the floor with the legs stretched out in front, especially if someone is sitting in front.

It is considered impolite to eat or drink while walking about in public except at picnics or fairs.

During the Islamic fasting (Puasa) month, Muslims do not take any food from sunrise to sundown. It would be inconsiderate to eat and drink in their presence during this period.

It is not customary for Muslims to shake hands with members of the opposite sex. Public display of affection such as kissing and hugging are seen to be in bad taste. Casual physical contact with the opposite sex will make Muslims feel uncomfortable.

In the relationship between sexes, Islam enforces strict legislation. If a non-Muslim is found in the company of a Muslim of the opposite sex in a secluded place rather than where there are a lot of people, he/she could be persecuted.

If you are found committing 'khalwat' that is seen in a compromising position with a person of the opposite sex who is a Muslim, you could be deported.

When walking in front of people, especially the elderly and those senior in rank or position, it is a gesture of courtesy and respect for one to bend down slightly, as if one is bowing, except this time side way to the person or persons in front of whom one is passing. One of the arms should be positioned straight downwards along the side of the body.

Leaning on a table with someone seated on it especially if he/she is an official or colleague in an office is considered rude.

Resting one's feet on the table or chair is seen as overbearing. So is sitting on the table while speaking to another person who is seated behind it. To touch or pat someone, including children, on the head is regarded as extremely disrespectful.

The polite way of beckoning at someone is by using all four fingers of the right hand with the palm down and motioning them towards yourself. It is considered extremely impolite to beckon at someone with the index finger.

SUPPLEMENTS

IMPORTANT LAWS OF BRUNEI

ACT / ORDER	CHAPTER / NOTIFICATION NO.	DATE OF COMMENCEMENT	STATUS
ADMIRALTY JURISDICTION ACT [2000 Ed.]	CAP. 179	01-10-1996	
ADOPTION OF CHILDREN ORDER 2001	S 16/2001	26-03-2001	
AGRICULTURAL PESTS AND NOXIOUS PLANTS ACT [1984 Ed.]	CAP. 43	01-08-1971	
AIR NAVIGATION ACT [1984 Ed., Amended by S 21/97, S 41/00, S 42/00, Repealed by S 63/06 - Civil Aviation Order]	CAP. 113	01-03-1978	REPEALED w.e.f. 20-05-06
AIRPORT PASSENGER SERVICE CHARGE ACT [2000 Ed.]	CAP. 188	01-05-1999	
ANTI-TERRORISM (FINANCIAL AND OTHER MEASURES) ACT [2008 Ed.]	CAP. 197	14-06-2002	
ANTIQUITIES AND TREASURE TROVE ACT [2002 Ed.]	CAP. 31	01-01-1967	
APPLICATION OF LAWS ACT [2009 Ed.]	CAP. 2	25-04-1951	
ARBITRATION ACT [1999 Ed.]	CAP. 173	24-04-1994	
ARBITRATION ORDER, 2009	S 34/2009		not yet in force
ARMS AND EXPLOSIVES ACT [2002 Ed.]	CAP. 58	08-04-1927	
ASIAN DEVELOPMENT BANK ACT [2009 Ed.]	CAP. 201	25-04-2006	
AUDIT ACT [1986 Ed., Amended by S 39/03]	CAP. 152	01-01-1960	
AUTHORITY FOR INFO-COMMUNICATIONS TECHNOLOGY INDUSTRY OF BRUNEI DARUSSALAM ORDER 2001 [Amended by S 13/03, S 35/03]	S 39/2001	01-01-2003	
BANISHMENT ACT [1984 Ed.]	CAP. 20	31-12-1918	
BANKERS' BOOKS (EVIDENCE) ACT [1984 Ed., Amended by S 29/93, Repealed by S 13/06]	CAP. 107	17-04-1939	REPEALED w.e.f. 12-02-06
BANKING ACT [2002 Ed., Repealed by S 45/06 - Banking Order]	CAP. 95	01-01-1957	REPEALED w.e.f. 04-03-06
BANKING ORDER, 2006	S 45/2006	04-03-2006	
BANKRUPTCY ACT [1984 Ed., Amended by S 12/96, S 52/00]	CAP. 67	01-01-1957	
BILLS OF EXCHANGE ACT [1999 Ed.]	CAP. 172	03-05-1994	
BILLS OF SALE ACT [1984 Ed.]	CAP. 70	16-01-1958	
BIOLOGICAL WEAPONS ACT [1984 Ed.]	CAP. 87	11-04-1975	
BIRTHS AND DEATHS REGISTRATION ACT [1984 Ed.]	CAP. 79	01-01-1923	

BISHOP OF BORNEO (INCORPORATION) ACT [1984 Ed.]	CAP. 88	25-04-1951	
BRETTON WOODS AGREEMENT ACT [2000 Ed.]	CAP. 176	30-09-1995	
BROADCASTING ACT [2000 Ed., Corrigendum S 41/07]	CAP. 180	15-03-1997	
BRUNEI ECONOMIC DEVELOPMENT BOARD ACT [2003 Ed., Amended by S 11/03]	CAP. 104	11-04-1975	
BRUNEI FISHERY LIMITS ACT [1984 Ed., Amended by S 25/09]	CAP. 130	01-01-1983	
BRUNEI INVESTMENT AGENCY ACT [2002 Ed., Amended by S 14/03, S 64/04, S 15/08, S 78/08]	CAP. 137	01-07-1983	
BRUNEI MALAY SILVERSMITHS GUILD (INCORPORATION) ACT [1984 Ed.]	CAP. 115	15-07-1959	
BRUNEI NATIONAL ARCHIVES ACT [1984 Ed.]	CAP. 116	01-08-1981	
BRUNEI NATIONAL PETROLEUM COMPANY SENDIRIAN BERHAD ORDER 2002 [Amended by S 6/2003, S 12/2003]	S 6/2002	05-01-2002	
BRUNEI NATIONALITY ACT [2002 Ed., Amended by S 55/2002]	CAP. 15	01-01-1962	
BUFFALOES ACT [1984 Ed.]	CAP. 59	01-01-1909	
BURIAL GROUNDS ACT [1984 Ed.]	CAP. 49	01-01-1932	
BUSINESS NAMES ACT [1984 Ed., Amended by S 30/88]	CAP. 92	01-03-1958	
CENSORSHIP OF FILMS AND PUBLIC ENTERTAINMENTS ACT [2002 Ed.]	CAP. 69	21-08-1962	
CENSUS ACT [2003 Ed.]	CAP. 78	07-06-1947	
CENTRE FOR STRATEGIC AND POLICY STUDIES ORDER, 2006	S 64/2006	01-07-2006	
CHILD CARE CENTRES ORDER 2006	S 37/06	04-03-2006	
CHILDREN AND YOUNG PERSONS ORDER, 2006 [Corrigendum S 24/06, Amended by S 60/08]	S 9/2006		not yet in force
CHILDREN ORDER 2000 [Amended by S 84/00, S 48/03]	S 64/2000	01-09-2000	
CHINESE MARRIAGE ACT [1984 Ed., Amended by S 44/89]	CAP. 126	31-07-1955	
CIVIL AVIATION ORDER, 2006	S 63/2006	20-05-2006	
COIN (IMPORT AND EXPORT) ACT [1984 Ed.]	CAP. 33	01-01-1909	
COMMISSIONS OF ENQUIRY ACT [1984 Ed., Amended by S 35/05]]	CAP. 9	28-04-1962	
COMMISSIONERS FOR OATHS ACT [1999 Ed.]	CAP. 169	26-08-1993	
COMMON GAMING HOUSES ACT [2002 Ed., Amended by S 20/08]	CAP. 28	01-01-1921	
COMPANIES ACT [1984 Ed., Amended by S 26/98, S 23/99, S 69/01, S 10/03, S 45/06, S	CAP. 39	01-01-1957	

96/08]			
COMPULSORY EDUCATION ORDER, 2007	S 56/2007	24-11-2007	
COMPUTER MISUSE ACT [2007 Ed.]	CAP. 194	21-06-2000	
CONSTITUTION OF BRUNEI DARUSSALAM [2004 Ed., Amended by S 14/06] Article 8A, 9(2), 9(4), 9(5) - suspended by S 15/06 w.e.f. 21/02/06	CONST. I	29-09-1959	
CONSTITUTION [FINANCIAL PROCEDURE] ORDER [2004 Ed., Amended by S 14/08, S 36/08]	CONST. III	01-01-1960	
CONSULAR RELATIONS ACT [1984 Ed.]	CAP. 118	01-01-1984	
CONTINENTAL SHELF PROCLAMATION [1984 Ed.]	SUP. II		
CONTRACTS ACT [1984 Ed., Amended by S 60/02]	CAP. 106	17-04-1939	
CO-OPERATIVE SOCIETIES ACT [1984 Ed.]	CAP. 84	01-07-1975	
COPYRIGHT ORDER 1999	S 14/2000	01-05-2000	
CRIMINAL CONDUCT (RECOVERY OF PROCEEDS) ORDER 2000 [Amended by S 30/07]	S 52/2000	01-07-2000	
CRIMINAL LAW (PREVENTIVE DETENTION) ACT [2008 Ed.]	CAP. 150	26-11-1984	
CRIMINAL PROCEDURE CODE [2001 Ed., Amended by S 63/02, GN 273/02, S 62/04, S 32/05, S 6/06, S 9/06, S 4/07]	CAP. 7	01-05-1952	S 6/06 & S 9/06 not yet in force
CRIMINALS REGISTRATION ORDER, 2008	S 42/2008	01-04-2008	
CURRENCY ACT [1984 Ed., Repealed by S 16/04 - Currency and Monetary Order]	CAP. 32	Please refer Act	REPEALED w.e.f. 01-02-04
CURRENCY AND MONETARY ORDER 2004 [Corrigendum S 71/04; Amended by S 59/05, S 39/07]	S 16/2004	01-02-2004	
CUSTOMS ACT [1984 Ed., Amended by S 23/89, S 82/00, S 52/01, S 39/06, Repealed by S 39/06 - Customs Order]	CAP. 36	01-01-1955	REPEALED w.e.f. 04-03-06
CUSTOMS ORDER, 2006 [Amended by S 98/08]	S 39/06	04-03-2006	
DANA PENGIRAN MUDA MAHKOTA AL-MUHTADEE BILLAH FOR ORPHANS ACT [2000 Ed.]	CAP. 185	25-08-1998	
DEBTORS ACT [2008 Ed.]	CAP. 195	16-10-2000	
DEFAMATION ACT [2000 Ed.]	CAP. 192	17-08-1999	
DESCRIPTION OF LAND (SURVEY PLANS) ACT [1984 Ed.]	CAP. 101	03-09-1962	
DEVELOPMENT FUND ACT [1984 Ed.]	CAP. 136	01-01-1960	
DIPLOMATIC PRIVILEGES (EXTENSION) ACT [1984 Ed.]	CAP. 85	02-12-1949	

DIPLOMATIC PRIVILEGES (VIENNA CONVENTION) ACT [1984 Ed.]	CAP. 117	01-09-1982	
DISAFFECTED AND DANGEROUS PERSONS ACT [1984 Ed.]	CAP. 111	29-07-1953	
DISASTER MANAGEMENT ORDER 2006	S 26/06	01-08-2006	
DISSOLUTION OF MARRIAGE ACT [1999 Ed.]	CAP. 165	29-04-1992	
DISTRESS ACT [2009 Ed.]	CAP. 199	16-10-2000	
DOGS ACT [1984 Ed., Amended by S 14/90]	CAP. 60	17-04-1939	
DRUG TRAFFICKING (RECOVERY OF PROCEEDS) ACT [2000 Ed., Amended by S 29/07]	CAP. 178	30-03-1996	
EDUCATION ORDER 2003 [Amended by S 86/06]	S 59/2003	20-12-2003	
EDUCATION (BRUNEI BOARD OF EXAMINATIONS) ACT [1984 Ed.]	CAP. 56	01-01-1975	
EDUCATION (NON-GOVERNMENT SCHOOLS) ACT [1984 Ed., Repealed by S 59/03 - Education Order]	CAP. 55	01-01-1953	REPEALED w.e.f. 20-12-03
ELECTION OFFENCES ACT [1984 Ed.]	CAP. 26	28-04-1962	
ELECTRICITY ACT [2003 Ed. Amended by S 68/05]	CAP. 71	05-03-1973	
ELECTRONIC TRANSACTION ACT [2008 Ed.]	CAP. 196	01-05-2001	except Part X
EMBLEMS AND NAMES (PREVENTION OF IMPROPER USE) ACT [1984 Ed.]	CAP. 94	18-01-1968	
EMERGENCY REGULATIONS ACT [1984 Ed.]	CAP. 21	21-02-1933	
EMPLOYMENT AGENCIES ORDER, 2004	S 84/2004	20-12-2004	
EMPLOYMENT INFORMATION ACT [1984 Ed.]	CAP. 99	15-05-1974	
EVIDENCE ACT [2002 Ed., Amended by S 1/06, S 13/06]	CAP. 108	17-04-1939	
EXCHANGE CONTROL ACT [1984 Ed., Repealed by S 70/00]	CAP. 141	01-01-1957	REPEALED w.e.f. 01-07-00
EXCISE ACT [1984 Ed., Repealed by S 40/06 - Excise Order]	CAP. 37	01-01-1925	REPEALED w.e.f. 04-03-06
EXCISE ORDER 2006	S 40/06	04-03-2006	
EXCLUSIVE ECONOMIC ZONE, Proclamation of	S 4/94	20-07-1993	
EXTRADITION (MALAYSIA AND SINGAPORE) ACT [1999 Ed.]	CAP. 154	19-05-84 [S] 01-11-83 [M]	
EXTRADITION ACT [1984 Ed., Repealed by S 10/06 - Extradition Order]	CAP. 8	09-12-1915	REPEALED w.e.f. 07-02-06
EXTRADITION ORDER 2006	S 10/06	07-02-2006	
FATAL ACCIDENTS AND PERSONAL INJURIES ACT [1999 Ed.]	CAP. 160	01-02-1991	

FINANCE COMPANIES ACT [2003 Ed., Amended by S 41/06]	CAP. 89	01-08-1973	
FINGERPRINTS ENACTMENT [Repealed by S 42/08 - Criminals Registration Order, 2008]	17 of 1956	01-01-1957	REPEALED w.e.f. 01-04-08
FIRE SERVICES ACT [2002 Ed., Amended by S 79/06] now become FIRE AND RESCUE w.e.f. 1/8/2006	CAP. 82	04-08-1966	
FISHERIES ACT [1984 Ed., Amended by S 20/02, Repealed by S 25/09 - Fisheries Order, 2009]	CAP. 61	05-03-1973	REPEALED w.e.f. 30-05-09
FISHERIES ORDER, 2009	S 25/2009	30-05-2009	
FOREST ACT [2002 Ed., Amended by S 47/07]	CAP. 46	30-10-1934	
GENEVA AND RED CROSS ACT [1984 Ed.]	CAP. 86	12-12-1938	
GENEVA CONVENTION ORDER, 2005	S 40/2005		not yet in force
GUARDIANSHIP OF INFANTS ACT [2000 Ed.]	CAP. 191	01-08-1999	
GURKHA RESERVE UNIT ACT [1984 Ed.]	CAP. 135	09-05-1981	
HALAL CERTIFICATE AND HALAL LABEL ORDER, 2005 [Amended by S 75/08]	S 39/2005	01-08-2008	
HALAL MEAT ACT [2000 Ed., Amended by GN 274/02]	CAP. 183	17-04-1999	
HIJACKING AND PROTECTION OF AIRCRAFT ORDER 2000	S 41/2000	24-05-2000	
HIRE PURCHASE ORDER, 2006	S 44/06	04-03-2006	
IMMIGRATION ACT [2006 Ed., Amended by S 34/07]	CAP. 17	01-07-1958	
INCOME TAX ACT [2003 Ed., Amended by S 51/08, S 52/08, S 13/09]	CAP. 35	31-12-1949	
INCOME TAX (PETROLEUM) ACT [2004 Ed.]	CAP. 119	18-12-1963	
INDUSTRIAL CO-ORDINATION ORDER 2001	S 44/2001	01-06-2001	
INDUSTRIAL DESIGNS ORDER 1999	S 7/2000	01-05-2000	
INFECTIOUS DISEASES ORDER 2003 [Amended by S 27/06]	S 34/2003	08-05-2003	
INSURANCE ORDER, 2006 [Amended by S 88/06, S 28/07, S 54/07]	S 48/2006	04-03-2006	
INTERMEDIATE COURTS ACT [1999 Ed., Amended by S 57/04, S 74/04, S 80/06]	CAP. 162	01-07-1991	
INTERNAL SECURITY ACT [2008 Ed.]	CAP. 133	01-04-1983	
INTERNATIONAL ARBITRATION ORDER, 2009	S 35/2009		not yet in force
INTERNATIONAL BANKING ORDER 2000 [Amended by S 9/01]	S 53/2000	01-07-2000	
INTERNATIONAL BUSINESS COMPANIES ORDER 2000 [Amended by S 37/03]	S 56/2000	01-07-2000	

INTERNATIONAL INSURANCE AND TAKAFUL ORDER 2002	S 43/2002	01-07-2002	
INTERNATIONAL LIMITED PARTNERSHIP ORDER 2000 [Amended by S 7/01]	S 45/2000	01-07-2000	
INTERNATIONAL TRUSTS ORDER 2000	S 55/2000	01-07-2000	
INTERNATIONALLY PROTECTED PERSONS ACT [1984 Ed.]	CAP. 16	08-07-1995	
INTERPRETATION AND GENERAL CLAUSES ACT [2006 Ed.]	CAP. 4	29-09-1959	
INTOXICATING SUBSTANCES ACT [1999 Ed., Amended by S 58/07]	CAP. 161	01-05-1992	
INVENTIONS ACT [1984 Ed., Amended by S 28/97]	CAP. 72	01-03-1952	
INVESTMENT INCENTIVES ACT [1984 Ed., Repealed by S 48/01 - Investment Incentives Order]	CAP. 97	01-05-1975	REPEALED w.e.f. 01-06-01
INVESTMENT INCENTIVES ORDER 2001	S 48/2001	01-06-2001	
ISLAMIC ADOPTION OF CHILDREN ORDER 2001	S 14/2001	26-03-2001	except section 3
ISLAMIC BANKING ACT [1999 Ed., Repealed by S 96/08 - Islamic Banking Order, 2008]	CAP. 168	02-12-1992	REPEALED w.e.f. 30-09-08
ISLAMIC BANKING ORDER, 2008	S 96/2008	30-09-2008	
ISLAMIC FAMILY LAW ORDER 1999 [Corrigenda S 42/04, Amended by S 17/05]	S 12/2000	26-03-2001	except section 3
KIDNAPPING ACT [1999 Ed.]	CAP. 164	22-02-1992	
KOLEJ UNIVERSITI PERGURUAN UGAMA SERI BEGAWAN ORDER, 2008	S 84/2008	30-08-2008	
LABOUR ACT [2002 Ed., Amended by GN 274/02, S 84/04]	CAP. 93	01-02-1955	
LAND ACQUISITION ACT [1984 Ed.]	CAP. 41	03-01-1949	
LAND CODE [1984 Ed., Amended by S 29/09]	CAP. 40	06-09-1909	
LAND CODE (STRATA) ACT [2000 Ed., Amended by S 28/09]	CAP. 189	01-07-2009	
LAW REFORM (CONTRIBUTORY NEGLIGENCE) ACT [1984 Ed., Repealed by S 4/91]	CAP. 53	25-04-1951	REPEALED w.e.f. 01-02-91
LAW REFORM (PERSONAL INJURIES) ACT [1984 Ed., Repealed by S 4/91]	CAP. 10	25-04-1951	REPEALED w.e.f. 01-02-91
LAW REVISION ACT [2001 Ed., Amended by S 93/00]	CAP. 1	01-01-1984	
LAYOUT DESIGNS ORDER 1999	S 8/2000	01-05-2000	
LEGAL PROFESSION ACT [2006 Ed.]	CAP. 132	01-01-1987	

LEGISLATIVE COUNCIL AND COUNCIL OF MINISTERS ACT (REMUNERATION AND PRIVILEGES) [1984 Ed., Amended by S 46/05, S 12/06]	CAP. 134	30-01-1965	
LEGITIMACY ORDER 2001	S 33/2001	21-04-2001	
LICENSED LAND SURVEYORS ACT [1984 Ed.]	CAP. 100	01-07-1980	
LIMITATION ACT [2000 Ed.]	CAP. 14	01-09-1991	
LUNACY ACT [1984 Ed.]	CAP. 48	09-07-1929	
MAINTENANCE ORDERS RECIPROCAL ENFORCEMENT ACT [2000 Ed.]	CAP. 175	25-02-1998	
MARITIME OFFENCES (SHIPS AND FIXED PLATFORMS) ORDER, 2007	S 61/2007	17-12-2007	
MARRIAGE ACT [1984 Ed., Amended by S 42/05]	CAP. 76	03-08-1948	
MARRIED WOMEN ACT [2000 Ed.]	CAP. 190	01-08-1999	
MEDICAL PRACTITIONERS AND DENTISTS ACT [1984 Ed., Amended by GN 273/02]	CAP. 112	29-07-1953	
MEDICINES ORDER, 2007	S 79/2007	01-01-2008	sec.1(2)(a) only
MERCHANDISE MARKS ACT [1984 Ed.]	CAP. 96	07-10-1953	
MERCHANT SHIPPING ACT [1984 Ed., Repealed by S 27/02 - Merchant Shipping Order]	CAP. 145	01-09-1984	REPEALED w.e.f. 16-05-02
MERCHANT SHIPPING ORDER, 2002 [Amended by S 23/09]	S 27/2002	16-05-2002	
MERCHANT SHIPPING (CIVIL LIABILITY AND COMPENSATION FOR OIL POLLUTION) ORDER, 2008	S 54/2008	17-04-2008	
MIDWIVES ACT [1984 Ed., Amended by S 47/02]	CAP. 139	01-01-1959	
MINING ACT [1984 Ed.]	CAP. 42	04-03-1920	
MINOR OFFENCES ACT [1984 Ed., Amended by S 26/90, S 43/98, S 89/06, S 82/08]	CAP. 30	29-07-1929	
MISCELLANEOUS LICENCES ACT [1984 Ed., Amended by S 43/08, S 85/08]	CAP. 127	01-01-1983	
MISUSE OF DRUGS ACT [2001 Ed., Amended by S 7/2002, GN 273/02, S 59/07, S 5/08]	CAP. 27	01-07-1978	
MONEY CHANGING AND REMITTANCE BUSINESS ACT [1999 Ed.]	CAP. 174	01-01-1995	
MONEY LAUNDERING ORDER 2000	S 44/2000	01-07-2000	
MONEYLENDERS ACT [1984 Ed., Amended by S 53/00, S 45/06]	CAP. 62	01-01-1922	
MONOPOLIES ACT [2003 Ed.]	CAP. 73	13-12-1932	
MOTOR VEHICLES INSURANCE (THIRD PARTY RISKS) ACT [1984 Ed., Amended by S 28/98, S 48/08 (corrig)]	CAP. 90	28-02-1950	

Act	Cap/No	Date	Notes
MUNICIPAL BOARDS ACT [1984 Ed.]	CAP. 57	01-01-1921	
MUTUAL ASSISTANCE IN CRIMINAL MATTERS ORDER, 2005	S 7/2005	01-01-2006	
MUTUAL FUNDS ORDER 2001	S 18/2001	01-01-2001	
NATIONAL BANK OF BRUNEI BERHAD; NATIONAL FINANCE SENDIRIAN BERHAD ACT [1999 Ed.]	CAP. 156	19-11-1986	
NATIONAL REGISTRATION ACT [2002 Ed.]	CAP. 19	01-03-1965	
NEWSPAPERS ACT [2002 Ed., Amended by S 36/05, S 86/08]	CAP. 105	01-01-1959	
NORTH BORNEO (DEFINITION BOUNDARIES) ORDER IN COUNCIL 1958 [1984 Ed.]	Sup. III		
NURSES REGISTRATION ACT [1984 Ed.]	CAP. 140	01-01-1968	
OATHS AND AFFIRMATIONS ACT [2001 Ed.]	CAP. 3	08-09-1958	
OFFENDERS (PROBATION AND COMMUNITY SERVICE) ORDER, 2006 [Amended by S 80/08]	S 6/2006		not yet in force
OFFICIAL SECRETS ACT [1988 Ed., Amended by S 52/05]	CAP. 153	02-01-1940	
OLD AGE AND DISABILITY PENSIONS ACT [1984 Ed., Amended by GN 273/02, GN 649/03, S 38/08]	CAP. 18	01-01-1955	
PASSPORTS ACT [1984 Ed., Amended by S 6/86, S 2/00, S 44/03, S 24/04, S 54/05, S 33/07]	CAP. 146	14-12-1983	
PATENTS ORDER, 1999	S 42/99		not yet in force
PAWNBROKERS ACT [1984 Ed., Repealed by S 41/05 - Pawnbrokers Order]	CAP. 63	01-01-1920	REPEALED w.e.f. 01-08-05
PAWNBROKERS ORDER 2002 [Amended by S 41/05]	S 60/2002	01-08-2005	
PENAL CODE [2001 Ed.]	CAP. 22	01-05-1952	
PENSIONS ACT [1984 Ed., Amended S 23/87, S 37/08]	CAP. 38	01-03-1959	
PERBADANAN TABUNG AMANAH ISLAM BRUNEI ACT [1999 Ed., Amended by S 15/03, S 29/04]	CAP. 163	29-09-1991	
PERSATUAN BULAN SABIT MERAH NEGARA BRUNEI DARUSSALAM (INCORPORATION) ACT [1999 Ed., Amended by S 40/05]	CAP. 159	28-11-1999	S 40/05 not yet in force
PETROLEUM MINING ACT [2002 Ed.]	CAP. 44	18-11-1963	
PETROLEUM (PIPE-LINES) ACT [1984 Ed.]	CAP. 45	04-03-1920	
PHARMACISTS REGISTRATION ORDER 2001	S 21/2001	01-07-2001	
POISONS ACT [1984 Ed., Amended by S 16/96, S 28/01]	CAP. 114	01-07-1957	
PORTS ACT [1984 Ed., Amended by S 17/88, S 26/02, S 18/05]	CAP. 144	01-01-1986	

Act	Cap/No.	Date	Notes
POST OFFICE ACT [1984 Ed., Amended by S 17/97]	CAP. 52	01-05-1988	
POWERS OF ATTORNEY ACT [2002 Ed.]	CAP. 13	01-01-1922	
PRESERVATION OF BOOKS ACT [1984 Ed.]	CAP. 125	18-01-1967	
PREVENTION OF CORRUPTION ACT [2002 Ed.]	CAP. 131	01-01-1982	
PREVENTION OF POLLUTION OF THE SEA ORDER, 2005	S 18/2005	28-03-2005	
PRICE CONTROL ACT [2002 Ed.]	CAP. 142	13-03-1974	
PRIME MINISTER'S INCORPORATION ORDER 1984 [Amended the Constitution (Mentri Besar Incorporation) Order 1960 (S 55/60)]	S 5/84	01-01-1984	
PRISONS ACT [1984 Ed., Amended by S 12/89]	CAP. 51	01-07-1979	
PROBATE AND ADMINISTRATION ACT [1984 Ed.]	CAP. 11	01-02-1956	
PROTECTED AREAS AND PROTECTED PLACES ACT [1984 Ed.]	CAP. 147	01-12-1983	
PUBLIC ENTERTAINMENT ACT [2000 Ed.]	CAP. 181	01-06-1997	
PUBLIC HEALTH (FOOD) ACT [2000 Ed., Amended by S 73/00, S 64/02]	CAP. 182	01-01-2001	
PUBLIC OFFICERS (LIABILITIES) ACT [1984 Ed., Repealed by S 40/00]	CAP. 80	25-02-1929	REPEALED w.e.f. 24-05-00
PUBLIC ORDER ACT [2002 Ed., Amended by S 33/05]	CAP. 148	01-11-1983	
PUBLIC SERVICE COMMISSION ACT [1984 Ed.]	CAP. 83	01-01-1983	
QUARANTINE AND PREVENTION OF DISEASE ACT [1984 Ed., Repealed by S 34/03 - Infectious Diseases Order]	CAP. 47	09-08-1934	REPEALED w.e.f. 08-05-03
RECIPROCAL ENFORCEMENT OF FOREIGN JUDGMENTS ACT [2000 Ed.]	CAP. 177	27-03-1996	
REGISTERED AGENTS AND TRUSTEES LICENSING ORDER 2000	S 54/2000	01-07-2000	
REGISTRATION OF ADOPTIONS ACT [1984 Ed., Amended by S 15/01]	CAP. 123	01-01-1962	
REGISTRATION OF GUESTS ACT [1984 Ed.]	CAP. 122	01-07-1974	
REGISTRATION OF MARRIAGES ACT [2002 Ed.]	CAP. 124	01-01-1962	
RELIGIOUS COUNCIL AND KADIS COURTS ACT [1984 Ed., Amended by S 1/88, S 31/90, S 37/98, S 12/00, S 24/03, S 17/05, S 26/05]	CAP. 77	01-02-1956	
ROAD TRAFFIC ACT [2007 Ed., Amended by S 39/04, S 59/08]	CAP. 68	01-01-1956	S 39/04 not yet in force
ROYAL BRUNEI ARMED FORCES ACT [1984 Ed., Amended by S 2/06]	CAP. 149	01-01-1984	
ROYAL BRUNEI POLICE FORCE ACT [1984 Ed.]	CAP. 50	31-12-1983	

ROYAL ORDERS AND DECORATIONS [1984 Ed.]	Sup. V		
RUBBER DEALERS ACT [1984 Ed.]	CAP. 64	01-01-1921	
SALE OF GOODS ACT [1999 Ed.]	CAP. 170	03-05-1994	
SARAWAK (DEFINITION OF BOUNDARIES) ORDER IN COUNCIL 1958 [1984 Ed.]	Sup. IV		
SEAMEN'S UNEMPLOYMENT INDEMNITY ACT [1984 Ed.]	CAP. 75	02-10-1939	
SECOND-HAND DEALERS ACT [1984 Ed.]	CAP. 65	01-01-1934	
SECURITIES ORDER 2001 [Amended by S 33/02, S 43/05]	S 31/2001	01-03-2001	
SECURITY AGENCIES ACT [2000 Ed.]	CAP. 187	01-06-2000	
SEDITION ACT [1984 Ed., Amended by S 34/05]	CAP. 24	06-04-1948	
SMALL CLAIMS TRIBUNALS ORDER, 2006	S 81/2006		not yet in force
SOCIETIES ACT [1984 Ed., Repealed by S 1/05 - Societies Order]	CAP. 66	04-10-1948	REPEALED w.e.f. 04-01-05
SOCIETIES ORDER, 2005	S 1/2005	04-01-2005	
SPECIFIC RELIEF ACT [1984 Ed., Amended by S 59/04]	CAP. 109	17-04-1939	
STAMP ACT [2003 Ed.]	CAP. 34	01-01-1909	
STATISTICS ACT [1984 Ed.]	CAP. 81	01-08-1977	
STATUTORY DECLARATION ACT [1984 Ed.]	CAP. 12	11-01-1951	
STATUTORY FUNDS APPROPRIATION ENACTMENT 1959 [Amended by S 63/63, 7 of 1966, 19 of 1967, 4 of 1975, S 50/76, S 49/76, S 110/79, S 12/82, S 13/82, S 42/84, S 13/86, S 22/93, S 22/03, S 39/08]	9 of 1959	01-01-1960	
SUBORDINATE COURTS ACT [2001 Ed., Amended by S 56/04, S 73/04, S 9/06, S 60/08]	CAP. 6	01-01-1983	S 9/06 and S60/08 not yet in force
SUBSCRIPTION CONTROL ACT [1984 Ed.]	CAP. 91	15-12-1953	
SUCCESSION AND REGENCY PROCLAMATION 1959 [2004 Ed., Amended by S 16/06, S 78/06]	CONST. II	29-09-1959	
SUMMONSES AND WARRANTS (SPECIAL PROVISIONS) ACT [1999 Ed.]	CAP. 155	19-05-84 [S] 01-11-83 [M]	
SUNGAI LIANG AUTHORITY ACT [2009 Ed.]	CAP. 200	06-04-2007	
SUPREME COURT ACT [2001 Ed., Amended by S 55/04, S 61/04, S 72/04]	CAP. 5	16-09-1963	
SUPREME COURT (APPEALS TO PRIVY COUNCIL) ACT [1999 Ed., Amended by S 45/05]	CAP. 158	01-02-1990	
SUSTAINABILITY FUND ORDER, 2008	S 36/2008	11-03-2008	

SYARIAH COURTS ACT [2000 Ed., Amended by S 17/05]	CAP. 184	26-03-2001	
SYARIAH COURTS CIVIL PROCEDURE ORDER, 2005 [available in Malay text only] - PERINTAH ACARA MAL MAHKAMAH-MAHKAMAH SYARIAH, 2005	S 26/2005	06-04-2005	
SYARIAH COURTS EVIDENCE ORDER, 2001	S 63/2001	15-10-2001 except s.5	
SYARIAH FINANCIAL SUPERVISORY BOARD ORDER, 2006 [Amended by S 65/07]	S 5/2006	17-01-2006	
TABUNG AMANAH PEKERJA ACT [1999 Ed., Amended by S 9/99, S 9/00, S 16/03, S 2/07]	CAP. 167	01-01-1993	
TAKAFUL ORDER, 2008	S 100/2008	30-09-2008	
TELECOMMUNICATIONS ACT [1984 Ed. Repealed by S 38/01 - Telecommunication Order]	CAP. 54	01-12-1974	REPEALED w.e.f. 01-04-06
TELECOMMUNICATIONS ORDER 2001	S 38/2001	01-04-2006	
TELECOMMUNICATION SUCCESSOR COMPANY ORDER 2001 [Corrigendum S 25/06]	S 37/2001	01-04-2006	
TERRITORIAL WATERS OF BRUNEI ACT [2002 Ed.]	CAP. 138	10-02-1983	
TOBACCO ORDER 2005	S 49/2005	01-06-2008	
TOKYO CONVENTION ACT [2008 Ed.]	CAP. 198	24-05-2000	
TOWN AND COUNTRY PLANNING (DEVELOPMENT CONTROL) ACT [1984 Ed.]	CAP. 143	19-09-1972	
TRADE DISPUTES ACT [1984 Ed.]	CAP. 129	21-01-1962	
TRADE MARKS ACT [2000 Ed.]	CAP. 98	01-06-2000	
TRADE UNIONS ACT [1984 Ed.]	CAP. 128	20-01-1962	
TRAFFICKING AND SMUGGLING OF PERSONS ORDER, 2004	S 82/2004	20-12-2004	
TRANSFER OF FUNCTIONS OF THE MINISTER OF LAW ACT [2000 Ed.]	CAP. 186	16-09-1998	
TRAVEL AGENTS ACT [1984 Ed.]	CAP. 103	01-01-1982	
TREATY OF FRIENDSHIP AND CO-OPERATION [1984 Ed.]	SUP. I		
TRESPASS ON ROYAL PROPERTY ACT [1984 Ed.]	CAP. 23	01-01-1918	
UNDESIRABLE PUBLICATIONS ACT [1984 Ed., Amended by S 60/07]	CAP. 25	01-12-1986	
UNFAIR CONTRACTS TERMS ACT [1999 Ed.]	CAP. 171	18-06-1994	
UNIVERSITI BRUNEI DARUSSALAM ACT [1999 Ed., Amended by S 22/00, S 17/03, S 84/06]	CAP. 157	01-07-1988	

UNIVERSITI ISLAM SULTAN SHARIF ALI ORDER, 2008	S 71/2008	14-08-2008	
UNLAWFUL CARNAL KNOWLEDGE ACT [1984 Ed.]	CAP. 29	15-01-1938	
VALUERS AND ESTATE AGENTS ORDER, 2009	S 30/2009	01-07-2009	
VETERINARY SURGEONS ORDER, 2005	S 30/2005	02-06-2008	
VICAR APOSTOLIC OF KUCHING (INCORPORATION) ACT [1984 Ed.]	CAP. 110	11-08-1973	
WATER SUPPLY ACT [1984 Ed.]	CAP. 121	01-01-1968	
WEIGHTS AND MEASURES ACT [1986 Ed.]	CAP. 151	01-01-1987	
WILD FAUNA AND FLORA ORDER, 2007	S 77/2007	31-12-2007	
WILD LIFE PROTECTION ACT [1984 Ed.]	CAP. 102	01-08-1981	
WILLS ACT [2000 Ed.]	CAP. 193	21-10-1999	
WOMEN AND GIRLS PROTECTION ACT [1984 Ed., Amended by GN 649/03]	CAP. 120	19-04-1973	
WORKMEN'S COMPENSATION ACT [1984 Ed., Amended by GN 273/02]	CAP. 74	01-04-1957	
YAYASAN SULTAN HAJI HASSANAL BOLKIAH ACT [2008 Ed.]	CAP. 166	05-10-1992	

STRATEGIC GOVERNMENT CONTACT IN BRUNEY

Prime Minister's Office
E-Mail: PRO@jpm.gov.bn
Telephone: 673 - 2 - 229988
Fax: 673 - 2 - 241717
Telex: BU2727
Address:
Prime Minister's Office
Istana Nurul Iman
Bandar Seri Begawan BA1000

Audit Department
Prime Minister's Office
Jalan Menteri Besar
Bandar Seri Begawan BB 39 10
Brunei Darussalam
Telephone: (02) 380576
Facsimile: (02) 380679
E-mail: jabaudbd@brunet.bn

Information Department
Prime Minister's Office
Berakas Old Airport
Bandar Seri Begawan
BB 3510
Brunei Darussalam.
E-mail:- pelita@brunet.bn
Fax: 673 2 381004
Tel: 673 2 380527

Narcotics Control Bureau
Prime Minister's Office
Jalan Tungku Gadong
Bandar Seri Begawan BE 2110
Tel No: 02-448877 / 422479 / 422480 / 422481
Fax No: 02-422477
E-mail: ncb@brunet.bn

One-Stop Agency
The Ministry of Industry and Primary Resources
Bandar Seri Begawan 1220
Brunei Darussalam

Telefax: (02) 244811
Telex: MIPRS BU 2111
Cable: MIPRS BRUNEI

Head Policy and Administration Division
Ministry of Industry and Primary Resources
Jalan Menteri Besar, Bandar Seri Begawan 1220
Brunei Darussalam
Tel: (02) 382822

Secretary of Public Service Commission
Old Airport
Bandar Seri Begawan BB 3510

Tel No: 02-381961
E-mail: bplspa@brunet.bn

Semaun Holdings Sdn Bhd
Unit 2.02, Block D, 2nd Floor
Yayasan Sultan Haji Hassanal Bolkiah Complex
Jalan Pretty
Bandar Seri Begawan BS8711
Brunei Darussalam
E-mail address: semaun@brunet.bn

Department of Agriculture
Ministry of Industry & Primary Resources
BB3510
Brunei Darussalam
Telephone: + 673 2 380144
Fax: + 673 2 382226
Telex: PERT BU 2456

Land Transport Department
KM 6, Jalan Gadong,
Beribi BE1110,
Brunei Darussalam.
Tel : (673-2) 451979
Fax : (673-2) 424775
Email : latis@brunet.bn

FOREIGN MISSIONS

AUSTRALIA

Australian High Commission
(His Excellency Mr. Neal Patrick Davis - High Commissioner)
4th flr Teck Guan Plaza, Jln Sultan
Bandar Seri Begawan BS8811
Brunei Darussalam
or
P.O. Box 2990
Bandar Seri Begawan, BS8675
Brunei Darussalam
Tel: 673 2 229435/6
Fax: 673 2 221652

AUSTRIA

Austrian Consulate General
No. 5 Taman Jubli, Spg 75,
Jalan Subok,
Bandar Seri Begawan BD2717
Brunei Darussalam
or
P.O. Box 1303,
Bandar Seri Begawan, BS8672
Brunei Darussalam

Tel : 673 2 261083
Email: austroko@brunet.bn

BANGLADESH

High Commission of People's Republic of Bangladesh
(His Excellency Mr. Muhammad Mumtaz Hussain - High Commissioner)
AAR Villa, House No. 5,
Simpang 308, Jalan Lambak Kanan, Berakas,
BB1714
Brunei Darussalam
Tel: 673 2 394716
Fax: 673 2 394715

BELGIUM

Consulate of Belgium
2nd Floor, 146 Jln Pemancha
Bandar Seri Begawan BS8711
Brunei Darussalam
or
P.O.Box 65,
Bandar Seri Begawan, BS8670
Brunei Darussalam
Tel: 673 2 222298
Fax: 673 2 220895

BRITAIN

British High Commission
(His Excellency Mr. Stuart Laing - High Commissioner)
Unit 2.01, Block D of Yayasan Sultan Hassanal Bolkiah
Bandar Seri Begawan BS8711
Brunei Darussalam
or
P.O.Box 2197
Bandar Seri Begawan, BS8674
Brunei Darussalam
Tel: 673 2 222231
Fax: 673 2 226001

CAMBODIA

Royal Embassy of Cambodia
(His Highness Prince Sisowath Phandaravong - Ambassador)
No. 8, Simpang 845
Kampong Tasek Meradun, Jalan Tutong, BF1520
Brunei Darussalam
Tel: 673 2 650046
Fax: 673 2 650646

CANADA

High Commission of Canada
(His Excellency Mr. Neil Reeder - High Commissioner)
Suite 51 - 52, Britannia House, Jalan Cator
Bandar Seri Begawan, BS8811
Brunei Darussalam
Tel: 673 2 220043
Fax: 673 2 220040

CHINA

Embassy of People's Republic of China
(His Excellency Mr. Wang Jianli - Ambassador)
No. 1, 3 & 5, Simpang 462
Kampong Sungai Hanching,
Jln Muara, BC2115
Brunei Darussalam
or
P.O.Box 121
M.P.C, Berakas BB3577
Brunei Darussalam
Tel: 673 2 339609
Fax: 673 2 339612

DENMARK

Consulate of Denmark
Unit 6, Bangunan Hj Tahir,
Spg 103, Jln Gadong
Bandar Seri Begawan
Brunei Darussalam
or
P.O.Box 140
Bandar Seri Begawan, BS8670
Brunei Darussalam
Tel: 673 2 422050, 427525, 447559
Fax: 673 2 427526

FINLAND

Consulate of Finland
Bee Seng Shipping Company
No.7 1st Floor Sufri Complex
KM 2, Jalan Tutong
Bandar Seri Begawan, BA2111
Brunei Darussalam
or
P.O.Box 1777
Bandar Seri Begawan, BS8673
Brunei Darusslaam
Tel: 673 2 243847
Fax: 673 2 224495

FRANCE

Embassy of the Republic of France
(His Excelleny Mr. Jean Pierre Lafosse - Ambassador)
#306-310 Kompleks Jln Sultan,
3rd Floor, 51-55 Jln Sultan
Bandar Seri Begawan BS8811
Brunei Darussalam
or
P.O.Box 3027
Bandar Seri Begawan, BS8675
Brunei Darussalam
Tel: 673 2 220960 / 1
Fax: 673 2 243373

GERMANY

Embassy of the Federal Republic of Germany
(His Excellency Klaus-Peter Brandes - Ambassador)
6th flr, Wisma Raya Building
Lot 49-50, Jln Sultan
Bandar Seri Begawan, BS8811
Brunei Darussalam
or
P.O.Box 3050
Bandar Seri Begawan, BS8675
Brunei Darussalam
Tel: 673 2 225547 / 74
Fax: 673 2 225583

INDIA

High Commission of India
(His Excellency Mr. Dinesh K. Jain - High Commissioner)
Lot 14034, Spg 337,
Kampong Manggis, Jln Muara, BC3515
Brunei Darussalam
Tel: 673 2 339947 / 339751
Fax: 673 2 339783
Email: hicomind@brunet.bn

INDONESIA

Embassy of the Republic of Indonesia
(His Excellency Mr. Rahardjo Djojonegoro - Ambassador)
Lot 4498, Spg 528
Sungai Hanching Baru, Jln Muara, BC3013
Brunei Darussalam
or
P.O.Box 3013
Bandar Seri Begawan, BS8675
Brunei Darussalam
Tel: 673 2 330180 / 445
Fax: 673 2 330646

IRAN

Embassy of the Islamic Republic of Iran
No. 2, Lot 14570, Spg 13
Kampong Serusop, Jalan Berakas, BB2313
Brunei Darussalam
Tel: 673 2 330021 / 29
Fax: 673 2 331744

JAPAN

Embassy of Japan
(His Excellency Mr. Hajime Tsujimoto - Ambassador)
No 1 & 3, Jalan Jawatan Dalam
Kampong Mabohai
Bandar Seri Begawan, BA1111
Brunei Darussalam
or
P.O.Box 3001
Bandar Seri Begawan, BS8675
Brunei Darussalam
Tel: 673 2 229265 / 229592, 237112 - 5
Fax: 673 2 229481

KOREA

Embassy of the Republic of Korea
(His Excellency Kim Ho-tae - Ambassador)
No.9, Lot 21652
Kg Beribi, Jln Gadong, BE1118
Brunei Darussalam
Tel: 673 2 650471 / 300, 652190
Fax: 673 2 650299

LAOS

Embassy of the Lao People's Democratic Republic
(His Excellency Mr. Ammone Singhavong - Ambassador)
Lot. No. 19824, House No. 11
Simpang 480, Jalan Kebangsaan Lama
Off Jalan Muara, BC4115
Brunei Darussalam
or
P.O.Box 2826
Bandar Seri Begawan, BS8675
Brunei Darussalam
Tel: 673 2 345666
Fax: 673 2 345888

MALAYSIA

Malaysian High Commission
(His Excellency Wan Yusof Embong - High Commissioner)
No.27 & 29, Simpang 396-39
Kampong Sungai Akar
Jalan Kebangsaan, BC4115
Brunei Darussalam
or
P.O.Box 2826
Bandar Seri Begawan, BS8675
Brunei Darussalam
Tel: 673 2 345652
Fax: 673 2 345654

MYANMAR

Embassy of the Union of Myanmar
(His Excellency U Than Tun - Ambassador)
No. 14, Lot 2185 / 46292
Simpang 212, Kampong Rimba, Gadong BE3119
Brunei Darussalam
Tel: 673 2 450506 / 7
Fax: 673 2 451008

NETHERLANDS

Netherlands Consulate
c/o Brunei Shell Petroleum Co. Sdn Bhd
Seria KB3534
Brunei Darussalam
Tel: 673 3 372005, 373045

NEW ZEALAND

New Zealand Consulate
36A Seri Lambak Complex,
Jalan Berakas, BB1714
Brunei Darussalam
or
P.O.Box 2720
Bandar Seri Begawan, BS8675
Brunei Darusslam
Tel: 673 2 331612, 331010
Fax: 673 2 331612

NORWAY

Royal Norwegian Consulate
Unit No. 407A - 410A
4th Floor, Wisma Jaya
Jalan Pemancha
Bandar Seri Begawan, BS8811
Brunei Darussalam
Tel: 673 2 239091 / 2 / 3 / 4
Fax: 673 2 239095/6

OMAN

Embassy of the Sultanate of Oman
(His Excellency Mr. Ahmad Moh,d Masoud Al-Riyami - Ambassador)
No.35 Simpang 100,
Jalan Tungku Link
Kampong Pengkalan, Gadong BE3719
Brunei Darussalam
or
P.O.Box 2875
Bandar Seri Begawan, BS8675
Brunei Darussalam
Tel: 673 2 446953 / 4 / 7 / 8
Fax: 673 2 449646

PAKISTAN

Pakistan High Commission
(His Excellency Major General (Rtd) Irshad Ullah Tarar - High Commission)
No.5 Kampong Sungai Akar
Jalan Kebangsaan, BC4115
Brunei Darussalam
Tel: 673 2 6334989, 339797
Fax: 673 2 334990

PHILIPPINES

Embassy of the Republic of Philippines
His Excellency Mr. Enrique A. Zaldivar - Ambassador)
Rm 1 & 2, 4th & 5th floor
Badiah Building, Mile 1 1/2 Jln Tutong
Brunei Darussalam, BA2111
or
P.O.Box 3025
Bandar Seri Begawan, BS8675
Brunei Darussalam
Tel: 673 2 241465 / 6
Fax: 673 2 237707

SAUDI ARABIA

Royal Embassy of Kingdom of Saudi Arabia
No. 1, Simpang 570
Kampong Salar
Jalan Muara, BU1429
Brunei Darusslam
Tel: 673 2 792821 / 2 / 3
Fax: 673 2 792826 / 7

SINGAPORE

Singapore High Commission
(His Excellency Tee Tua Ba - High Commissioner)
No. 8, Simpang, 74,
Jalan Subok, BD1717
Brunei Darussalam
or
P.O.Box 2159
Bandar Seri Begawan, BS8674
Brunei Darussalam
Tel: 673 2 227583 / 4 / 5
Fax: 673 2 220957

SWEDEN

Consulate of Sweden
Blk A, Unit 1, 2nd Floor
Abdul Razak Plaza,
Jalan Gadong,
Bandar Seri Begawan, BE3919
Brunei Darussalam
Tel: 673 2 448423, 444326
Fax: 673 2 448419

THAILAND

Royal Thai Embassy
(His Excellency Thinakorn Kanasuta - Ambassador
No. 2, Simpang 682,
Kampong Bunut, Jalan Tutong, BF1320
Brunei Darussalam
Tel: 673 2 653108 / 9
Fax: 673 2 262752

UNITED STATE OF AMERICA

Embassy of the United States of America
3rd Flr, Teck Guan Plaza,
Jalan Sultan
Bandar Seri Begawan BS8811
Brunei Darussalam
Tel: 673 2 229670
Fax: (02) 225293

VIETNAM

Embassy of the Socialist Republic of Vietnam
(His Excellency Tran Tien Vinh - Ambassador)
No. 10, Simpang 485
Kampong Sungai Hanching
Jalan Muara,BC2115
Brunei Darussalam
Tel: 673 2 343167 / 8
Fax: 673 2 343169

BRUNEI'S MISSIONS IN ASEAN, CHINA, JAPAN AND KOREA

CAMBODIA
Embassy of Brunei Darussalam
No : 237, Pasteur St. 51
Sangkat Boeung Keng Kang I
Khan Chamkar Mon
Phnom Penh
Kingdom of Cambodia
Tel : (855) 23211 457 & 23211 458
Fax : (855) 23211 456
E-Mail : Brunei@bigpond.com.kh

CHINA
Embassy of Brunei Darussalam
No. 3 Villa, Qijiayuan Diplomatic Compound
Chaoyang District
Beijing 100600
People's Republic of China 1000600
Tel : 86 (10) 6532 4093 - 6
Fax : 86 (10) 6532 4097
E-Mail : bdb@public.bta.net.cn

INDONESIA
Embassy of Brunei Darussalam
Wisma GKBI
 (Gabungan Koperasi Batik Indonesia)
Suite 1901, Jl. Jend. Sudirman No. 28
Jakarta 10210
Indonesia
Tel : 62 (21) 574 1437 - 39 / 574 1470 - 72
Fax : 62 (21) 574 1463

JAPAN
Embassy of Brunei Darussalam
5-2 Kitashinagawa 6-Chome
Shinagawa-ku
Tokyo 141
Japan
Tel : 81 (3) 3447 7997 / 9260
Fax : 81 (3) 344 79260

REPUBLIC OF KOREA
Embassy of Brunei Darussalam
7th Floor, Kwanghwamoon Building
211, Sejong-ro, Chongro-Ku
Seoul
Republic of Korea.
Tel : 82 (2) 399 3707 / 3708
Fax : 82 (2) 399 3709
E-Mail : kbrunei@chollian.net

LAOS
Embassy of Brunei Darussalam
No. 333 Unit 25 Ban Phonxay
Xaysettha District
Lanexang Avenue
Vientiane
Laos People's Democratic Republic
Tel : (856) 2141 6114 / 2141 4169
Fax : (856) 2141 6115
E-Mail : kbnbd@laonet.net

MALAYSIA
High Commission of Brunei Darussalam
Tingkat 8 Wisma Sin Heap Lee (SHL)
Jalan Tun Razak
50400 Kuala Lumpur
Malaysia.
Tel : 60 (3) 261 2828
Fax : 60 (3) 263 1302
E-Mail : Sjtnbdkl@tm.net.my

THE UNIION OF MYANMAR
Embassy of Brunei Darussalam
No : 51 Golden Valley
Bahan Township
Yangon
The Union of Myanmar.
Tel: 95 (1) 510 422
Fax: 95 (1) 512 854

PHILIPPINES
Embassy of Brunei Darussalam
11th Floor BPI Building
Ayala Avenue, Corner Paseo De Roxas
Makati City, Metro Manila
Philippines
Tel : 63 (2) 816 2836 - 8
Fax : 63 (2) 816 2876
E-Mail : kbnbdmnl@skynet.net

SINGAPORE
High Commission of Brunei Darussalam
325 Tanglin Road
Singapore 247955
Tel : (65) 733 9055
Fax : (65) 737 5275
E-Mail : comstbs@singnet.com.sg

THAILAND
Embassy of Brunei Darussalam
No. 132 Sukhumvit 23 Road
Watana District
Bangkok 10110
Thailand
Tel : 66 (2) 204 1476 - 9
Fax : 66 (2) 204 1486

VIETNAM
Embassy of Brunei Darussalam
No. 4 Thien Quang Street
Hai Ba Trung District

Hanoi
Vietnam
Tel : (84) 4 826 4816 / 4817 / 4818

Fax : (84) 4 822 2092
E-Mail : bruemviet@hotmail.com

FOOD AND RESTAURANTS

Brunei restaurants, including western style fast food centres, cater to a wide range of tastes and palates.
Visitors can also sample authentic local food offered at the tamu night market in the capital.
The market, along the Kianggeh river, is actually open from early morning. It takes on a special atmosphere at night when crowds throng its alleys to shop and eat at the lowest prices in town.
Tropical fruits like watermelon, papaya, mango and banana are also available.
Locals are fond of the Malay-style satay, bits of beef or chicken in a stick, cooked over low fire and dipped in a tangy peanut sauce.

Brunei's first Chinese halal restaurant is Emperor's Court, owned by Royal Brunei Catering, which caters to Cantonese and Western tastebuds.

A list of restaurants in the capital and Seria-Kuala Belait areas follows:
Bandar Seri Begawan
Aumrin Restaurant, 1 Bangunan Hasbullah, 4 Jalan Gadong
Airport Restaurant, Brunei International Airport
Coffee Tree, Unit 3, top floor ,Mabohai Shopping Complex
Emperor's Court, 1st Floor, Wisma Haji Mohd Taha, Jalan Gadong
Excellent Taste, G5 Gadong Properties Centre, Jalan Gadong
Express Fast Food, 22/23 Jalan Sultan
Ghawar Restaurant, 3 Ground Floor Bang Hasbullah 4
Jade Garden Chinese Restaurant, Riverview Inn, Km 1 Jalan Gadong
Jolibee Family Restaurant, Utama Bowling Centre, Km 11/2 Jalan Tutong
Kentucky Fried Chicken (B) Sdn Bhd, G15-G16 Plaza Athirah
Lucky Restaurant, Umi Kalthum Building, Jalan Tutong
McDonald's Restaurant, 10-12 Block H, Abdul Razak Complex, Simpang 137, Gadong
Phongmun Restaurant, Nos. 56-60, 2nd Floor Teck Guan Plaza
Pizza Hut, Block J, Unit 2 & 3 Abdul Razak Complex
Pondok Sari Wangi, 12 Blk A, Abdul Razak Complex, Jalan Gadong
Popular Restaurant, 5, Ground floor, PAP Hajjah Norain Building
QR Restaurant, Blk C, Abdul Razak Complex, Jalan Gadong
Rainbow Restaurant, 110 Jalan Batu Bersurat, Gadong
Rasa Sayang Restaurant, 607 Bangunan Guru-Guru Melayu
Rose Garden Restaurant, 8 Blk C, Abdul Razak Complex, Jalan Gadong
Season's Restaurant, Gadong Centrepoint
SD Cafe, 6-7 Bangunan Hj Othman, Simpang 105, Jalan Gadong
Seri Kamayan Restaurant, 4 & 5 Bangunan Hj Tahir ,Simpang 103, Jalan Gadong
Seri Maradum Baru, Block C6, Abdul Razak Complex
Sugar Bun Fast Food, Lot 16397 Mabohai Complex, Jalan Kebangsaan
Schezuan's Dynasty Restaurant, Gadong Centrepoint
Swensen's Ice Cream and Fine Food Restaurant, 17-18 Ground Floor Bagunan Halimatul Sa'adiah, Gadong
Tenaga Restaurant, 6 1st Floor Bangunan Hasbollah 4
The Stadium Restaurant, Stadium Negara Hassanal Bolkiah
Tropicana Seafood Restaurant, Block 1 Ground Floor, Pang's Building,Muara
Kuala Belait/Seria
Belait Restaurant, Jalan Bunga Raya
Buccaneer Steak House, Lot 94 Jalan McKerron
Cottage Restaurant, 38 Jalan Pretty
Jolene Restaurant, 83,1st Jalan Bunga Raya
New China Restaurant, 39/40 3rd Floor, Ang's Building, Jalan Sultan Omar Ali, Seria
New Cheng Wah Restaurant, 14 Jalan Sultan Omar Ali, Seria
Orchid Room, B5, 1st Floor, Jalan Bunga Raya
Red Wing Restaurant, 12 Jalan Sultan Omar Ali, Seria

Tasty Cake Shop/Pretty Inn, 26 Jalan Sultan Omar Ali, Seria
Tasconi's Pizza, Simpang 19, Jalan Sungai Pandan

WHERE TO SHOP

For many travellers one of the pleasures of visiting another country is finding something of interest and value for one's self, family or friends. There are many shops in Brunei offering a wide variety of goods at competitive prices. These range from modern department stores to small market stalls where bargaining is still commonly practised.

Modern department stores are found in the major towns of Bandar Seri Begawan, Tutong, Kuala Belait and Seria. In addition to these departmental stores there is a wide variety of old-fashioned shophouses as well as more modern air-conditioned shops.

Most items ranging from the latest electronic goods and imported luxury goods to common household items and groceries can be conveniently found in these shops.

Traditional items that reflect the culture of Brunei like the brass cannon, kris and kain songket, better known as "jong sarat" are excellent souvenirs to bring home from a visit to the country. These can be purchased at the Arts and Handicrafts Centre which is located off Kota Batu, and also at the airport.

Before leaving Brunei make sure you stop by the Duty Free shops at the airport. These offer a wide range of luxury goods, garments, jewellery, writing instruments, perfumes, handicrafts, Brunei souvenirs, books and chocolates at very reasonable prices.

SHOPPING CENTRES

Hua Ho Department Store, Jln Gadong, Bandar Seri Begawan

Kota Mutiara Department Store, Bangunan Darussalam, Bandar Seri Begawan

Lai Lai Department Store, Mile 1 Jln Tutong, Bandar Seri Begawan

Millimewah Department Store (BSB), Bangunan Darussalam, Bandar Seri Begawan

Millimewah Department Store (Tutong),Tutong

Millimewah Department Store (Seria), Seria

Princess Inn Department Store, Mile 1 Jln Tutong , Bandar Seri Begawan

Tiong Hin Superstore,Jln Muara, Bandar Seri Begawan

Megamart,Jln Gadong, Bandar Seri Begawan

Wisma Jaya Complex, Jln Pemancha, Bandar Seri Begawan

First Emporium & Supermarket, Mohammad Yussof Complex, Jln Kubah Makam DiRaja, Bandar Seri Begawan

Seria Plaza, Seria

Seaview Department Store, Jln Maulana, Kuala Belait

TRAVEL AGENTS

BANDAR SERI BEGAWAN

Antara Travel & Tours Sdn Bhd 02-448805/808
Anthony Tours & Travel Sdn Bhd 02-228668
Borneo Leisure Travel Sdn Bhd 02-223420
Brunei Travel Services Sdn Bhd 02-236006
Century Travel Centre Sdn Bhd 02-227296
Churiah Travel Service 02-224422
Darat Dan Laut 02-426321
Freme Travel Services Sdn Bhd 02-234277
Halim Tours & Travel Sdn Bhd 02-226688
Intan Travel & Trading Agencies 02-427340
Jasra Harrisons (B) Sdn Bhd 02-236675
JB Travel & Insurance Agencies 02-239132
JJ Tour Service (B) Sdn Bhd 02-224761
Ken Travel & Trading Sdn Bhd 02-223127
Mahasiswa Travel Service 02-243452
Oriental Travel Services 02-226464
Overseas Travel Services Sdn Bhd 02-445322
Sarawak Travel Service Sdn Bhd 02-223361
Seri Islamic Tours & Travel Sdn Bhd 02-243341
Straits Central Agencies (B) Sdn Bhd 02-229356
Sunshine Borneo Tours & Travel Sdn Bhd 02-441791
SMAS 02-234741
Travel Centre (B) Sdn Bhd 02-229601
Travel Trade Agencies Sdn Bhd 02-229601/228439
Tai Wah Travel Service Sdn Bhd 02-224015
Tenega Travel Agency Sdn Bhd 02-422974
Titian Travel & Tours Sdn Bhd 02-448742
Twelve Roofs / Perusahaan Hj. Asmakhan 02-340395
Wing On Travel & Trading Agencies 02-220536
Zizen Travel Agency Sdn Bhd 02-236991
Zura Travel Service Sdn Bhd 02-234738

KUALA BELAIT

Freme Travel Services Sdn Bhd 03-335025
Jasra Harrisons Sdn Bhd 03-335391
JJ Tour Service Sdn Bhd 03-334069
Limbang Travel Service Sdn Bhd 03-335275
Overseas Travel Service Sdn Bhd 03-222090
Southern Cross Travel Agencies Sdn Bhd 03-334642
Straits Central Agencies Sdn Bhd 03-334589
Usaha Royako Travel Agency 03-334768

SELECTED COMPANIES

- Advance Computer Supplier and Services
- AJYAD Publishing
- Akitek SAA Home Page

- Amalgamated Electronic Sdn. Bhd.
- Anthony Tours & Travel Agency
- Baharuddin & Associates Consulting Engineers
- Beseller Sdn Bhd Homepage
- BIT Computer Services
- BruDirect Business Centre
- Brunei Hotel
- Brupost
- CfBT Homepage
- Compunet Computer & Office Systems
- Dalplus Technologies, Brunei
- DN Private Investigation and Security Consultant
- DP Happy Video House
- Elite Computer Systems Sdn. Bhd.
- Fabrica Interior Furnishing Co
- Glamour Homepage
- HSBC
- HSE Engineering Sdn. Bhd.
- Indah Sejahtera Development & Services
- Insurans Islam Taib
- Interhouse Marketing Sdn. Bhd.
- International School Brunei
- IP and Company
- ISS Thomas Cowan Sdn. Bhd.
- Jerudong Park Medical Centre
- Kristal
- L & M Prestressing Sdn. Bhd.
- Megamas Training Company Sdn. Bhd.
- Mekar General Enterprise Homepage
- Micronet Computer School
- National Insurance Company Berhad
- Paotools Supplies & Services Co.
- Petar Perunding Sdn. Bhd.
- Petrel Jaya Sdn Bhd
- Phongmun Restaurant Homepage
- Poh Lee Trading Company
- Q-Carrier
- Sabli Group of Companies - Brunei Darussalam
- Scanmark Design Sdn Bhd
- SDS System (B) Sdn. Bhd.
- SEAMEO VOCTECH Homepage
- Singapore Airlines
- Sistem Komputer Alif Sdn Bhd
- SPCastro And Associates Sdn Bhd
- Sunshine Borneo Tour & Travel Sdn.Bhd.
- Survey Service Consultants
- Syabas Publishers
- Syarikat Suraya Insan
- Syarikat Intellisense Technology
- Tabung Amanah Islam Brunei
- Tang Sung Lee Sdn. Bhd.

- The Lodge Resort (In Brunei)
- Trinkets Enterprise
- Twelve Roofs / Perusahaan Hj. Asmakhan
- Unicraft Enterprises
- Utama Komunikasi

BASIC TITLES ON BRUNEI

IMPORTANT!
All publications are updated annually!
Please contact IBP, Inc. at ibpusa3@gmail.com for the latest ISBNs and additional information
Global Business and Investment Info Databank: www.ibpus.com

Title
Brunei A "Spy" Guide - Strategic Information and Developments
Brunei A "Spy" Guide - Strategic Information and Developments
Brunei Air Force Handbook
Brunei Air Force Handbook
Brunei Business and Investment Opportunities Yearbook
Brunei Business and Investment Opportunities Yearbook
Brunei Business and Investment Opportunities Yearbook Volume 1 Strategic Information and Opportunities
Brunei Business and Investment Opportunities Yearbook Volume 2 Leading Export-Import, Business, Investment Opportunities and Projects
Brunei Business Intelligence Report - Practical Information, Opportunities, Contacts
Brunei Business Intelligence Report - Practical Information, Opportunities, Contacts
Brunei Business Law Handbook - Strategic Information and Basic Laws
Brunei Business Law Handbook - Strategic Information and Basic Laws
Brunei Business Law Handbook - Strategic Information and Basic Laws
Brunei Business Law Handbook - Strategic Information and Basic Laws
Brunei Company Laws and Regulations Handbook
Brunei Constitution and Citizenship Laws Handbook - Strategic Information and Basic Laws
Brunei Country Study Guide - Strategic Information and Developments
Brunei Country Study Guide - Strategic Information and Developments
Brunei Country Study Guide - Strategic Information and Developments Volume 1 Strategic Information and Developments
Brunei Customs, Trade Regulations and Procedures Handbook
Brunei Customs, Trade Regulations and Procedures Handbook
Brunei Diplomatic Handbook - Strategic Information and Developments
Brunei Diplomatic Handbook - Strategic Information and Developments
Brunei Ecology & Nature Protection Handbook
Brunei Ecology & Nature Protection Handbook
Brunei Ecology & Nature Protection Laws and Regulation Handbook
Brunei Energy Policy, Laws and Regulation Handbook
Brunei Energy Policy, Laws and Regulations Handbook
Brunei Energy Policy, Laws and Regulations Handbook
Brunei Export-Import Trade and Business Directory
Brunei Export-Import Trade and Business Directory
Brunei Foreign Policy and Government Guide
Brunei Foreign Policy and Government Guide
Brunei Immigration Laws and Regulations Handbook - Strategic Information and Basic Laws

For additional analytical, business and investment opportunities information, please contact Global Investment & Business Center, USA at (703) 370-8082. Fax: (703) 370-8083. E-mail: ibpusa3@gmail.com
Global Business and Investment Info Databank - www.ibpus.com

Title
Brunei Industrial and Business Directory
Brunei Industrial and Business Directory
Brunei Investment and Business Guide - Strategic and Practical Information
Brunei Investment and Business Guide - Strategic and Practical Information
Brunei Investment and Business Guide - Strategic and Practical Information
Brunei Investment and Business Guide - Strategic and Practical Information
Brunei Investment and Business Guide Volume 2 Business, Investment Opportunities and Incentives
Brunei Investment and Trade Laws and Regulations Handbook
Brunei Labor Laws and Regulations Handbook - Strategic Information and Basic Laws
Brunei Land Ownership and Agriculture Laws Handbook
Brunei Mineral & Mining Sector Investment and Business Guide - Strategic and Practical Information
Brunei Mineral & Mining Sector Investment and Business Guide - Strategic and Practical Information
Brunei Mining Laws and Regulations Handbook
Brunei Oil & Gas Sector Business & Investment Opportunities Yearbook
Brunei Oil & Gas Sector Business & Investment Opportunities Yearbook
Brunei Oil and Gas Exploration Laws and Regulation Handbook
Brunei Recent Economic and Political Developments Yearbook
Brunei Recent Economic and Political Developments Yearbook
Brunei Recent Economic and Political Developments Yearbook
Brunei Starting Business (Incorporating) in....Guide
Brunei Sultan Haji Hassanal Bolkiah Mu'izzaddin Waddaulah Handbook
Brunei Sultan Haji Hassanal Bolkiah Waddaulah Handbook Economic and Foreign Policy Handbook
Brunei Tax Guide Volume 1 Business Taxation
Brunei Tax Guide Volume 2 Personal Taxation
Brunei Taxation Laws and Regulations Handbook
Brunei Telecommunication Industry Business Opportunities Handbook
Brunei Telecommunication Industry Business Opportunities Handbook
Brunei: How to Invest, Start and Run Profitable Business in Brunei Guide - Practical Information, Opportunities, Contacts

INTERNATIONAL BUSINESS PUBLICATIONS, USA
ibpusa@comcast.net. http://www.ibpus.com

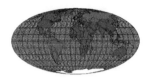

WORLD ISLAMIC BUSINESS LIBRARY
Price: $149.95 Each

Islamic Banking and Financial Law Handbook
Islamic Banking Law Handbook
Islamic Business Organization Law Handbook
Islamic Commerce and Trade Law Handbook
Islamic Company Law Handbook
Islamic Constitutional and Administrative Law Handbook
Islamic Copyright Law Handbook
Islamic Customs Law and Regulations Handbook
Islamic Design Law Handbook
Islamic Development Bank Group Handbook
Islamic Economic & Business Laws and Regulations Handbook
Islamic Environmental Law Handbook
Islamic Financial and Banking System Handbook vol 1
Islamic Financial and Banking System Handbook Vol. 2
Islamic Financial Institutions (Banks and Financial Companies) Handbook
Islamic Foreign Investment and Privatization Law Handbook
Islamic Free Trade & Economic Zones Law and Regulations Handbook
Islamic International Law and Jihad (War(Law Handbook
Islamic Labor Law Handbook
Islamic Legal System (Sharia) Handbook Vol. 1 Basic Laws and Regulations
Islamic Legal System (Sharia) Handbook Vol. 2 Laws and Regulations in Selected Countries
Islamic Mining Law Handbook
Islamic Patent & Trademark Law Handbook
Islamic Taxation Law Handbook
Islamic Trade & Export-Import Laws and Regulations Handbook

For additional analytical, business and investment opportunities information, please contact Global Investment & Business Center, USA at (202) 546-2103. Fax: (202) 546-3275. E-mail: rusric@erols.com

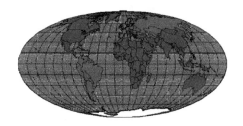

WORLD CRIMINAL LAWS, REGULATIONS AND PROCEDURES HANDBOOKS LIBRARY
Price: $99.95 Each

World Business Information Catalog: http://www.ibpus.com

TITLE
Afghanistan Criminal Laws, Regulations and Procedures Handbook - Strategic Information, Regulations, Procedures
Albania Criminal Laws, Regulations and Procedures Handbook - Strategic Information, Regulations, Procedures
Algeria Criminal Laws, Regulations and Procedures Handbook - Strategic Information, Regulations, Procedures
Angola Criminal Laws, Regulations and Procedures Handbook - Strategic Information, Regulations, Procedures
Argentina Criminal Laws, Regulations and Procedures Handbook - Strategic Information, Regulations, Procedures
Armenia Criminal Laws, Regulations and Procedures Handbook - Strategic Information, Regulations, Procedures
Aruba Criminal Laws, Regulations and Procedures Handbook - Strategic Information, Regulations, Procedures
Australia Criminal Laws, Regulations and Procedures Handbook - Strategic Information, Regulations, Procedures
Austria Criminal Laws, Regulations and Procedures Handbook - Strategic Information, Regulations, Procedures
Azerbaijan Criminal Laws, Regulations and Procedures Handbook - Strategic Information, Regulations, Procedures
Bahamas Criminal Laws, Regulations and Procedures Handbook - Strategic Information, Regulations, Procedures
Bahrain Criminal Laws, Regulations and Procedures Handbook - Strategic Information, Regulations, Procedures
Bangladesh Criminal Laws, Regulations and Procedures Handbook - Strategic Information, Regulations, Procedures
Barbados Criminal Laws, Regulations and Procedures Handbook - Strategic Information, Regulations, Procedures
Belarus Criminal Laws, Regulations and Procedures Handbook - Strategic Information, Regulations, Procedures
Belgium Criminal Laws, Regulations and Procedures Handbook - Strategic Information, Regulations, Procedures
Belize Criminal Laws, Regulations and Procedures Handbook - Strategic Information, Regulations, Procedures
Benin Criminal Laws, Regulations and Procedures Handbook - Strategic Information, Regulations, Procedures
Bermuda Criminal Laws, Regulations and Procedures Handbook - Strategic Information, Regulations, Procedures
Bhutan Criminal Laws, Regulations and Procedures Handbook - Strategic Information, Regulations, Procedures
Bolivia Criminal Laws, Regulations and Procedures Handbook - Strategic Information, Regulations, Procedures
Bosnia and Herzegovina Criminal Laws, Regulations and Procedures Handbook - Strategic Information, Regulations, Procedures
Botswana Criminal Laws, Regulations and Procedures Handbook - Strategic Information, Regulations, Procedures
Brazil Criminal Laws, Regulations and Procedures Handbook - Strategic Information, Regulations, Procedures
Brunei Criminal Laws, Regulations and Procedures Handbook - Strategic Information, Regulations, Procedures
Bulgaria Criminal Laws, Regulations and Procedures Handbook - Strategic Information, Regulations, Procedures
Burkina Faso Criminal Laws, Regulations and Procedures Handbook - Strategic Information, Regulations, Procedures
Burundi Criminal Laws, Regulations and Procedures Handbook - Strategic Information, Regulations, Procedures
Cambodia Criminal Laws, Regulations and Procedures Handbook - Strategic Information, Regulations, Procedures
Cameroon Criminal Laws, Regulations and Procedures Handbook - Strategic Information, Regulations, Procedures
Canada Criminal Laws, Regulations and Procedures Handbook - Strategic Information, Regulations, Procedures
Cape Verde Criminal Laws, Regulations and Procedures Handbook - Strategic Information, Regulations, Procedures
Caribban Countries Crime Prevention and Security Strategy Handbook - Strategic Information, Programs and Regulations
Cayman Islands Criminal Laws, Regulations and Procedures Handbook - Strategic Information, Regulations, Procedures
Central African Republic Criminal Laws, Regulations and Procedures Handbook - Strategic Information, Regulations, Procedures
Chad Criminal Laws, Regulations and Procedures Handbook - Strategic Information, Regulations, Procedures
Chile Criminal Laws, Regulations and Procedures Handbook - Strategic Information, Regulations, Procedures

---

For additional analytical, business and investment opportunities information,
Please contact Global Investment & Business Center, USA
at (202) 546-2103. Fax: (202) 546-3275. E-mail: rusric@erols.com

China Criminal Laws, Regulations and Procedures Handbook - Strategic Information, Regulations, Procedures
Colombia Criminal Laws, Regulations and Procedures Handbook - Strategic Information, Regulations, Procedures
Comoros Criminal Laws, Regulations and Procedures Handbook - Strategic Information, Regulations, Procedures
Congo Criminal Laws, Regulations and Procedures Handbook - Strategic Information, Regulations, Procedures
Congo, Democratic Republic Criminal Laws, Regulations and Procedures Handbook - Strategic Information, Regulations, Procedures
Cook Islands Criminal Laws, Regulations and Procedures Handbook - Strategic Information, Regulations, Procedures
Costa Rica Criminal Laws, Regulations and Procedures Handbook - Strategic Information, Regulations, Procedures
Cote d'Ivoire Criminal Laws, Regulations and Procedures Handbook - Strategic Information, Regulations, Procedures
Croatia Criminal Laws, Regulations and Procedures Handbook - Strategic Information, Regulations, Procedures
Cuba Criminal Laws, Regulations and Procedures Handbook - Strategic Information, Regulations, Procedures
Cyprus Criminal Laws, Regulations and Procedures Handbook - Strategic Information, Regulations, Procedures
Czech Republic Criminal Laws, Regulations and Procedures Handbook - Strategic Information, Regulations, Procedures
Denmark Criminal Laws, Regulations and Procedures Handbook - Strategic Information, Regulations, Procedures
Djibouti Criminal Laws, Regulations and Procedures Handbook - Strategic Information, Regulations, Procedures
Dominica Criminal Laws, Regulations and Procedures Handbook - Strategic Information, Regulations, Procedures
Dominican Republic Criminal Laws, Regulations and Procedures Handbook - Strategic Information, Regulations, Procedures
Ecuador Criminal Laws, Regulations and Procedures Handbook - Strategic Information, Regulations, Procedures
Egypt Criminal Laws, Regulations and Procedures Handbook - Strategic Information, Regulations, Procedures
El Salvador Criminal Laws, Regulations and Procedures Handbook - Strategic Information, Regulations, Procedures
Equatorial Guinea Criminal Laws, Regulations and Procedures Handbook - Strategic Information, Regulations, Procedures
Eritrea Criminal Laws, Regulations and Procedures Handbook - Strategic Information, Regulations, Procedures
Estonia Criminal Laws, Regulations and Procedures Handbook - Strategic Information, Regulations, Procedures
Ethiopia Criminal Laws, Regulations and Procedures Handbook - Strategic Information, Regulations, Procedures
Fiji Criminal Laws, Regulations and Procedures Handbook - Strategic Information, Regulations, Procedures
Finland Criminal Laws, Regulations and Procedures Handbook - Strategic Information, Regulations, Procedures
France Criminal Laws, Regulations and Procedures Handbook - Strategic Information, Regulations, Procedures
Gabon Criminal Laws, Regulations and Procedures Handbook - Strategic Information, Regulations, Procedures
Gambia Criminal Laws, Regulations and Procedures Handbook - Strategic Information, Regulations, Procedures
Georgia Criminal Laws, Regulations and Procedures Handbook - Strategic Information, Regulations, Procedures
Germany Criminal Laws, Regulations and Procedures Handbook - Strategic Information, Regulations, Procedures
Ghana Criminal Laws, Regulations and Procedures Handbook - Strategic Information, Regulations, Procedures
Greece Criminal Laws, Regulations and Procedures Handbook - Strategic Information, Regulations, Procedures
Guatemala Criminal Laws, Regulations and Procedures Handbook - Strategic Information, Regulations, Procedures
Guinea Criminal Laws, Regulations and Procedures Handbook - Strategic Information, Regulations, Procedures
Guinea-Bissau Criminal Laws, Regulations and Procedures Handbook - Strategic Information, Regulations, Procedures
Guyana Criminal Laws, Regulations and Procedures Handbook - Strategic Information, Regulations, Procedures
Haiti Criminal Laws, Regulations and Procedures Handbook - Strategic Information, Regulations, Procedures
Honduras Criminal Laws, Regulations and Procedures Handbook - Strategic Information, Regulations, Procedures
Hungary Criminal Laws, Regulations and Procedures Handbook - Strategic Information, Regulations, Procedures
Iceland Criminal Laws, Regulations and Procedures Handbook - Strategic Information, Regulations, Procedures
India Criminal Laws, Regulations and Procedures Handbook - Strategic Information, Regulations, Procedures
Indonesia Criminal Laws, Regulations and Procedures Handbook - Strategic Information, Regulations, Procedures
Iran Criminal Laws, Regulations and Procedures Handbook - Strategic Information, Regulations, Procedures
Iraq Criminal Laws, Regulations and Procedures Handbook - Strategic Information, Regulations, Procedures
Ireland Criminal Laws, Regulations and Procedures Handbook - Strategic Information, Regulations, Procedures
Israel Criminal Laws, Regulations and Procedures Handbook - Strategic Information, Regulations, Procedures
Italy Criminal Laws, Regulations and Procedures Handbook - Strategic Information, Regulations, Procedures
Jamaica Criminal Laws, Regulations and Procedures Handbook - Strategic Information, Regulations, Procedures
Japan Criminal Laws, Regulations and Procedures Handbook - Strategic Information, Regulations, Procedures
Jordan Criminal Laws, Regulations and Procedures Handbook - Strategic Information, Regulations, Procedures
Kazakhstan Criminal Laws, Regulations and Procedures Handbook - Strategic Information, Regulations, Procedures
Kenya Criminal Laws, Regulations and Procedures Handbook - Strategic Information, Regulations, Procedures
Korea, North Criminal Laws, Regulations and Procedures Handbook - Strategic Information, Regulations, Procedures

For additional analytical, business and investment opportunities information,
Please contact Global Investment & Business Center, USA
at (202) 546-2103. Fax: (202) 546-3275. E-mail: rusric@erols.com

Korea, South Criminal Laws, Regulations and Procedures Handbook - Strategic Information, Regulations, Procedures
Kosovo Criminal Laws, Regulations and Procedures Handbook - Strategic Information, Regulations, Procedures
Kurdistan Criminal Laws, Regulations and Procedures Handbook - Strategic Information, Regulations, Procedures
Kuwait Criminal Laws, Regulations and Procedures Handbook - Strategic Information, Regulations, Procedures
Kyrgyzstan Criminal Laws, Regulations and Procedures Handbook - Strategic Information, Regulations, Procedures
Laos Criminal Laws, Regulations and Procedures Handbook - Strategic Information, Regulations, Procedures
Latvia Criminal Laws, Regulations and Procedures Handbook - Strategic Information, Regulations, Procedures
Lebanon Criminal Laws, Regulations and Procedures Handbook - Strategic Information, Regulations, Procedures
Lesotho Criminal Laws, Regulations and Procedures Handbook - Strategic Information, Regulations, Procedures
Liberia Criminal Laws, Regulations and Procedures Handbook - Strategic Information, Regulations, Procedures
Libya Criminal Laws, Regulations and Procedures Handbook - Strategic Information, Regulations, Procedures
Liechtenstein Criminal Laws, Regulations and Procedures Handbook - Strategic Information, Regulations, Procedures
Lithuania Criminal Laws, Regulations and Procedures Handbook - Strategic Information, Regulations, Procedures
Luxembourg Criminal Laws, Regulations and Procedures Handbook - Strategic Information, Regulations, Procedures
Macao Criminal Laws, Regulations and Procedures Handbook - Strategic Information, Regulations, Procedures
Macedonia, Criminal Laws, Regulations and Procedures Handbook - Strategic Information, Regulations, Procedures
Madagascar Criminal Laws, Regulations and Procedures Handbook - Strategic Information, Regulations, Procedures
Madeira Criminal Laws, Regulations and Procedures Handbook - Strategic Information, Regulations, Procedures
Malawi Criminal Laws, Regulations and Procedures Handbook - Strategic Information, Regulations, Procedures
Malaysia Criminal Laws, Regulations and Procedures Handbook - Strategic Information, Regulations, Procedures
Maldives Criminal Laws, Regulations and Procedures Handbook - Strategic Information, Regulations, Procedures
Mali Criminal Laws, Regulations and Procedures Handbook - Strategic Information, Regulations, Procedures
Malta Criminal Laws, Regulations and Procedures Handbook - Strategic Information, Regulations, Procedures
Marshall Islands Criminal Laws, Regulations and Procedures Handbook - Strategic Information, Regulations, Procedures
Mauritania Criminal Laws, Regulations and Procedures Handbook - Strategic Information, Regulations, Procedures
Mauritius Criminal Laws, Regulations and Procedures Handbook - Strategic Information, Regulations, Procedures
Mexico Criminal Laws, Regulations and Procedures Handbook - Strategic Information, Regulations, Procedures
Micronesia Criminal Laws, Regulations and Procedures Handbook - Strategic Information, Regulations, Procedures
Moldova Criminal Laws, Regulations and Procedures Handbook - Strategic Information, Regulations, Procedures
Monaco Criminal Laws, Regulations and Procedures Handbook - Strategic Information, Regulations, Procedures
Mongolia Criminal Laws, Regulations and Procedures Handbook - Strategic Information, Regulations, Procedures
Morocco Criminal Laws, Regulations and Procedures Handbook - Strategic Information, Regulations, Procedures
Mozambique Criminal Laws, Regulations and Procedures Handbook - Strategic Information, Regulations, Procedures
Myanmar Criminal Laws, Regulations and Procedures Handbook - Strategic Information, Regulations, Procedures
Namibia Criminal Laws, Regulations and Procedures Handbook - Strategic Information, Regulations, Procedures
Nauru Criminal Laws, Regulations and Procedures Handbook - Strategic Information, Regulations, Procedures
Nepal Criminal Laws, Regulations and Procedures Handbook - Strategic Information, Regulations, Procedures
Netherlands Criminal Laws, Regulations and Procedures Handbook - Strategic Information, Regulations, Procedures
New Zealand Criminal Laws, Regulations and Procedures Handbook - Strategic Information, Regulations, Procedures
Nicaragua Criminal Laws, Regulations and Procedures Handbook - Strategic Information, Regulations, Procedures
Niger Criminal Laws, Regulations and Procedures Handbook - Strategic Information, Regulations, Procedures
Nigeria Criminal Laws, Regulations and Procedures Handbook - Strategic Information, Regulations, Procedures
Northern Mariana Islands Criminal Laws, Regulations and Procedures Handbook - Strategic Information, Regulations, Procedures
Norway Criminal Laws, Regulations and Procedures Handbook - Strategic Information, Regulations, Procedures
Oman Criminal Laws, Regulations and Procedures Handbook - Strategic Information, Regulations, Procedures
Pakistan Criminal Laws, Regulations and Procedures Handbook - Strategic Information, Regulations, Procedures
Palestine (West Bank & Gaza) Criminal Laws, Regulations and Procedures Handbook - Strategic Information, Regulations, Procedures
Panama Criminal Laws, Regulations and Procedures Handbook - Strategic Information, Regulations, Procedures
Papua New Guinea Criminal Laws, Regulations and Procedures Handbook - Strategic Information, Regulations, Procedures
Paraguay Criminal Laws, Regulations and Procedures Handbook - Strategic Information, Regulations, Procedures
Peru Criminal Laws, Regulations and Procedures Handbook - Strategic Information, Regulations, Procedures
Philippines Criminal Laws, Regulations and Procedures Handbook - Strategic Information, Regulations, Procedures
Pitcairn Islands Criminal Laws, Regulations and Procedures Handbook - Strategic Information, Regulations, Procedures

For additional analytical, business and investment opportunities information,
Please contact Global Investment & Business Center, USA
at (202) 546-2103. Fax: (202) 546-3275. E-mail: rusric@erols.com

Poland Criminal Laws, Regulations and Procedures Handbook - Strategic Information, Regulations, Procedures
Portugal Criminal Laws, Regulations and Procedures Handbook - Strategic Information, Regulations, Procedures
Qatar Criminal Laws, Regulations and Procedures Handbook - Strategic Information, Regulations, Procedures
Romania Criminal Laws, Regulations and Procedures Handbook - Strategic Information, Regulations, Procedures
Russia Criminal Laws, Regulations and Procedures Handbook - Strategic Information, Regulations, Procedures
Rwanda Criminal Laws, Regulations and Procedures Handbook - Strategic Information, Regulations, Procedures
Samoa (Western) Criminal Laws, Regulations and Procedures Handbook - Strategic Information, Regulations, Procedures
Sao Tome and Principe Criminal Laws, Regulations and Procedures Handbook - Strategic Information, Regulations, Procedures
Saudi Arabia Criminal Laws, Regulations and Procedures Handbook - Strategic Information, Regulations, Procedures
Senegal Criminal Laws, Regulations and Procedures Handbook - Strategic Information, Regulations, Procedures
Serbia Criminal Laws, Regulations and Procedures Handbook - Strategic Information, Regulations, Procedures
Seychelles Criminal Laws, Regulations and Procedures Handbook - Strategic Information, Regulations, Procedures
Sierra Leone Criminal Laws, Regulations and Procedures Handbook - Strategic Information, Regulations, Procedures
Singapore Criminal Laws, Regulations and Procedures Handbook - Strategic Information, Regulations, Procedures
Slovakia Criminal Laws, Regulations and Procedures Handbook - Strategic Information, Regulations, Procedures
Slovenia Criminal Laws, Regulations and Procedures Handbook - Strategic Information, Regulations, Procedures
Solomon Islands Criminal Laws, Regulations and Procedures Handbook - Strategic Information, Regulations, Procedures
Somalia Criminal Laws, Regulations and Procedures Handbook - Strategic Information, Regulations, Procedures
South Africa Criminal Laws, Regulations and Procedures Handbook - Strategic Information, Regulations, Procedures
Spain Criminal Laws, Regulations and Procedures Handbook - Strategic Information, Regulations, Procedures
Sri Lanka Criminal Laws, Regulations and Procedures Handbook - Strategic Information, Regulations, Procedures
Sudan Criminal Laws, Regulations and Procedures Handbook - Strategic Information, Regulations, Procedures
Suriname Criminal Laws, Regulations and Procedures Handbook - Strategic Information, Regulations, Procedures
Swaziland Criminal Laws, Regulations and Procedures Handbook - Strategic Information, Regulations, Procedures
Sweden Criminal Laws, Regulations and Procedures Handbook - Strategic Information, Regulations, Procedures
Switzerland Criminal Laws, Regulations and Procedures Handbook - Strategic Information, Regulations, Procedures
Syria Criminal Laws, Regulations and Procedures Handbook - Strategic Information, Regulations, Procedures
Taiwan Criminal Laws, Regulations and Procedures Handbook - Strategic Information, Regulations, Procedures
Tajikistan Criminal Laws, Regulations and Procedures Handbook - Strategic Information, Regulations, Procedures
Tanzania Criminal Laws, Regulations and Procedures Handbook - Strategic Information, Regulations, Procedures
Thailand Criminal Laws, Regulations and Procedures Handbook - Strategic Information, Regulations, Procedures
Togo Criminal Laws, Regulations and Procedures Handbook - Strategic Information, Regulations, Procedures
Trinidad and Tobago Criminal Laws, Regulations and Procedures Handbook - Strategic Information, Regulations, Procedures
Tunisia Criminal Laws, Regulations and Procedures Handbook - Strategic Information, Regulations, Procedures
Turkey Criminal Laws, Regulations and Procedures Handbook - Strategic Information, Regulations, Procedures
Turkmenistan Criminal Laws, Regulations and Procedures Handbook - Strategic Information, Regulations, Procedures
Uganda Criminal Laws, Regulations and Procedures Handbook - Strategic Information, Regulations, Procedures
Ukraine Criminal Laws, Regulations and Procedures Handbook - Strategic Information, Regulations, Procedures
United Arab Emirates Criminal Laws, Regulations and Procedures Handbook - Strategic Information, Regulations, Procedures
United Kingdom Criminal Laws, Regulations and Procedures Handbook - Strategic Information, Regulations, Procedures
United States Criminal Laws, Regulations and Procedures Handbook - Strategic Information, Regulations, Procedures
Uruguay Criminal Laws, Regulations and Procedures Handbook - Strategic Information, Regulations, Procedures
Uzbekistan Criminal Laws, Regulations and Procedures Handbook - Strategic Information, Regulations, Procedures
Venezuela Criminal Laws, Regulations and Procedures Handbook - Strategic Information, Regulations, Procedures
Vietnam Criminal Laws, Regulations and Procedures Handbook - Strategic Information, Regulations, Procedures
Yemen Criminal Laws, Regulations and Procedures Handbook - Strategic Information, Regulations, Procedures
Zambia Criminal Laws, Regulations and Procedures Handbook - Strategic Information, Regulations, Procedures
Zimbabwe Criminal Laws, Regulations and Procedures Handbook - Strategic Information, Regulations, Procedures

**For additional analytical, business and investment opportunities information,
Please contact Global Investment & Business Center, USA
at (202) 546-2103. Fax: (202) 546-3275. E-mail: rusric@erols.com**